Trade Unions in British Politics:
the first 250 years

Trade Unions in British Politics: the first 250 years

Edited by Ben Pimlott and Chris Cook

Second Edition

LONGMAN
London and New York

Longman Group UK Limited,
Longman House, Burnt Mill, Harlow,
Essex CM20 2JE, England
and Associated Companies throughout the world.

Published in the United States of America by Longman Inc., New York

First Published 1982
Second Edition 1991

British Library Cataloguing in Publication Data
Trade unions in British politics: the first 250 years – 2nd ed.
  1. Great Britain. Politics. Role. History of in trade
  unions
  I. Pimlott, Ben   II. Cook, Chris *1945–*
  322.20941

  ISBN 0–582–08155–6
  ISBN 0–582–06298–5 pbk

Library of Congress Cataloging-in-Publication Data
Trade unions in British politics: the first 250 years/edited by Ben
  Pimlott and Chris Cook. — 2nd ed.
      p.   cm.
  Includes index.
  ISBN 0–582–08155–6 (cased): £24.00. — ISBN 0–582–06298–5 (pbk.):
  £12.95
  1. Trade-unions—Great Britain—Political activity—History.
  I. Pimlott, Ben, 1945–   II. Cook, Chris, 1945–
  HD6667.T7   1991
  322′.2′0941—dc20
                                                          90–46397
                                                          CIP

Set in 10/12 pt Bembo
Produced by Longman Singapore Publishers (Pte) Ltd.
Printed in Singapore

Contents

Preface to the Second Edition

When *Trade Unions in British Politics* was first published in 1982, the political role of unions was in crisis. On the one hand, unions were under pressure from a hostile government and, in the new conditions of mass unemployment, were finding it hard to defend themselves; on the other, following the bitter row with the Callaghan government over wages policy, they had increased their direct involvement in the Labour Party which (partly as a result) was in disarray. The post-war consensus, which had brought unions close to government decision-taking, seemed at an end: yet unions remained at the centre of political debate.

Much has happened since. The same party is in power (with a new Prime Minister) but the climate is quite different, partly because of changes in government–union and union–Labour Party relations. In some ways unions are weaker than at the beginning of the last decade, but they have also shown their ability to adapt. New union attitudes are certainly one reason for the rapid evolution of the Labour Party, in which the unions have – in a remarkable departure from tradition – voluntarily accepted a reduced involvement. If Labour returns to power in 1991 or 1992, its relationship with the union movement now seems likely to be much less suffocating than in the 1970s.

This new edition takes full account of the changes that have taken place, as well as of those in prospect. The introduction has been revised and expanded. Part One (the main historical section) has been amended in a number of places to take account of recent research, and Ken Coates's essay on early post-war developments (Chapter 8) is now included in this half of the book. In Part Two, Robert Taylor has extensively revised his chapter on unions in the 1960s and 1970s, while Chapters 10 to 13 also contain some revisions.

The most important change in this edition is the inclusion of three entirely

new chapters. These look at the growing importance of Europe and the
Community to British trade unionism, at the political role of unions up to
the end of Mrs Thatcher's premiership, and at recent aspects of the Labour
Party–union relationship. The three essays – each by a leading expert from
a different professional background – bring the coverage of the book fully
up to date. They also alter its balance. The emphasis in the first edition was
on trade union history before 1960. The present volume is evenly divided
between historical analysis and discussions of contemporary or recent
issues affecting unions in politics. Its aim is to provide as wide-ranging
an introduction to an ever-changing field as possible.

Ben Pimlott
Chris Cook

Abbreviations

ACAS	Advisory, Conciliation and Arbitration Service
ACTT	Association of Cinematograph, Television and Allied Technicians
AEU	Amalgamated Engineering Union
Ag. Hist. Rev.	*Agricultural History Review*
ASE	Amalgamated Society of Engineers
ASLEF	Associated Society of Locomotive Engineers and Firemen
ASTMS	Association of Scientific, Technical and Managerial Staffs
AUEW	Amalgamated Union of Engineering Workers
BEC	British Employers' Confederation
Bodl. Lib.	Bodleian Library
Brit. Jrnl. Soc.	*British Journal of Sociology*
BL	British Library
CBI	Confederation of British Industry
CDS	Campaign for Democratic Socialism
CGT	Confédération Générale du Travail
CND	Campaign for Nuclear Disarmament
CRE	Commission for Racial Equality
DWRGWU	Dock, Wharf, Riverside and General Workers' Union
Ec. Hist. Rev.	*Economic History Review*
EEC	European Economic Community
EETPU	Electrical, Electronic, Telecommunications and Plumbing Union
EOC	Equal Opportunities Commission
ETUC	European Trade Union Confederation
GGLU	Gasworkers' and General Labourers' Union
GMB	General Municipal and Boilermakers

GMWU	General and Municipal Workers' Union
GNCTU	Grand National Consolidated Trades Union of Great Britain and Ireland
Hist. Jrnl.	*Historical Journal*
HC Debs	House of Commons Debates
HCP	House of Commons Papers
HLRO	House of Lords Record Office
HMSO	Her Majesty's Stationery Office
ICFTU	International Confederation of Free Trade Unions
ILP	Independent Labour Party
IMF	International Monetary Fund
Jrnl. Cont. Hist.	*Journal of Contemporary History*
LRC	Labour Representation Committee
MFGB	Miners' Federation of Great Britain
MSC	Manpower Services Commission
MSF	Manufacturing, Science and Finance
NALGO	National Association of Local Government Officers
NAPL	National Association for the Protection of Labour
NATFHE	National Association of Teachers in Further and Higher Education
NCL	National Council of Labour
NEC	National Executive Committee (of Labour Party)
NEDC	National Economic Development Council
NIC	National Incomes Commission
NJAC	National Joint Advisory Council
NUGMW	National Union of General and Municipal Workers
NUM	National Union of Mineworkers
NUPE	National Union of Public Employees
NUR	National Union of Railwaymen
NUWM	National Unemployed Workers' Movement
OBU	Operative Builders' Union
OEEC	Organization for European Economic Co-operation
PLP	Parliamentary Labour Party
PRO	Public Record Office
PRO FO	Public Record Office (Foreign Office)
SDF	Social Democratic Federation
SDP	Social Democratic Party
SLADE	Society of Lithographic Artists, Designers and Engravers
SOGAT	Society of Graphical and Allied Trades
TGWU	Transport and General Workers Union
TUC	Trades Union Congress
USDAW	Union of Shop, Distributive and Allied Workers
Welsh Hist. Rev.	*Welsh History Review*

Introduction

Ben Pimlott

This book is about trade union political power – and the lack of it. Such a subject immediately poses conceptual problems. One is reminded of Gilbert Ryle's puzzled foreigner confronting a game of cricket. Having learnt the functions of the bowlers, the batsmen, the umpire and the scorers, he then says 'But there is no one left on the field to contribute the famous element of team-spirit. I see who does the bowling, the batting and the wicket-keeping; but I do not see whose role it is to exercise *esprit de corps*.'[1] A student of British industrial history is likely to be similarly perplexed. Having examined the functions of the TUC, the Labour Party Conference, trade union officials, shop stewards and sponsored MPs, the question is still likely to remain: 'But where is this thing called trade union power and who has the role of exercising it?'

The authors of these chapters present a variety of answers, looking always at the specifically political aspects of union behaviour. There have been many studies of individual unions, partly reflecting the increased availability of union archives and some interesting general histories of trade unionism. Yet no definitive history of unions in their political context has been written; nor does any study examine comprehensively their contemporary political role. We have tried to fill this gap. Our aim has been to cover the development of the political relationships of British unions from eighteenth-century beginnings to the present day; and to consider the crisis of confidence which has created a widening gulf between leaders and conferences of major unions, on the one hand, and successive governments, on the other.

In one sense this book is an introduction. No previous knowledge of unionism or labour history has been assumed. However, writers have been chosen for their specialist knowledge, and each chapter, based on original research, is intended as a contribution to scholarship. Partly for this reason, the editors have imposed no unifying theme. Most of the key developments in union political history over the last two hundred and fifty years are discussed, with a concentration on the twentieth century and on the period since 1945 in particular. However, writers vary widely in their backgrounds, interests and perspectives. Contributors include historians and political scientists; a media sociologist; a former Permanent Secretary at the Department of Employment; an international trade union official; several journalists; and a Euro MP. Few books about trade unions, we believe, have provided a better range. All contributors have some sympathy for their subject matter; but all are, at the same time, critical friends.

The book is divided into two parts. Part One is arranged chronologically, taking the story from earliest times up to 1960. The second part looks at post-war aspects of government–union relations, and examines more broadly the political role and behaviour of unions in contemporary Britain. As the reader progresses, he will find not only that it is impossible to locate the political power of trade unions in terms of individuals or groups, but that trade union power is not a single commodity.

Three types of political interest and involvement may be identified:

1. Involvement stemming from concern about government action or inaction in industrial matters (e.g. over wages, trade union rights, working conditions or the settlement of disputes).
2. Involvement arising from concern about government action or inaction in matters which, while not strictly industrial, are related to the protective function of unions (e.g. pensions, social security, and other welfare provisions).
3. Involvement based on ideological or other commitments with little direct relevance to the industrial role of unions. Foreign policy would be included here; so would moral, constitutional or 'socialist' demands (such as the abolition of the House of Lords or nationalization without compensation).

The overlap between these categories is, of course, very great. Workers' control is clearly an industrial issue – but there is a large ideological element in it as well. There are other problems of classification. The traditional demand of the Miners' Federation for the nationalization of coal probably falls into the first category. But what of the campaign in the 1970s and 1980s to take Britain out of the EEC? It will quickly be seen that many matters outside the immediate sphere of unions in fact concern them indirectly. An issue like nuclear disarmament, for example, in which trade unions have taken a close interest, apparently has little to do with industrial affairs. Yet as Chapter 10 seeks to show, part of the force of the union commitment in the 1980s came from the economic crisis, summed up in the slogan 'Jobs Not Bombs'.

All the same, there is an important difference between a trade union battle for, say, an employment protection act, and a campaign against the purchase of South African goods. In fact, there is a shading off from matters which affect unions and their members on a daily basis, and issues which spring from the wider political idealism of union activists. The co-existence of these types of involvement is an important feature of British unionism. Once the distinction is noted, it will be seen that British unions behave very differently from many of their Continental, and more especially, their American, equivalents; and that to regard trade unions as the counterpart of capital, management or even of government (as in Edward Heath's electorally disastrous question: 'Who governs Britain?') is dangerously misleading.

Trade unions have always been regarded suspiciously by governments. As John Stevenson points out, from the mid-nineteenth century (if not earlier) a major aim of nascent unionism was to be regarded as respectable and to avoid making enemies. 'Trade unionists were conscious of their ambivalent legal status and wished to avoid provoking the authorities into acting against them', he writes of unions in the 1840s; 'at the same time, the more sophisticated trade unionists, like many popular radicals, were coming to recognize that "public opinion" was an important factor in industrial disputes, in the battle for full legal recognition and in the campaign for political rights.'

Respectability involved limiting demands. One thing that militated against respectability was the presence of popular leaders and agitators who wished to bring sweeping changes to society in general. In the early and mid-nineteenth century such pressures came from within the working class, especially from the Chartists. Later there was a middle-class involvement, and as John Lovell shows, the early socialist societies which came into existence in the 1880s were often far removed from the world of manual labour. Yet the socialists had an undoubted appeal for union leaders. The ILP, in particular, recruited many trade union members. It was a sign of the growing significance of this new body that in 1894 Tom Mann gave up his position as full-time President of the dockers' union to become Secretary of the ILP. What attracted unionists to the socialist groups? Lovell argues that the unions were successfully permeated not because of the relevance of socialism itself, but because the ideology implied a militant *industrial* posture. This (by no means necessary) connection between the desire to overturn society and the desire to beat employers has meant that in the twentieth century industrial militancy has often been combined with a radical political philosophy of an apparently unrelated kind. Yet, as Robert Taylor points out, there is actually a contradiction between the egalitarianism implied by socialism and the *laissez-faire* view of collective bargaining implied by most forms of industrial militancy.

The Labour Party, founded in 1900 as the Labour Representation

Committee, was scarcely a socialist body. Even Keir Hardie declared that, when acting in the House of Commons, Labour MPs should be 'neither Socialists, Liberals, nor Tories, but a Labour Party'. It was a political affront to the trade unions – the Taff Vale verdict of 1901 – that did most to get the new organization off the ground. In its earliest days, the Labour Party was a sectional trade union body mainly concerned with the election of working men to the House of Commons. One of the most fascinating developments of twentieth-century history was the transformation of this party into an organization which adopted socialism as its official doctrine, successfully challenged major political parties for the control of government, and *inter alia*, adopted members of the professional middle class, and even the aristocracy, as its leaders. What brought about the change? As David Rubinstein indicates, after a period of industrial peace following the election of the Asquith Government in 1906, the eruption of 1910–14 had a radicalizing effect on important sections of the union rank-and-file, injecting doctrines which were to re-emerge during the First World War. It was a Conservative leader, Bonar Law, who declared in the House of Commons in 1912: 'I should like to see the trade unions become stronger, because I think that, as a rule, they tend to the diminution of disputes'. Another feature of these crucial years, as Rubinstein points out, was the increasing involvement of government in industrial affairs. There had been little direct government intervention before the 1890s. By 1907–12, the Liberal administration was being brought into most of the major disputes that took place.

Rubinstein quotes Lenin in 1913: 'In Britain a change has taken place in the relation of social forces, a change which cannot be expressed in figures but which everyone feels.' Perhaps this was wishful thinking. What is undoubtedly true is that the First World War, like the Second, transformed the position of unions in British society, and produced an intensity of political interest that had never existed before. According to Chris Wrigley, the attack on the status and security of skilled workers led to a widening support for socialist tendencies within the rapidly strengthening Labour Party. Nevertheless, the party reorganization which made electoral victory possible was built on a trade union scaffolding in the constituencies. Wrigley quotes Arthur Henderson's remark to C.P. Scott in 1917, on Labour's ability to field 500 candidates: 'They were better equipped for doing this than either of the other two great parties, because they had an existing trade-union organization in every town.' This trade union base has continued to provide ballast for the Labour Party throughout its history.

The First World War put socialism firmly onto the union agenda. It also gave the unions – temporarily – a status which they had never had before. The requirements of war production created a new basis for consultation. However this did not long survive the Armistice in 1918, and the period of militancy which followed was accompanied by government policies aimed at confrontation rather than co-operation. Moreover, the increasing electoral success of the Labour Party scarcely turned the House of Commons into the main channel for union grievances. As Patrick Renshaw points out, the Labour Party, embarrassed by an industrial upheaval over which it had no control, played only a minor role during the General Strike. Far more was heard of Liberal than of Labour leaders. Indeed, one of the ironies of the inter-war period is that the dwindling Liberal Party was a much more fertile source of practical ideas and schemes for dealing with unemployment and the problems of sickness and old age than the expanding Labour Party.

The impact of mass unemployment in the 1930s demonstrated the limits of trade union power – industrial and political – as Richard Shackleton shows. Trade union membership reached its nadir in 1933. The behaviour of the unions in the 1930s may, indeed, be compared with their behaviour in the Great Slump of the 1980s: at both times, weakness *vis-à-vis* employers and the government concentrated trade union political interest and influence on the Labour Party, and at the same time encouraged unions temporarily to back left-wing demands.

'The depression did not lead the unions towards any head-on clash with the government or the capitalist system', notes Shackleton, 'but it did make them less hostile and in some cases positively receptive to the ideas for structural change emanating from the left.' The 1930s, like the 1980s, were also a decade in which the constituency parties increased their power – partly through the benevolence of the trade union leaders. There are similarities, indeed, between the revolutionary Party Conference of 1980, following electoral defeat and a rapid growth in unemployment, and the Conference of 1932, when union delegates demanded 'definite socialist legislation' including the nationalization of the joint stock banks.

Yet unions did have some influence on public affairs in the 1930s. A trade union campaign against the Unemployment Assistance Board forced the government to retrench. Moreover, the backing given by Bevin, Citrine and other leaders to Dalton's campaign within the Labour Party for a strong foreign policy, and for rearmament, paved the way for the coalition of May 1940, based on a patriotic front.

The Second World War produced less industrial unrest than the First – partly because inflation was kept to a much lower level. As Denis Barnes and Eileen Reid show, more than half of all the strikes that did occur were over wages. Yet a partnership between government and trade unions was achieved that proved more durable than after the First World War. The election of a Labour government in 1945 clinched the deal. 'The trade union movement finally and triumphantly achieved the political power which had prompted the formation of the Labour Party in 1900', suggest Barnes and Reid. Ken Coates takes a different view. Coates accepts that the war had brought the TUC into direct consultation with the government on a wide variety of public issues and that: 'The aspirations stimulated by

Ernest Bevin and Walter Citrine . . . after the defeat of the General Strike in 1926 had, in the main, become material facts.' However, he points out that union influence on government was concentrated in the hands of a few individual leaders, and he suggests that union power over policy diminished as the government moved towards a strategy based on wage restraint. Coates concludes that the real extent of the post-war consensus rested on full employment, and would last only so long as full employment was maintained.

Arguably, however, it was inflation rather than unemployment which broke the consensus. In the 1960s and 1970s, unions became the scapegoats of relative economic decline – denounced for forcing up wage rates far above levels of improved labour productivity. From 1956, when he became General Secretary of the TGWU, Frank Cousins became, in Robert Taylor's words, 'the union bogeyman to make the flesh creep', and one of the most important changes of the years that followed was the gradual switch of trade unions away from automatic support for the PLP leadership, a change that was encouraged by the altering pattern of the block vote, with white-collar and large general unions replacing coal, rail and cotton. Labour's crisis in the 1980s stemmed, indeed, far more from a radicalization of the unions, which dominated the Party Executive as well as Conference, than from any changes in the constituencies.

The last quarter of a century has seen successive attempts alternately to control, and to reach an arrangement with, trade unions. The failure of *In Place of Strife* was followed by the disaster of the Conservatives' Industrial Relations Act. The failure of incomes policy was followed by the illusion of the 'social contract', which (as Taylor points out) was only a pale imitation of the partnerships between government and unions that dominated politics in Scandinavia, Austria and West Germany. During this period, the notion of an over-mighty, baronial, union leadership gained currency in the media. Opinion polls suggested that Jack Jones, General Secretary of the TGWU in succession to Cousins, was the most powerful man in Britain. Yet the reality was very different. 'The intractable nature of our trade union "problem" stems not from the supposed overweening power or pretension of the trade union movement', Taylor concludes, 'but from its weaknesses which grew more obvious under conditions of rising inflation and dominant work-place bargaining during the 1960s and 1970s.' Bonar Law had said something similar in 1912.

One of the paradoxes of the 1970s was that unions continued to grow in numerical strength while becoming progressively less popular with the general public – which increasingly meant trade unionists themselves. This apparent contradiction is reflected in the findings of public-opinion polls. According to one survey at the end of the decade, 82 per cent of adults believed that unions had too much power; yet 78 per cent of the same sample also thought that unions performed an essential function. Two prime ministers fell from power because they failed to appreciate the nature of public attitudes towards trade unions: Edward Heath underestimated sympathy for the miners in 1974, while Callaghan failed to allow for a public reaction against the breakdown of wage restraint at the end of 1978.

If unions tend to be unpopular, are they to blame, or do they get unfairly treated in the press? Jean Seaton suggests the latter, while arguing that unions themselves take too little care of their own public relations. When a union calls a strike, the popular press often personalizes the consequences – focusing on a pensioner stricken by hypothermia through lack of electricity, or a house burnt down through lack of fire protection. This kind of presentation is seldom given to the impact of major decisions by a Rowlands or a Goldsmith. As a result unions tend to regard the media warily, exacerbating the problem of misrepresentation. 'Obliged to defend entirely honourable objectives as if they were excusing crimes', Seaton concludes, 'the unions have become over-defensive.'

When Barry Hindess published *The Decline of Working-Class Politics* in 1971, he began a controversy about the withering away of Labour's traditional basis of support. In Chapter 11, Hindess re-examines his own arguments in the light of later developments and concludes that he neglected the role of locally affiliated trade union branches – which provide an important layer of working-class political participation. Henry Drucker also stresses the influence of trade unions in his discussion of the 'ethos' of the Labour Party – to be distinguished from the 'doctrine' which members profess to believe. As Drucker points out, 'The ethos of the Labour Party provides a language – not simply a rhetoric – for party debate.' Anybody with first-hand knowledge of the Labour Party will, indeed, be aware of the importance of unions as a reference point in almost every discussion. Despite middle-class accretions, the Labour Party continues to see itself as working class, and does not forget Bevin's dictum that it originated from 'the bowels of the trade-union movement'. The union connection is reflected not just in money, organic links and block votes. It is also to be seen in union-derived organizational practices, and in the special moral authority that trade union activists can often exercise at Labour Party branch level.

How much influence do unions exercise over Labour Party policy making? It used to be believed that, outside their own industrial sphere, unions would tend to follow rather than initiate or dictate. As Chapter 13 shows, however, the second-wave debate on nuclear disarmament in the 1980s presented a different pattern. The unilateralist campaign did not originate in the unions, and was indeed often linked to what Frank Parkin described as 'middle-class radicalism'.[2] However, when the first movement subsided in the early 1960s, it left behind a residue of latent trade union support, which provided a powerful base for the revived campaign two decades later: it was indeed the unions, as early as 1972, which brought it back to the attention of the Labour Party by backing unilateralist resolutions at Conference. As with the EEC, so with defence, the attitude of the Labour Party on a primarily non-industrial issue was determined by the union movement, rather than the other way round.

The accusation of union dominance had, of course, long been one of the Right's most effective weapons against Labour. The apparent truth of the allegation from the 1970s became a debilitating electoral weakness. A particularly ironic aspect was that, increasingly, the union members whose numerical strength gave unions their constitutional power at Labour Party Conferences, voted at general elections for other parties. This was partly because trade unionism had moved into white collar occupations which did not have a strong tradition of Labour voting, and partly because of Labour's weakening grip on the manual working class. Whatever the reason, the fall in rank-and-file union support for Labour over a twenty-year period was dramatic. Whereas in 1964, the year Harold Wilson became Prime Minister, 73 per cent of union members voted Labour, only 51 per cent did so in 1979, the year of James Callaghan's defeat. The low point was reached in 1983 when (as Philip Bassett reminds us) only one trade union member in three voted for the party the unions had created. By this time, Labour found itself offering an approach that was more than ever 'unionist' in tone, yet one which was rejected by the majority of trade unionists themselves. Since then, there has been a partial recovery: how far it has gone the next election will show. But the gradual realization that too much interest in Labour Party affairs was likely to mean hostile Tory governments in perpetuity, has brought a remarkable transformation in the attitudes of many unions.

For unions, the 1980s was certainly a traumatic period. 'In the course of a decade', points out William Brown, 'their political influence has tumbled', along with their legal status. Shunted to the political margins and facing a workforce which was often sceptical about the supposed economic advantages to union membership, some union leaders began to re-think their relationship both with the government and with the Labour opposition. After the disappointment of the 1987 election result – which did, however, re-establish Labour as the only available alternative government – the revival of the Labour Party became a serious priority. At the same time, the old commitments which had earned trade unions the media's 'dinosaur' tag no longer seemed so pressing. As the impossibility of re-nationalizing many of the newly privatized companies (let alone others which had not previously been state-owned) became apparent, the symbolic importance of public ownership faded. The anti-politician mood in unions which followed the 1978–79 'winter of discontent', and which had helped to provide union backing for the mandatory re-selection of Labour MPs, passed, and unions edged towards the old right-wing Labour demand of one-member-one-vote in constituency selections. Meanwhile, not only unilateralism but – even more dramatically – the unions' long-standing hostility to the European

Community, gave way to a new spirit of realism. The influence of Jacques Delors, and a realization of the opportunities offered by the Social Charter, both played a part; so, probably, did Mrs Thatcher's open xenophobia. By 1990, as Denis MacShane indicates, unions were looking to Europe and European unions as allies in their battles against an unfriendly government in London.

At home, a revival of Labour Party confidence was combined with an increasingly serious desire to see it in office, on almost any terms. If the involvement of unions in the Party contributed to its electoral weakness, then a degree of withdrawal was required: such was the reasoning of progressive leaders such as John Edmonds of the General and Municipal, and Tom Sawyer of NUPE. This view, as Philip Bassett points out, was not unwelcome either in the Leader's office, or at Walworth Road. The result has been a package of constitutional reforms which are as radical as any in the past, yet have aroused much less animosity – including a reduction in the size of the bloc vote, and the delegation of policy formulation to an elected National Policy Forum. It is too soon to judge the effects of these changes. They could, however, be a watershed in union–Labour Party relations, and in the unions' own perception of their political role. Hitherto, even when the unions have stood back from direct political interference, they have jealously protected their constitutional rights within the Labour Party. The possibility of continuing, and irreversible, reductions in the unions' involvement opens new vistas.

There is the eventual option of complete separation. This has obvious attractions to the politicians: a party no longer attached to its union roots would be more adaptable (it may be argued) and more appealing to middle-ground and middle-class voters. Such a party might be able to put behind it some of the encrusted rhetoric which Henry Drucker describes in his essay about the party's (essentially unionist) 'ethos'. Yet Labour leaders would be unwise to ignore Ernest Bevin's famous reminder that the Party came from 'the bowels of the trade union movement'.

They should not forget that what one historian has called Labour's 'bowel problem'[3] has also been a bowel advantage. Those who point to the electoral unpopularity of unions need to be reminded that it was *support* for unions that turned Labour into a major party in the first place. As Ross McKibbin showed in his seminal *The Evolution of the Labour Party, 1910–1924,*[4] it was the organizational capacity and class identity of local trades councils – from which local Labour Parties were formed – which gave Labour its national lift-off in the 1920s and ensured the Labour loyalty of mining areas and manufacturing centres even after a new breed of graduate, middle-class MPs gained prominence. The classic doorstep response, 'Of course we're Labour – we're working- class', comes from the same heritage. For much of the present century it has been a strange truth that among the working class the supposed political power of the unions has been widely condemned;

yet Labour has continued to get support because of an association with the working class and working-class values which comes, ultimately, from the trade unions which were responsible for the Party's foundation.

The unions have been blamed (with some justice) for the 1981 Labour split: but without the union-derived, working-class loyalty which we have described, it is doubtful whether the party could have beaten off the Alliance challenge. Not only did the unions continue to pay the bills; it was Labour's out-of-date, oft-derided, cloth-cap image which enabled the party to go on piling up big majorities in the poorest parts of the United Kingdom while the SDP and Liberals gained spectacular near-misses almost everywhere.

The new constitutional and policy-making arrangements by no means take all, or even most, of the 'labour' out of Labour, and from every point of view – party and union – they seem an advance. Yet it is a path that needs to be trod with caution. For how long, it may be asked, will a trade union movement continue to finance a semi-detached party whose pursuit of non-working-class votes may lead it further and further away from the role of trade union advocate? For how long will proletarian voters give automatic support to lawyers and dons whose only link with their constituents is a pro-underdog philosophy? These are points which Labour's planners would do well to ponder. Labour seems likely to recapture much lost working-class support in 1991 or 1992. Whether the strategy of moving away from the unions provides a formula for retaining this support next time the party suffers a nervous breakdown, is another matter.

Obviously a great deal depends on the outcome of the next election – a contest which is set to generate more excitement than any previous one for a generation. If Labour wins, it will find itself governing a country with a changed working class since 1979, and trade unions with different expectations, in an utterly different industrial and economic environment. Whether it manages its industrial relations better than in the 1960s and 1970s may be the critical test of its period of office. But even if Labour loses, William Brown is surely right that government hostility towards unions cannot continue indefinitely, and that the 1990s will be the decade in which government – of whatever hue – starts courting unions once again.

Trade union entitlements within the Community, together with the crisis in the pay structure of the public services, the chronic problem of occupational training and – above all – the failure of what Brown calls 'the 1980s formula of high unemployment and radical labour legislation' to tame Britain's inflationary tendencies, all point in this direction. The Conservative governments of the 1980s have tried to take the unions out of politics: whoever is in power at the end of the twentieth century is likely to find the unions a powerful, and continuing, political presence.

NOTES AND REFERENCES

1. G. Ryle, *The Concept of Mind*, Penguin, London, 1963, p. 18.
2. *Middle-class Radicalism*, Manchester University Press, 1968.
3. A.J. Taylor, *Trade Unions and the Labour Party*, Croom Helm, London, 1987, p. 1.
4. Oxford University Press, Oxford, 1974.

Part one

HISTORICAL PERSPECTIVES

1 Early trade unionism: radicalism and respectability

John Stevenson

The history of the trade unions has traditionally been associated with the rise of the working classes as a whole. But although the identification of the early trade societies and, later, trade unions with 'the making of the English working class' is hard to escape, escape it must, for the early trade unions can most readily be understood in the context of small, sectional groups of workers, many of them craft-based, who, beginning with the trade societies of the eighteenth century, very slowly expanded their membership and, even in the mid-nineteenth century, only embraced a small fraction of the total working population.

EIGHTEENTH-CENTURY TRADE UNIONISM

Until very recently the eighteenth century remained something of a 'dark age' of trade union history. The Webbs' *History of Trade Unionism* occupied a central position with their account of the origins of trade unionism and the impact of the Combination Acts of 1799 and 1800.[1] But as several subsequent historians recognized, the Webbs made only limited investigations into the origins of trade union development in the eighteenth century, their main concern being with the period after 1800. An important supplement to the Webbs, however, was and remains J.L. and B. Hammond's *The Skilled Labourer, 1760–1832*, first published in 1919, a series of studies which included chapters on the experience of groups of workers in the textile trades and an important chapter on the activities of the coal-miners of the Tyne and Wear. Although it has tended to be overshadowed by their wide-ranging studies of the growth of the factory system in *The Town Labourer* and the transformation of agriculture in *The Village Labourer, The Skilled Labourer* remains one of the most important accounts of early industrial organization. It retained, however, the character of a disconnected series of studies in which the Hammonds' primary preoccupation was with the disruptive effects of industrialization upon the 'social economy' of the skilled craftsmen rather than a coherent account of trade union development in the late eighteenth and early nineteenth centuries.[2] In spite of the significant clues which their work provided for an analysis of early trade unionism the literature on the early trade unions remained remarkably slight. As several historians noted, criticism could justly be directed at those who followed the Webbs and the Hammonds for failing to devote the same degree of attention to the earlier phases of trade union history as to its later stages. Writing in 1964, Eric Hobsbawm noted the striking recovery of interest in nineteenth-century trade union history but commented that 'eighteenth-century unionism or its equivalent has been hardly touched upon by labour historians since the Webbs surveyed it . . .'.[3] Thus, in his comprehensive survey of trade union history, first published in 1963, Henry Pelling did no more than reflect the general state of the historiography in dealing with the whole of trade union development from its 'Origins' to 1825 in a single chapter, devoting only twelve pages out of a total of 260 to the period before 1815. A decade later, while Professor Musson could refer to 'a mounting pile of books and articles' on nineteenth-century trade union history, to which he provided a judicious review in his pamphlet of 1972, he chose as his starting point the almost traditional date of 1800, the year of the definitive Combination Act which amended the statute of 1799 and was to remain in force until 1824.[4]

Fortunately, the position has altered substantially in recent years, not least because of the efforts of some of the historians to which we have already referred. Hobsbawm's study of 'The Tramping Artisan' illustrated the way in which, from the eighteenth century, skilled workmen within particular crafts were able to move about the country during times of slack trade or unemployment using approved 'houses of call' or 'club houses' where they could receive temporary lodging, food and shelter, as well as assistance to find work from fellow members of their trade. Men who wished to leave their locality received a 'blank' or 'clearance' which attested to their good standing in their trade which was presented to the secretary of the society in the next town who would provide food and lodging, as well as news of employment opportunities. If work was unavailable the man tramped on, sometimes making journeys of hundreds of miles using the 'houses-of-call' as both temporary lodging houses and as informal labour exchanges. By the early nineteenth century the system of 'tramping' provided a remarkable example of mutual aid and organization by skilled crafts such as the printers, woolcombers, brushmakers, carpenters, tailors, hatters, and many others. At least as, if not more important, was Hobsbawm's article on

'The Machine Breakers', which, focusing on Luddism, argued that riots, machine-breaking and personal intimidation were not senseless episodes of violence but a more considered process of 'collective bargaining by riot' by which workmen sought to put pressure upon their employers, discipline their fellows, and draw attention to their grievances. Moreover, as he demonstrated, this form of activity had a long pedigree reaching at least as far back as the seventeenth century.[5] This approach to early labour violence, dismissed by many historians as a symptom of a 'primitive' stage of trade union development, fitted very well with the work of social historians such as George Rudé whose pioneering investigations of the 'mob' illustrated that ephemeral acts of violence or lawlessness were in fact often perfectly rational attempts by otherwise inarticulate sections of the populace to articulate grievances or negotiate with the authorities. Far from being 'primitive', they represented an often surprisingly sophisticated and flexible form of expression by the lower classes which could be used as an instrument of bargaining by workmen when other forms of action proved fruitless.[6] The Webbs' emphasis on formal trade union organization had led them to neglect these *ad hoc* forms of action by workmen. Hence, even where there is no obvious evidence of organized trade societies, as among many of the skilled trades of the eighteenth and early nineteenth centuries, groups of workmen could still organize effectively on an *ad hoc* basis to preserve traditional customs and practices or to raise wages.

On an empirical basis, we now have a growing amount of evidence about workmen's organizations in the eighteenth century. The most significant feature revealed is the sheer volume of activity. While historians have long been familiar with the behaviour of some of the prominent skilled trades of the capital, such as the Spitalfields weavers, printers, bookbinders, and tailors, we also have an increasing amount of information about the activities of hitherto little-known groups of provincial workmen. In a pioneering attempt at a comprehensive account of eighteenth-century industrial relations C.R. Dobson has located nearly 400 labour disputes in the British Isles between 1717 and 1800, involving a very wide selection of trades and occurring in almost every part of the country.[7] Moreover, Dobson's list of 'disputes', while the most complete we have available in print to date, undoubtedly understates the amount of activity by workmen, given that it omits several disputes which can be identified in individual trades through other secondary sources. In addition, any tabulation of 'disputes' represents only the tip of the iceberg of collective activity by eighteenth-century workmen. The existence of any form of organized pressure from workmen often only emerged into the full light of day when a strike or demonstration left some record behind in newspapers, pamphlets, or quarter-sessions papers. Indeed, such detailed research as we have suggests both a much greater volume of activity on the part of eighteenth-century workmen than has hitherto been appreciated and an often surprising ability to bargain effectively with local employers and to represent their case to local and national authorities. As A.E. Musson[8] has written:

The normal trade-society methods were to approach their employers verbally or in written 'memorials', and usually 'respectfully', to negotiate peacefully whenever possible, and, if the worst came to the worst, to come out on strike, giving due notice. They had no wish to undergo the hardships of unemployment or the rigours of the law, or to risk their meagre funds and imperil their friendly benefits, without good cause, and the typical 'craft' societies generally deplored mob-violence.

Tumultuous demonstrations and parades of workmen were a relatively common feature in the London skilled trades, as in the series of trade disputes among coal-heavers, silk-weavers, watermen, sailors, hatters, sawyers and tailors in the 1760s. For example, in the spring of 1768 between 5,000 and 6,000 striking sailors marched from St George's Fields in Southwark to St James's Palace 'with colours flying, drums beating and fifes playing' where they handed in a petition for an increase of wages. The remarkable feature of the London disputes of the 1760s was less the degree of violence they displayed than the evidence they offer of effective organization among many groups of workers, several of which proved perfectly capable of making orderly representations to the masters, to Parliament, or to the monarch and of organizing strikes and the collection of funds, accompanied, if necessary, by intimidation and violence both to prevent strike-breaking or to bring pressure to bear on the employers.[9] Similarly in the burgeoning coal trade of the North-East, keelmen, sailors and colliers had also proved themselves capable of orchestrating a wide range of tactics in order to bargain with the employers. The keelmen, who shipped coal down the Tyne and Wear in small boats or 'keels' to the waiting colliers at the river estuaries became notorious during the eighteenth century for the strength of their organization. Strikes, intimidation, riotous assembly, as well as petitions to the local authorities and to Parliament, punctuated their history. In 1787 the keelmen obtained an Act of Parliament regulating aspects of their trade which although far from bringing an end to disputes illustrated their ability to organize effectively and make the system of government work to their advantage.[10] Perhaps even more remarkable was the ability of the colliers of the North-East to conduct a six-week strike in the summer of 1765 against the coalowners' attempt to tighten their control over the colliers by extending the customary yearly bond into virtual life service. As well as maintaining the strike, the colliers countered an advertisement by the masters in the Newcastle papers by one of their own, emphasizing the legality of their proceedings and the justice of their cause.[11]

Thus by the end of the eighteenth century, many groups of workmen had displayed the ability to strike, to organize funds, to negotiate effectively, and to represent their grievances both by violent and non-violent means.

Moreover, the increasing development and complexity of the economy, an overall rise in prices, and fluctuations in trade, accentuated by the American and Revolutionary Wars, gave early trade organizations a renewed impetus. Dobson records that the number of trade disputes between 1781 and 1800 was 153, forty more than in the period 1761–80. The last decade of the eighteenth century accounted for nearly a third of the disputes listed by Dobson for the whole period 1717–1800, with activity in a very wide variety of trades. The years 1791–92 witnessed a veritable explosion of strike activity both in the capital and in the country with forty disputes recorded, including groups such as the ship carpenters at Liverpool, the seamen working the East Coast from Scotland to the Thames, and the colliers at Bristol, Sheffield, Wigan and Newcastle. Disputes continued throughout the 1790s, but especially in 1795, a year of high prices and trade dislocation when shipyard workers, tailors, coal-heavers and even some agricultural workers sought wage increases.[12]

On the eve of the Combination Laws then, trade disputes had become increasingly common, backed by various degrees of formal organization. In many provincial disputes, organization appears to have been little more than an *ad hoc* arrangement to prosecute a particular strike. Some groups, however, such as the textile trades, shipyard workers, keelmen, and seamen with a long tradition of labour conflict had acquired the rudiments of a formal trade union structure. The legalization of Friendly Societies in 1793 provided one means by which funds could be collected for use in strikes, a practice which Francis Place frankly admitted was the reason for the creation of a benefit society among his branch of the London tailoring trade in the early 1790s.[13] Indeed, it was among the skilled London artisans that organization had proceeded furthest. Often anticipating features regarded as the hallmarks of Victorian 'respectability', their distinction from the mass of common labourers lay in their possession of a skill and the higher status, income, and independence which it could command. Although some of these attributes could be possessed by other groups of workers who found themselves in a strong bargaining position because of their strategic importance in a particular trade or location – the unskilled London coal-heavers are an example of this type – it was these men who were in the forefront of organizing the earliest trade societies. By the end of the century, they were accustomed to using a variety of means to counter threats to their livelihood, whether by economic fluctuations or competition from cut-price labour. Friendly Benefit Societies were used to mitigate the threats of accident, sickness and old age. Houses-of-call and tramp networks offered an opportunity for artisans to move about the country and alleviate labour surpluses or withstand a period of strike. Above all, control of apprenticeship provided a crucial means of ensuring the status and bargaining power of individual trades. The utilization of these factors varied between different groups. The shipwrights, for example, founded the St Helena Benefit Society in 1794 with members from all thirty-seven shipyards on the Thames, some 2,000 men in all. As well as functioning as an effective trade union, the Society also paid out benefits for disablement and to widows 'at discretion'.[14] Another group, the London tailors, placed great reliance on the use of a strong union organization and a well-organized system of houses-of-call. As early as 1756 they proved strong enough to maintain a month-long strike and were later to obtain a parliamentary protection for their position. The same was true of the silk-weavers of the East End who, after a spate of 'collective bargaining by riot' in the 1760s, were able to obtain in the 1773 Spitalfields Act protection for their wage rates and control over entry to the trade.[15]

TRADE UNIONS AND THE COMBINATION LAWS

As we have seen, one of the most remarkable features of the years preceding the introduction of the Combination Laws was the number and even the success of groups of workmen in obtaining their ends through collective action. Attempts to check the growth of trade union action had already led to the passing of forty Acts outlawing combinations in individual trades prior to 1799. The Combination Act of 1799 was itself the result of a move by the master millwrights to obtain an Act against combination in the millwright's trade, which was taken up by Pitt's Government and turned into a general Act against all combinations of workmen. Its context is important because, as Professor Aspinall remarked, it was passed against what was regarded as 'a *growing* and illegal practice'.[16] The Act was designed for utility: its crucial feature lay in its provision for summary trial before a magistrate and its requirement for the evidence of only one witness to secure a conviction. Although, by contemporary standards, the penalties attached to the Act of 1799 were not particularly severe – three months in gaol or two months hard labour – they were certainly serious enough to deter many workmen. Above all, the Act offered a speedy recourse to the law for employers faced by any combination of workmen to improve conditions or raise wages, or any clear moves by their workmen in such a direction.

However, in spite of its reputation as an ingredient in Pitt's 'Reign of Terror', the Combination Act of 1799 was modified within a year by organized trade union pressure channelled through sympathetic MPs in Parliament. The Lord Mayor of London presented to the Commons a petition from the journeymen workmen of the Cities of London and Westminster asking for the repeal of the 'injurious, unjust and oppressive' law. Further petitions came from Liverpool, Manchester, Bristol, Plymouth, Bath, Lancaster, Leeds, Derby, Nottingham and Newcastle upon Tyne. Supported by the Whig MPs Richard Brinsley Sheridan and Sir Francis Burdett a new Act modified the original measure. Although it retained the principal features of the earlier legislation, cases had now to be heard before two magistrates, who could not be employers in the trade of the men charged, and provision was made for arbitration. This limited success in modifying the Combination Laws was testimony to the ability of workmen by the end of the eighteenth century to influence Parliament and to manipulate some of the levers of political power.[17]

Moreover, historians have modified the original impression of the Hammonds that the Combination Laws marked a full-scale 'war' on trade unions. In a famous article, Dorothy George argued that the Act of 1800 'was in practice a very negligible instrument of oppression'.[18] She pointed to the frequent reluctance of employers to invoke the law in industrial disputes, their fear of cases being referred to the quarter sessions, and their preference, in serious cases, for the older law of conspiracy and the law of master and servant. The true picture of trade unionism under the Combination Laws is undoubtedly a complex one. It is clear that the Combination Laws were sometimes invoked, as in the celebrated case of the *Times* printers in 1810. Equally, there seems little doubt that some groups of workers were placed in a disadvantageous position by the threat of summary conviction before local magistrates. During the campaign of the shearmen in the South-West woollen industry against the introduction of gigmills, a campaign which involved the use of petitions, appeals to the magistracy, test cases, threatening letters, and only occasional violence, a London magistrate sent to the area to supervise the conviction of large numbers of shearmen commented: 'Two or more Justices meet daily at one or other of the Manufacturing Towns and as the Combination Act affords a very convenient pretext for summoning and examining upon Oath any suspected persons I have continually some before them. It answers the double purpose of keeping the Magistrates at their Post and of alarming the disaffected.'[19]

Elsewhere, however, there is ample evidence that trade union activity continued under the Combination Laws through the agency of Friendly Societies, clandestine meetings and *ad hoc* combinations. The Webbs pointed out that the London craft trades were never more completely organized than between 1800 and 1820 and, although there were prosecutions against combinations of workmen under the Combination Laws or other legislation, magistrates were often prepared to tolerate strikes provided there was no serious disorder.[20] The London tailors were able to obtain rises in wages through combinations in 1795, 1802, 1807, 1810 and 1813 and retained sufficient funds and organization to pay unemployment relief to members. Other trades also saw a strengthening of organization, with increased emphasis on wage-bargaining machinery among groups such as carpenters, brushmakers, basketmakers, compositors, silk-weavers and tinplate workers. The wartime years in London have been characterized by Iowerth Prothero as seeing 'unprecedented inflation, unprecedented wage demands and an unprecedented number of strikes'. As a result the London trade societies 'emerged from the wars far more strongly than when they had begun'.[21]

Among the most well-organized trades were the shipyard workers crucial to the war effort. The shipyard workers in the Government dockyards had a history of disputes reaching far back into the eighteenth century. Petitions for higher wages and strikes had characterized the 1790s. In 1795 the shipwrights had achieved a 50 per cent wage rise from the standard 3s. 6d. per day, itself almost 50 per cent higher than the rate paid in 1784, to 5s. 3d. under the plea of the higher price of provisions and the pressure of war. The Combination Laws, notwithstanding, the shipyard workers were involved in a series of petitions and disputes in 1799–1801, culminating in a national dispute in April–May 1801, which immobilized all the Government dockyards on the South Coast and on the Thames. In February 1801 as the Government was preparing a naval expedition against the League of Armed Neutrality in the Baltic, the men of Plymouth, Portsmouth, Chatham, Sheerness, Woolwich and Deptford presented a joint petition for a doubling of wages. The strike was broken by the firm action of John Jarvis, Earl St Vincent, who locked-out the men and called out the troops in Portsmouth to quell the strike. The following year the shipwrights in the civilian yards conducted a strike, backed by petitions, advertisements in the press and a pamphlet by their chief organizer John Gast, defending the men's case and conduct.[22] Though this strike was unsuccessful, other trades proved relatively successful in their recourse to the metropolitan authorities for increases in wages. Appeals to quarter sessions for wage rises were made by the London tailors in 1800, carpenters in 1803, and shoemakers in 1804. The Spitalfields silk-weavers were also able to obtain modifications of the Acts regulating their trade by collective action in 1792 and 1811.

Elsewhere in the country the Tyne keelmen organized a successful three-week strike in 1809 to increase piecework rates.[23] The handloom weavers of the North, increasingly finding their position undermined by the introduction of power looms and by the flooding of the labour market with cheap unskilled labour, tried petitioning Parliament for a Minimum Wage Bill in 1799 and 1800 and again in 1807, when 130,000 signatures were obtained in Lancashire, Cheshire and Yorkshire. News of the rejection of the Bill in May 1808 led to disturbances in Manchester when thousands of weavers assembled and sent delegates to the manufacturers and town officials to demand some redress for their grievances. A strike was begun which spread through the cotton district in which the men sought an increase in wages of a third. By June 1808 over 60,000 looms were idle and the employers were eventually forced to come to an agreement. Although there was some violence, including incidents of finished work being destroyed by vitriol, the strike was conducted relatively peacefully.

Only a few of the weavers were prosecuted for minor offences and the overall impression of the dispute remains the attempt by the local authorities not to exacerbate the situation by a rigorous prosecution of the law.[24]

Nor was trade union organization confined to the older groups of craftsmen. The first organizations of cotton-spinners had appeared in the 1780s and 1790s. As early as 1785 the Friendly Society of Cotton Spinners at Stockport told its members not to work 'below the normal prices', though the first unions of factory spinners do not seem to have existed before 1792. In that year the first regular organization was formed among the Manchester mule-spinners with rules which prohibited members from working in a shop where a strike had taken place and laying down that 'strangers' should pay 10s. 6d. to join the Society. In 1795 the Manchester cotton-spinners conducted two strikes for wage increases, the latter lasting a month and proving successful. Further disputes are recorded in 1799, 1800, 1802, though in 1803 the masters raised a fund of £20,000 to defeat another strike. In 1810, however, the men took advantage of a surge in production to create a wider organization. Federating their unions, 30,000 spinners struck work organized by a congress at Manchester. Supported by contributions totalling £17,000 collected from spinners still working, the strike lasted four months before funds ran out and the men were forced back to work.[25]

The Luddite outbreaks which affected much of the North and Midlands in 1811–12 have been increasingly recognized as more than a mere blind and spasmodic episode of resistance to technological change. In an important article Eric Hobsbawm placed the Luddite outbreaks within the context of earlier episodes of 'collective bargaining by riot'. Subsequently, historians have spent much of their effort in discussion of how far political motives penetrated into what was clearly a complex and many-sided movement which, as well as covering a wide geographical area, involved different groups of workers, and showed significant changes over time. A certain consensus has emerged that the frame-breaking which began in Nottinghamshire, Leicestershire and Derbyshire in 1811 fits most readily within the tradition of 'collective bargaining by riot'. By 1811 attempts by the framework-knitters of the area to achieve regulation of their trade had failed to achieve any results at a time when unemployment, wage cuts, and high prices bore increasingly hard upon the men. Although the framework-knitter's leader Gravenor Henson had little choice but to disavow the violence which took place, there is little doubt that the campaign of frame-breaking was seen by many workers as a continuation of wage-bargaining by other means. Most reports emphasized the selectivity of the machine-breakers who concentrated on the frames of masters who either underpaid, or produced cheap 'cut-up' stockings using unskilled workers, and the discipline of the bands, meeting secretly, then proceeding from village to village to do the frame-breaking. Many of the documents from the Luddites breathed the familiar language of eighteenth-century trade societies, an appeal to protective legislation of the past and to the authorities to intervene on their behalf. Significantly, too, violent and more peaceful methods appeared to move in cadence with each other. When the first and major wave of machine-breaking was crushed by the stationing of 2,000 troops in the Midlands, a 'United Committee of Framework-Knitters' was formed to promote a parliamentary Bill to regulate the trade. When the Bill was rejected in the Lords and the framework-knitters prosecuted under the Combination Laws in July 1814, frame-breaking was resumed.[26]

In Yorkshire, to which Luddism spread in 1812, it occurred in the aftermath of the failure of a joint campaign by the 'croppers' of the South-West and Yorkshire to enforce the Tudor statutes against the use of machinery and unapprenticed labour. The two areas had co-operated through delegates and had put a Bill before Parliament in 1805 backed by several petitions. In the event, the croppers' agitation failed. Annual Suspending Acts allowed manufacturers to introduce machinery until a general repeal of paternalistic regulation of the woollen trade was passed in 1809. Frustrated in constitutional and peaceful methods, the Yorkshire croppers turned to machine-breaking in the midst of unemployment and high prices. Although there is *some* evidence of political, even insurrectionary undertones to Yorkshire Luddism, their activities were only a variation upon the other means of resisting the erosion of the bargaining position of the workers. It was significant that in another part of the country in 1812, the Scottish weavers conducted one of the most impressive strikes in early trade union history, bringing 40,000 looms to a stand-still for six weeks in an area stretching from Carlisle to Aberdeen.[27]

From one point of view the history of trade unions in the wartime years can be read as a doleful chronicle of defeat and repression. The repeal and evasion of existing protective legislation in pursuit of *laissez-faire* economic principles and the use of the army and the law to break resistance certainly added up to a series of defeats for the workmen concerned. But resistance had been born out of, and also promoted, organization, and was sometimes formal, often *ad hoc*. Strikes and disputes continued to ripple through the manufacturing areas even during the bleak post-war depression. A six-week strike among the seamen of the North-East ports in the autumn of 1815 to obtain higher wages and agreed manning levels has been noted by one historian both for the degree of organization among the men and the moderation of the authorities in dealing with it.[28] There is growing evidence even among less-skilled groups of workers such as colliers, ironworkers, lead-miners, and cotton-operatives that strikes were increasingly replacing food riots as the primary means of defending living standards. In South Wales, the ironworkers' strike against wage reductions in 1816, as well as using traditional features such as marching gangs and attacks on work and masters' houses, was characterized by a high degree of organization among the men.[29] In 1819 the magistrates of the St. Helens' area were surprised by the sophisticated tactics used by the local colliers in a strike. The men used the technique of 'strike in detail', a succession of strikes in different pits, so that working miners could support those on strike.[30] Equally significant was the strike of Manchester cotton operatives in 1818. By the end of July 20,000 workers were idle. The spinners' strike was organized by a committee of twelve to manage funds collected from sympathetic trade groups in other parts of the country. Orderly parades were organized through the centre of Manchester, the very discipline of which alarmed the local authorities. As strike funds ran low, the General Union of Spinners attempted to organize a General Union of Trades, also known as the Philanthropic Society. Letters were sent out to various trades asking them to join and a General Meeting of Trades was held on 19 August with representatives of fifteen trades which passed a series of resolutions. Although the Philanthropic Society lapsed within a month, two spinners' delegates were sent to London to obtain the support of John Gast, the Secretary of the London Shipwrights' Club, who was the leader of the movement for a general union in London, the 'Philanthropic Hercules', set up in December 1818 with Gast as President.[31]

While these movements towards a General Union were short-lived, they were to recur with greater strength in the 1830s. In spite of their failure, they emphasized the wider ambitions of trade unionists in the post-war period and the extent to which unions whether clandestine, in the guise of Friendly Societies, or operating more or less openly, had begun to seek a wider focus for their activities. The repeal of the Combination Laws in 1824 through the efforts of Francis Place and Joseph Hume was, in a backhanded way, testimony to the growing power of trade unions. Place's arguments that the Combination Laws actually promoted disputes and strikes and that their removal would lead to their withering away was convincing to employers and MPs in a context where they recognized that the trade union organization, far from being crushed, was highly active.

The 1824 Act not only swept away the Combination Laws, but also freed trade unions from the threat of prosecution for conspiracy. The effect was almost as if a safety valve had been released: trade unions bounded into open conflict, with strikes and some violence in support of wage increases. The result was a hasty reconsideration of the 1824 Act and a threat that the Combination Laws would be reimposed. With Place as chief wire-puller, backed by strong trade union protests, a compromise was reached in the 1825 Act. The Act exempted from prosecution only those combinations of workmen which met together solely to agree what wages or hours of employment to require or demand. Combinations for any other objects were unlawful. Trade societies could be prosecuted for violence, threats, intimidation, molestation or obstruction and were, once again, made subject to the common law of conspiracy. The overall effect of the statute was to enforce a narrow definition of the lawful activities of a trade union, confining these to peaceful collective bargaining over wages and hours only. Combination to negotiate outside these limits was liable at law not only as contravening the terms of the statute, but as criminal conspiracy at common law 'in restraint of trade'. In addition many of the methods which a union might employ in furtherance of its objectives were liable to prosecution, as well as being so vaguely defined as to cause considerable difficulties in the practical operation of collective bargaining. Although the legislation of 1825 was a legal landmark for trade unionism, it did not prevent numerous prosecutions for trade unionists in the future.

RADICALISM AND REFORM

The formation of the first political societies by working men and the rise of a popular reform movement added a new dimension to the political activities of trade unions. The influence of the French Revolution and the writings of Thomas Paine had been followed by the formation of political societies in scores of towns and cities in Britain. At least eighty such societies existed in England by the mid-1790s and in the case of the London Corresponding Societies, founded in January 1792, as many as ninety 'divisions' were in existence by 1795. Although these societies were sometimes dominated by middle-class reformers, in places such as London, Sheffield and Norwich they were artisan-based. Division lists of the London Corresponding Society show their members as being drawn predominantly from the London skilled trades. Moreover, their forms of organization, with General Committees, Treasurers and delegates and 1d. a week subscriptions, clearly owed a great deal to the traditions of the existing trade societies. Francis Place, a leading light in the London Corresponding Society from 1794 to 1797, was already a veteran of the world of trade clubs and Friendly Societies. In Sheffield, a town of small masters and artisans where trade societies were strong, the Sheffield Society for Constitutional Information had an estimated 2,000 members by the summer of 1792 drawn largely from its skilled trades. The East Anglian textile trades supported many independent artisans whose talents for organization had already expressed themselves in strong craft unions which proved durable enough to force up their wage rates during the Napoleonic Wars, even when the trade was in evident decline. The Norwich artisans supported at least forty small tavern clubs and *The Cabinet*, an intellectual journal which reflected the attitudes of some of the most enthusiastic supporters of the French Revolution.[32]

As early as 1793 the principal artisan societies had espoused a radical political programme which included universal suffrage and annually-elected parliaments. Some of the more detailed lists of resolutions also included economic and social grievances, complaints against taxes, high food prices, the game laws, and the prosecutions of workmen for participating in trade union activities. Although the conventional picture of the 1790s ends with the disintegration of the lower-class reform societies under the twin pressures of disillusionment and government repression, E.P. Thompson has stressed the importance of the decade after the French Revolution for its role in the creation of a wider 'working-class consciousness' which embraced both political and trade union activities, writing '. . . at any time before the 1840s it is a mistake to segregate in our minds political disaffection and industrial organization'.[33]

The claim is an important one, not least because it has been the subject of much criticism by historians who find it essential to draw distinctions between trade union activities and those specifically directed towards political ends. Such disputes have focused around the existence of a 'revolutionary underground' in the years 1799–1812 and the interpretation of episodes such as Luddism. The difficulties are very great, partly because historians have often been operating from quite different ideological perspectives – essentially Marxist and non-Marxist – and because the evidence itself is often of a highly contentious nature: spy reports, confessions, upper-class opinions, agitational literature and oral traditions. At the very least it can be said that in *some* areas, at *some* times, and for *some* people, there was an overlap of trade union and political action in what might pass for a 'working-class consciousness'; and Thompson and some who have followed him have highlighted parts of Lancashire, Yorkshire and Wales as beginning to display these characteristics by the Napoleonic Wars. In truth, an often more accurate phrase would be an 'artisan consciousness', for it was frequently the skilled workmen who provided the backbone of early radical societies and who spawned the most persistent trade societies. Often, however, the picture is less clearcut; trade unions before and after 1825 could and did operate without any reference to the prevailing aspirations of the more committed popular radicals. In areas such as the North-East, Nottingham and parts of London, trade unions seem frequently to have come into existence and acted quite independently of radical politics. Even in areas favoured by some historians for the display of a 'working-class consciousness' there was often a failure of trade union and political action to march together. A running together of every riot, strike and radical handbill in a particular town does not necessarily indicate the presence of an incipient 'working-class movement'. However, the question of interpretation is primarily one of *a priori* assumptions and perspectives. Those who are prepared to accept a distinction between 'class in itself' and 'class for itself' will be prepared to adduce even the most sectional and fragmentary actions as evidence of the growth of 'working-class consciousness' and the growth of class conflict in early nineteenth-century Britain. Those, on the other hand, who argue that an effective working class is a more convincing construct for the later years of the nineteenth century than for the earlier, inevitably insist upon the important distinctions to be drawn between industrial and political activity.[34]

Nonetheless, in the years which followed the Napoleonic Wars there is little doubt that increasing numbers of workmen were recruited to the cause of parliamentary reform. Groups such as the hand-loom weavers who had made repeated attempts to secure economic remedies to their distress without obvious success were increasingly being driven to consider political remedies. In 1817, the year of the March of the Blanketeers, Professor Read has demonstrated how the Lancashire weavers began to turn their attention to parliamentary reform. In their petitions of that year they complained of the failure of their frequent petitions to the King, the Prince Regent and the House of Commons to provide relief for their sufferings. These evils, they concluded, could only be ended by parliamentary reform.[35] These sentiments echoed the strenuous efforts by radical journalists such as William Cobbett, whose cheap edition of the *Political Register*, or 'Twopenny Trash', first appeared at the end of 1816. Cobbett's message was simple and direct: that the sufferings of the labourer derived from a corrupt Parliament and that parliamentary reform was the key to easing the burdens upon the poor and improving their standard of living. The same message was being spread by the mushrooming radical journals of the post-war years, the *Black Dwarf*, the *Cap of Liberty*, the *Republican*, and the *Gorgon*. The first Hampden Club had been founded in 1812 and during the next three years the veteran reformer Major John Cartwright made tours of the manufacturing districts to carry his message to all who would listen. By 1816 Hampden Clubs and Union Clubs were springing up in the North and Midlands, many of them formed entirely by working men, often subscribing a small sum to purchase pamphlets and newspapers and meeting in chapels, cottages and alehouses. The great reform campaigns of the years 1816–19 undoubtedly witnessed the involvement of thousands of working men, some of whom were also trade unionists, as well as others who were not. In 1817 more than 700 petitions for reform were presented from over 350 towns, many of them the unrepresented manufacturing towns, while in 1818 there were over 500.[36]

At the tragic Peterloo meeting of August 1819, some 60,000 weavers attended, along with representatives of other trades. It appears that many of the weavers had wavered in their attachment to reform in the months after the dispersal of the Blanketeers, frightened off by the repressive stance of the government. The weavers, unlike the spinners, dissociated themselves from the radical leaders during the strikes of 1818. By the same token, however, the spinners were giving a hearing to radical orators and gradually by 1819 most of the important groups of workmen in Lancashire were prepared to throw their weight behind the radical cause.[37] In the aftermath of 'Peterloo', the reform campaign in Lancashire began to ebb. Improved trade, government repression, and divisions within the radical movement all played a part. Elsewhere there was a similar story. For a time, trade unionists had become involved in political agitation, but while the demand for reform ebbed and flowed very much in accordance with the trade cycle, trade union organization continued in existence, often increasing in strength in periods of expansion where reform depended upon the bitter lesson of 'distress' to obtain its followers.

Trade societies played a significant part in the agitation which surrounded the passing of the Reform Act of 1832. Francis Place wrote that: 'The systematic way in which the people proceeded, their steady perseverence, their activity and skill astounded the enemies of reform. Meetings of almost every description of persons were held in cities, towns and parishes; by journeymen tradesmen in the clubs, and by common workmen who had no trade clubs or associations of any kind. . .'. Monster demonstrations in London, Birmingham and elsewhere were organized by middle-class reformers which depended for their intimidatory aspect upon the attendance of thousands of artisans and labourers. Although the political unions which dominated the reform agitation were led by the middle classes, scores of 'low unions' sprang into existence in 1831 which were almost entirely organized by the working classes. The National Union of the Working Classes in the capital offered a more potent threat of insurrectionary activity, sufficient for the government to ban its paramilitary proceedings. Even after the Reform Act was passed, working-class radicals remained organized in places such as London and Manchester ready to implement a further stage in franchise reform. Spring 1833 witnessed a revival of reform activity with a mass meeting at Birmingham attended by an estimated 180,000 people. On 13 May 1833 the NUWC planned a mass meeting at Cold Bath Fields to discuss preparations for a National Convention. Broken up by police, one of whom was killed, the Convention plans had to be suspended. Nonetheless, the seeds had been sown among some of the better-organized sections of workmen for a further campaign for political reform in which trade unions were to provide one of the most important elements among an increasingly wide range of working-class organizations.[38]

THE GENERAL UNIONS

The early 1830s were also marked by the development of movements for a general union, whose origins lay in the ideas of men such as John Doherty, the cotton-spinners' organizer, and John Gast, the London artisan leader. Ten years after the 'Philanthropic Society' had been formed in Lancashire and the 'Philanthropic Hercules' in London, a renewed impulse came in 1829 when Doherty called a conference to establish a Grand General Union of the Operative Spinners of Great Britain and Ireland at which the resolution was passed 'That one grand general union of all the operative spinners in the United Kingdom be now formed, for the mutual support and protection of all.' Shortly after, Doherty launched a Union of Trades, recruiting widely in parts of the North, Staffordshire and South Wales. In April 1830 it adopted the name of the National Association for the Protection of Labour (NAPL). By 1831 the NAPL was in difficulties. The General Spinners' Union had collapsed after an unsuccessful series of strikes, demoralizing many NAPL supporters, one of its secretaries made off with funds, and there were arguments over tactics between Doherty and the Manchester-based Executive Committee. By 1832 the NAPL had broken up; it failed to capture wide support outside Lancashire and was broken up by the defeat of the cotton-spinners who proved its main support. More ambitious attempts at General Unionism were to follow. In 1827 a General Union of Bricklayers and Carpenters was established and in 1832 converted into the Operative Builders' Union (OBU), which organized a twice-yearly 'Builders' Parliament,' and was involved in a series of strikes and lock-outs to enforce union recognition. But while Doherty had been primarily concerned with using general unions as a means of strengthening the bargaining power of his followers by building up national organization and obtaining help from other trades, the OBU was influenced by Owenism, proposing to offer not only Friendly Society benefits but also to compete with the master builders by offering to organize direct work. Their high hopes, however, were destroyed in a protracted lock-out in 1833 when some of the building trades split off into individual craft societies and others were driven out of existence.

The most important of the movements towards General Unionism was the Grand National Consolidated Trades' Union of Great Britain and Ireland. In February 1834 a conference of trade union delegates met in London to consolidate all trade unions into a single united body. Its impulse came from the experience of the Derby 'Turn-Out' of 1833 when the Derby employers had attempted to break combinations in the local trades by declaring that they would stop employing union members and not re-employ any person who had not repudiated union membership. Lock-outs occurred in other towns and fund-raising activities to support the men were organized by the Birmingham Committee of Trades. The Derby workers also appealed to London which led to the calling of the conference out of which the Grand National was born. At another level, however, it drew upon the growing political and idealistic aims of groups of workers who were increasingly involved in a wide range of activities from support for parliamentary reform to local trade union activity. Owenite ideas also played a part, though many of the supporters of the GNCTU may have looked no further than providing a means of supporting strikes. The resolutions passed at the conference in 1834 reflected both practical and Owenite emphases, calling for: unity of action of all unions; settlement of workers on the land; lodges of GNCTU to set up workrooms to employ strikers and unemployed; lodges to set up funds for sick and aged and for funeral expenses; lodges to set up depots for provision of necessary goods; lodges to furnish means of respectable entertainment; Lodges of Industrious Females to be an integral part of unions; and District Miscellaneous Lodges to be set up to cover trades without existing organization. Owen promoted the GNCTU for ideological purposes, as the vehicle for the creation of a new society, but the delegates probably had more immediate and pragmatic aims in view. Thus the first action of the GNCTU was to decree a levy of 1s. per member to help the 'turn-outs' of Derby and Worcester.[39]

The membership was dominated by the skilled trades, chief among them being the London tailors, described by Francis Place as 'Owenized and union mad'; the London shoemakers also played a prominent part. Other London trades included the cabinetmakers; saddlemakers; silk-weavers; tinplate workers; wood-turners; ropemakers; shipwrights; and bookbinders. But the membership did not include the OBU, the potters, the cotton-spinners or the woollen-workers of Yorkshire. The Webbs' view that the GNCTU had as many as 500,000 members has been rejected subsequently, only 16,000 paid-up members having been discovered, 11,000 of them in London.[40] Sympathy was certainly wider. John Foster's description of the mood of the Oldham workmen in 1833–34 certainly suggests a flavour of near-millenarian expectation in which the newly articulated concept of the 'Grand National Holiday' or 'General Strike' captured the imagination of thousands of operatives and craftsmen.[41] In the event, calls by Doherty and other leaders for a general strike in April 1834 in support of the GNCTU received only patchy response in Lancashire, Yorkshire and the Midlands. One by one, the strikes in the major centres of GNCTU strength collapsed during the summer of 1834. By the end of June, the Derby movement was crushed and the men forced to renounce union action. The London tailors were also broken by a strike in June 1834. In Yorkshire, the Woollen Trades Union of Leeds was dissolved as were the unions associated with it.

But the bleak story of the failure of General Unionism did not extinguish trade union influence. The story of the 'Tolpuddle Martyrs', six Dorsetshire agricultural workers convicted in March 1834 for administering illegal oaths in connection with an Agricultural Labourers' Friendly Society and sentenced to seven years transportation, while often cited as an illustration of the persecution of working men who sought to organize themselves, was perhaps even more remarkable for the significant display of organized pressure by trade unions and other sympathizers against the sentences. Protest meetings were held all over the country, while in London 25,000 men marched through the streets in the most orderly demonstration of organized working-class pressure seen since the Reform crisis. Though the sentence was not rescinded as a result of these demonstrations, they confirmed the growing ability of trade unionists and radical sympathizers to orchestrate a campaign of protest against the authorities. The collection of subscriptions for the Glasgow cotton-spinners convicted of intimidation and arson in 1837 further illustrated this capacity.

Moreover, many local craft unions and Friendly Societies remained in existence and others were soon to revive. As Malcolm Thomis has indicated, continuity with the 1820s was seen in the build-up of small unions, 'town by town, craft by craft' during the 1830s and the build-up of wider district organization, as in the county units among the miners in Northumberland, Durham, Lancashire and Yorkshire.[42] Trade unionists were also involved in the campaign for factory legislation and the opposition to the New Poor Law. The Factory Commissioners in 1833 said of the leaders of the Ten Hours movement that it was led by 'the same men who in every instance of rash and headlong strikes have assumed the command of the discontented members of the operative body . . .'. At the local level, too, Foster has shown how in towns such as Oldham trade unionists were by the mid-1830s already beginning to manipulate the machinery of local government to their own advantage, through parish vestries, watch committees and, ultimately, town councils.[43]

FROM CHARTISM TO LABOURISM

While the future lay with the steady development of better-organized and more widely-based trade societies and the growing involvement of trade unionists in local government and ameliorative campaigns, the Chartist movement was the most impressive of the popular agitations of the late 1830s and 1840s. The People's Charter with its articulation of a programme of radical parliamentary reform based on the premises of universal suffrage, annual Parliaments, and vote by ballot became the focus of a mass campaign between 1839 and 1848. Chartism was a highly complex and multi-faceted movement which grew out of many different strands of working-class activity in the 1830s and which, at the local level, displays an almost bewildering range of attitudes and organizations. The relationship between Chartism and trade unionism was extremely complex. Asa Briggs put forward the view that still commands major support, of a 'pendulum swing' by workmen between economic action through trade unions and political action through Chartism. Support by working men for Chartism was indeed subject to many factors, the economic position of particular trades, the character of local politics, and the movements of the trade cycle. Most historians have accepted that the core of the Chartist movement lay in the skilled artisans who had formulated the Charter following disillusionment with the Reform Act of 1832 and their experiences in the 1830s, to which in the years of economic depression, 1839, 1842 and 1848 were attached large masses of workers who had hitherto played little part in any organized political activity.[44]

Detailed analysis has suggested that Chartism was strongest in two types of area: vulnerable centres of craft industry such as the West Country woollen centres and the centres of outwork and hand-loom weaving in the North and Midlands and some of the medium-sized industrial towns such as Stockport and Bolton. It tended to be the old, handicraft industries which supported Chartism rather than the more 'modern' sectors of the economy, represented by places such as St Helens and Crewe.[45] It was the outworkers of the weaving, knitting, woolcombing and nailmaking trades who in August 1839 accepted the call for a 'Sacred Month', a general strike, from the Chartist Convention. Factory operatives were far less enthusiastic; although some adhered to Chartism at the depths of the depression in 1838–39 and 1842, they soon moved back into trade unionism. Moreover, some of the most skilled and organized sections of the workforce were often split over support for Chartism. Some, such as the trades which supported the London Working Men's Association, had played a leading part in the formulation of the People's Charter. Other groups, however, dropped out of Chartism when it became tainted with violence in the aftermath of the Newport 'rising' of November 1839 and some, like the potters' union, became antagonistic to Chartism.[46]

The tensions between Chartism and trade unionism were well illustrated in the summer of 1842 when the Chartists sought to turn the stoppages of that summer into a 'general strike' for the Charter. The strike movement was largely spontaneous in character, a reaction to wage cuts, high prices, unemployment, and truck payments which spread from the North Staffordshire coalfield to Cheshire, Lancashire, Yorkshire, the Midlands and the North-East. Some local strike leaders had already endorsed the Charter, but the declaration by trade delegates in Manchester in August 1842 of a general strike for the Charter was certainly an attempt to capitalize upon the strike movement which would have been taking place in any case. By the end of the month, however, support for the strike was crumbling; few trades had sufficient funds to maintain their members during a season of high prices and unemployment.[47] The strike movement of 1842 was evidence to the well-tried tactics of the industrial workers. Delegate conferences and co-ordinated strike action had been used before but were used here, for a time, in sup- port of broader political objectives. However, several groups of strikers maintained far more interest in their immediate economic objectives than in the Charter. The cotton-operatives, miners, and potters were less well represented among the trade delegates and their adherence to the Charter was patchy and temporary. The factory operatives of Ashton and Stalybridge were among the most strenuous opponents of turning the movement into a strike for the Charter. Another group, the potters, resented the intrusion of Chartist orators into their affairs and blamed them for inciting violence.

Active Chartists were often aware that trade societies would not always throw their weight behind the movement. The 'upper trades' in particular drew the hostility of men such as Feargus O'Connor and Ernest Jones for the pursuance of narrow sectional aims at the expense of the wider movement.[48] Many unions, however, remained reluctant participants in what was increasingly seen as a violent and 'unrespectable' movement. 'No politics' rules and a concentration upon immediate problems of employment and wages frequently diverted organized labour from the more ambitious and idealistic courses charted for it by ideologues such as Ernest Jones. Other causes, such as the Anti-Corn Law movement, temperance and co-operation often tempted ambitious and committed working-class men as much as, if not more than, Chartism.

With the ebbing of the Chartist movement after the defeats and suppression of the 1840s, the period of 'labourism' and 'model unionism' was ushered in. Some historians have argued that the years after 1848 did mark a decisive break with the 'insurgent' movements of the 1830s and 1840s. From this perspective, State force and economic power coerced a highly vulnerable workforce into acceptance of the dominant economic and ideological assumptions of expansive Victorian capitalism. In truth, however, radical alternatives had never captured the degree of support in the 1830s and 1840s which would make such an interpretation viable. Piecemeal and sectional action had been the hallmark of trade union action almost from the beginning. While there were undoubtedly minorities of workmen who at one time or another accepted visions for a Paineite, Owenite or Chartist reconstruction of society, they remained minorities. The majority of trade societies which formed the single most important and persistent unit of working-class organization in most towns had very early recognized the need for accommodation with the authorities, an acceptance of 'respectability', and protection for their place in society.

The first generation of notable trade union leaders, men such as John Gast, John Doherty and Thomas Hepburn were, at least in public, opposed to violence. Moreover, while men like Gast certainly associated with reformers and even ultra-radicals and were prepared to support them in their legal campaigns, they concentrated upon the development of more effective union organization and the kind of stance which might produce concessions from government and employers. Men such as Doherty remained wedded to peaceful methods of organization as the principal means of obtaining their ends. Similarly in the great miners' strikes in the North-East in 1831–32, Thomas Hepburn adopted as his watchwords moderation and abstention from violence, on the grounds that these offered the greatest hope of obtaining public sympathy. Hepburn urged his men to refrain from violence even under the provocation of strike-breaking and eviction from their cottages.[49]

These strikes illustrated features which were to characterize trade union-ism in later years. Trade unionists were conscious of their ambivalent legal status and wished to avoid provoking the authorities into acting against them; at the same time, the more sophisticated trade unionists, like many popular radicals, were coming to recognize that 'public opinion' was an important factor in industrial disputes, in the battle for full legal recognition, and in the campaign for political rights. In this context, it was hardly surprising that many trade unionists in the 1840s stood aloof from Chartism and proved all too ready to embrace with open arms the fruits of 'respectability' in the mid-Victorian period.

Thus, one of the most striking characteristics of industrial bargaining from the 1840s was the increasing emphasis placed by union leaders on 'respectability' and non-violence. To take one example, the formation of county unions in the coal-mining industry led in 1842 to the creation of the Miners' Association of Great Britain and Ireland, which within two years could claim 70,000 members. Largely eschewing the Chartist movement, the Miners' Association began a campaign for better wages and working conditions which in 1844 produced a bitter four-month conflict in the North-East and other coalfields. From the outset, the strikers determined to keep the peace as much as possible and even newspapers hostile to their cause commented on the self-discipline and restraint. Although there were attacks on blacklegs, the union leaders tried to deal with the problem at source by sending representatives to other areas in order to discourage them from providing strike-breaking labour, publishing notices in newspapers to inform people that the strike was taking place and explaining the issues involved. A principal fear of the union leaders was that violent proceedings would be turned against them in the courts and press. Numerous resolutions were passed to keep the peace, with warnings that anyone who did not do so would be deemed a traitor to the cause.[50]

As in earlier disputes, it was difficult to prevent unrest at the spate of mass evictions ordered by some of the coalowners. Faced with the eviction notices one of their leaders urged the strikers: 'Stay in the House, your families around, lock the door (as against an ordinary housebreaker), sit down or go to bed, firmly and quietly state that you have read in a book that "an Englishman's home is his castle". Beyond that, offer no resistance whatever. Let them *carry* you out.' Although this advice was not always followed, the *Newcastle Courant* admitted that it would be 'unjust to the great body of men not to state that distinctly their general demeanour is remarkable peaceful'.[51]

The general determination of union leaders to preserve an officially 'moderate' tone was partly conditioned by the vague legal status of trade unions, and it was the Miners' Association solicitor, W.P. Roberts, 'the Pitmen's Attorney-General', who had done much to shape this policy in 1844. Similar determination to win a strike without resort to violence was shown by the Amalgamated Association of Operative Cotton Spinners who struck work in 1853–54. A successful strike in Stockport supported by funds from other districts was followed by a protracted dispute in Preston. Almost equally matched in funds and determination, the masters and men were locked in a dispute from October 1853 to May 1854. But it was not until strike-breaking labour was brought in from Ireland in February that any disturbances occurred. Almost as soon as they did, the local magistrates began to arrest the strike leaders on charges of 'molesting and obstructing' the imported labour. Even so, Dickens, who visited the town in February 1854, was deeply impressed by the peaceful atmosphere and the good order of the strike meetings.

By the 1860s there was a revival of mining trade unionism in Northumberland. Although there were evictions and conflicts with bailiffs during a fifteen-week strike at Cramlington in 1865, this dispute has been described as 'the last strike in the mould of 1832 and 1844'. Increasingly, union leaders such as Thomas Burt sought to organize 'model unions' based on high subscriptions and dependable members, their aim being to avoid strikes and secure union recognition. One of the most notable examples of a disciplined and publicity-conscious strike occurred during the campaign of the engineers on Tyneside to reduce working hours in 1871. The 'Nine Hours' League' was sufficiently strong to prevent its men returning to work on compromise terms during a protracted dispute and went to considerable lengths to avoid disturbances in the face of the introduction of blackleg labour and the prosecution of union members for breach of contract. Some disturbances occurred, but the strike leaders vigorously and publicly declared their opposition to such incidents; and although they knew full well that their words would have little effect on their more militant members and sympathizers, they maintained a strenuous defence of moderation and non-violence in order to appeal to public sympathy. The historians of this dispute have written: 'It would be ingenuous indeed to accept at face value all assurances given by Leaguers that their activities were invariably peaceful. The combination of a skilful and conspicuously non-violent leadership equipped with a large supply of emollient phrases, together with a good deal of successful intimidation was a singularly effective one.'[52]

That respectability could still display another face was shown by increasing concern about trade union 'Outrages', the most famous of which occurred in Sheffield in 1866. The Sheffield incidents arose out of a series of attacks on non-union members of the cutlery trades. A long series of instances of intimidation had preceded what was to become a *cause célèbre* of trade union history, the blowing-up of a workman's house by gunpowder in October 1866. Bitterly attacked in the newspapers, the trade unions found themselves being subjected to a Royal Commission of Inquiry which investigated many aspects of trade union practice; the evidence collected provided many examples of restrictive practices and minor forms of 'outrage', especially in the building trades.[53] In their evidence before the commission, however, trade unionists concentrated on the beneficial functions of the unions and their peaceful intentions; they also used the enquiry as a platform from which to air their grievances about their legal disabilities. As a result, the Majority Report of the Commission came out in favour of legalizing trade unions, a proposal which was enshrined in the trade union legislation of the 1870s.[54]

The mid-Victorian era has generally been regarded as the heyday of 'New Model Unionism' among the highly-paid artisans. The formation of the Amalgamated Society of Engineers (ASE) in 1851 has been taken as marking the demonstration of this tendency in an expanding sector of industry with emphasis upon high subscription fees and tight organization. Groups such as the carpenters and bricklayers in London soon followed, but 'model unionism' tended to be less important outside London where small local unions remained the rule. Only a minority of the London and provincial craftsmen were even in a union at all, 10 per cent being one estimate in 1867 for all London trades and figures of between 10 and 19 per cent being given for the provincial trades such as carpenters and bricklayers. Nonetheless, membership grew in the mid-Victorian era, the ASE quadrupling in size between 1850 and 1880. Provincial unions could still, however, lead a highly fluctuating existence, dependent upon the local fortunes of trades and disputes.[55]

With the formation of the TUC in 1868 trade unions were increasingly being recognized as significant pressure groups in national and local politics, more and more prepared to represent their interests through political parties, local government and extra-parliamentary organizations. Trade unionists had allied with middle-class radicals of the Reform League to obtain the Second Reform Act in 1867. It was the demonstrations of trade unionists and workmen in 1866 and 1867 in London which, if not decisive in forcing a Reform Act through Parliament, had at least contributed to a sense of urgency about the question of a further extension of the suffrage.[56] By the 1860s, too, trade councils became a new municipal forum for the organized section of the working class, predominantly the skilled workers, in cities such as London, Sheffield, Birmingham, Edinburgh, Glasgow, Liverpool and Manchester.[57]

The situation had been reached by 1870 where the better-paid, most highly-organized and best-educated sections of the workforce had established themselves with sufficiently strong organization, and sufficient means of articulating their grievances, both industrial and political, to have been assimilated into the existing framework of society. While vast numbers of unskilled workers, women, children and the whole of the agricultural workforce remained virtually unorganized a small group had made very significant advances indeed. It was, however, to take almost another half-century before even a majority of unskilled workers came into union membership. Meanwhile, the trade unions, so often looked on as the standard-bearers of an industrial working class, had steadily eschewed the most radical political options of the previous century and had instead become models of 'success'. At least one historian has noted the irony of their position, one which still influences their historiography:[58]

As a successful cause, trade unionism automatically became entitled to the patronage with which successful causes are endowed within the Whig tradition. And as they gained new friends for deflecting the working classes from direct action, industrial sabotage and revolutionary conspiracy, towards more acceptable modes of conduct, so did the unions lose old friends for precisely the same reason, selling out to the establishment and robbing the working-class movement of its revolutionary potential.

NOTES AND REFERENCES

1.   S. and B. Webb, *The History of Trade Unionism*, Longmans, Green, London (rev. edn), 1920.
2.   J.L. and B. Hammond, *The Skilled Labourer, 1760–1832*, Longmans, Green, London, 1919.
3.   E.J. Hobsbawm, 'Trade union historiography', *Bulletin of the Society for the Study of Labour History*, no. 8 (spring 1964) p. 32.
4.   H. Pelling, *A History of British Trade Unionism*, Penguin Books, Harmondsworth, 1963; A.E. Musson, *British Trade Unions, 1800–1875*, Macmillan, London, 1972.
5.   E.J. Hobsbawm, 'The tramping artisan' and 'The machine breakers' in *Labouring Men*, Weidenfeld and Nicolson, London, 1964.
6.   See G. Rudé, *The Crowd in History*, Wiley, New York, 1964 and E.P. Thompson, 'The moral economy of the English crowd in the eighteenth century', *Past and Present*, 50 (1971).
7.   C.R. Dobson, *Masters and Journeymen: a prehistory of industrial relations, 1717–1800*, Croom Helm, London, 1980.
8.   A.E. Musson, *British Trade Unions*, op. cit., p. 15.
9.   See W.A.J. Shelton, *English Hunger and Industrial Disorders: a study of social conflict during the first decade of George III's reign*, Macmillan, London, 1973, pp. 165–202.
10.   See J.M. Fewster, 'The Keelmen of Tyneside in the eighteenth century', *Durham University Journal* (new ser.), 19 (1957–58).
11.   J.L. and B. Hammond, *The Skilled Labourer*, op. cit., pp. 12–17.
12.   See C.R. Dobson, *Masters and Journeymen*, op. cit., pp. 20–29; and J. Stevenson, *Popular Disturbances in England, 1700–1870*, Longman, London, 1979, pp. 127–34.

13. See St John G. Ervine, 'Francis Place, 1771–1854' in M. Katanka (ed.), *Radicals, Reformers and Socialists*, Charles Knight, London, 1973, pp. 38–42.

14. For the shipwrights see D. Wilson, 'Government dock-yard workers in Portsmouth, 1793–1815', Warwick University Ph.D. thesis, 1975 and I.J. Prothero, *Artisans and Politics in Early Nineteenth-Century London: John Gast and his times*, Dawson, Folkestone, 1979, pp. 33–39.

15. See L.D. Schwartz, 'Conditions of life and work in London, c. 1770–1820, with special reference to East London', D.Phil., Oxford University, 1976.

16. A. Aspinall, *The Early English Trade Unions*, Batchworth, London, 1949, p. xii.

17. See C.R. Dobson, *Masters and Journeymen*, op. cit., pp. 146–48.

18. M.D. George, 'The combination laws', *Economic History Review*, VI (1936); see also her 'The combination laws reconsidered', *Economic History*, no. 2 (May 1927).

19. J.L. and B. Hammond, *The Skilled Labourer*, op. cit., p. 176.

20. S. and B. Webb, *The History of Trade Unionism*, op. cit., p. 83.

21. I.J. Prothero, *Artisans and Politics*, op. cit., pp. 40–46.

22. See J. Gast, *Calumny Defeated or a Compleat Vindication of the working shipwrights during the late disputes with their employers*, London, 1802.

23. D.J. Rowe, 'The strikes of the Tyneside keelmen in 1809 and 1819', *The International Review of Social History*, 13 (1968), pp. 58–66.

24. J.L. and B. Hammond, *The Skilled Labourer*, op. cit., pp. 72–81 and D. Bythell, *The Handloom Weavers*, Cambridge University Press, Cambridge, 1969, pp. 189–91.

25. See R.G. Kirkby and A.E. Musson, *The Voice of the People: John Doherty 1798–1854*, Manchester University Press, Manchester, 1975, pp. 13–14.

26. See J. Stevenson, *Popular Disturbances*, op. cit., pp. 155–57. For discussion of Henson's role see E.P. Thompson, *The Making of the English Working Class*, Penguin, Harmondsworth, 1968, pp. 924–34 and R.A. Church and S.D. Chapman, 'Gravenor Henson and the making of the English working class' in E.L. Jones and G.E. Mingay (eds), *Land, Labour and Population in the Industrial Revolution*, Routledge and Kegan Paul, London, 1967.

27. See J. Stevenson, *Popular Disturbances*, op. cit., pp. 157–62.

28. See D.J. Rowe, 'Trade Unions and Strike Action in the North-East before 1871' in E. Allen, J.F. Clarke, N. McCord, and D.J. Rowe, *The North-East Engineers' Strikes of 1871*, Frank Graham, Newcastle upon Tyne, 1971 pp. 65–70.

29. See D.J.V. Jones, *Before Rebecca: popular protests in Wales, 1793–1835*, Allen Lane, London, 1973, pp. 69–85.

30.   See T.C. Barker and J.R. Harris, *A Merseyside Town in the Industrial Revolution, St. Helens, 1750–1900*, Liverpool University Press, Liverpool, 1954, pp. 159–63.

31.   See R.G. Kirkby and A.E. Musson, *The Voice of the People*, op. cit., pp. 20–23 and I.J. Prothero, *Artisans and Politics*, op. cit., pp. 100–02.

32.   See A. Goodwin, *The Friends of Liberty*, Hutchinson, London, 1979 and G.A. Williams, *Artisans and Sans-Culottes*, Edward Arnold, London, 1968.

33.   E.P. Thompson, *The Making of the English Working Class*, op. cit., p. 546.

34.   See, for example, the discussion in M.I. Thomis, *The Town Labourer and the Industrial Revolution*, Batsford, London, 1974, pp. 184–97.

35.   D. Read, *Peterloo: The 'Massacre' and its background*, Manchester University Press, Manchester, 1958, pp. 19–24.

36.   See E.P. Thompson, *The Making of the English Working Class*, op. cit., pp. 703–11.

37.   D. Bythell, *The Handloom Weavers: a study in the English cotton industry during the Industrial Revolution*, Cambridge University Press, Cambridge, 1968, pp. 212–13.

38.   See E.P. Thompson, *The Making of the English Working Class*, op. cit., pp. 887–905.

39.   See G.D.H. Cole, *Attempts at a General Union 1818–1834*, Macmillan, London, 1953.

40.   W.H. Oliver, 'The consolidated trades of '34', *Economic History Review* (2nd ser.), **18** (1964).

41.   See I.J. Prothero, 'William Benbow and the concept of the "general strike"', *Past and Present*, **63** (1974); J. Foster, *Class Struggle and the Industrial Revolution*, Methuen, London, 1974, pp. 107–14.

42.   M. Thomis, *The Town Labourer*, op. cit., p. 132.

43.   J. Foster, *Class Struggle*, op. cit., pp. 51–64.

44.   See A. Briggs, *Chartist Studies*, Macmillan, London, 1959, pp. 13–15.

45.   Ibid., pp. 2–10; F.C. Mather, *Chartism*, Historical Association, London, 1965, pp. 9–15.

46.   See, for example, J.F.C. Harrison on Leeds in A. Briggs, *Chartist Studies*, op. cit., pp. 65–98, and W.H. Warburton, *The History of Trade Unionism in the Potteries*, Lawrence and Wishart, London, 1931, pp. 118–39.

47.   See F.C. Mather, 'The General Strike of 1842' in J. Stevenson and R. Quinault (eds), *Popular Protest and Public Order: six studies in British history, 1790–1920*, George Allen and Unwin, London, 1974, pp. 115–40.

48.   See D.J.V. Jones, *Chartism and the Chartists*, Allen Lane, London, 1975, pp. 138ff.

49.   E. Allen *et al.*, *The North-East Engineers' Strikes*, op. cit., pp. 70–74.
50.   Ibid., pp. 76–83 and R. Challinor and B. Ripley, *The Miners' Association: a trade union in the age of the Chartists*, Lawrence and Wishart, London, 1968.
51.   Ibid., pp. 164–65.
52.   E. Allen *et al.*, *The North-East Engineers' Strikes*, op. cit., p. 143.
53.   See S. Pollard, 'The ethics of the Sheffield outrages', *Transactions of the Hunter Archaeological Society*, **17** (1953–54) and R.N. Price, 'The other face of respectability: violence in the Manchester brick-making trade, 1859–1870', *Past and Present*, **66** (1975).
54.   See H.W. McCready, 'British Labour and the Royal Commission on Trade Unions, 1867–69', *University of Toronto Quarterly*, **24** (1955).
55.   G.D.H. Cole, 'Some notes on British trade unionism in the third quarter of the nineteenth century', *International Review of Social History*, **2** (1937).
56.   See R. Harrison, *Before the Socialists*, Routledge and Kegan Paul, London, 1965 and G. Himmelfarb, 'The politics of democracy: the English Reform Act of 1867', *Journal of British Studies*, **6** (1966).
57.   See H. Browne, *The Rise of British Trade Unions*, Longman, London, 1979, pp. 37–39.
58.   M. Thomis, *The Town Labourer*, op. cit., p. 126.

2 Trade unions and the development of independent labour politics 1889–1906

John Lovell

The period 1889–1906 has a very special significance in the history of trade union involvement in British politics. It was the period that witnessed the forging of the 'labour alliance' – the linking-up of trade unions and socialist political societies to form an independent party of labour. The story of this momentous development has usually been told from the standpoint of the socialist wing of the alliance. This is not unreasonable since, as the author of the standard history of the origins of the Labour Party has observed, the socialists were the one political group interested in bringing the party of labour into being.[1] Union leaders remained for long unconvinced of the necessity for political action independent of the two major parties, not least because many of them had a deep attachment to the Liberal Party. In the process that brought the Labour Party into being, therefore, the socialists are seen as making the running and as ultimately achieving success in their objective of converting the unions to a belief in political independence. It would be misleading, however, to regard the role of the unions as a purely passive one. Their conversion to political independence owed much, it is true, to an increasing acceptance of the socialist gospel by the younger generation of union activists, but it resulted also from the unions' determination to strengthen their position in industry through action in the political sphere. This determination made it possible for the unions to make common cause with the socialist societies, but it did not in itself imply a shift in ideology. The unions entered the 'labour alliance' on their own terms.

The traditional starting point for accounts of the emergence of the Labour Party is 1880 or thereabouts, since the decade of the 1880s saw the revival of socialism in Britain.[2] The socialist societies set up at this time were at the outset largely middle class in composition. This was particularly true of the Fabian Society. The Social Democratic Federation (SDF) did succeed in recruiting a number of talented working men – Mann, Burns, Thorne and others – but its leader, H.M. Hyndman, had been educated at Eton and Trinity College, Cambridge, and was, as various historians have observed, a curious figure to find at the head of a socialist party. The membership of these societies was insignificant and it was only the events of 1889 that rescued them from the obscurity to which they would otherwise have been condemned. This year, and the year that followed, witnessed a remarkable increase in the level of trade union membership. A good deal of this increase resulted from the growth of existing trade unions, but it was the contribution made by newly-created organizations that attracted most attention. These new unions set out to recruit the mass of unskilled and semi-skilled workers left unorganized by the established unions. Since the latter showed relatively little interest in the task of organizing the unorganized, and the unskilled themselves found it difficult to provide from among their own ranks sufficient numbers of men with the education and administrative skills necessary to run an organization, socialists stepped in to fill the vacuum.

The great upheaval among unorganized workers had its origins in London, where first the match-girls at Bryant and May's factory, then the Beckton gasworkers, and finally the London dockers won spectacular victories against their employers. The great London dock strike of 1889 was of particular importance, for it achieved tremendous publicity and the ultimate triumph of the men stimulated unorganized workers into activity throughout the country. In this strike, as in the earlier movements of match-girls and gasworkers, the small band of socialists played a major part, compensating for their lack of numbers by their dedication and ability. Furthermore, as implied above, their influence extended beyond the initial disputes into the formation and administration of new trade unions for the unskilled. Out of the movements of London gasworkers and dockers there arose the Gasworkers' and General Labourers' Union (GGLU) and the Dock, Wharf, Riverside and General Workers' Union (DWRGWU) which, as their names imply, recruited on a general basis among unskilled workers and quickly spread beyond London to various provincial centres. Socialists made important contributions to both organizations. Tom Mann, although a skilled engineer by trade, became the first President of the DWRGWU and another socialist working man, Will Thorne, became General Secretary of the GGLU. Thorne had actually worked as a gas-stoker and was obliged to place considerable reliance in the union's early days on socialists who had had the advantage of an education. Eleanor Marx, in fact, taught him to read and became an officer in the union. H.H. Champion, a former army officer and leading member of the SDF in the 1880s, was another who played an important part in launching the new unions in London. His paper, the *Labour Elector*, became for a time the official organ of both the GGLU and DWRGWU. Champion also helped to found the General Railway Workers' Union (GRWU), an organization that recruited casual railway labourers excluded from membership of the existing Amalgamated Society of Railway Servants. The expansion of the new organizations into the provinces also received assistance from socialist activists, the GGLU in particular being assisted in the West Riding of Yorkshire by members of the Socialist League, a breakaway group from the SDF. League members formed branches of the union in the area and undertook the necessary secretarial duties. Examples of socialist involvement in the creation and administration of new organizations could be multiplied, and the leading historian of these unions has concluded that socialists 'founded, inspired, or rapidly took over all but perhaps one of the "general" unions of 1889'.[3]

The new unions of 1889 were often viewed at the time, and have been viewed by many writers since, as embodying a new idea of trade unionism. In such a view the 'new unionism' presented a challenge to the ideas and methods of existing trade unions. New unions were portrayed as being militant, class-conscious, socialist, open in their recruitment policy and devoid of Friendly Society functions – the antithesis of the 'old unionism'. While there may be some truth in this view, the fact remains that the attitude of the mass of unskilled workers towards these new organizations was purely instrumental in character. They joined them in their thousands not because of any socialist – or even class – commitment, but because they expected to benefit in bread-and-butter terms, and while the trade boom of 1889–90 lasted these expectations were to a certain extent fulfilled. When the boom broke and the depression of the 1890s undermined the bargaining strength of the organizations, there was a mass exodus. A similar pattern of membership fluctuation had occurred in the 1870s. Socialists at the time, whatever their aspirations may have been, were, of course, alive to the limitations of their position in relation to the general membership of new unions. Champion noted with reference to the great dock strike that socialists were welcomed by the strikers not for their socialism but because of their talents as organizers. Later on, Mann presided over a DWRGWU that put the sectional interests of dockers first, even when these interests brought the union into conflict with Thorne's GGLU. Hobsbawm, the leading historian of the general unions of 1889 and one sympathetic to the socialist aspirations of their leadership, nonetheless characterizes them as 'offspring of a marriage between the class unionism of the socialists and the more modest plans of the unskilled themselves', and it was undoubtedly within the framework set by the 'modest plans of the unskilled' that socialist leaders had to operate.[4] As time passed the apparent contrast between the old unionism and the new came to be less and less credible and the new organizations settled into a routine trade union existence indistinguishable from that of established unionism. Furthermore, as a result of their disproportionately heavy membership losses from the early 1890s, the new unions came to constitute but a fraction of the union movement as a whole; at the end of the 1890s they accounted for less than one-tenth of all trade unionists.[5]

Despite their limitations from a socialist standpoint the new unions are accorded a place of great importance in the story of Labour's march to political independence. Ben Tillett, the General Secretary of the DWRGWU, was to write in his autobiography that the new unionism 'marked the beginning of that close alliance in thought and purpose between the Trade Union Movement and the Socialist Movement which produced in due time the Labour Party'.[6] As the last part of this remark concedes, however, there was a significant time lag between the flowering of the new unionism and the conversion of the trade union movement to a belief in political independence. Socialist delegates from the new unions, and also from trades councils, certainly made an immediate impact on the TUC, and at the 1890 Congress succeeded in getting a resolution passed in favour of an eight-hour day by legislative action. Even in 1890, however, new-union delegates were in no position to achieve a really fundamental shift in TUC policy and thereafter the numerical decline of the new organizations weakened their position within the movement. Furthermore, in 1895 the basis of representation at Congress was changed; trades councils were excluded, votes were to be proportionate to union membership, and delegates had to be either full-time union officials or still working at their trade. The change was certainly not designed to benefit the socialists, although in practice it is doubtful whether it made a significant difference to their position.[7] In any event, socialists did not 'capture' the TUC in the wake of the new-unionist upsurge, nor did they get within measurable distance of doing so. The contribution of new unionism to political independence was less immediate and less direct, and it is possible that it has been exaggerated.

A period of roughly ten years separates the high-water mark of the new-unionist movement from the setting up of the Labour Representation Committee – the forerunner of the Labour Party. That there is a thread running through the 1890s, linking these two developments, few would wish to deny, but the connection between new unionism and the formation of the Labour Party is perhaps less obvious than is sometimes assumed. The principal event normally taken to connect the two developments is the formation of the ILP in 1893, the new unions being held to have been a major factor leading to the formation of the ILP, which in its turn is seen as the most important influence working for the creation of the 'labour alliance'. The ILP represented an attempt to join together on a national basis the numerous local groups of working-class political activists that had sprung up in the provinces in the early 1890s. These local groups were largely socialist in outlook and committed to independent labour political activity, and they had tended to develop in areas of the country where there was a Radical Nonconformist political tradition. The more secularist brand of socialism advocated by the SDF held limited appeal in such areas, although the SDF made headway in London and Lancashire where political conditions were quite different. A major part in the promotion and co-ordination of this provincial socialist boom was played by an emerging labour press. The most notable papers were Robert Blatchford's *Clarion*, published in Manchester, the *Yorkshire Factory Times* and the *Workman's Times*, edited by Joseph Burgess. This last paper was deliberately used by Burgess as a means of promoting independent labour groups across the country. The centre of the movement was the West Riding of Yorkshire, and Bradford in particular. The Bradford Labour Union, formed in April 1891, was a pioneer in this kind of independent labour political activity and a model for others to follow. With its backing Ben Tillett of the DWRGWU stood as Independent Labour candidate for West Bradford at the general election of 1892 and, while not elected, received a more than respectable share of the poll. Given the strength of the movement in the city, it was of course to Bradford that the delegates from the various labour political groups came in January 1893 to form the ILP.

It is clear that the movement that resulted in the creation of the ILP coincided with, and drew strength from, the new-unionist upsurge, but the ILP can hardly be regarded as the creation of the new unions. At the foundation conference of the party it has been estimated that over one-third of the delegates came from the Labour parties and clubs in the woollen-manufacturing area of Yorkshire, and as noted above Bradford – the hub of this area – was very much the hub of the independent labour movement.[8] Yet the woollen-textile area was hardly a strongpoint of new or any other kind of unionism. In contrast to the cotton-textile district across the border in Lancashire the woollen district of the West Riding was weakly unionized prior to 1889, and although the great strike that occurred at the Manningham Mills in Bradford in the winter of 1890–91 helped to trigger-off the vigorous political activity in the area, its impact on industrial organization was much less impressive. The strike was lost, and although the union involved succeeded in raising its membership from a mere 700 in 1888 to 4,700 in 1892, numbers quickly fell away again to 1,800 by 1900. This union was the West Yorkshire Power-Loom Weavers (the General Union of Textile Workers after 1900). Formed in 1883 it qualifies as a 'new' union by reason of its emergence from obscurity during the 1888–92 period. Furthermore, it was led by a group of men – Gee, Drew and Turner – who were committed to independent labour politics and socialism. Drew in particular played a leading part in the formation of the Bradford Labour Union and later the ILP. Whatever their triumphs in the political arena, however, in industry these men faced nothing but disappointment. The very places that were renowned for their political vitality were at the same time deserts for the union organizer. Turner described Bradford as 'the most heartbreaking district for Trades Union organizing that ever I came across', Halifax as a 'hopeless area' and Keighley as a 'blackleg area'.[9] The contrast between the industrial and political aspects of the region at this period appears so great as almost to suggest an inverse relationship between the degree of industrial success of new unions and the extent of their leaders' commitment to independent labour politics and socialism. Such a relationship would seem, however, to be somewhat implausible in view of the experience of West Ham in London's dockland. West Ham was an important area of recruitment for both the DWRGWU and the GGLU and indeed so far as the former was concerned it was the most important district of the union down to 1900. In this case new-unionist strength seems to have had a direct bearing on political activity, for West Ham elected Keir Hardie to Parliament in 1892 as an Independent Labour candidate (albeit largely with Liberal votes), while in 1898 the local branches of the SDF and ILP won control of West Ham Borough Council. If the experience of West Ham indicates a direct connection between new unions and political independence, and if also, as the authors of the standard history of trade unionism in this period argue, the overall record of new unionism in increasing the number of labour representatives on local bodies was an impressive one, one is still, nonetheless, left with the position that the ILP had its origins in an area where unionism was chronically weak.[10] One must conclude therefore, that in addition to the stimulus provided by the upsurge of new organizations, the movement that produced the ILP had a momentum of its own. The role of the West Riding apart, it is in any case clear that some of those who made the most important contributions to the formation of the party did so from positions outside the new unions. Champion, Burgess, Blatchford and Jowett may all have been connected to a greater or lesser degree with new unionism, but they were not themselves a part of it. Even Hardie, the most important figure of all, while he had begun his campaign for labour independence as a Scottish miners' delegate and had carried the argument forward within the forum provided by the TUC, found himself excluded from that body in the 1890s because he did not qualify as a union delegate.

In its early days the new national party did possess some close links with the new unions of 1889. Tom Mann, who gave up his position as full-time President of the DWRGWU, was elected as Secretary of the ILP in 1894, and in that year the council of the party included Pete Curran of the GGLU and Ben Tillett. These links did not long survive at national level, however, and by the end of the 1890s the new-union men had been replaced by journalist-politicians such as Ramsay MacDonald, Philip Snowden and Bruce Glasier. This weakening of the ties with the unions was a cause of concern to Hardie, who continued as the party's chairman and dominant figure.[11] Hardie had always believed that the ILP would succeed only to the extent that it managed to win over the general body of trade unionists – 'new' and 'old' – to the principle of independent labour politics. This commitment to the winning of trade union support was one of the features that distinguished the new party from the earlier socialist groups founded in the 1880s. It was a commitment manifest in the very title of the party, from which the word 'socialist' had deliberately been excluded in order not to offend a trade union movement that still remained suspicious of socialism and socialists. Despite its broader approach, however, the ILP was no more successful than the SDF in building up a mass following. Regarded as a national political party, it was in fact a failure. At the 1895 general election all its twenty-eight candidates went down to defeat, including Hardie, who lost his seat at West Ham. In the later 1890s its membership was dwindling and by 1900 it was virtually bankrupt.[12] Ironically it was at this point, when its fortunes had reached almost their lowest ebb, that the party finally succeeded in joining with the trade unions to form the Labour Representation Committee. At this juncture it is perhaps easier to appreciate how the ILP might have been rescued from oblivion by its association with the unions than to see how it could have been the major influence bringing the alliance into being.

While the ILP as a national party may not, indeed, have been the most important factor contributing to the formation of the Labour Party it did, nonetheless, play a part greater than its reduced circumstances in 1900 would appear to indicate. This was due to the influence exercised by ILP members operating within the unions themselves. Although the total membership of the ILP went into decline after 1895, the curious fact is that its influence within the unions actually increased. It was this success of the socialists in infiltrating individual trade unions that rendered futile the attempt of the TUC establishment to eliminate their influence from Congress by excluding trades councils and outside delegates under the new standing orders of 1895. Their positions of leadership in the new organizations of 1889 had, of course, given the socialists a foothold in the union movement even before the establishment of the ILP in the early 1890s. Although, as we have seen, these new organizations were quickly forced onto the defensive by economic depression and employers' counter-attacks, the composition of their leaderships remained to a large extent unchanged through the 1890s and the influence of socialists at all levels was reinforced by the emergence of the ILP, with its specific appeal to trade unionists. Since the new unions were so small a section of the union movement the influence of socialists would, however, have remained extremely limited had it been confined within their boundaries. In fact, ILP members made their presence felt in a wide variety of older organizations: these included the boot and shoe operatives', the railway servants', the carpenters and joiners', the boilermakers', and the engineers'.[13] In coal and cotton, the main bastions of the trade union movement in the 1890s and 1900s, they met with less success, although they did secure important footholds in the Durham and Scottish miners' organizations. In contrast to their position in the new unions, in the older societies socialists were often in the position of an opposition group, embattled against an ageing Lib-Lab leadership. Even in the 1890s, however, they were beginning to push through into positions of leadership. In 1896 George Barnes, an ILP man, was elected to the post of Secretary of the engineers', and four years later another ILP member, D.C. Cummings, became Secretary of the boilermakers'. In the case of the railway servants', a union of growing importance in the 1890s, socialists benefited from a system of union government which ensured a rapid turnover of executive members. By 1897 they had achieved a position of considerable influence on the executive and in the following year they were able to use this to secure the appointment of an ILP man as editor of the union journal. In 1899 socialists on the executive of this union were to play a vital part in the sequence of events that led to the formation of the Labour Representation Committee.

The success of the socialists in infiltrating a wide range of unions, at a time when the membership of the ILP was actually in decline and when the total membership of all socialist societies was little more than 10,000, is, on the face of things, somewhat surprising. One historian has concluded that this success was attributable to what he sees as the particular relevance of socialist ideology to union practice at this period.[14] Socialism is thus held to have possessed an attraction for union activists that it did not possess for the population at large. It may, of course, be further supposed that this appeal was felt particularly strongly by the younger generation of activists, who were in the nature of the case more receptive to the influence of new ideas. Socialism is held to have been of particular relevance to trade unionists because it provided a convincing analysis of developments taking place in late nineteenth-century industry. Increasing technical change that threatened the position of craft-workers corresponded well with the Marxist view that increasing mechanization would reduce the skilled to the level of the unskilled. The socialist theory of capitalist concentration also appeared convincing at a time when important mergers were taking place in industries such as shipbuilding and armaments, and when employers in a number of industries were forming organizations capable of inflicting severe defeats on organized labour – a capacity demonstrated in dramatic fashion by the great engineering lock-out of 1897–98. These aspects of socialist analysis gained further credibility from developments across the Atlantic, where the processes of mechanization and concentration had proceeded farther and faster than in the United Kingdom. The progress of American industry received widespread publicity in this country and it was perhaps natural for people to assume that the current state of affairs in America represented the future state of Britain.[15] Since American trade unionism was undeniably weaker than its counterpart in Britain this assumption provided little comfort for union activists. However, if socialist analysis could claim to identify the new tendencies appearing in late nineteenth-century industry it could also, so it has been argued, suggest ways in which organized labour could meet this challenge.[16] The theory of capitalist concentration suggested that unions in their turn should draw together in larger units capable of matching the enhanced power of capital. In this view socialism provided the unions with a modernization programme; a programme of amalgamation, federation and rationalization that would adapt a nineteenth-century union structure to the realities of twentieth-century industry.

How far this apparent relevance of socialism accounted for its following within the unions is hard to say. It must undoubtedly have been a factor, but it is likely that other influences were also at work. In unions that they did not actually control the role of the socialists was by no means unambiguously progressive during this period.[17] In the engineers' and boot and shoe operatives' they took the lead in rank-and-file movements that opposed technical and organizational change in industry. That such changes threatened the relatively privileged status of skilled workers was clear, but it was less obvious that the mass of semi- and unskilled workers stood to lose. Industrial change was in any case an inescapable feature of an advanced industrial economy, particularly one so dependent on international trade as the United Kingdom. If the primary attraction of socialism was its relevance, it is hard to see why socialists should have been so active in fighting a losing battle in defence of craft privilege. The truth was, of course, that socialists were concerned primarily with building up a following within a union structure that was given, so that in craft societies they were prepared to take the part of disaffected craft-workers even though the aims of such workers had little to do with a socialist programme of modernization. While this may have made some tactical sense it did not make the task of reforming socialists any easier when they finally secured positions of leadership in such unions. Barnes, in fact, resigned his post as General Secretary of the engineers' in 1908, because resistance to central authority within the union had made his position impossible. Arguably, the main reason for the relatively successful permeation of the unions was not so much the compelling relevance of socialist doctrine as the well-known ability of a dedicated minority of activists to achieve an influence out of all proportion to their numbers. Turning to more recent times one would not, presumably, account for the degree of success achieved by the communists in infiltrating the unions in the years following the Second World War primarily in terms of the relevance of communist doctrine. This is not, of course, to imply that *any* well-organized minority could make an impact of this kind. What socialists, and later syndicalists and communists, had in their favour was that their ideologies implied a militant posture in relation to the employers.

There is, however, one important distinction to be made between the ILP (or SDF) as an activist minority within the unions in the later-nineteenth century and minorities such as the communists in more recent times. This concerns the way in which the determinants of union membership have been modified over time.[18] As unions gradually became institutionalized so the act of joining a union tended to lose its voluntary character. Closed-shop arrangements ensured that workers were unionists regardless of their attitudes to unions and society in general. In this situation it has been the apathy of the membership that has permitted minorities to move into positions of influence. In the later-nineteenth century this institutionalization was not far advanced so that the act of joining a union was still to some extent a voluntary one. Of course, the position varied greatly as between different trades and industries, for the process of institutionalization was an uneven one, but in the newer and weaker sectors of organization, at any rate, union membership was likely to entail a risk and so to require a positive commitment. Social, political and economic attitudes were thus likely to have a bearing on whether or not people joined unions, and the weaker the union was the greater would be the part such attitudes played in determining membership. It is reasonable to assume that this situation worked in favour of socialist influence in the weaker or less well-established unions. The ILP's brand of socialism undoubtedly entailed a commitment to trade unionism. To say all this may not be to say very much, and it is certainly not being suggested that even in the weakest of unions the majority of the membership was socialist. Nonetheless, the precarious nature of unionism in many sectors of employment may well have had the effect of selecting for union membership those who, even if not socialists themselves, had some sympathy with socialist aspirations.

The extent of socialist influence within various unions has been discussed at some length because it had an important bearing on the political initiative taken by the TUC in 1899. Unresponsive to promptings from outside socialist propagandists, Congress finally moved at the instigation of one of its affiliated unions. The union in question was, of course, the Amalgamated Society of Railway Servants. The General Secretary of this organization, Richard Bell, was a somewhat less than fervent advocate of independent labour politics (although he was subsequently obliged to play an inglorious part in them) but he was unable to dominate his executive, a body on which, as we have already seen, socialists were strongly represented. Thomas Steels, an ILP man who had served his two-year term on the union's executive in 1897–98, persuaded his branch in 1899 to adopt a resolution calling upon the Parliamentary Committee of the TUC to convene a conference of trade unions and other interested organizations with a view to devising 'ways and means for securing the return of an increased number of labour members to the next Parliament'. The executive accepted the resolution with only one dissentient and it was duly forwarded to the 1899 Congress, where it was moved by James Holmes, a regional organizer of the union and an ILP member.[19] This resolution has, of course, become famous as the first step in the formation of the Labour Party, but even at the time it was, despite its modest wording, seen to be of great importance. It was debated for three hours and its passage by Congress was greeted by its supporters with an outburst of enthusiastic cheering and hat-waving. A further indication that this resolution was not just another of Congress's 'hardy annuals' was provided by the relative closeness of the voting figures – 546,000 for to 434,000 against on a card vote.

It is clear that the socialists had been responsible for the introduction of the resolution, but the question arises as to whether theirs had been the critical influence in securing the majority – a question fundamental to an evaluation of the role of socialism in the formation of the Labour Party. In the case of the seven important unions that are assumed to have voted in favour, socialism certainly played a part. Four of these were new unions with socialist leaderships, and the other three – the railway servants, the boot and shoe operatives and the carpenters and joiners – have already been referred to in connection with the progress made by the ILP within the unions. The most important union in which socialists were a major influence, the engineers, had disaffiliated from Congress and so played no part in the decision. The seven unions must have made a vital contribution, but between them they accounted for less than half of the total vote in favour of the resolution. The difference must have been made up by the support of most of the smaller unions. Some of these would have been socialist in inclination, but it is rather unlikely that the favourable vote of all of them stemmed from socialist influence. It would seem reasonable to conclude that while the ILP's role was of vital importance, it was not able to carry the day unaided.

One suggestion is that the resolution passed because the trade union establishment did not exert itself to oppose it.[20] The most powerful elements in the movement, the coal and cotton unions, did cast their considerable votes against, but it has been argued that their leaders made little attempt to combat the arguments of the socialists and so win-over neutral opinion. In this situation the votes of the small unions went the other way and decided the issue. This is not as negative an interpretation of the 1899 Congress as might at first sight appear. In his history of the Labour Party's origins, Pelling claims that the 1899 decision indicated a real change in the attitude of the unions to political action, and the apparent reluctance of the Lib-Lab establishment to mobilize all its forces in opposition to the resolution can be regarded as one manifestation of this change.[21] The shift in opinion was not primarily a matter of ideology although it did have the effect of drawing socialists and non-socialists closer together. Both before the 1899 Congress, and for some years after it, the majority of trade union leaders were Liberal in political outlook. Continued adherence to Liberalism did not, however, preclude a reappraisal of the political situation, and there were two influences at work in the late 1890s encouraging such a reappraisal.

The first was the simple fact that the political influence of the trade union movement had not kept in step with its numerical expansion. The total number of trade unionists had risen from about 750,000 in 1888 to just under 2,000,000 by 1899, yet the number of trade union MPs had only risen from 8 to 11 in the same period. Parliamentary representation was not, it is true, the only measure of union political influence and the cotton operatives' societies in particular were well organized for the purpose of lobbying Parliament from the outside. Nonetheless, ever since the extension of the franchise to working people in 1867 unions had attached importance to having their own men returned to Westminster and the first union MPs had entered Parliament in 1874. It appears to be generally agreed that the failure to increase the number of these MPs in step with the growing size of the movement resulted from the inadequacies of the Liberal Party as an instrument of the labour interest. Despite the sympathy shown by the party's leaders and managers at national level the local associations in the constituencies remained unresponsive to labour's claims and persistently refused to adopt trade unionists as candidates. The loyalty of union leaders to the party was thus placed under severe strain while the case for an independent approach to politics was considerably strengthened.

The second influence complemented the first. At a time when union leaders were unable to view the state of their parliamentary representation with any degree of satisfaction various developments were taking place which appeared to emphasize the need for a strong union presence at Westminster. The need to review the political situation thus acquired a certain urgency. The developments in question concerned the behaviour of employers and the courts, and combined together they threatened to weaken severely the unions' position in industry. So far as the courts were concerned the second half of the 1890s witnessed a series of adverse decisions that eroded the legal settlement of 1875. In 1899 the worst of these decisions was yet to come, but things had already gone far enough to cause disquiet. The activities of the courts provided an ominous backcloth for the growth of employer organizations, another feature of the decade that has been mentioned above. Although most employers' organizations were prepared to deal with unions, the collective bargaining machinery that they were instrumental in establishing in this period was not to the taste of many of the unionists involved, and can indeed be regarded as an outcome of union weakness rather than strength. In no industry was this truer than in engineering, where the national procedure agreement was imposed on the union at the conclusion of the disastrous lock-out of 1897–98. This victory of the federated engineering employers over the ASE, the most prestigious of all British unions, was in itself an event that disturbed the entire trade union movement. Furthermore, in its aftermath there came the formation of the Employers' Parliamentary Council. This organization was designed to match the TUC in lobbying MPs and governments, and it was clear from the beginning that it took a keen interest in the legal restriction of the unions' industrial power.

In a valuable article on unions and politics written some years ago, Flanders argued that the political aims and activities of trade unions are circumscribed by their institutional needs as industrial organizations.[22] To push these aims and activities beyond a certain point would be to risk dividing the membership and undermining the unity so essential to the unions' industrial purposes. However, Flanders also argued that there is a certain minimum level of commitment to political activity that unions cannot avoid. This arises from their need to create and maintain a legal and economic framework conducive to their industrial activity. This notion of a minimum level is of obvious relevance to the situation at the turn of the century, when unions felt that their position was being threatened by the various developments outlined above. At such a time political involvement was inescapable, and it is this consideration that provides the context for the vote at the 1899 Congress.

Those who had been most active in support of the 1899 resolution felt that one of its strongest and most essential points was that it took the issue of labour representation out of the hands of the Lib-Labs who dominated the Parliamentary Committee. The responsibility of that body was to end with the calling of the conference of interested organizations. In thus removing the matter from the direct control of the TUC the resolution took advantage of a recent precedent, for the issue of industrial federation had been resolved by setting up an outside organization – the General Federation of Trade Unions. Valuable as this tactic may have been, viewed from the socialist standpoint, it did not, of course, obviate the need to win the support of the individual unions themselves. The Parliamentary Committee duly called a general conference on labour representation, and this assembled on 27 February 1900 in the Memorial Hall, Farringdon Street. In addition to the three socialist bodies, unions with a combined membership of about 570,000 were represented. This figure was less than half of the total affiliated to the TUC, and was slightly less than might have been anticipated on the basis of the vote at the 1899 Congress, for the engineers' – absent from Congress – were present at the Memorial Hall conference. The outcome of the conference was, of course, the Labour Representation Committee (LRC), an organization highly satisfactory to the ILP but one whose political effectiveness depended on its progress in securing trade union affiliations. At the beginning progress was slow. There was to be no rush by the unions into independent labour politics. In February 1901, after a full year's existence, the number of unionists affiliated to the LRC stood at 353,000 and by June the same year the figure was 383,000. This was significantly less than the number represented at the original conference.

It is clear that by mid-1901 concern about the direction of legal and industrial developments had not reached a level sufficient to propel the majority of important unions into active support for independent labour politics. The limited number of unions that had affiliated to the LRC by this stage were either subject to strong socialist influence or had other special reasons for joining.[23] In short, the boundary of union support for political independence had not been extended since the 1899 resolution and Memorial Hall conference, and indeed it had not even been consolidated. Thus the engineers', who had certainly been expected to affiliate, failed to do so. In their ballot on the question the verdict was favourable but the total of votes was so small that the executive decided not to act.[24] The apathy shown by members of this union is in itself an interesting comment on the limitations of the forces making for independent labour politics.

In the event, however, mid-1901 proved to be the turning point. In July the House of Lords handed down its decision in the famous Taff Vale case. This established that unions could be sued for damages, and before very long heavy damages were indeed being awarded against them in the courts. There could be no doubting the gravity of this legal setback. It is not possible to be absolutely precise about the impact of the House of Lords' decision upon trade union affiliations to the LRC. Some of the unions that affiliated after the decision would no doubt have done so anyway, the timing of their action being dictated by the cumbersome nature of their constitutional machinery rather than by the impact of outside events. Furthermore, as we have seen in the case of the engineers', the apathy of the membership on political questions drew out the process of affiliation. It appears, incidentally, that this apathy was not much modified by the Taff Vale decision, for when the membership of the engineers' voted again on the question of joining the LRC, a vote taken shortly after the judgement, less than 7,000 members participated out of a total union membership of around 85,000.[25] Even this represented an improvement on the ballot held earlier and this time the union joined. Whatever may have been the impact upon the mass of unionists, however, the judgement really does seem to have had a decisive influence on union leaders. Affiliations to the LRC rose from 383,000 in June 1901 to 626,000 in May 1902, and by the time of the LRC's third annual conference in February 1903 the figure had reached 847,000.[26] At that conference a parliamentary fund was established for the support of labour candidates. This was in itself a vital step in the direction of creating a genuine national Labour Party and also served as a valuable bargaining counter in negotiations with the Liberals. The conclusion of the secret electoral pact with that party, in September 1903, finally set the stage for the emergence of the Labour Party at the general election of 1906.

The debt of the infant Labour Party to the Amalgamated Society of Railway Servants was a considerable one. That union had not only sponsored the 1899 resolution on labour representation, it had also, in the summer of 1900, given official backing to the strikers on the Taff Vale Railway. Even more remarkable was the role of the union's regional organizer, James Holmes, for he both moved the resolution at the 1899 TUC and played the principal part in launching the Taff Vale strike in the summer of 1900. It is not, of course, being suggested that Holmes or his union embarked on the strike with any idea of the momentous legal and political consequences that would flow from it, it is rather one of history's ironies that the union that had taken the lead in the creation of the LRC should have inadvertently contributed most to the latter's success by embroiling itself in costly litigation arising out of its industrial activities. Nor was the special part that this union had to play in the story of labour representation over with the conclusion of the damages case that followed the Taff Vale judgement. For it was one of its members, W. Osborne, who attempted to stem the tide of union support for independent labour politics by taking another case through to the House of Lords, and securing a judgement that prohibited unions from spending their funds for political purposes. The Osborne judgement of December 1909 proved, however, to be but a temporary setback for the Labour Party: it was the influence of Holmes rather than Osborne that endured,

The Taff Vale case was of critical importance in securing trade union affiliations to the LRC, and because this was so it is possible to argue that the trade union commitment to the Labour Party reflected simply the minimum level of political involvement discussed by Flanders in the chapter already commented upon. In this view the Labour Party was the political instrument chosen by the unions to defend their legal status and hence their industrial bargaining power. But just as Flanders' argument carries the implication that unions in practice will advance their political activities beyond the minimum level necessary for their industrial survival, so the realities of the situation at the turn of the century suggest that it would be wrong to take too restricted a view of the unions' interest in politics. The disabilities imposed upon the unions by the Taff Vale and other cases of the period were removed by the 1906 Trade Disputes Act, yet trade union support for the Labour Party went on growing after the legal threat had been lifted. Of supreme importance was the affiliation of the Miners' Federation in 1909. In 1910 the miners contributed no less than 550,000 to a total affiliated union membership of about 1,400,000, and it was the mining constituencies that seemed to provide the best prospects for the expansion of the party in Parliament.[27] The miners' response to the setting up of the LRC in 1900 had been to establish their own separate political fund, and their initial lack of sympathy for the new party was not removed by the shock of the Taff Vale judgement. Although the Lancashire miners broke away and affiliated in 1903, and although the cotton unions also joined up in that year, the Miners'Federation continued to operate its separate scheme outside the LRC. Supporters of the LRC within the Miners' Federation managed to arrange a ballot on the affiliation issue in 1906, but the outcome was unfavourable, and it required a further ballot in 1908 before the miners finally threw in their lot with the Labour Party.

The affiliation of the Miners' Federation was of vital importance for the future of the Labour Party. In understanding the Federation's decision to join it is important to remember the miners' longstanding commitment to political activity. Like the cotton and railway industries, the coal industry had long been the subject of special legislation, so that the desirability of having their own men at Westminster had been recognized by the miners for many years. The more recently unionized coalfields also believed in political action as a means of supplementing collective bargaining, and from its foundation at the end of the 1880s the Miners' Federation had campaigned for the legal enactment of the eight-hour day in the mines. The concentration of miners in distinct communities made them a more potent electoral force than any other occupational group, and the strength of support for Liberalism in most mining communities outside Lancashire provided a further element of political cohesion. In the end, however, it was the problems posed by this Liberal connection that paved the way for the affiliation to the Labour Party. The reluctance of Liberal constituency associations to adopt trade unionists as candidates has already been commented upon, and given the size of their organization and its political potential this reluctance must have been especially frustrating to the miners' leaders – the more so in view of the number of coalowners who sat as Liberal MPs. Liberal resistance to the miners' claims was felt in the coal fields of Yorkshire, Durham, South Wales and Scotland, and it was only in the prosperous East Midlands region that the constituency associations showed a willingness to adopt miners as candidates.[28] Significantly, this area remained loyal to the Liberals for some years after the Miners' Federation joined the Labour Party. Indeed, the continued strength of Liberal support within the Miners' Federation as a whole resulted in much tension in its relations with the Labour Party in the early days of affiliation. Initially the decision to join the Labour Party was not perceived by many of the miners' leaders and their members as a real move in the direction of political independence. Instead it reflected a recognition that the LRC operating from outside had been able to drive a much better electoral bargain with the Liberal Party than had the miners from within.[29] Furthermore, since the 1903 electoral deal between the Liberals and the LRC contributed to the selection of moderate trade union rather than socialist candidates in the latter party, it had the effect of reducing ideological objections to affiliation.[30]

Despite their limited perception of the role of the new party, once in the miners stayed in as did all those lesser organizations that had affiliated earlier. Staying in meant accepting that the Labour Party was indeed an independent party, with an organization – if not a policy – clearly distinguishable from that of the Liberals at all levels from the constituency upwards. Acceptance proved hard in the miners' case, but it was aided by the continued progress of the socialists within the federation. Independent Labour Party activists had played a major role in securing the favourable vote in the 1908 ballot, and after 1912 the federation had a socialist President, Robert Smillie. In the years 1912–14 Smillie was able to go a long way towards finally severing the Liberal connection.[31] Ordinary miners, it is true, continued to vote Liberal in large numbers, whatever their union might say, but as the historian of mining politics in this period has pointed out, the still-restricted franchise tended to exclude the younger men who were less likely to possess Liberal sympathies.[32] This limited franchise, of course, worked in the same direction in other industries, and it was not until it was reformed in 1918 that the Labour Party was able to realize its full potential.[33]

Consideration of the miners has carried us well beyond 1906, the terminal date of this study, but it has been necessary because of their great importance, and because their history indicates how slow was the process whereby unions were converted to a belief in political independence. In that process it is clear that various elements were at work. In the first place there was the apathy of the majority of union members towards political affairs, an apathy to which the restricted franchise no doubt contributed and which was revealed in some of the ballots on affiliation to the LRC and, outside our period, on the issue of the political levy. The Webbs complained in 1897 that the unions 'are perpetually meddling with wide issues of general politics, upon which the bulk of their constituents have either no opinions at all, or are marshalled in the ranks of one or another of the political parties'.[34] On balance it would seem that this apathy was of assistance to the second influence running through our period, the role of socialists within the unions. Socialists were committed to independent labour politics and they exerted an influence within the unions out of all proportion to their numbers: this was a particularly striking phenomenon in the period 1895–1900 when the total membership of socialist societies was in decline. A third influence was the undermining of the unions' industrial position by adverse legal decisions, the Taff Vale judgement above all. Even had the unions operated in practice on the basis of a minimum level of political involvement this development would have necessitated a political response, and the evidence, in fact, indicates that it was the unions' response to Taff Vale that established the LRC on a permanent footing. But Taff Vale, as a recent writer has observed, is a story with a happy ending, for the 1906 Trade Disputes Act not only reversed the judgement but gave the unions everything that they desired in the way of freedom from legal interference in their industrial affairs.[35] What then sustained the cause of labour representation after 1906?

Having been led to set up their own political arm by an external threat union executives saw no reason to dismantle it once that threat had been lifted. This was because they possessed a continuing interest in political affairs. The tactic of employing political means to secure industrial ends was well established in the trade union world long before the advent of the Labour Party. In their analysis of trade unionism in the 1890s the Webbs referred to the tactic as the Method of Legal Enactment, and compared it with the other trade union 'methods' – collective bargaining and mutual insurance.[36] Institutions within the trade union movement, such as the TUC itself, the United Textile Factory Workers' Association, and in its early days perhaps even the Miners' Federation, existed primarily for the purpose of promoting legislation favourable to labour. Given a trade union political interest, the representation of that interest at Westminster was a natural-enough development. Labour representation, however, as distinct from outside pressure-group activity, raised the problem of party allegiances. Hitherto, trade union candidates had had to be elected under the auspices of one or other of the two major parties, and in practice this meant the Liberals. The Liberal connection was, however, unwelcome to the substantial number of union members who were Conservative in sympathy. In any case, as we have seen, Liberal Party constituency organizations dominated by middle-class groups were reluctant to adopt trade union candidates. The Labour Party represented a solution to the problem of party allegiances in that it distanced itself from existing political creeds and focused on labour representation as an end in itself. 'They had fixed upon a common denominator', Keir Hardie stated in 1903, 'that, when acting in the House of Commons, they should be neither Socialists, Liberals, nor Tories, but a Labour party.'[37] Defining itself in this way, the party chose not to adopt a political programme of its own, and in fact continued its existence without such a programme down to 1918.[38] Such a situation was satisfactory enough to the moderate union leaders who viewed politics simply as an extension of their industrial activities, but it was hardly what the more advanced socialists had had in mind when they acclaimed the formation of the labour alliance at the turn of the century.

NOTES AND REFERENCES

1. H. Pelling, *The Origins of the Labour Party 1880–1900*, Clarendon Press, Oxford (1965 edn), p. 216.
2. Ibid. See also P. Adelman, *The Rise of the Labour Party 1880–1945*, Longman, London, 1972.

3.   E.J. Hobsbawm, 'Trade union history', *Economic History Review* (2nd ser.), **20**, 2 (August 1967), p. 361.
4.   E.J. Hobsbawm, *Labouring Men*, Weidenfeld and Nicolson, London, 1964, p. 182.
5.   H.A. Clegg, A. Fox and A.F. Thompson, *A History of British Trade Unions since 1889*, vol. 1, Clarendon Press, Oxford, 1964, p. 97.
6.   Ben Tillett, *Memories and Reflections*, Long, London, 1931, p. 116.
7.   H.A. Clegg et al., *A History of British Trade Unions*, op. cit., p. 294.
8.   H. Pelling, *Origins of the Labour Party*, op. cit., p. 116.
9.   H.A. Clegg et al., *A History of British Trade Unions*, op. cit., p. 184.
10.   Ibid., p. 286.
11.   H. Pelling, *Origins of the Labour Party*, op. cit., p. 176.
12.   F. Bealey and H. Pelling, *Labour and Politics, 1900–1906*, Macmillan, London, 1958, p. 160.
13.   H.A. Clegg, et al., *A History of British Trade Unions*, op. cit., pp. 291–304.
14.   E.J. Hobsbawm, 'Trade union history', op. cit.
15.   H. Pelling, *America and the British Left*, Adams & Charles Black, London, 1956, Ch. 5.
16.   E.J. Hobsbawm, 'Trade union history', op. cit.
17.   H.A. Clegg et al., *A History of British Trade Unions*, op. cit., pp. 297 and 302.
18.   R. Kornhauser, 'Some social determinants and consequences of union membership', *Labor History*, **2** (winter 1961), pp. 51–52.
19.   H.A. Clegg et al., *A History of British Trade Unions*, op. cit., pp. 268 and 296.
20.   Ibid., p. 303.
21.   H. Pelling, *Origins of the Labour Party*, op. cit., p. 206.
22.   A. Flanders, 'Trade unions and politics', in Flanders, *Management and Unions*, Faber and Faber, London, 1970.
23.   H.A. Clegg et al., *A History of British Trade Unions*, op. cit., p. 374.
24.   F. Bealey and H. Pelling, op. cit., p. 37.
25.   Ibid., p. 88.
26.   H.A. Clegg et al., *A History of British Trade Unions*, op. cit., p. 375.
27.   R. McKibbin, *The Evolution of the Labour Party 1910–24*, Oxford University Press, London, 1974, p. 1.
28.   R. Gregory, *The Miners and British Politics 1906–14*, Oxford University Press, London, 1968, p. 62.
29.   Ibid., pp. 26–27.
30.   F. Bealey and H. Pelling, *Labour and Politics*, op. cit., p. 159.

31. R. Gregory, *The Miners and British Politics*, op. cit., p. 38.
32. Ibid., pp. 189–90.
33. R. McKibbin, *The Evolution of the Labour Party*, op. cit., p. xv.
34. S. and B. Webb, *Industrial Democracy*, Longmans, London (1920 edn), p. 838.
35. R. Currie, *Industrial Politics*, Oxford University Press, Oxford, 1979, p. 67.
36. S. and B. Webb, *Industrial Democracy*, op. cit., Pt. Two.
37. Quoted in R. Currie, *Industrial Politics*, op. cit., p. 69.
38. Ibid., p. 77.

3 Trade unions, politicians and public opinion 1906–1914[1]

David Rubinstein

The period between 1906 and 1914 marked a sharp change in the history of British trade unions. It was during this brief span that union members and their leaders became fixtures on the political scene. The behaviour of politicians, civil servants, the press and the middle- and upper-class public differed sharply from that of their predecessors. Unions held much less influence with Government than they were to do after two great wars and the concomitant rise of political Labour, but changes in their status before 1914 formed the essential background to the gains which followed 1918 and 1945.

Although unions had secured the right to exist and function in the 1870s, and the Labour Party was well represented in Parliament from 1906, they constituted at the beginning of the new century a democratic plum in an undemocratic pudding, a political and social system run by a traditional governing class. For the system reflected not a nominally liberal form of Government but the reality of contemporary social forces; the upper class retained a predominance grossly disproportionate to their numbers. The writer Sidney Low commented in *The Governance of England* (1904, p. 185): 'The effective power continues to be retained in the hands of a comparatively small body of persons, many of them born to politics and brought into it young. Roughly speaking, this class is composed almost entirely of persons who form part of what is called Society.' Low's view was echoed four years later in another standard work by A.L. Lowell of Harvard University, who observed that the upper classes ruled in England 'by the sufferance of the great mass of the people . . . [E]ven among the Liberals', Lowell added, 'social influence is a power, and a power that does not seem likely to pass away'.[2]

Political inequality interacted with the profound gulf between social classes whose narrowing is one of the most important facts of British life in the past three-quarters of a century. Shrewd contemporaries commented on this gulf, which most of them inevitably took for granted. Charles Masterman, one of the sharpest social observers among Liberal politicians of his day, wrote in *The Condition of England* (1909, p. 111): 'To-day, even national distinctions seem less estranging than the fissure between the summit and basis of society.' Arthur D. Lewis, a well-informed student of labour unrest throughout Europe, wrote in *Syndicalism and the General Strike* (1912, p. 171): 'If you talk of a class-war in England, every one raises pious hands of horror; but in no country is there so much instinctive distrust between class and class and so much effort to keep the classes apart . . .'.

Despite the rise of Labour, most politically active working-class voters still thought of themselves in 1906 as Liberals. The behaviour of the Liberal Government elected in that year is therefore of particular interest and significance. During the trade union agitation of 1867–75 many leading Liberals displayed ignorance, suspicion and hostility towards unions, as indicated in their speeches, writing and the ambiguous legislation of 1871. By the 1890s politics were more closely concerned with social questions, but the policies of the Liberal Governments of 1892–95 remained largely in the Gladstonian mould in the primacy afforded to Irish Home Rule and imperial questions. The most important trade union issue to arise in Parliament during the period, the eight-hour day for miners, was brushed aside despite a favourable second reading in the House of Commons in 1893.

By the late 1890s the progressive New Liberalism, which was to be so prominent a feature of the Edwardian period, had already made its appearance. The Liberal Party, however, was by no means wholly free from anti-union associations by the turn of the century. Joseph Walton and Sir Christopher Furness, for example, stood as Liberals at by-elections in Barnsley and York in 1897–98, where their protestations could not protect them from strong attack as opponents of trade unionism. (Walton, who nonetheless enjoyed the support of the leaders of the Yorkshire miners, was elected by a large majority; Furness was narrowly defeated.) As employers, Walton and Furness were by no means unusual among Liberal MPs. One calculation suggests that 41 per cent of Liberal members in 1906 were businessmen; another suggests 36–37 per cent and that after 1910 this proportion dropped to 33–34 per cent. In addition, the Liberal parliamentary ranks contained large numbers of landowners, lawyers, writers and journalists, but no more than a handful of trade unionists.[3] But after 1906 Liberal candidates rarely put themselves in a position to be attacked as hostile to trade unions. To take a prominent example, D.A. Thomas, a wealthy Liberal coalowner, moved his parliamentary seat from the mining constituency of Merthyr Tydfil to Cardiff before the Cambrian

Combine dispute, in which he was a principal combatant, blazed forth in 1910. Thomas was not a candidate in the second election of that year.

From the start, with the appointment of the former trade unionist and socialist John Burns to a Cabinet post, the Liberal Government courted the support of the unions. The success of its social legislation required a considerable degree of union participation as the responsible ministers, Sydney Buxton, Churchill and Lloyd George, all recognized. This was particularly true of the operation of labour exchanges and National Insurance.[4] Lloyd George wrote to Sir Robert Morant, the Chairman of the new National Health Insurance Commission, on 12 January 1912: 'Your report on the Trades Union meeting is highly satisfactory. Their support is essential to success: if the Trades Union had been either hostile or sulky, we could not have hoped to overcome successfully the resistance of the doctors and the employers might even have been encouraged to strike.'[5] Part of the process of securing trade union support involved the appointment of union leaders to posts in government service in unprecedented numbers. By the end of 1912, according to Élie Halévy's calculation, nearly 400 posts had been created by the Liberals and staffed by trade unionists in the Factory Inspectorate, the Board of Trade, the Home Office, the National Insurance administration and elsewhere in the civil service.[6]

Ministers adopted a new Fair Wages resolution in 1909, encouraging the payment of union wage rates in government contracts. They also encouraged unions in government employment; as early as February 1906 the TUC's Parliamentary Committee recorded its thanks to Buxton, then Postmaster-General, for allowing Post Office employees to be represented by their unions. A.H. Gill, MP, told the 1907 TUC from the President's chair that a number of meetings and conferences had been held with Cabinet ministers in the past year:

The result is that we are now in closer connection with the various Government Departments than ever we were previously. Trade Union officials are recognized by the Post Office, Admiralty, and War Departments, and are allowed to represent their members with regard to any grievances from which they suffer from time to time. This privilege has been fought for for many years, and has been stoutly and persistently refused by successive Governments until now. I look upon this as a notable achievement . . .

Meetings with ministers became more frequent, more informal and more productive than in the past, and as in the case of a meeting convened by Asquith in August 1911 to discuss labour unrest, the initiative to hold them did not always stem from the union side.[7]

In addition to the above measures, a number of Acts of Parliament were passed which directly affected union interests. Ministers were noticeably less eager, however, to strengthen the legal and political position of the unions and the Labour Party than to harness union support for Liberal social reforms and smooth industrial relations in government employ. Given the unions' political and financial support for the Labour Party, it is not surprising that the legislation required the strong pressure of the Labour Party, the impact of unforeseen events, or, in the case of the miners' eight-hour day in 1908, the threat of a strike.[8] The 1906 Trade Disputes Act, which freed the unions from the shackles of the Taff Vale decision and strengthened the right of peaceful picketing, payment of MPs in 1911, and the Trade Union Act of 1913, which reversed the Osborne judgement of 1909 by permitting unions to spend money on political objects under certain conditions, were relevant in this context.

Ministerial doubts and divisions did not prevent a number of expressions of confidence in trade unionism. Campbell-Bannerman told the House of Commons on 30 March 1906 during a debate on the Trade Disputes Bill that 'dread and suspicion' had yielded to a general acknowledgement of 'the beneficent nature of the trade-union organization', and that there had been 'a great revolution in the attitude of public feeling' (HC Deb., col. 52). The Osborne judgement led to a number of attempts by ministers to assess the proper political role of unions. There was 'an exhaustive debate' in Cabinet, as Asquith told King George V,[9] and several debates in the House of Commons, during one of which Churchill declared (30 May 1911, col. 1017): 'I consider that every workman is well advised to join a trade union.'

Ministers were as actively involved in industrial relations as in legislation, and their involvement and that of their officials in the strengthened conciliation service will be considered later. What deserves attention here is the motivation for the remarkable change in Liberal behaviour after 1905. Undoubtedly part of the explanation lay in a growing social conscience among the upper social classes, including both the Liberal leaders and influential civil servants. But social conscience did not exist in a void. It was partly the result of an increasingly articulate working class which had created its own political party. The Labour Representation Committee was a small body, but it was important enough to be recognized by the Liberals in an electoral agreement in 1903. This agreement, by which Labour Representation Committee candidates were free from Liberal competition in a number of constituencies in return for Labour 'friendliness' elsewhere, was largely responsible for the important gains of the Labour Representation Committee (shortly to be renamed the Labour Party) in the general election of 1906.

Even more important than the Labour gains was the momentum created by the Liberals themselves, for their huge majority changed the political scene more abruptly and sweepingly than could have been anticipated a year or two previously. The Liberal leadership, notably Campbell-Bannerman, Prime Minister until 1908, and Asquith, his successor, were careful during the election campaign not to make lavish promises of public expenditure, but certain gestures were made; Campbell–Bannerman in particular held out hope of social reform in an important speech.[10] The rank-and-file had been subject to no such restraint, and enthusiastically committed themselves to new departures, many of them looking to retrenchment in imperial and military expenditure as a means of financing social reform.[11] The Liberal majority, which included many lively, radical MPs, and the equally lively radical press, encouraged the Government to act on novel lines and to contribute to the change in 'tone, spirit, temper, and tendency' of public policy to which Campbell–Bannerman had prophetically referred during the campaign.[12]

The 1906 election took place near the start of a prolonged period of heated domestic political controversy, the long preoccupation with imperial questions finally subsiding after the end of the South African war in 1902. Discussion of free trade, land ownership, the House of Lords, poverty, socialism, the rights of labour, women and the Irish all reached a climax during these years.[13] The constant political discussions of the house painters in Robert Tressell's *The Ragged Trousered Philanthropists*, probably written between 1907 and 1909, were thus more realistic in the context of their time than they would have been in a later period. Sir George Askwith, the Government's chief labour conciliator, observed in a paper submitted to the Cabinet in 1911 that 'social questions are becoming more and more matters of politics, and are thus continually coming under public discussion'. The high-Tory Stephen Reynolds concluded that as a result of the controversy over free trade and other issues, 'the working classes have been made aware of the existence of economics', and the Liberal Seebohm Rowntree also drew attention to the plethora of nostrums offered to the working class, including tariff reform, land reform and socialism.[14] Publications like *Riches and Poverty* by Leo Chiozza Money, MP, with its graphic illustrations of the inequalities of existing society, encouraged controversy; the book was first published in October 1905 and was in its eleventh printing by March 1914. Arthur Ponsonby's *The Camel and the Needle's Eye* (1909) was another example of the genre by another Liberal MP.

Above all, the spectacle of a Chancellor of the Exchequer acting as social agitator caught the national imagination. The Conservative press and political leaders bitterly attacked Lloyd George for arousing class hatred with his Budget of 1909 and his speeches at Limehouse and elsewhere[15] (and were in turn reprobated by Lloyd George for encouraging violence over the reform of the House of Lords and the Irish question), but socialists also appreciated the Chancellor's activities. 'A man who doesn't pay attention to a socialist orator is caught by the Chancellor of the Exchequer', R.H. Tawney mused,[16] and J.R. Clynes, a future Labour Home Secretary, told the House of Commons on 15 February 1912 (col.60): 'The present Chancellor of the Exchequer, perhaps more than any man in history, has directed public attention to these extremes of riches and poverty.'

The fevered atmosphere of the Edwardian years was the background to the sharp rise in numbers of trade unionists, from 1,559,000 when figures were officially compiled in 1893, to 2,022,000 in 1900, 2,565,000 in 1910 and 4,145,000 in 1914. Between 1900 and 1909 there were relatively few industrial disputes and, apart from a cotton-workers' lock-out in 1908 which cost nearly 5,000,000 days, relatively few working days were lost. Not only did trade union membership grow at an unprecedented rate between 1910 and 1914, but industrial turmoil reached a level never previously experienced over so long a period.[17] The same years experienced a transformation of the trade union movement, after a relatively long period of calm.

One of the most important aspects of this transformation was the breach which had opened between the union leadership and some of the rank-and-file, among whom shop stewards had begun to be active in certain industries. The Government in its pioneering gropings towards an industrial policy had to cope not with trade union leaders alone, but with a leadership poised uneasily between employers and an increasingly restive membership. Beatrice and Sidney Webb had detected signs of this breach as early as 1894, and by 1910, when *The Times* wrote of 'a partial breakdown' of trade unionism, it had grown a good deal sharper.[18] Syndicalism, partly cause and partly effect, was widely blamed, not least by the trade union leaders themselves.[19] Politicians and officials were in no doubt as to what was happening. Sydney Buxton, President of the Board of Trade, told his Cabinet colleagues in 1912: 'The leaders no longer possess the confidence, and are not allowed the executive authority that used to be reposed in them . . . . The leaders have lost influence and consequently self-confidence, and naturally are unwilling to take the same responsibility as they would gladly have taken, and did take, under former conditions.'[20] Austen Chamberlain, a Conservative leader, told the House of Commons on 16 August 1911 (cols. 1947–48), when industrial turmoil was at its height: 'I think the most prominent feature of the present unrest is the extent to which agreements made under the arbitration of the Board of Trade have failed to obtain acceptance by the men after their leaders have signed them.'

Part of the explanation of the rank-and-file rebellion lies in the growing 'respectability' of the unions, the apparent conservatism of many union leaders and the willingness of employers to recognize unions and collective bargaining between 1890 and 1914, especially in the later years of the period.[21] Askwith calculated in 1910 that less than a quarter of workers in industry were directly covered by collective agreements, but that many others were indirectly affected. Another writer put the total percentage of industrial workers affected by collective bargaining in 1914 at about half.[22] As formal systems of union–employer relations developed in nearly every industry but the railways, both employers and previously hostile elements of the press felt increasingly that the best hope of industrial peace lay in strong trade unions. The *Quarterly Review*, an influential Conservative journal, wrote in October 1911 (p. 598) that no better method of reconciling labour's claims with economic realities and social peace than collective bargaining had yet been suggested. The *Daily Mail* wrote on 20 September 1913 that most businessmen regarded unions as 'a necessity of modern industrialism' and 'conciliatory and conservative organisations', and the *Morning Post* commented on 8 July 1914 that union leaders were moderates, who opposed syndicalism and preferred industrial peace to war.

A number of businessmen spoke in terms of qualified approval of trade unions to the Royal Commission on Trade Disputes and Trade Combinations, and the same Sir Christopher Furness who had lost the York by-election in 1898 because of union hostility told a union audience a decade later: 'I am a sincere friend of Trades-Unionism . . .'.[23] Andrew Bonar Law, the Conservative leader, bluntly told the House of Commons on 23 July 1912 (col. 1124): 'I should like to see the trade unions become stronger, because I think that, as a rule, they tend to the diminution of disputes.' The view that unions meant peace was given authoritative support by the Industrial Council, a semi-official body consisting of twenty-six leading employers and trade unionists, which issued a report published as a parliamentary paper in 1913. The council concluded that where strong unions faced strong employers' organizations, as in the steel trade, 'breaches of agreements rarely occur' or were quickly settled, but where, as in baking, organization was weak, agreements were 'constantly imperilled owing to the inability of either side to take effective action in the event of a breach of the agreement occurring'.[24] Although this statement underestimated the occurrence of strikes and lock-outs in well-organized industries, it could not have made cheerful reading for militants, who saw trade unions as fighting rather than pacific organizations.

The most interesting feature of books, articles and parliamentary speeches of the period from 1910 is the constant reiteration that not only the trade union movement but the working class itself had been transformed, a transformation which in 1910 appeared to be part of a worldwide phenomenon. Contemporaries attributed the unrest partly to the much-publicized failure of wages to keep pace with rising prices between 1900 and 1910, but they were even more impressed by the change in the nature of working-class demands, the insistence upon emancipation from the harsh constraints of poverty. The upper classes, many commentators noted, were spending more lavishly and flamboyantly than ever before, thanks to the rising income of the minority who paid income tax and to increased company profits at a time of falling real wages.[25] Seebohm Rowntree pointed out in the *Contemporary Review* (Oct. 1911, pp. 459–60) that the working classes 'read in the papers that imports and exports have exceeded all previous records, and that never before have railway returns been so high. They have been like men watching a rich feast, in the provision of which they had played an important part, but in which they might not share.' The symbol of upper-class arrogance and extravagance was generally taken to be the motor car, a point to which the Liberal backbencher Eliot Crawshay-Williams drew the attention of the House of Commons in launching a debate on industrial unrest on 8 May 1919 (col. 495): 'At this very time, when the poor man's cottage has been dusted by motor cars and his hedge has been whitened, he has been given an increasingly efficient education, and a larger area of thought . . .'.

For it was education, including both teaching and the spread of mass communications, to which the militancy of the working class was generally attributed. The Liberal economist George Paish asserted: '. . . the education, instruction, and amusement of everyone in the past generation or two by the circulation of newspapers, magazines, and books is nothing short of a revolution. Never did the average man and woman advance in knowledge and intellectual attainments as in modern times . . .' (*Sociological Review*, July 1911, p. 182). W.C. Anderson, a leader of the ILP, wrote in the *Socialist Review* (Oct. 1911, p. 99):

If social conditions were to remain unchallenged, no working-class school should have been opened, no cheap books should have been printed, no working-class meetings should have been permitted, and every man or woman who showed any reforming impulse should have been hanged immediately . . . Education, even an entirely inadequate education, has helped to create in him certain new wants which, though neither extravagant nor expensive, are beyond the reach of his purse. In short, the worker begins to think, and this process is at the root of the Labour unrest and will mark the beginning of many changes.

Conservatives, as might be expected, were not unanimously enthusiastic about the results of educating the working classes, but they recognized what had taken place and in some cases at least claimed credit. Henry FitzHerbert Wright, a Conservative backbencher, wrote to his leader, Bonar Law, in 1913: 'During the last 20 years we have, & rightly, done much by the way the educational system has been administered to broaden their outlook & their interests: it is only natural they now want those interests to be met.'[26]

Adult education also played its part. The breakaway from Ruskin College in 1909 which established the Plebs League and the Central Labour College injected a Marxist element into the movement. Rowland Kenney, a socialist journalist, wrote in the *English Review* in March 1912 (pp. 690, 692) that more and more trade unionists spent their spare time and money in gaining knowledge which would serve working-class interests. Through the Central Labour College, he added, 'an army of workers' was being educated to believe in antagonism between classes. The Workers'

Educational Association, founded in 1903, was less consciously militant than the Central Labour College, but its students were independent spirits who thought for themselves. R.H. Tawney, then a Workers' Educational Association tutor, asked a Northumberland miner in May 1912 to explain labour unrest and was told: 'People have discovered that human society is flexible: they have got the idea of evolution; and they do not see why social institutions should not be adapted in accordance with their desires.'[27]

Falling real wages, the luxuries of upper-class life, more widely available means of communication, and education both formal and informal added up to an explosive mixture. Stephen Reynolds, the intimate of Devon fishermen, anticipated the result, the strike-bound summer of 1911, when he put these words into the mouth of one of his working-class characters: ' "Have you ever thought to yourself, sir," he said, "why 'twas you was born to smoke these here expensive fags, an' to have money, an' be sent to college, an' ride in motor-cars, an' hae all sorts o' advantages that I can't get for my kids, no matter how hard I works?" ' 'Silently,' Reynolds added, 'so far as the reading public is concerned,' working people had been 'learning to question the whole of the present system of wages and earnings and social position.'[28]

Politicians, journalists and social observers, especially but not exclusively those on the liberal-left, were quick to draw sweeping conclusions from the labour unrest. J.A. Hobson wrote after the election of January 1910 that the organized working class had become concerned about poverty and social injustice and, two years later, that class hostility had grown more acute. C.P. Trevelyan and C.F.G. Masterman, rising Liberal politicians, saw the labour unrest in terms of 'a great wave of hope', 'the most incalculable of disturbing forces', sweeping through the working class. This was an analysis shared by a group of advanced Liberals which included Hobson and three Rowntrees, who urged on the Cabinet Committee on Industrial Unrest the need for sweeping measures of social reform: '. . . we would urge in Lincoln's words that "a country cannot remain half-slave, half-free".' G.K. Chesterton pointed out that 'for those that influence the State' the working class was unnoticed until it stopped working, and that strikes were the inevitable consequence. Strikes, moreover, stirred public opinion far more than they had done in the past, as the *New Statesman* commented, contrasting unconcern with the miners' prolonged lock-out in 1893 with the resounding effect of the shorter but more widespread strike of 1912.[29]

The *Fortnightly Review, The Nation* and the author George Sturt concurred in assessing the labour unrest as the start of a social revolution, in which political and social power was passing into the hands of the working class. To the individualist Harold Cox it seemed to be 'one of those great movements which from time to time seize hold of mankind, and profoundly affect the whole course of history'. Beatrice and Sidney

Webb returned from a world tour in April 1912 to find 'a new England', 'an awakened England'. Edward Cadbury, the Liberal manufacturer, and Fabian Ware, the Conservative journalist, saw the unrest as signifying the demand of the worker to control his own life and to rise to occupations previously closed to him. Christian social observers like the clergyman A.J. Carlyle and the writer Gilbert Slater discerned a revolt against the conditions of working-class life and a demand for amenities enjoyed by other social classes, a diagnosis shared by the *Westminster Gazette*, which in a report from Tyneside surmized that the labour unrest was a demand for the water closet and the high living standard which this implied: 'Deep down in his soul is blind revolt against life as he finds it.'[30] These assessments may have been confused and the expectations exaggerated, but such comments bore ample witness to the manner in which trade union action had upset the social balance and caused social philosophies to be amended or adjusted.

The Liberal Government intervened in most of the major industrial disputes between 1907 and 1912.[31] This was a more remarkable development than might appear, since formal government involvement had begun only with the miners' lock-out in 1893. Lloyd George played a more important role as conciliator than any other minister, but Asquith, Buxton, Churchill and others also took part in attempts to avoid or settle such disputes as the threatened railway and cotton strikes in 1907, the South Wales coal strike in 1910–11, waterfront, labourers' and railway strikes in 1911, and coal and dock strikes in 1912. Where politicians kept clear, civil servants took part. The Board of Trade's Labour Department had intervened systematically in industrial disputes since the passage of the Conciliation Act in 1896, but after 1906 both the degree of its involvement and its rate of success in resolving disputes rose to impressive heights. The leading civil servant conciliator was Sir George Askwith, who as Chief Industrial Commissioner from 1911 acquired not only increased personal prestige but a reorganized department with greater resources. The Department also encouraged the creation of voluntary conciliation boards, whose numbers rose from 105 in 1896 to 325 in 1913.[32] This intervention by civil servants was important, but it was the activity of politicians which was to have longer-lasting effects on both politics and trade unions.

Historians have debated how close Britain was to civil strife or revolution between 1910 and 1914,[33] and the subject will not be confronted directly here. But two points should be made. The first is that during the Cambrian Combine coal strike in South Wales in 1910–11, the summer strikes of 1911 and the national coal strike in March and April 1912, tensions and apprehensions ran very high. Violence flared in South Wales in 1910, when large numbers of police and troops were drafted into Tonypandy and the surrounding area, and one man died during fighting with the police. In summer 1911 violence was much more serious. Rioting took place in many parts of the country and troops were enthusiastically despatched to actual and potential trouble spots by the Home Secretary, Winston Churchill. Thousands of troops were stationed in London, giving an impression of a city under martial law. Two men were shot by troops in Liverpool and two in Llanelly, where several others died after the explosion of an ammunition van. The mining strike was relatively free from civil strife; here the causes of apprehension were not actual violence but the fear both of provoking the miners and of allowing them to dictate the terms of conflict, the geographical and human scale of the strike, and the crucial nature of the commodity involved.[34]

The second point is that in the eyes of most contemporaries the labour unrest was no longer an immediate threat or promise after the failure of the London dock strike in summer 1912. The Government rapidly lost interest in the subject, and the massive coverage in the press, government papers and *Hansard* of 1910–12 did not extend to the Midlands strikes of 1913 or the troubles in building and coal in 1914. Even the bitter Dublin dispute of 1913–14 failed to arouse outside Ireland the same emotions as in 1910–12. The subject was never forgotten: the strike wave had been too massive and frightening, and the industrial situation remained too turbulent (see Pratten, Ch. IX). Both the numerous disputes of 1913–14 and the formation of the Triple Industrial Alliance in 1914 led to considerable concern. The Liberal *Daily News*, for example, wrote as late as 21 July 1914 in a leading article entitled 'Labour and Revolution': 'It is idle to ignore the possibility that any spark may in the present state of this labour world cause a vast conflagration. Sparks are not wanting.' But other organs of opinion were less disturbed; *The Times*, indeed, saw the Triple Alliance as more likely to lead to industrial peace than war (19 June 1914). In any case the threat remained shapeless, potential rather than actual.

It would be a mistake to take at face value the reactions of contemporaries during a period of high excitement. Nevertheless, lasting results did ensue from the strike wave of 1910–12 which deserve examination. One indication of the state of mind of the governing classes during the dock and rail strikes of 1911 can be found in the leading articles of *The Times*. On 11 August it wrote: 'Mob law is in fact supreme as far as the food of London is concerned, and the outlook is of the gravest kind.' On 16 August: 'These trade unionists in their crazy fanaticism or diseased vanity are prepared to starve the whole population . . .'. On 18 August it referred to the behaviour of the railway strike-leaders as 'reckless and treasonable madness'. The next day the strike had become 'this reckless revolt against society' and on 23 August, with the railway strike uneasily concluded, the August wave seemed '[t]he greatest labour upheaval that this country has seen'. The conservative *Morning Post*, writing on 14 August, thought that 'open revolution' was closer than at any time in living memory, and proclaimed: 'The time has come for the "whiff of grape shot" which is the only final answer of authority to the clamour of an undisciplined mob.' Two days later, however, it blamed the strikes on the summer's excessive heat and saw the 'best remedy' as ten days' cold rain (see also Pratten, pp. 123–26, 154–68).

Winston Churchill, always inclined to dramatize political occasions, had every reason to exaggerate the scale and seriousness of the strikes when defending himself in the House of Commons on 22 August. Even so, his words portrayed a serious situation, reflecting both press comment and the panicky calls for help of local authorities.[35] Had the railway strike not been quickly ended, Churchill declared (cols. 2326–28), industrial England 'would have [been] hurled . . . into an abyss of horror which no man dare to contemplate . . . . I do not know whether in the history of the world a similar catastrophe can be shown to have menaced an equally great community . . . . Employment, wages, food and the lives of many millions of people were threatened and at stake.'

The railway strike with its widespread violence followed Asquith's abrasive treatment of the railwaymen's leaders and his threat that the railways would be kept open by whatever means were necessary (*The Times*, 18 Aug. 1911). The result was an intensification of the existing panic.[36] Political, business and press leaders were deeply relieved when Lloyd George repaired the damage and persuaded the union leaders to call off the strike. Asquith was one of the most relieved and paid a lavish private tribute to Lloyd George's settlement of one of the Government's 'most formidable problems'; his wife wrote to Sydney Buxton the next day: 'I cd hardly breathe or sleep for anxiety & misery these last 2 weeks.'[37] But from the union point of view the inauguration of a government industrial relations policy by strike-breaking troops hardly heralded the new Jerusalem. Their chief gain was parliamentary rather than governmental, for, on the initiative of Ramsay MacDonald, the House of Commons passed a resolution on 22 November urging direct discussions between unions and employers. This was a considerable victory, since employer failure to recognize the railway unions had been the principal cause of the strike, though Asquith maintained his careful insistence that he was not advocating recognition (cols 1209–1328).

At the end of 1911 it could not be said that after six reforming Liberal years the attitude of government to industrial relations had fundamentally altered, though the scale and seriousness of strikes had dictated direct government intervention in their solution. This position was to change under the impact of the miners' strike, which began on 1 March 1912. As in August 1911 the gravity of the situation was universally recognized, and leading articles bordered on panic as the deadline approached. *The Economist*, which afterwards claimed to have kept its head (6 Apr., p. 739), wrote in advance that a national coal strike would be 'a calamity which would paralyse practically every branch of English industry' (24 Feb., p. 398), and *The Times* declared on 26 February that the strike was 'the greatest catastrophe that has threatened the country since the Spanish Armada' (see Pratten, pp. 190–92, 200–201).

The strike was characterized by a general absence of violence and a relative lack of privation, but the high note of hysteria sounded in August 1911 was heard again. Sir Henry Seton-Karr, a former Conservative MP, volunteered through the pages of *The Times* on 8 March to play his part in fighting socialist trade unionism, by resorting if necessary to 'siege rations, martial law, and organized support of starving families'. A.J. Balfour, who had recently been superseded as Conservative leader, told the House of Commons on 21 March (col. 2078) that the country had never been 'face to face with a peril of this character or of this magnitude', Lord Robert Cecil, a rising Conservative star, wrote privately to Balfour's successor, Bonar Law, warning that 'a victory by the miners would really mean anarchy & ultimately actual fighting', and Austen Chamberlain was told by a friend that revolvers were being sold in large numbers, presumably to those who upheld civil peace against the threat of working-class violence.[38] The prosecutions which the government undertook against the so-called 'Don't Shoot' leaflet, a syndicalist publication appealing for support from soldiers, and the over-reaction to the syndicalist pamphlet *The Miners' Next Step*[39] helped to keep tension high during the strike.

The miners' action forced upon the government the realization that the days of non-intervention were over and that a minimum wage would have to be sanctioned by Parliament in an industry whose workers were relatively well-paid, strongly-organized men. Not only ministers but opposition leaders were reluctantly persuaded that Parliament could not, in Chamberlain's words of 21 March (col. 2178), 'maintain that attitude of indifference to the great combinations of labour and of capital which it has sought to preserve in the past'. Asquith, by no means an interventionist in these matters, told the House of Commons on 19 March (col. 1733) that the principle of the minimum wage could no longer be denied, and he was echoed two days later by Sir Edward Grey (col. 2185) who, though Foreign Secretary, played an important role in the strike negotiations. The reason for this philosophical shift was given by Asquith to the House with startling frankness on 21 March (col. 2096):

It is impossible that we should allow the whole life, industrial and social, of this country to be brought to a deadlock and a standstill. There we are agreed. Having that common end in view, are we not right, indeed are we not bound, to obtain from Parliament a legislative declaration of the reasonableness of the claim for a minimum wage, subject to adequate safeguards for the employer?

Cherished Liberal beliefs had been forced to yield under the weight of social and economic reality. The principle of non-intervention retained a figleaf, however, for Asquith (col. 2096) insisted that the Bill was 'provisional and temporary' and refused, against the opposition of the miners and some of his Cabinet colleagues, to allow the inclusion of a schedule of wage figures.[40]

The 1912 Act, which set up machinery to award miners a minimum wage determined locally, was not a precedent since the future did not lie with the statutory determination of the wages of male trade unionists. The significance of the discussion of the minimum wage lay in the fact that, at a time when political crises followed each other thick and fast, a trade union issue had become the most pressing topic of the day. Asquith told the House of Commons when he introduced the Bill on 19 March (col. 1724): 'I cannot remember ever to have exerted the same pains and persistence in the pursuit of a single object' and a week later broke down in the House under the strain.[41] Grey wrote that the strike marked the beginning of a revolution in which power was passing from the House of Commons to the trade unions. Lloyd George may have meant much the same when he told his friend Lord Riddell that the strike marked the end of the old Liberal Party.[42] The behaviour of Herbert Samuel is an illustration of the contradictory position in which ministers were placed; as Postmaster-General he was naturally anxious to end the dispute, but as Liberal MP he raised £10,000 on behalf of his Cleveland mining constituents, thus enabling the miners to receive strike pay and the strike to be prosecuted more effectively.[43] Conventional opinion, which might have been expected to oppose government intervention in the strike, was forced by events to adopt a different tone. Thus *The Times* declared on 4 March:

Whatever may be thought of government interference in the abstract, it may be hoped that the exceptional character of the present crisis will induce those who view it with disapproval to suppress their objections . . . It is the duty of all who have national interests at heart to put aside political differences and to do all that they can to strengthen the hands of the Government.

As already mentioned, the two years before the outbreak of war in August 1914 marked an anti-climax in terms of government involvement in industrial disputes. Politicians withdrew with alacrity from a problem which they were no better able to resolve than their successors have proved to be. Conservative leaders demonstrated their uncertainty in the face of industrial crisis during the coal strike, when they were critical of the Government's minimum wage legislation but unable to offer a convincing alternative (see Chamberlain, p. 441; Pratten, p.211). Bonar Law, with a frankness which rivalled Asquith's, admitted to the House of Commons on 19 March 1912 (col. 1740): 'Let me say at once that I am thankful the responsibility rests with right hon. Gentlemen opposite.' Law had written the previous day to a parliamentary supporter, who had urged the abolition of peaceful picketing and the protection of potential strike-breakers: '. . . at present I cannot see my way clearly as to what action we should take', and he wrote to another Conservative MP in May that he was grateful not to have had to speak in a parliamentary debate on industrial unrest.[44]

The Government had no more notion how to proceed than had Opposition leaders, though it was unwilling to limit the right to strike and picket as some Conservatives and some employers wished to do.[45] The Cabinet Committee on Industrial Unrest set up in the spring of 1912 held several hearings but came to no conclusions and abandoned their task in favour of a narrower inquiry by the Industrial Council.[46] Members of Parliament repeatedly but unsuccessfully pressed both Asquith and Lloyd George to present a report or conclusions from the Cabinet Committee; the last such question was asked of Asquith on 28 July 1914 (col. 1110). The Cabinet was told that the distress caused by the coal strike was unexpectedly light,[47] and the disinclination to take decisive measures may have been strengthened by the picture which Sydney Buxton presented to his colleagues of the industrial situation as fraught with uncertainty and danger. Most of the Cabinet appear to have shared Buxton's conclusion, which advocated a policy of inaction:

The whole question of industrial unrest is obviously one abounding in difficulties of all sorts. It appears clear that the Government cannot safely or effectively move in the direction of legislative, or even administrative, action without much fuller information than they have at their disposal, and after much greater consideration of the question than they have yet been able to give.[48]

Asquith told both the House of Commons and a dinner of bankers that he welcomed suggestions as to how best to deal with industrial relations. Neither Buxton nor any other member of the Government ever put forward a convincing plan for major legislation, though a proposal that collective agreements once made should be legally binding on both sides of industry found a measure of support.[49] Buxton's final thought on the matter, a Cabinet paper written in January 1914, was that the government should promote comprehensive voluntary agreements and set up courts of inquiry to strengthen conciliation procedures.[50] Not even these fairly modest suggestions were taken up by the Cabinet. The danger of intervention seemed greater than the danger of inaction, and after an unsuccessful attempt by Lloyd George and other ministers to settle the London dock strike in late spring and summer 1912, political leaders did not participate in solving labour disputes until after the beginning of the war. Government involvement in industrial relations in peacetime had become established in a mould which entailed muddling through particular crises, where possible by the combination of 'conferences, conciliation, compromise and *common sense*'[51] recommended to Asquith by a Cabinet colleague after the railway strike of 1911. It was a mould which long endured.

Viewed by the standards of its predecessors, the Liberal Government took unprecedentedly bold steps between 1906 and 1914 in the fields of social and labour legislation and in forging links with trade union leaders. In terms of industrial relations the Government was less successful; its unintended achievement was to preside over the sudden entry of the subject 'into the sphere of practical politics', in the words of the *Economic Journal*. The result was as far-reaching as it was unplanned. The attitude of politicians and governments towards trade unions and working-class living standards underwent an important alteration. As the *Economic Journal* (whose editor was J.M. Keynes) pointed out (June 1912, p. 345), a further manifestation of *laissez-faire* had been overthrown and 'a further advance [taken] in a direction which we may or may not choose to call Socialistic'. A similar view was taken by the authors of an authoritative contemporary book, who suggested that government involvement in industrial disputes might come to be regarded as 'the most important development in economic matters in this country in the last fifty years'.[52]

The conclusion that the State must be involved in industrial relations was not limited to outside analysts or to the left of the political spectrum. The Unionist (i.e. Conservative) Social Reform Committee, which included Stanley Baldwin and several other future ministers, issued a report in June 1914 which significantly advocated improved conciliation procedures, minimum wages, steps towards the abolition of casually employed labour and other reforms, and declared: 'It is incontestably the right and duty of statesmanship to supervise and control the conditions of employment in the interests of the State as a whole . . . . [I]t is the right and duty of statesmanship to intervene between employer and employed in the case of industrial dispute to protect the interests of the community . . .'.[53]

In August 1913 Lloyd George addressed a large meeting of miners in Sutton-in-Ashfield. F.B. Varley, Vice-President of the Nottinghamshire Miners' Association, commented in his own speech to the meeting that Lloyd George was probably the first Cabinet minister who had ever addressed the association. This was a development, Varley added, which 'gave the impression that the State was beginning to recognize that the working classes were the vital part of the nation'.[54] This comment suggests the nature of the advance made in these years. By 1914 press and politicians were forced to direct much anxious attention to the problems and uncertainties brought about by a militant working class. Trade unions, the representative institutions of the working class, had doubled their membership and greatly increased their influence and importance. 'In Britain a change has taken place in the relation of social forces,' Lenin wrote in January 1913, 'a change which cannot be expressed in figures, but which everyone feels.'[55] No more than a foundation had yet been laid, but it was a foundation upon which much was to be built.

NOTES AND REFERENCES

1.   I am grateful for the generous assistance which I have received from Geoff Brown and David Martin and from Mrs E. Clay of Hassocks, who kindly permitted access to the papers of her grandfather, Sydney Buxton. I am also grateful to my many predecessors in this crowded field; in particular to Geoff Brown, Peter Clarke, H.V. Emy, Ross Martin, Peter Rowland and Chris Wrigley. The reader should also be directed to J.D. Pratten, 'The Reaction to Working Class Unrest, 1911–1914', University of Sheffield, unpublished doctoral thesis, 1975, in which a number of the subjects treated here are considered at greater length.

2.   A.L. Lowell, *The Government of England*, vol. II, Macmillan, New York, 1908, pp. 508–513. For further consideration of the influence of 'society' on Liberal politicians and the Liberal Government of 1906–14, see J.A. Hobson, *Traffic in Treason*, T. Fisher Unwin, London, 1914, pp. 61–62, and Lord Riddell, *More Pages from my Diary*, Country Life, London, 1934, p. 59.

3.   There are several analyses of the social composition of the 1906–14 Parliaments, the most detailed of which is J.A. Thomas, *The House of Commons 1906–1911*, University of Wales Press, Cardiff, 1958. For the figure of 41 per cent, see W.L. Guttsman, *The British Political Elite*, McGibbon & Kee, London, 1963, p. 90. The other figures are from H.V. Emy, *Liberals, Radicals and Social Politics 1892–1914*, Cambridge University Press, Cambridge, 1973, pp. 101–103, 280.

4.   Ross M. Martin, *TUC: the Growth of a Pressure Group 1868–1976*, Clarendon Press, Oxford, 1980, pp. 99–102; José Harris, *Unemployment and Politics*, Clarendon Press, Oxford, 1972, Ch. VI; José Harris, *William Beveridge*, Clarendon Press, Oxford, 1977, pp. 154–55, 182–83.

5.   Lloyd George Papers (HLRO), C/6/2/1.

6.   Élie Halévy, *A History of the English People, Epilogue vol. II*, Benn, London (English trans. 1934), pp. 438–39; Martin, *TUC*, op. cit., p. 105.

7.   V.L. Allen, *Trade Unions and the Government*, Longman, London, 1960, pp. 84, 88–89; Brian Bercusson, *Fair Wages Resolutions*, Mansell, London, 1978, Ch. 6; TUC Parliamentary Committee *Minutes*, 14 February 1906, 16 August 1911; TUC *Annual Report*, 1907, pp. 44–45; Martin, *TUC*, op. cit., pp. 99, 130.

8.   Élie Halévy, *A History of the English People*, op. cit., p. 237.

9.   Asquith's Cabinet Letter to King George V, copy in Asquith Papers (Bodl. Lib), 5/f.248, 22 November 1910. Ministers' papers on the Osborne judgement are filed in the PRO, Cab. 37/103 and 104, and are briefly summarized by Emy, *Liberals, Radicals and Social Politics*, op. cit., p. 251.

10. *Liberal Policy*, a speech by Sir Henry Campbell-Bannerman on 21 December 1905, pp. 8–10; *The Economist*, 12 October 1907, p. 1710.

11. A.K. Russell, *Liberal Landslide: the General Election of 1906*, David & Charles, Newton Abbot, 1973, pp. 65–77, 195; P. Rowland, *The Last Liberal Governments: the Promised Land, 1905–1910*, Barrie & Rockliff/Cresset, London, 1968, p. 34n; Stephen Koss, *Fleet Street Radical: A.G. Gardiner and the Daily News*, Allen Lane, London, 1973, p. 92.

12. Quoted in Russell, *Liberal Landslide*, op. cit., p. 117.

13. Many of these issues are vividly discussed in G. Dangerfield's *The Strange Death of Liberal England*, Smith & Haas, New York (first published 1935).

14. Askwith: G.R. Askwith, 'The Present Unrest in the Labour World', PRO, Cab. 37/107/70, 25 June 1911, p. 9; Reynolds: Stephen Reynolds and Bob and Tom Woolley, *Seems So! a Working-Class View of Politics*, Macmillan, London, 1911, p. 172; Rowntree: Seebohm Rowntree, *The Way to Industrial Peace and the Problem of Unemployment*, T. Fisher Unwin, London, 1914, pp. 11–12.

15. For example, *Morning Post*, 21 March 1912.

16. J.M. Winter and D.M. Joslin (eds), *R.H. Tawney's Commonplace Book*, Cambridge University Press, Cambridge, 1972, p. 8. Tawney was writing on 29 April 1912.

17. H. Pelling, *A History of British Trade Unionism*, Penguin, Harmondsworth, 1963, pp. 261–62; H.A. Clegg, A. Fox and A.F. Thompson, *A History of British Trade Unions since 1889: vol. I, 1889–1910*, Clarendon Press, Oxford, 1964, pp.459–60.

18. S. and B. Webb, *The History of Trade Unionism*, Longmans, London, 1894, pp. 454–58; The *Times*, 9 November 1919, See also *Punch*, 17 August 1910, p. 111; 14 September 1910, p. 191.

19. For example, J.H. Thomas to Cabinet Committee on Industrial Unrest, 24 April 1912; Lloyd George Papers, C/21/1/12.

20. 'Industrial Unrest', Cab. 37/110/62, 13 April 1912, p. 4.

21. S. and B. Webb, *Industrial Democracy*, vol. I, Longmans, London, 1897, p. 238; H.A. Clegg *et al.*, *A History of British Trade Unions*, op. cit., pp. 362–63, 471; R. Price, *Masters, Unions and Men*, Cambridge University Press, Cambridge, 1980, Ch. 5–7.

22. PP 1910, vol. XX, Cd, 5366, pp. iii–iv; C.M. Lloyd, *Trade Unionism*, Adam & Charles Black, 1915, p. 136.

23.   PP 1906, vol. LVI, Cd. 2826, evidence of Sir Benjamin Browne, William Bagley, Sir George Livesey, M.C. James, James Samuel Beal, Thomas Warburton; also G.R. Askwith, the Government labour conciliator; Sir Christopher Furness, *Industrial Peace and Industrial Efficiency*, Alexander Salton, West Hartlepool, 1908, pp. 20, 31.

24.   PP 1913, vol. XXVIII, Cd. 6952, para. 18. For the Industrial Council see R. Charles, *The Development of Industrial Relations in Britain, 1911–1939*, Hutchinson, London, 1973, Pt One.

25.   One of the most perceptive and informative of such comments was by the Liberal economist W.T. Layton in *The Economist*, 26 August 1911, pp. 440–42. A valuable modern assessment is provided by T.R. Gourvish, 'The Standard of Living, 1890–1914', in Alan O'Day (ed.), *The Edwardian Age*, Macmillan, London, 1979, pp. 13–34.

26.   Bonar Law Papers (HLRO), 29/1/3, 1 February 1913. The comments by Paish, Anderson and Wright, written from widely varying points of view, stand for a host of others. One of the most perceptive was by H.G. Wells, writing in a series entitled *What the Worker Wants*, [1912], reproduced from the *Daily Mail* and partly reprinted in D. Read, *Documents from Edwardian England, 1901–1915*, Harrap, London, 1973, pp. 274–76.

27.   J.M. Winter and D.M. Joslin (eds); *R.H. Tawney's Commonplace Book*, op. cit., p. 10.

28.   S. Reynolds and B. and T. Woolley, *Seems So!*, op. cit., pp. 114, 183.

29.   Hobson: *Sociological Review*, vol. III, April 1910, p. 115; *Industrial Unrest*, National Liberal Club, London, 1912, p.2; Trevelyan: A.J.A. Morris in A.J.A. Morris (ed.), *Edwardian Radicalism*, Routledge and Kegan Paul, London, 1974, p. 144 and in *C.P. Trevelyan*, Blackstaff Press, Belfast, 1977, p. 88; Masterman: *The Times*, 18 September 1911; advanced Liberals: *Labour Unrest and Liberal Social Policy*, 1912, in Lloyd George Papers, C/21/1/17 (see also Emy, *Liberals, Radicals and Social Politics*, op. cit., pp. 271–72); Chesterton: *Illustrated London News*, 26 August 1911, p. 327 (also *Daily News*, 19 August 1911); *New Statesman*, 27 September 1913, p. 772.

30.   *Fortnightly Review* vol CX, 1 September 1911, pp. 381–90; *The Nation*, 19 August 1911, p. 725; Sturt: E.D. Mackerness (ed.), *The Journals of George Sturt 1890–1927*, vol. 2, Cambridge University Press, Cambridge, 1967, p. 662–69; Cox: Harold Cox, *Labour Unrest*, British Constitution Association, London, 1912, p. 1; Webbs: J.M. Winter, *Socialism and the Challenge of War*, Routledge & Kegan Paul, London, 1974, pp. 13, 31 (also Henrietta Barnett, *Canon Barnett*, Murray, London, 1921 edn., p. 728); Cadbury: *Sociological Review*, vol. VII, April 1914, p. 105; Ware: Fabian Ware, *The*

Worker and his Country, Edward Arnold, London, 1912, p. 252;
Carlyle and Slater: *William Temple* (intro.), *The Industrial Unrest
and the Living Wage*, P.S. King, London, 1913, pp. 56–60, 106–8;
Westminster Gazette: 11 October 1910.

31. C. Wrigley, *David Lloyd George and the British Labour Movement*,
Harvester, Hassocks, 1976, Ch. III; Roger Davidson, 'Sir Hubert
Llewellyn Smith and Labour Policy, 1886–1916', unpublished doc-
toral thesis, University of Cambridge, 1971, pp. 176–97.

32. Lord Askwith, *Industrial Problems and Disputes*, Murray, London,
1920, p. 179; Lord Amulree, *Industrial Arbitration in Great Britain*,
Oxford University Press, London, 1929, Ch. XII; Ian G. Sharp,
Industrial Conciliation and Arbitration in Great Britain, Allen & Unwin,
London, 1950, Pt Two, Ch. II; Roger Davidson, 'Social Conflict
and Social Administration: The Conciliation Act in British Industrial
Relations', in T.C. Smout (ed.), *The Search for Wealth and Stability*,
Macmillan, London, 1979, pp. 175–97.

33. G. Dangerfield, *The Strange Death of Liberal England*, op. cit. esp.
Pt Two, Ch. IV, Pt Three, Ch. IV; H. Pelling, *Popular Politics and
Society in Late Victorian Britain*, Macmillan, London, 1968, Ch. 9;
G.A. Phillips, 'The Triple Industrial Alliance in 1914', *Economic
History Review*, vol. XXIV, February 1971, pp. 55–67; S. Meacham,
' "The Sense of an Impending Clash" ', *American Historical Review*,
vol. 77, December 1972, pp. 1343–64; R. Holton, *British Syndicalism,
1900–1914*, Pluto Press, London, 1976.

34. The best available account of the labour unrest can be found in R.
Holton, *British Syndicalism*, op. cit.; D. Smith, 'Tonypandy 1910',
Past & Present, **87**, May 1980, pp. 158–84, sensitively analyses the
background to the South Wales disturbances.

35. PRO, HO 45/10654/212470; PP 1911, vol. XLVII, HCP 323. See
also Randolph S. Churchill, *Winston S. Churchill, vol. II, Companion
Part 2, 1907–1911*, Heinemann, London, 1969, pp. 1268–93, esp.
pp. 1274–75.

36. A vivid example of the intensity of public concern was provided by
the *Illustrated London News*, which devoted sixteen of its thirty pages
of editorial matter on 19 August to the dock strikes and twenty-three
of twenty-nine-and-a-half pages on 26 August to the rail strike.

37. Asquith: quoted in J. Grigg, *Lloyd George: the People's Champion,
1902–1911*, Eyre Methuen, London, 1978, p. 293; original in Lloyd
George Papers, C/6/11/9, 20 August 1911; Margot Asquith: Buxton
Papers (Hassocks, Sussex), letter file for 1911, 21 August 1911.

38. Bonar Law Papers, 25/3/19, 9 March 1912; Austen Chamberlain,
Politics from Inside, Cassell, London, 1936, p. 444.

39. R. Holton, *British Syndicalism*, op. cit., Ch. 5, 7.

40. Wrigley, *David Lloyd George*, op. cit., pp. 68–72.

41.   *Daily Mail* and *Morning Post*, 27 March 1912; Askwith, *Industrial Problems and Disputes*, op. cit., pp. 216–17; Austen Chamberlain *Politics from Inside*, op. cit., p. 462.

42.   Grey: G.M. Trevelyan, *Grey of Fallodon*, Longman, London, 1937, pp. 176–77; Lloyd George: Riddell, *More Pages*, op. cit., pp. 42, 47, 49.

43.   Herbert Samuel Papers (HLRO), A/156/402, Samuel to his mother (Clara Samuel), 17 March 1912.

44.   Bonar Law Papers, 25/3/40 (16 March 1912); 33/4/23 (18 March 1912); 26/3/29 (17 May 1912); 33/4/39 (23 May 1912).

45.   R.V. Sires, 'Labor Unrest in England', *Journal of Economic History* vol. XV, September 1955, p. 263.

46.   Clues to the progress of the committee can be found in the Lloyd George Papers, C/21/1 and C/3/10, and in a letter to Lloyd George from Herbert Samuel dated 13 June 1912 (C/7/9/2).

47.   John Burns, 'Effect of Coal Dispute', Cab. 37/110/56, 30 March 1912. See also *Economic Journal*, vol. XXII, June 1912, pp. 343–44; September 1912, pp. 367–87; *Board of Trade Labour Gazette*, vol. XX, April 1912, pp. 125–28; May 1912, pp. 165–66. Some of the working class suffered severely from the strike, but as *The Nation* wrote on 6 April, 'the motor classes have simply not felt it' (p. 5).

48.   'Industrial Unrest', Cab. 37/110/62, 13 April 1912, p. 7 and *passim*.

49.   H.C. Deb., 23 July 1912, cols. 1114–17; 10 March 1913, cols. 38–39; *The Times*, 9 May 1912; Wrigley, *David Lloyd George*, op. cit., p. 75.

50.   'Industrial Disputes', Cab. 37/118/14, 23 January 1914. See also Peter Rowland, *The Last Liberal Governments: Unfinished Business, 1911–1914*, Barrie & Jenkins, London, 1971, pp. 296–97; Wrigley, *David Lloyd George*, op. cit., 76–77.

51.   Joseph A. Pease to Asquith, Asquith Papers, 24/f. 47 (12 September 1911).

52.   Charles Watney and James A. Little, *Industrial Warfare*, Murray, London, 1912, p. 235. See also Keith Middlemas, *Politics in Industrial Society*, Deutsch, London, 1979, p. 64.

53.   Unionist Social Reform Committee, *Industrial Unrest: a Practical Solution*, Murray, London, 1914, pp. 5, 15–37.

54.   Lloyd George Papers, C/36/1/15, typescript copy of article in *Nottinghamshire Free Press*, 15 August 1913.

55.   V.I. Lenin, *On Britain*, Foreign Language Publishing House, Moscow, 1959, p. 152.

4 Trade unions and politics in the First World War

Chris Wrigley

In April 1918 Arthur Balfour, the Foreign Secretary, showed considerable interest in two papers written on the theme 'Democracy and International Relations' which argued that the nature of diplomacy would be transformed by the new strength of the labour movement arising from the war. The author of the memoranda commented in the first of them, 'Hitherto the relations of one country with another have been matters in which the two Governments concerned exercised an almost absolute discretion. Even where a system of real democratic government prevailed foreign policy was regarded as comparatively outside the sphere of party disputes and, as contrasted with domestic policy, displayed in its general features a marked continuity . . .'. Now, with the rise of labour, he felt 'democracy is everywhere replacing the representative by the delegate' and subsequently in future negotiations governments would have to carry popular approval at every stage, 'It would probably be impossible . . . for our Government to make a peace greatly different from the declared war aims of the Labour Party.' Balfour was sufficiently impressed to ask for a second memorandum with practical suggestions as to what should be done about this.[1]

The strength of the labour movement's position in a society with its economy geared to 'a war of production' was increasingly recognized in British governing circles as the First World War proceeded. The government found that it *needed* to recognize the labour movement as a force in the land in virtually all areas of State activity. During the war the trade union side of the movement carried by far the most weight. The enhanced position of labour in the labour market was reflected by a rapidly growing trade union membership: from 4,145,000 in 1914 to 6,533,000 in 1918 (and 8,348,000 at the peak of the post-war boom in 1920). Trade union financial strength also grew dramatically – not just reflecting the increase in members and higher subscriptions but also a reduction in the provision of strike pay in a period of less official strikes.

From early on in the war the government naturally paid special attention to the unions in areas of output crucial to the war. With the need for a massive expansion of munitions production the government required changed working conditions in large sectors of the engineering industry. After the employers and unions failed to agree to major changes the government organized a meeting to discuss the matter at the Treasury in March 1915. After the Treasury Conference Lloyd George took great pains to involve the engineering trade union leadership (and Arthur Henderson) in bringing about drastic changes in the workshop practices of their own members.[2] More generally, the government paid increased attention to the labour movement's national bodies – such as the War Emergency Workers' National Committee, formed the day after the outbreak of the war, and the Joint Committee on After-the-War Problems, formed in 1916.[3]

The enhanced position of labour was also reflected in the offices offered to Labour MPs and to trade union leaders. With the formation of the first Coalition Government in May 1915 Arthur Henderson was brought into the Cabinet (nominally, until August 1916, as President of the Board of Education) and was utilized to help resolve the government's labour difficulties; and two other Labour MPs were given minor office then. When Lloyd George was trying to form a government in December 1916 he needed Labour support and gave more lavish inducements. Henderson was given a seat in the War Cabinet, John Hodge and George Barnes were given ministerial office, and three minor posts were given to other Labour MPs. Moreover, Labour was given other things it had been pressing for – an improved policy of food distribution, State control of the mines and shipping, and the introduction of a Ministry of Labour. Lloyd George, as Prime Minister, was especially willing to appoint trade union figures to major posts. He tried, unsuccessfully, to bring the miners' leader, Robert Smillie, and the railwaymen's leader, J.H. Thomas, into his government. While Lloyd George often claimed that in his government posts were given on grounds of merit and not political expediency, in reality posts were given to Labour men and Tory backwoodsmen because of Lloyd George's political needs. At the time of the 1918 general election, when the labour movement had disengaged from his government, leaving him only with renegade Labour figures, Lloyd George confessed to Bonar Law that the Labour men 'are not ministers because they are the most suitable men, but because they represent a large class who should have a voice in the government of the country'.[4]

In a long war with massive casualties on the Western Front the government became increasingly concerned about manpower allocation. The government had to make tough decisions in late 1917 and 1918 as to whether to take further men from the mines and munitions at the expense of output or to run the risk of depleting the army on the Western Front. At the same time the government was aware of mounting discontent over conscription, rising prices and changes in workplace practices among the working class. As a result Labour's attitude to reconstruction not just at home but internationally had to be taken very seriously indeed by the government. So the Webbs could write in 1920, before the post-war boom had ended, 'We may . . . not unfairly say that Trade Unionism has . . . won its recognition by Parliament and the government, by law and by custom, as a separate element in the community, entitled to distinct recognition as part of the social machinery of the State, its members being thus allowed to give – like the clergy in Convocation – not only their votes as citizens, but also their concurrence as an order or estate.'[5]

THE RESPONSE TO GOVERNMENT INDUSTRIAL POLICY

In such a war between industrial powers the government soon became involved in organizing the economy in order to maximize production in many key areas and in allocating labour, raw materials and other resources according to the needs of the time. In order to achieve increased output in crucial areas such as the engineering and mining industries, the government soon came to control them. As a result the government became directly involved in a high proportion of industrial disputes.

The government's role in industry led to the trade union leadership coming increasingly into contact with Whitehall and Westminster. In the opening months of the war employers and unions tried to resolve difficulties on their own. The skilled unions naturally tried to respond to manpower shortages by expedients which least transgressed their accepted practices. Thus in the hosiery trade the union, which was faced with a shortage of men who had completed their apprenticeships after many had left for the army, first transferred men from shop to shop and also allowed those nearest to the completion of their apprenticeships to take on skilled work.[6] However, in most industries, faced with an absolute shortage of labour and greatly increased demand, sooner or later the manpower problem had to be resolved by the State. Trade unionists naturally resented employers' attempts to get them to waive trade union practices on private work for profit on the grounds of the war. Thus in engineering, after the failure of negotiations between the employers and the unions the government stepped in; and the trade union leaders soon found, having made a voluntary agreement with the government at the Treasury Conference and its successors, that voluntary measures were transformed into statutory measures with the passing of the Munitions of War Act in June 1915.

The involvement of the engineering trade union leadership in carrying out government policies led to serious tensions between them and their membership. Lloyd George first succeeded in manoeuvring the leaders into taking the onus on themselves to provide proposals for increasing munitions production which would seriously change the working conditions of their members, and then succeeded in getting them to form a committee (the National Advisory Committee on Labour) which was to be deeply involved in implementing the policy. They joined with the staff of the Ministry of Munitions to carry out the dilution of labour (the upgrading of semi- and unskilled labour to do skilled workers' jobs) – a policy which was always recognized as being liable to cause serious unrest in the engineering work-shops. Thus these trade union leaders were transformed from men who represented their members' grievances to employers and the government to men who quite literally saw to it that the government's policy on removing restrictive practices and bringing unskilled labour to their members' places of work was carried out – even in the face of their members' violent opposition as on the Clyde in 1915 and 1916. The impact of such policies was, of course, felt on the shop floor. Such policies were especially a shock to craftsmen in those areas hitherto largely untouched by modern production methods – and in these there was a conservative revolt against the trade union leadership. The leadership of shop-floor dissent naturally passed to shop stewards – and in some engineering centres a revolutionary shop-stewards' movement emerged.[7]

So the attack on skilled workers' status and security led to a widening support for socialist and revolutionary socialist leaders. The shop-stewards' movement widened the political debate among activists in the labour movement and won wider working-class support in a few areas such as the Clyde. Many of the leading figures in the shop-stewards' movement were to be founding members of the Communist Party of Great Britain in 1921. For many in the trade union movement the experience of State intervention in their industries and the witnessing of government action against socialist figures such as John Maclean removed the mask from the face of 'the benevolent state'. The Socialist Labour Party's manifesto of 1903 had decried 'what is variously called "State Socialism", "Public Ownership" or "Municipalism" – that is the ownership of certain public utilities by a community in which capitalism is still dominant. A worker is as much exploited by a capitalist state or corporation as by a private employer . . .'.[8] The experience of State control during the First World War in the 'controlled establishments' did much to confirm such critiques among some trade unionists. In particular workmen in controlled establishments deeply resented the munitions tribunals, where they could be disciplined for a whole range of matters – from bad time-keeping to strikes. More generally, during the war the State lost its liberal guise, with the use of spies and crude propaganda and with the severe treatment of dissenters, be they socialists or pacifists. The government's use of a range of extraordinary powers horrified many. Thus Lord Shaw of Dunfermline, a former Liberal

Lord Advocate, complained in January 1918 that 'the Defence of the Realm Act . . . did not warrant, and Parliament unless it had been tricked could not have sanctioned, the implications that compliant Governments have put upon it . . .'.[9]

In contrast to the engineering trade union leaders' willingness to co-operate with the government in reorganizing their industry, the miners' leaders were recalcitrant. The miners' leaders had left the Treasury Conference at an early stage, refusing to become involved in such discussions. The South Wales miners' strike of July 1915, which undermined the Munitions of War Act within a fortnight of it reaching the statute book, warned the government against undue optimism in attempting to achieve good industrial relations by legislation. With the miners there was no marked division between the leadership and the rank-and-file, and no movement comparable to the shop-stewards' movement in engineering emerged. The problem of coping with industrial unrest among the miners was the major reason for the State taking over control of the South Wales and later the other mines.

Responses to State intervention in industry were very varied among trade unions. There was a certain 'beggar-thy-neighbour' attitude among many of them. The Amalgamated Society of Engineers (ASE) went its own way during the war – much to the resentment of other unions. Privileges were gained from the government at the expense of other trade unionists. On the issue of conscription the ASE for a brief period gained the right to issue cards to its members to exempt them from military service. When this right was soon withdrawn Lord Derby, the Secretary of State for War, warned Lloyd George, 'If we do not call up the members of the ASE the men of the unskilled unions will strike; if we do call up the ASE they will strike; and if we call up neither we shall get no recruits . . .'.[10] In fact such a position underlined a weakness of British trade unionism during the First World War. There were considerable divisions between the unions. Lloyd George was to be adept at dividing and ruling.

Overall there was a major political failure on the part of British trade union leaders to achieve widespread social concessions in return for agreeing to forego the right to strike. If they had not given up the right to strike the unions would have been in a very powerful position in a labour market which by the time of the Armistice had lost some 5,700,000 men to the armed forces. As a result of responding to the patriotic call for sacrifices at home while soldiers died at the Front the unions in many key industries failed to maintain real wages until at least 1917. In the case of agriculture the farm labourers failed to benefit from the shortage of labour, and acquiesced while the government supplied alternative labour in large quantities ('blackleg labour on a large scale', as Lord Ernle was later to put it).[11] They only gained when the government presented them with minimum wages in the Corn Production Act 1917, a package aimed at increasing agricultural output. During the First World War, while Labour agreed to drastic changes in workshop practices and did not make the most of the changed conditions in the labour market it nevertheless faced soaring prices and much evidence of profiteering. In the Second World War the trade union movement and the government were much more sensitive to the need for broad social concessions to be made if trade unionists were to forego the right to strike and many of their customary trade practices. This is well illustrated in Table 1 in the contrast between the control of the cost of living in the two wars (though it needs to be recognized that the government in the Second World War controlled items on the cost of living index but allowed others to soar in price).[12]

TRADE UNIONS AND THE LABOUR PARTY

The experience of the war led to the Labour Party's aims, both short- and long-term, becoming more radical in the last year of the war. This was in spite of the fact that socialists in the Labour Party were viewed with considerable suspicion by pro-war trade union leaders. Less frequently commented on than this, is the way trade unionism gave succour to the Labour Party at the grassroots.

Just as the trade unions' status was enhanced nationally by war needs, so it was locally. Trade unionists, often to the horror of local middle- and upper-class dignatories, took their place on increasing numbers of local committees: from those relieving distress to those hearing the pleas of conscientious objectors. Once local trade unionists took part in such local bodies they were often radicalised; they found the powers of the bodies unduly restricted or that labour's representation on them was inadequate.[13]

Similarly in most industries the war brought added status to trade unions in the work-place. This stemmed from the enhanced position of labour in the economy and the need of the government for a spirit of conciliation in industry. This led the government to insist that employers recognize the unions and set up joint committees with the unions – and this sometimes occurred in industries where hitherto unionization had been weak. Thus in the Midlands the hosiery industry enjoyed a boom and trade union membership probably quadrupled. The unions' success in achieving war bonuses attracted new members – and these bonuses were achieved painlessly, often through government arbitrators. The government insistence on working through representative bodies led to national collective bargaining and eventually to a national Whitley Council. In dealing with the industry, be it drawing up regulations for introducing female labour or allocating raw materials, the government dealt with the unions.[14]

The expansion of trade union membership during the war and its aftermath coincided with the coming of a larger electorate. At the time

TABLE 1

	Wholesale prices Average Jan./July 1914 = 100	Cost of living index July 1914 = 100	Wage rates July 1914 = 100
Jan. 1915	117	110–15	
July 1915	129	125	105–10
July 1916	158	145	115–20
July 1917	214	180	135–40
July 1918	233	205	175–80
July 1919	250	210	210–15
July 1920	308	252	260

	Wholesale prices Aug. 1939 = 100	Cost of living index 1 Sept. 1939 = 100	Wage rates Beginning Sept. 1939 = 100
Jan. 1940	128	112	103–04
July 1940	142	121	112–13
July 1941	156	128	122
July 1942	163	129	131
July 1943	167	129	136
July 1944	170	130	143
July 1945	174	134	149
July 1946	180	132	161

of the Liberal landslide in the 1906 general election there had been 7,300,000 electors; in 1918 there were 21,400,000 electors. At the local level – as well as at the national – this greatly enhanced the political powers of the trade unions, especially in towns or areas dominated by one industry. Not all the additional trade union members had the vote; this is especially true of women, for those between twenty-one and thirty were denied the vote until the 1929 election. But even in the case of women they were nevertheless 40 per cent of the 1918 electorate and were a sizeable portion of union membership in industries such as hosiery. So politicians of all parties in 1918 found it expedient to take pains to be amenable to the local leaders of the unions in the key industry or industries of their constituencies.

Where the Labour Party was strong in 1918 and subsequent elections its strength usually stemmed from a strong trade union presence in the constituency. Arthur Henderson, in conversation with C.P. Scott, editor of the *Manchester Guardian*, in December 1917, expressed the hope of running 500 candidates in the next general election. With considerable optimism Henderson commented that 'They were better equipped for doing this than either of the other two great parties because they had an existing trades union organization in every town. As to the country districts [they had] the assistance of the co-operators, if they should decide to work with them, as, in many of the country districts . . . eight out of ten households were co-operators.'[15]

The trade unions played a crucial role in working-class areas of London in the 1918 general election and the 1919 LCC and local elections. Local trade unionists during the war became involved in campaigns on food prices, profiteering, conscription and other wartime issues. The impact of the war in the community and at the workplace radicalized many trade unionists. In Battersea the ruling Progressive Council split in 1915 over tensions arising from the war – and the great majority of councillors who had hitherto stood as Progressives stood as Labour candidates in the 1919 municipal elections and won a landslide victory. In Battersea, as in the East End, the trade unions dominated labour politics – and socialists who had antagonized the local trade union leaders were liable to suffer in selection meetings.[16] In many provincial towns Labour's post-war electoral success also owed much to trade union organization, and especially to the role of the trades councils.[17] In some areas Labour did flourish without strong trade union roots in such places as the Colne Valley where it rested on advanced radicalism. But on the whole the Labour Party was strong where trade unionism was strong, and weak where trade unionism was weak.[18]

At the national level the trade union leaders also asserted their strength in the Labour Party. Trade union dominance of the Labour Party had always seen that the socialists were effectively controlled, that their aims were subordinated to the practicalities of achieving labour legislation in Parliament. With much of the ILP being anti-war the trade union leaders looked askance at the socialists in the Labour Party. At the 1916 TUC Conference the most pro-war elements tried to get a specifically trade union party formed. This was defeated, but this strand of thinking in the trade union movement was sufficiently strong to attract Lloyd George, Milner and others to believe that it was worthwhile to foster a 'patriotic labour' movement.

If the TUC recoiled from forming a purely trade union party the union leaders were happy to take even more power within the Labour Party into their own hands. At the January 1917 Labour Party Conference trade union votes succeeded in passing a motion that the whole Conference would vote on all the places on the national executive (thereby ending the system whereby each section of the party elected its own members to the appropriate section of the national executive).[19] This was established in the new Labour Party constitution adopted in February 1918. Increased control of the party by the trade union leaders was a blow to the anti-war socialists. In January 1917 Sidney Webb talked with Ramsay MacDonald about this, and wrote to Beatrice Webb, 'He said the trade unions were now a terrible incubus on the Labour Party, but that it had been inevitable to have them. Only by them could the Party have got mass support, and money (the Labour Party has now actually £20,000 in hand). He said that the present organisation of the party failed totally to represent the rank-and-file; and he looked more and more to the trades councils and similar local bodies.'[20]

The new Labour Party constitution of 1918 was brought in with due deference to the fears of many trade union leaders that changes in the organization of the party could lead to it slipping out of trade union control. However, with the creation of a mass electorate in the offing (with the Representation of the People Bill going through Parliament), Henderson, in late 1917, was able to impress upon the trade unions the need to organize working-class voters in a more effective manner and thereby create the opportunity for the labour movement to control the post-war reconstruction of society. The bringing in of Clause 4, which pledged 'to secure for the workers by hand or by brain the full fruits of their industry and the most equitable distribution thereof that may be possible, upon the basis of the common ownership of the means of production and the best obtainable system of popular administration and control of each industry and service', gave the Labour Party long-term objectives which distinguished it from other parties yet was sufficiently generalized to be acceptable to most currents of socialist thought of the time.[21] The acceptance of these aims by men such as Henderson was in part due to the impetus given to socialist ideas by the war generally and the Russian revolutions in particular; though Henderson and many others saw democratic socialist remedies to be a very desirable alternative to revolutionary socialist action such as the Bolsheviks had taken in Russia.

Sidney Webb was to make much of the PLP being a safeguard against Bolshevism during his 1918 general election campaign.[22]

The latter part of the war also saw the Labour Party adopting a more socialist short-term programme than hitherto. In the policy statement *Labour and the New Social Order*, 1918, the party's promises included the nationalization of the land, most of the transport system, electric power and the industrial insurance companies, the extension of municipal ownership, the extension of social welfare provisions, the provision of work for all who wanted it, and the introduction of a capital levy. In this Labour was offering, as Ralph Miliband has commented, 'a piecemeal collectivism, within a predominantly capitalist society' as 'the key to more welfare, higher efficiency and greater social justice'.[23]

However, whatever the limitations of the 1918 programme may be deemed to be, it was much more than the trade union leaders would have swallowed before the war or even before 1916. The experience of the war forced the trade union leaders to think seriously how society should be organized. From the start of the war they had worked with socialists on the War Emergency Workers' National Committee; there all could readily work together to find remedies for distress arising from the war. As the war went on, trade unionists, whether they liked it or not, were confronted by the need to offer suggestions for post-war reconstruction. The introduction of conscription of labour for the services, at a time of inflation and widespread profiteering, led to a widespread support in the labour movement for the policy of 'conscription of riches'. Overall, the wartime experience of State intervention in the economy made many trade unionists wish for more. As Royden Harrison has observed, labour came to demand that the State '*should* manage the economy and that it should manage it upon equalitarian lines'.[24] The example of Russia showed that the possibility of labour controlling the state was not just wishful thinking; yet it was also a warning that too-timid proposals could leave too much ground to the revolutionary left.

THE TRADE UNIONS AND WAR AIMS

The trade unions affected government policy on war aims basically because it was essential for the government to carry their support in maintaining maximum industrial production if Britain was to achieve outright victory rather than a negotiated peace. The introduction of conscription, the evidence of profiteering and the lack of results on the Western Front by late 1916 had begun seriously to undermine working-class support for the war. In 1917 and 1918 the government's need to define democratic war aims was inextricably linked to domestic considerations.

Trade unionists, like the rest of the labour movement, displayed a wide range of attitudes to the war. Among prominent trade union leaders one finds Havelock Wilson, the seamen's leader, at one extreme. He was rabidly pro-war. His hatred of the Germans, a hatred fuelled by the submarine campaign against British shipping, was reflected in such actions as his union preventing anti-war socialists going to Russia as part of a Labour delegation in June 1916, even though they had government permission to go. Whereas in contrast to Wilson, there was Robert Smillie of the miners, who was opposed to the war, though Smillie, in spite of his words at the time of the Leeds Convention in 1917, did not positively obstruct the war effort or campaign against it.[25] However, the great majority of the trade union leaders supported the war to a greater or lesser extent.

This was reflected by the actions of the TUC. The TUC Conference due to be held in September 1914 was cancelled but the Parliamentary Committee of the TUC issued a manifesto giving strong support to the war and endorsed the recruiting campaign. At the 1916 Conference delegates voted down the suggestion that the TUC should co-operate with Samuel Gompers and the American Federation of Labour in organizing an international labour conference of delegates from all countries (including enemy ones) to discuss peace terms.

Given the prevailing attitude among trade union leaders on the war, the succession of Arthur Henderson to the leadership of the PLP on the resignation of Ramsay MacDonald at the outset of the war was a major factor in maintaining the unity of the political and trade union wings of the labour movement during the war. Henderson's entry into Asquith's Cabinet, and later into Lloyd George's War Cabinet, reinforced trade union leaders' willingness to support the war effort. As Beatrice Webb shrewdly observed, in a characteristically patronizing yet scathing entry in her diary, the majority of Labour men held 'the illusion that the mere presence of Labour men in the government, apart from anything they may do or prevent being done, is in itself a sign of democratic progress'.[26]

Henderson and the TUC warmly welcomed the overthrow of the Czar in the February Revolution of 1917 and they hoped that it would lead to Russia fighting the war with renewed vigour. Henderson, when visiting Russia in June and early July 1917, became convinced that the Provisional Government was in real trouble with Russia's internal problems and that support for the proposed conference of European socialists at Stockholm was essential to maintain it in office and Russia in the war. He also saw the conference as an opportunity for British labour to make clear its war aims and thereby refute Bolshevik statements as to the imperialist nature of the war.[27]

However, by the time Henderson returned from Russia, Lloyd George and the War Cabinet had become firm opponents of British delegates going to Stockholm. As a result of their differing views Henderson and the government parted ways. The Stockholm incident did not lead to the Labour Party breaking with the government or to the government collapsing, as Lloyd George appears to have feared at the time.[28] But it did further damage relationships between trade union leaders and the government. There was widespread resentment in trade union circles at the way Henderson had been treated. In the event the Stockholm conference never took place; but, following the various debates on it, the TUC did decide to extend its activities into international affairs in the future.

With the Stockholm incident there was increasing fear on the part of traditional vested interests that labour was emerging as an independent and even decisive power in the land. Leo Amery wrote to Lloyd George in August 1917 warning, 'Even if the Conference itself did no great harm it would only be the beginning of a claim on the part of a sectional organisation to be consulted at every step affecting the conclusion of peace, which might end up by landing us in an intolerable situation – a second "Soviet" in fact.'[29]

After the introduction of conscription in 1916 the government had become alarmed at the influence pacifist propaganda was having on the trade unions' members. Men such as E.D. Morel, Chairman of the No Conscription Fellowship, realized that trade union support for their aims would be crucial for success. Thus in August 1916 he commented, 'If the Triple Alliance could be won over, if not in whole at any rate in part, to the definite programme of peace by negotiation, the effect ought to be very great, and combined with the steady operating force of economic factors, casualties, rising prices it might be decisive.'[30] The government was equally aware of this. When the War Cabinet was reviewing propaganda in October 1917 it was pointed out in the discussion 'That the only really efficient system of propaganda at present existing in this country was that organized by the pacifists, who had large sums of money at their disposal and who were conducting the campaign with great vigour.' Earlier in the year, in May, the War Cabinet had authorized the spending of Treasury money on domestic propaganda – and in August the government had set up the National War Aims Committee. This body, which had Lloyd George, Asquith, Bonar Law and Barnes as its presidents and at first was funded by private subscription, also received funds from the Treasury from October 1917.[31] Thus, as the government became more aware of the need to pay attention to Labour's views on the war so it also became more and more concerned with organizing propaganda within Britain.

When on 5 January 1918 Lloyd George made his major pronouncement on war aims it was to a meeting of trade union leaders and not to Parliament. By late 1917 the government needed to make a statement of its war aims for international and domestic reasons.[32] Internationally there was a need to respond to President Woodrow Wilson's message to Congress of 4 December, to the publication in the *Manchester Guardian* (from 12 December) of the secret treaties released by the Bolshevik government, and the declaration of war aims by the Central Powers (25 December 1917). A liberal statement of war aims would help to stop any drift to co-operation between the Germans and Russians, moderate French declarations, and encourage liberals and socialists in enemy countries to oppose their own governments. Moreover, the British government was no longer confident of being able to deliver the 'knock-out blow' to Germany and was willing to consider negotiations.

However, for all this, there is good reason to see internal pressures as being of paramount importance. The government at this time was in a corner over manpower. It needed to recruit more men from British industry – for Russia had been knocked out of the war, France had reached the limit of her resources, and American troops would not arrive in considerable numbers until the summer. So in spite of all its pledges to the skilled unions, the government found it essential to 'comb out' more men from reserved occupations. The government had tried to appease skilled workers on the issue of their eroded differentials – but the award of 12.5 per cent wage increases to them had been badly handled and led to a succession of strikes. Hence it was very appropriate that Lloyd George should make his declaration of war aims to a meeting of trade unionists called to discuss manpower problems.

The appeal to the trade unionists was politically important also in that it gave Lloyd George the chance to divide moderate trade unionism from the revolutionary movement in Britain. The government carefully monitored the activities of revolutionary groups and the spread of anti-war feeling among the working class; and while permitting the Leeds conference of June 1917 to take place, censored what were deemed to be 'the dangerous passages in the speeches' in the national press.[33] At a time when Henderson was uniting the bulk of the Labour Party behind moderate war aims Lloyd George was able to make a pronouncement in line with the Labour Party's aims. Thus Lloyd George told the trade union leaders, 'Last week I had the privilege not merely of perusing the declared war aims of the Labour Party but also of discussing in detail with the Labour leaders the meaning and intention of that declaration . . .'. and generally made the most of the situation.[34]

While Lloyd George's declaration of war aims was prompted by the need to make 'a counter offensive' to the Central Powers' declaration, it was very much a response to the pressure of the labour movement, above all to the need to appease the skilled unions over the government's scrapping of pledges on recruitment. It needed Lloyd George's diplomacy and charm to get his Tory colleagues to allow such a recognition of the power of organized labour to take place. The War Cabinet minutes record:[35]

It was suggested, and generally admitted, that there would be some adverse criticism to a statement made to the trade unionists . . . on the ground that it would give undue importance to the trade unionists as compared with other sections of the community who were equally affected. On the other hand it was pointed out that no other convenient opportunity offered itself and that it would be advisable to take advantage of it. On the whole, therefore, it was agreed that a statement to the trade unionists was desirable.

However, when the War Cabinet came to apologize to the United States Government for failing to consult them the British ambassador was instructed to inform the President 'that for the last week or two the Prime Minister and the War Cabinet have been in negotiation with the trade unions in regard to the release of the government from certain pledges made earlier in the war, such release being indispensable to the development of our man power for military purposes. The negotiations had reached a point at which success turned mainly on the immediate publication of statement of War Aims by the government.'[36] This was an excuse for the Americans – but nevertheless it is a true expression of Lloyd George's motivation in making such a speech when and where he did.

Whether Conservative politicians liked it or not, in the last two years of the war the labour movement was in a powerful position to influence the government's external policy. If the moderate trade union leadership had deserted the government then Britain's ability to continue the war would have been undermined. The May 1917 engineering strikes had been a warning as to the dangers to the war effort of industrial discontent at home.

A democratic peace was to be a unifying cause in the labour movement in the final year of the war. Distaste for Lenin and Trotsky was shared alike by moderate trade union leaders and the best-known ILP leaders. Henderson and MacDonald could come together on the issue of war aims. A meeting of Labour Party, Co-operative Movement and TUC leaders praised President Wilson's Fourteen Points, which he had announced to Congress on 8 January 1918; and the meeting issued a statement commending 'the moral quality and breadth of vision revealed in the President's speech'.[37] In contrast there was distrust of Lloyd George. In conversation with C.P. Scott on a future peace conference, Arthur Henderson observed 'George had given a promise that there should be . . . a special representative of Labour, but it [would] be useless if he appointed a tame Labour man like Barnes. Labour would claim to be consulted as to who should represent it.'[38] Moderate trade union leaders became warm supporters of President Wilson and his policies. The labour movement was to be the power behind the demand in Britain for a League of Nations.

LABOUR AT THE END OF THE WAR

By 1918 the labour movement was stronger and more confident that it should take power in Britain than it had been in 1914. The experience of the war had radicalized many in the labour movement and employers and the government were aware that labour was becoming increasingly antagonistic to capitalism itself.

The government and many employers responded to this by trying to foster a spirit of co-operation in industry. This was a recurring theme when the government was under serious pressure from industrial unrest, be it 1917, 1919 or 1911. During the pre-war labour unrest the government for a while had marshalled centre opinion behind the National Industrial Council, the declared aim of which was to bring together all those who shared the ideal of 'the substitution in the industrial sphere of co-operation for antago- nism in relations between employers and employed'. The Whitley Council scheme and the National Industrial Conference of 1919 were similar moves. During the war the government had skilfully incorporated certain trade union leaders into the governmental machine, had tried to press workshop committees on employers and unions, and had encouraged the assimilation of shop stewards more fully into the structure of the unions. Similarly, while the challenge of labour was strong many employers expressed the view that industry should be run as a team, with understanding between management and men, and that success in industry was for the good of the nation (with as little emphasis on private profit as possible).[39]

During the war the bulk of the trade union movement was prepared to forego making full use of its strength and to co-operate in the war effort. In doing this union leaders became accustomed to walking the corridors of power and being consulted in all matters affecting their members. When there was failure to consult them, as over the 1916 changes to National Insurance, they felt aggrieved; and in that case, in view of the unfavourable nature of the measure to many groups of workers, they successfully undermined it by a policy of non-co-operation.[40] The government needed to heed the unions' views not just on industrial matters but on war aims and post-war reconstruction during the war. Lloyd George was careful to be in tune with their aspirations in all these areas, even if he could avoid endorsing all that they wanted.

Labour's strength, as usual, was based on a favourable labour market; the war conditions and the post-war boom provided this. When the severe recession of 1921–22 came many of the gains of 1914–20 were lost. The number of trade unionists tumbled to below 5,000,000 by 1927 and many advances in wages, hours and conditions of work were lost. Even some of the much-heralded welfare provisions of the war were dismantled once the legal controls went. In the case of welfare provisions the unions' view was ambiguous, being suspicious of the inauguration of such schemes as likely to discourage trade union organization and as being motivated by a desire to increase output, yet often resentful when they were summarily scrapped by employers in the harsher climate after the war.

However, management was able to take advantage of the war to bring about various changes – and many of these were to stay. Premium bonus systems had been introduced increasingly into engineering firms before the war and had been opposed by the unions concerned and the TUC. During the war management men in government departments, notably the Ministry of Munitions, were eager to spread such systems. For all the strength of labour in the war the engineering unions still failed to co-ordinate consistent opposition to such systems.[41] Similarly, during the war there was a spread of 'scientific' management techniques, mostly derived from America (Taylorism and other such systems). While the spread of 'modern management' techniques faltered after the war in the strong mood for a return to pre-1914 conditions, nevertheless the ground was laid during the war and it was that much easier for employers to spread them between the wars when the labour market was unfavourable to the trade unions.[42]

Overall, the First World War enhanced the status of the trade unions in British society, both nationally and locally, and enabled them to exert considerable political pressure on the government. With the accompanying growth in the strength of the Labour Party they became by the Armistice realistic contenders for democratically elected power in Britain. However, the conditions which had led to them being consulted and flattered by government were transient; and they were not to receive this treatment again until the Second World War and the managed economy of 1945–79. But the continued trade union support, at national and local level, was vital in the Labour Party's development into a party which could attract support nationwide and be the alternative government.

NOTES AND REFERENCES

1.   The author of the memoranda was E.J. Phelan, Ministry of Labour. The first is dated 10 April 1918; PRO, FO 371–3442–6400. After he had 'read it with interest' on 19 April, Balfour asked for further details. The second memorandum is dated 24 April 1918 and in it Phelan urged the compilation of up-to-date information on the attitudes of the various sections of the labour movement to foreign policy; FO 371–3442–75987.

2.   C. Wrigley, *David Lloyd George and the British Labour Movement*, Harvester Press, Hassocks, 1976, Ch. 5, 6, 8 and 9.

3.   For the former see R. Harrison, 'The war emergency workers' national committee 1914–20' in A. Briggs and J. Saville (eds), *Essays in Labour History 1886–1923*, Macmillan, London, 1971, Ch. 9 and J.M. Winter, *Socialism and the Challenge of War*, Routledge and Kegan Paul, London, 1974, Ch. 7. For the TUC's position in the war see R.M. Martin, *TUC: the growth of a pressure group, 1868–1976*, Clarendon Press, Oxford, 1980, Ch. 6.

4. *Lord Riddell's Intimate Diary of the Peace Conference and After*, Gollancz, London, 1933, p. 4.
5. S. and B. Webb, *The History of Trade Unionism* (rev. edn, extended to 1920), Longmans, Green, London, 1920, p. 635.
6. Leicester Trimmers' Association E. C. minutes, 21 September 1914; Leicestershire County Record Office, DE 1655/1/12.
7. J. Hinton, *The First Shop Stewards' Movement*, Allen and Unwin, London, 1973.
8. Cited in R. Challinor, *The Origins of British Bolshevism*, Croom Helm, London, 1977, pp. 23–24.
9. In a letter to Herbert Samuel, 19 January 1918; HLRO, Samuel Papers, A/60/22.
10. Letter of 26 April 1917; HLRO, Lloyd George Papers F/14/4/39.
11. P.E. Dewey, 'Government provision of farm labour in England and Wales, 1914–1918', *Ag. Hist. Rev.*, **27**, 1979, pp. 110–21.
12. W.K. Hancock and M.M. Gowing, *British War Economy*, HMSO and Longmans, Green, London, 1949, p. 152.
13. A. Clinton, *The Trade Union Rank and File*, Manchester University Press, Manchester, 1977, pp. 54–55.
14. R. Gurnham, *A History of the Trade Union Movement in the Hosiery and Knitwear Industry, 1776–1976*, National Union of Hosiery and Knitwear Workers, Leicester, 1976, Ch. 4. For the similar example of the jute industry in Dundee see W.M. Walker, *Juteopolis*, Scottish Academic Press, Edinburgh, 1979, pp. 394–97.
15. Diary entry, 11–12 December 1917; T. Wilson (ed.), *The Political Diaries of C.P. Scott, 1911–1928*, Collins, London, 1970, p. 317.
16. C. Wrigley, *Changes in the Battersea Labour Movement, 1914–1919*, Loughborough University pamphlet, Loughborough, 1977 and Julia Bush, *Behind the Lines: East London Labour 1914–1919*, Merlin Press, 1984, pp. 148–54.
17. On Labour's electoral breakthrough see C. Cook, *The Age of Alignment*, Macmillan, London, 1975, Ch. 3 and 4, and on local organization see R. McKibbin, *The Evolution of the Labour Party, 1910–1924*, Clarendon Press, Oxford, 1974, Ch. 7.
18. D.G. Clark, *Colne Valley: Radicalism to Socialism*, Longman, London, 1981. For cities where Labour was weak see R.S.W. Davies, 'The Liverpool Labour Party and the Liverpool Working Class, 1900–39' in North West Labour History Society, *Bulletin 6*, 1979–80, pp. 2–14, in which he contrasts the different traditions of casual labour to other groups of workers, and also R.P. Hastings, 'The Birmingham labour movement, 1918–1945' in *Midland History*, **5**, 1979–80, pp. 78–92.
19. R. McKibbin, *The Evolution of the Labour Party*, op. cit., p. 90.

20. Letter of 23 January 1917; N. Mackenzie (ed.), *The Letters of Sidney and Beatrice Webb*, vol. 3, *Pilgrimage 1912–1947*, Cambridge University Press, Cambridge, 1978, p. 78. See also D. Marquand, *Ramsay MacDonald*, Jonathan Cape, London, 1977, pp. 229–31.
21. R. McKibbin, *The Evolution of the Labour Party*, op. cit., pp. 91–98.
22. See J.M. Winter, *Socialism and the Challenge of War*, op. cit., pp. 260–261, 273–74 and N. Mackenzie (ed.), *The Letters of Sidney and Beatrice Webb*, op. cit., pp. 110–13.
23. R. Miliband, *Parliamentary Socialism*, Allen and Unwin, London, 1961, pp. 61–62.
24. R. Harrison, 'The war emergency workers' national committee', op. cit., p. 255.
25. Ibid., p. 223.
26. M. Cole (ed.), *Beatrice Webb's Diaries, 1912–24*, Longmans, Green, London, 1952, p. 73.
27. The best account is in J.M. Winter, *Socialism and the Challenge of War*, op. cit., pp. 240–59.
28. On Lloyd George's attitude see C. Wrigley, *Lloyd George*, op. cit., pp. 211–16.
29. Letter, 7 August 1917; HLRO, Lloyd George Papers F/2/1/5.
30. Letter to C.P. Trevelyan, 26 August 1916; Newcastle University Library, C.P. Trevelyan Papers, Box 19.
31. War Cabinet (245) and War Cabinet (142) 4 October and 22 May 1917; PRO CAB 23–4–81 and CAB 23–2–179. See also I. Colvin, *The Life of Lord Carson*, vol. 3, Gollancz, London, 1936, p. 278.
32. The best account of the background to this is V.H. Rothwell, *British War Aims and Peacemaking, 1914–1918*, Clarendon Press, Oxford, 1971, pp. 143–53. For the underlying manpower issue see C. Wrigley, *Lloyd George*, op. cit., Ch. 14.
33. On the monitoring of labour questions by Scotland Yard, Military Intelligence, etc., see, for example, the minutes of a conference on labour intelligence, 15 April 1917, GT 733, PRO CAB 24–13–135. On the censor and the Leeds conference see I. Colvin (*Morning Post*) to Milner, 4 June 1917: Bodl. Lib., Milner Papers, vol. 144.
34. For Lloyd George's report to the War Cabinet on his meeting with the Labour Party's deputation see War Cabinet (308), 31 December 1917, PRO CAB 23–4–282. His speech to the trade unionists is printed as an appendix to War Cabinet (314), 4 January 1918, PRO CAB 23–5–16.
35. War Cabinet (313) 3 January 1918, 5 p.m., PRO CAB 23–5–12.
36. War Cabinet (315) 6 January, CAB 23–5–20.
37. A.J. Mayer, *Political Origins of the New Diplomacy, 1917–1918*, Yale University Press, New Haven, 1959, pp. 387–88.

38. C.P. Scott, unpublished diary, 7 January 1918; C.P. Scott Papers, BM Add. Mss 50,904, ff.234–36.
39. J. Child, *British Management Thought*, Allen and Unwin, London, 1969, pp. 44–50.
40. On this see N. Whiteside, 'Welfare legislation and the unions during the First World War', *Hist. Jrnl*, **23**, no. 4, 1980, pp. 857–74.
41. S. and B. Webb, *The History of Trade Unionism*, op. cit., pp. 484–86 and 576.
42. On Taylorism see C.R. Littler, 'Understanding Taylorism', *British Journal of Sociology*, **29**, no. 2, 1978, pp. 185–202.

5 The depression years 1918–1931

Patrick Renshaw

Trade unions, like most sections of the community, greeted the Armistice on 11 November 1918 with heartfelt relief. Yet they had made real advances during the war. Wages had been driven up, and the government had courted the TUC in the interests of good labour relations. Coalmines and railways had been taken under government control, while wartime collectivism made trade union solidarity, and even socialism, seem more acceptable. Now the war had been won, Britain could regain its overseas markets and re-establish itself as a financial and trading centre. Labour leaders looked forward to better things to come soon. These hopes were to be bitterly disappointed. The full cost of the war had yet to be paid, the reality of Britain's changed position in the world still to be seen. As a result, in the 1920s organized labour was to suffer the most severe economic depression since the Industrial Revolution. Fighting low wages and high unemployment, the TUC stumbled into, and lost, the General Strike of 1926, the most serious political crisis between the wars. Yet at the same time, trade unions were to grow more rapidly in experience and maturity than in any previous decade.

The political agent of this change was the Labour Party which, initially divided by the war, had gained strength from it. Though Arthur Henderson had joined Lloyd George's War Cabinet, the party decided to oppose the Coalition and fight the election of December 1918 independently. Labour was still a narrowly-based trade union pressure group. But by 1931 it had become the party of reform, replacing the Liberals and tasting the ambiguous and equivocal nature of power by forming two minority administrations. Impressed by the way the government had helped them during the war, trade unions in 1918 looked to Labour to make sweeping gains at the polls. The socialist programme on which it fought for the first time was perhaps the work of middle rather than working-class supporters.[1] More significant for a party seeking working-class support, 1918 was the first time it could appeal to a mass electorate. All men, and women householders over thirty, had just been given the vote. More people had been enfranchized than in all previous electoral reforms; and as eight years had elapsed since the last election, some three in five were casting their first ballot.

The significance of Labour's gains at the polls in 1918 was partially obscured by Lloyd George's crushing Coalition victory, and by the fact that several Labour leaders, including Henderson, Ramsay MacDonald and Philip Snowden, were unseated. Yet the sluggish increase in Labour MPs from thirty-nine to fifty-nine was based on a seven-fold rise in popular support since the election of 1910. With nearly 2,400,000 votes, or 22.7 per cent of those cast, Labour had clearly reached electoral take-off point, where a small increase in total votes would net a much larger increase in MPs. So it proved. Before Lloyd George's fall at the end of 1922, Labour had won fourteen by-elections and increased its vote almost everywhere. Within another twelve months Labour had won enough seats to form a government. Moreover, this political challenge was sharpened by more important events outside Parliament. Between 1913 and 1920 trade union membership doubled to top 8,000,000. Between 1918 and 1922 more than 2,000,000 trade unionists were involved in industrial disputes each year. At the same time, Labour was successful in hundreds of local elections, a trend which was often crucial, as Peter Stead has shown. Rising industrial unrest before 1921, and chronic mass unemployment after it, meant that control of local poor relief in helping jobless families counted for more than control of the Commons.[2]

Thus the post-war years saw trade unions working with the ILP, the Co-operative Movement, Clydesiders, Fabians and constituency activists to end the era of 'Lib-Labism'. Labour became a national party in the 1920s and many of its traditional political strongholds, such as the North-East or South Wales, date from this time rather than the pioneering days before 1914. The impact of Labour on the other parties was clear after the Spen Valley by-election in January 1920. Ross McKibbin's detailed study of Labour in evolution is somewhat dismissive of the use Maurice Cowling has made in his own work of 'gossip'.[3] Yet Cowling's use of correspondence is enlightening about Liberal and Tory reaction to the rise of Labour. It united, he argues, most other factions contending for power: Coalition Tories who admired Lloyd George as well as those who hated him; Asquithian Liberals beaten by his Coalition and those who backed it; and Tories who finally brought Lloyd George down in 1922. Yet the problem posed by Labour remained. Should one seek to outbid it, split it and form some centre coalition, or simply close ranks to crush it?[4]

All policies were tried, until the Tories were able to unite anti-Labour sentiment behind them as the party of resistance between 1925 and 1927.

Thus, though in the short-term the 1918 election was a triumph for Lloyd George, and in the medium-run an advance for Labour, its real importance was that it marked the return of the Tories. Though they now dominated Lloyd George's Coalition, they had not won an election since 1902. Yet they were to rule, alone or in coalition, for all but fourteen of the next fifty years. Although both parties faced the threat of Labour on equal terms, the Liberals disintegrated while the Tories prospered. The new government's immediate tasks revealed something of this. Lloyd George sensed the need to restore stability in the wake of the Russian Revolution and the collapse of authority all over Europe. Capital feared Labour as the spearhead of some similar kind of socialist revolution.

In fact, British Labour leaders like Henderson returned from Russia in 1917 convinced of the overriding need to create a democratic socialist movement at home. At the same time, the Prime Minister was eager to play-up the Bolshevik bogey to sustain Tory support for his Coalition, while the threat of disorder in Britain was real enough. Mutinies occurred in 1919, sometimes when troops were ordered to Russia, sometimes over bad conditions. The police struck in Liverpool and London. The strike rate soared, along with prices, in the post-war boom. Serious unrest in India and Ireland presaged the eventual break-up of Union and Empire. Military and police power was fully stretched. Tom Jones's *Whitehall Diaries*, and the Cabinet papers themselves, show that the Government took all this more seriously in 1919–20 than historians had known.

The first test for the new government came with strikes on the railways in 1919. The railwaymen were successful in resisting pay cuts, with financial help from the Co-operative Movement. Yet the government was able to restore the railways to private owners, who rapidly regrouped the industry into four large regional companies. When Lloyd George tried to restore the coal industry to private hands, however, the TUC brought the triple alliance out of mothballs. The mere threat of concerted action in docks, mines and railways was enough to persuade the government to retain control and set up the Sankey Commission to investigate the industry. So mining moved centre-stage, a position it occupied for much of the rest of the decade. This position was not surprising. Coal was Britain's largest and most important basic industry, on which more than one-tenth of the population was directly dependent. The Miners' Federation of Great Britain (MFGB) was the largest, most important and most militant trade union. The MFGB had hoped to use the triple alliance after 1914 to negotiate one national pay rise for all its million members, and eventually force the government to take mining into public ownership.

The war had prevented this, but now the MFGB hoped to revive the plan. What happened was quite different. Lloyd George's tactics were characteristically crafty. Miners, owners, industrialists and academics were represented equally on the Sankey Commission. The hearings gave socialist leaders of the MFGB a chance to pillory the system of private profit.[5] Yet the very equality with which all divergent interests were represented made it impossible for the Commission to issue an agreed report. So the government was free to do nothing beyond holding pay at current levels, reducing hours to seven a day and recommending improvements in conditions described as a scandal. G.D.H. Cole argued that the Sankey episode was crucial in defusing a potentially explosive situation in the post-war period, and in many ways this view remains valid.[6] The 'datum-line' strike in Yorkshire, and the failure of the 'mines for the nation' campaign in 1920, seem to show that, despite the sense of betrayal over the Sankey Report, MFGB members were more interested in immediate, mundane questions of wages, hours and conditions than in nationalization. Hamilton Fyfe, editor of the Labour *Daily Herald*, said that after Sankey the MFGB and the whole trade union movement became bogged down in the minutiae of coal tonnages, wages and hours rather than the broader questions of reorganization, ownership and control on which everything else really rested.[7]

Yet though the Sankey Commission no doubt gave the government time to pass the crisis, it is going too far to suggest that it was part of a well-planned counter-revolutionary programme. Some historians, notably Ralph Desmarais, see the post-war period as a time when the government and Civil Service scotched the socialist and trade union challenge by dismantling wartime planning, which might have helped the Left achieve its goals, replacing it by tough economic policies and a partially-concealed system of repressive control.[8] As we have seen, the government did help the TUC during the war. Afterwards, the Coalition used unrest in the army and police force, the post-war wave of strikes and the *Jolly George* incident – when dockers refused to load munitions for use against the Bolsheviks – to pass the Emergency Powers Act in 1920. But the Desmarais thesis is too simplistic. For a start, it overstates trade union militancy and solidarity. Nationalization had only limited appeal, even to the miners. Councils of Action, used over the *Jolly George*, may have reappeared during the General Strike. Yet this episode was misleading: it vindicated industrial action only against the threat of renewed war, not for any revolutionary objective. Finally, Desmarais overestimates the extent to which the nation's rulers saw prudent plans for dealing with possible future strikes as counter-revolution, or acted in a self-conscious, or even united, way in shaping policy.

BLACK FRIDAY

Indeed, from 1921 to 1927 events were largely shaped not by united action but by disputes over policy among both the nation's decision makers and its trade union leaders. Finance contended with industry for hegemony, exporters with those who sold on the home market. The TUC was split over concern with wages, on the one hand, and the workless on the other. The interests of both the MFGB and the coalowners were divided into export and domestic regions. The economic depression which struck in 1921 was really decisive, moulding trade union history for the next twenty years. Since the war had been paid for largely by inflation and the sale of overseas assets, the overriding objective of the financial world when it ended had been to restore Britain as a financial and trading centre. This was to be achieved by an immediate return to the pre-war gold standard of $4.86. But since this could only be secured by sudden and savage deflation, Lloyd George had been unwilling to pay the political price. So the decision was taken to let inflation run, while the Treasury and the Bank of England waited for the best moment to restore financial reality.

The collapse of the post-war boom at the start of 1921 was a major step along the way. Yet at first it looked like another dose of the old, familiar complaint of cyclical unemployment. Soon the truth became apparent to government, employers and trade unions alike. The war and changes in the terms of trade had eroded the competitive edge of coal-mining, engineering, shipbuilding and textiles – the very industries which had once made Britain the workshop of the world. Now, as C.L. Mowat put it, it was a case of 'the world's workshop on short time'.[9] In the coal trade, miners and owners alike had assumed that when peace returned they would struggle to divide the spoils of an expanding industry. But output per miner had fallen drastically, from 256 tons in 1913 to 178 tons in 1921. This falling productivity occurred partly because employers had refused to buy new equipment, partly because coal seams were wearing out, but partly because the MFGB had a vested interest during prosperity in maintaining high manning levels. Yet in the first three months of 1921 the industry lost £15,000,000. When Lloyd George hastened to divest his government of responsibility for such losses, by returning the mines to the owners, the triple alliance rumbled into action again. This time the consequences for the whole trade union movement were disastrous.

Black Friday – 15 April 1921 – is a familiar story, which need not be dealt with in detail here.[10] It destroyed the brittle unity of the triple alliance, which used divisions within the ranks of the MFGB as a pretext for calling off the strike. John Bromley and J.H. Thomas of the railwaymen, and Ernest Bevin of the transport workers and dockers, had lost patience. They were always expected to come to the aid of the miners, while the miners never helped them. Moreover, now the mines were back in private hands, railwaymen and transport workers could not coerce the coalowners. They could only threaten the government and hope they would intervene. The collapse of the triple alliance – or 'cripple alliance' as it was now bitterly called – ended an era of mounting trade union solidarity stretching back to the rail strike of 1911. Indeed, since 1889, the year of the strike for the 'docker's tanner', the birth of the 'new unionism' and the MFGB itself, trade union unity and strength had been growing.

Black Friday also discredited the MFGB Secretary Frank Hodges. Faced at a meeting of MPs with a question which forced him to choose between the 'national pool' to equalize profits, and higher wages, Hodges had chosen wages. Lloyd George used this answer skilfully to drive a wedge both between him and the rest of the miners' executive, and between the MFGB and their comrades in docks, railways and transport. Hodges – and to a lesser extent Thomas – bore the blame for Black Friday. Yet the choice of pay as first priority was to anticipate the TUC's later policy on unemployment, and that of the MFGB. To meet the threat of a national strike in 1921, the government made much more ominous preparations than in 1919, placing machine-guns near pitheads. The miners stayed out for three months before going back on terms worse than those offered at the start of the lock-out.

It was a decisive reverse. After Black Friday the mines were back in private hands, pay fell by as much as 50 per cent, and unemployment rose, never falling below a million until 1940. Trade union membership dropped from 8,500,000 in 1920 to 5,500,000 in 1924. The defeat of the MFGB was the start of an 'employers' offensive' which drove money wages down more steeply in 1920–21 than at any time in living memory. Sometimes with a strike, sometimes without one, workers in engineering, the docks, printing, the railways, shipbuilding and textiles were forced to accept lower pay. By the end of the year *The Economist* calculated that workers had lost three-quarters of their wartime wage increases, while the gap between skilled and unskilled rates was narrowed, never to be restored.

The effects of this deflation have been much debated by historians. W.B. Reddaway, for example, reckons that 1920–21 was the one time in modern British history when money wages fell at all fast.[11] But since the collapse of the post-war boom was not permanent, the domestic market recovered quickly. Wages fell, but so, too, did prices, so that real wages actually rose – perhaps by a fifth, perhaps by more – during the next decade or so. Critics of this view point out that such calculations neglect the extent to which average earnings were vitiated by higher unemployment, short-time and the loss of women's wages in the budgets of working-class homes.[12] Moreover, though it may be possible to prove that in simple accountancy terms wage workers were better off in 1931 than they had been in 1921, such calculations take no account of the bitterness created among trade unionists by the defeats of the 1920s. The problem for the historian of the working class in this period, as E.P. Thompson has pointed out in another context, is not only to determine whether they were better off at the end of the decade, but whether they *felt* so.[13]

Aside from such arguments, the response of the TUC to the events of 1921 and after is easier to explain. The TUC General Council moved, rather reluctantly at first, to fill the vacuum created by the demise of the triple alliance. Their motive, much as with the triple alliance in 1914, was to control militancy rather than to lead it. Bevin, 'the dockers' KC', had often been critical of the General Council in the past. After the collapse of the triple alliance in 1921 he steadily expanded his authority and that of the General Council. His ally was Walter Citrine, an electrical workers' leader and able bureaucrat, soon to become General Secretary of the TUC, who was described by Beatrice Webb as 'an intellectual of the scientific type . . . intent on real power'.[14] Bevin and Citrine were to prove key figures at the TUC between the wars. Yet the immediate prospect they faced as spokesmen of the emerging generation of leaders was not good. Between 1921 and 1924 the combined effects of the employers' offensive and the depression took their toll. Wages fell, unemployment ran at a steady million a year, or 10 per cent of the insured population, trade union membership fell by more than a third, the strike rate by nine-tenths.

LABOUR IN POWER

Political events reflected these jagged economic adjustments. Lloyd George, 'betrayer' of the Sankey Report and Black Friday, had lost the last vestige of the magic he had once exercised over the working class. When Tory Coalitionists turned against him at the end of 1922 his days were numbered. Yet he had pushed through unemployment insurance – the dole – in 1921, and this had now become the difference between life and death for the chronic jobless. When he fell, Bonar Law swept the Tories back into power alone for the first time since 1902, but then died within six months. Baldwin succeeded him as Prime Minister, until his snap election on Protection at the end of 1923 threw office to the first Labour Government.

In power, Labour faced the problem of how to treat the unions, its progenitors and paymasters. It showed small signs of being a creature of the TUC. From the trade union view, the important thing about the new set-up was that their sponsored MPs no longer dominated the parliamentary party, as they had in 1918. The ILP, the Co-operative Movement, Fabians and what might be called 'Lab-Libs' were part of the political coalition. MacDonald managed to reconcile these conflicting factions within the labour movement. He was now much the most impressive figure in the party, with a real flair for foreign affairs, and was to become with Baldwin one of the leaders who shaped inter-war history. Yet like Snowden at the Exchequer he was soon the captive of Treasury orthodoxy. Even without its dependence on Liberal votes in the Commons, Labour had no socialist solution to chronic unemployment. Socialism had essentially been about the distribution, rather than the creation, of wealth and work.

During its brief spell in office, the Labour Government did manage to do something.[15] In health and housing, John Wheatley had some really solid achievements, while abroad Britain recognized Soviet Russia. Nevertheless, the government alienated some trade unions. It agonized over the 'not genuinely seeking work' provisions of the dole,[16] failed to create new jobs and was quite prepared to take tough measures against strikers. Civil servants had been wary of sharing secret Emergency Powers Act plans for dealing with strikes when labour leaders like Thomas of the railwaymen might soon be leading the other side again once they left office. They need not have worried. Though Julian Symons has contended that Labour allowed the system to run down, the reverse would be nearer the truth.[17] MacDonald's Cabinet showed itself not only willing to improve the plans, but to use them against striking dockers and railwaymen. This latter dispute was especially instructive, for here was Thomas, leader of the victorious strike of 1919, now confronting a similar strike in government. Where the footplatemen's union ASLEF had struck with Thomas's NUR in 1919, the NUR now refused to return the favour in 1924, while the railway clerks once more remained at work. Such incipient divisions were to become crucial during the General Strike of 1926.

Yet the Labour Government's policies might have stimulated a more militant mood on the Left, and some historians have detected such a shift at the TUC in 1924–25. When Thomas resigned his seat on the General Council to join the new government, he was accompanied by Margaret Bondfield, J.R. Clynes and Tom Shaw. They were replaced by George Hicks, A.A. Purcell, A.J. Swales and Ben Tillett, all spokesmen of the Left. At the Hull TUC Conference in 1925, a 'Red Dawn' seemed to be breaking. The Communist boiler-maker Harry Pollitt made a fighting speech, and a fraternal delegate from the Soviet Union got a good reception.[18] Yet the detailed historical research of Daniel F. Calhoun into Soviet efforts to infiltrate the British labour movement shows how little they understood British conditions. It certainly fails to substantiate the traditional argument, advanced by Christopher Farman, Henry Pelling and others, that these events played an important part in shaping the confrontation between government and trade unions which occurred between 1925 and 1926.[19]

Any shift in political approach and attitude which occurred during this period clearly had the support of most elements in the TUC. For when the Labour Government fell at the end of 1924 Bondfield, Clynes, Shaw and Thomas soon won back their places on the General Council. Moreover, when confronted with the realities of power, Left-wingers like Swales apparently had little substantial to offer.[20] For what really counted was the evolving TUC attitude to unemployment. Since 1921 the General Council had faced a dilemma: how to choose between the interests of wage workers and the chronic unemployed? In a sense, this was the same problem Hodges had faced in his choice between the pool and wages on Black Friday. By 1925 the TUC had decided. In the words of Stephen Shaw, the most recent analyst of the topic, 'in any conflict between wages and unemployment, the protection of wages assumed primacy'.[21] It was the choice Hodges had made. It was the choice the MFGB made, even after they had cast Hodges into outer darkness for making it. The TUC for its part was prepared to back the miners in 1925–26, even though the wages the MFGB wanted would have closed hundreds of pits and thrown 200,000 miners on the dole.[22] In any wages/work trade-off, the TUC for all its apparent moderation did not really differ from the most intransigent miners' leaders, like Herbert Smith. This, rather than any 'Red Dawn', was the decisive element in the situation.

Yet although changes at the TUC may not have counted for much, Hodges' replacement as Secretary of the MFGB by A.J. Cook in 1924 had clearly been a decisive shift in leadership. Where Hodges had been pliable, a politician's politician whose talents were his making elsewhere, Cook listened to his rank-and-file members and then stuck out for what they wanted without compromise. Moreover, Cook's refusal to make concessions came at the very moment when they were going to be demanded most urgently. Before it fell, the Labour Government had been able to help the miners. French occupation of the Ruhr in 1923 had cut off supplies of German coal and driven British exports for a time to freakish levels. Emanuel Shinwell, the Minister for Mines, had used record profits to put pressure on the owners to raise pay by 13 per cent.

But then the Campbell Case brought Labour down, and while the party vote rose by more than a million at the general election, the Liberal vote fell by more as anti-socialist opinion stampeded behind the Tories. Baldwin returned at the head of the largest Tory majority for fifty years. So at the start of 1925 the moment seemed to have arrived to secure the overriding objective of the financial world and return to gold at $4.86. Chronic unemployment may have been a new problem, but the domestic market was buoyant and production actually 10 per cent higher than it had been in 1913. For the gold policy to work, more wage cuts would be necessary. But the Treasury, impressed by the speed with which money wages had been forced down in 1920–21, now believed the trick could be worked twice.[23] Even more important, officials like Sir Otto Niemeyer at the Treasury, and Montagu Norman at the Bank of England, argued that the whole purpose of the policy was to force trade unions and all British industry to abandon declining industries and seek new ways of earning abroad.[24]

Churchill resisted such arguments behind closed doors, hoping to make 'industry more content and finance less proud'. Privately, Baldwin was fighting mounting clamour to repeal trade union legal immunities, while in the House he scotched a Tory backbench bid to reverse the law on the political levy which linked Labour with the unions.[25] Historical arguments have centred on Baldwin's motives: was he playing for time, or seeking ways of educating both Labour and his own party? At this stage he was probably genuine in his desire to recreate in the nation at large the kind of industrial harmony he had known in the iron and steel trade of his Victorian youth. His 'peace in our time' speech was not all humbug. Yet industrial peace lasted less than a month. In his first Budget in April 1925, Churchill capitulated to the Treasury and the Bank of England and took Britain back onto gold. At $4.86 sterling was overvalued sufficiently to stop Britain's exports in their tracks, just as they were starting to move again.

This decision won the support of 'the best opinion', but the economist J.M. Keynes was not alone in his opposition. Manufacturers, especially exporters, agreed with Keynes, while Sir Alfred Mond, head of ICI, and Sir Allan Smith, President of the engineering employers, criticized the return. At the TUC Citrine seemed to accept it, but Bevin's hostility increased during the next five years. Moreover, there is sound reason for believing that Keynes was right, in the coal trade at least. The pound had been overvalued not by 2.5 per cent, as the Bank had argued, nor by 4.5 per cent, as the Treasury admitted, but by 10 per cent.[26] At all events, overvaluation, and failure to take account of the pound against the French franc or the German mark, shaped the next few months.[27]

THE GENERAL STRIKE

When the coalowners posted a 13 per cent pay cut at the end of June 1925, the MFGB called for TUC support and Baldwin backed down on 31 July, agreeing to pay a subsidy for nine months while the Samuel Commission investigated the industry once more. Much argument has ensued over Red Friday. The view 'We were not ready', which Baldwin gave his biographer G.M. Young, will not suffice. Cabinet papers show the government was fully prepared.[28] Public opinion, however, had not been shaped. The Macmillan Report, which had been published on 29 July, came down sharply on the miners' side and offered tart criticisms of the way the industry was managed. Baldwin's notorious statement 'All the workers in this country have got to take reductions in wages to help put industry back on its feet'[29] united trade union opinion at the very point at which it had split in 1921. But in the historical discussion of Red Friday, one point is often overlooked. The threat the TUC used in 1925 was not a strike but simply an *embargo* on the movement of coal by dockers, railwaymen and transport workers. Harder for employers and government to stop, it meant workers did not risk pay, pensions or jobs.

While the Samuel Commission – the third inquiry into mining in a year – deliberated, and the government perfected its plans for any future emergency, the TUC allowed itself to be persuaded to go for broke, as it were, and raise the bid from an embargo to a General Strike. Though unwilling, and unable, to do much by way of preparation for such an unprecedented step, the General Council went ahead with a policy which would lead to confrontation. Clearly, the tacit agreement between the TUC and the MFGB over work *versus* wages discussed above helped pattern the impending crisis. But John Lovell has thrown the most revealing light on the period July 1925 to May 1926 from the TUC perspective. With uncharacteristic lack of guile, Thomas missed the crucial meeting of the TUC policy committee formed to think about the immediate future. The miners insisted on strike backing; Bevin and Citrine were prepared to give it, providing they kept control.[30] If Red Friday were any guide, the threat of concerted action alone would be enough.

When the Samuel Commission reported on 6 March 1925, it recommended nationalization of royalties, sweeping reorganization and reforms. But all this was in the future. Its only immediate proposal was ending the subsidy and imposing the 13 per cent pay cut postponed in 1925. The miners would not look at this and the TUC would have to back them. And once the strike started, the TUC was on a loser whatever happened. If the General Strike succeeded, then syndicalism worked. Bevin, Citrine and Thomas had spent their lives in the trade union movement resisting such 'pernicious and absurd doctrines' as Beatrice Webb called direct action and workers' control.[31] Yet if the strike failed, as C.T. Cramp of the railwaymen believed it would, and Thomas believed it must, then the miners would be beaten, wages forced down, the TUC discredited, scapegoats sought. It would be Black Friday all over again, only worse. Faced with this choice, as Anthony Mason has put it, 'A short General Strike, called off as soon as could decently be done, was a kind of ironic compromise.'[32]

The details of 1926 need no rehearsal here.[33] The TUC's action in backing the miners was neither a constitutional threat, nor a revolutionary move, as the government claimed. The TUC was correct to call it a national strike: a remarkable and moving display of trade union solidarity on behalf of the MFGB. Of course, it was not entirely disinterested. Trade unionists felt that if miners' wages could be forced down, anyone's could, and their own would soon follow. Yet the strike ended after nine days in complete débâcle. A surrender more complete than Black Friday left the MFGB once more to fight on alone before going down to a defeat more serious than 1921. Bevin, Citrine and the General Council remained in charge throughout the nine days and must take responsibility. This at once raises the question: how were they able to retain command of the trade union movement after leading it to such a reverse? The short answer to that may be that their policies throughout commanded rank-and-file support.

Another way of looking at the problem is to ask why the TUC called off the strike so abruptly. Historians fall roughly into two groups on this: those who think it was failing, and those who think its very success alarmed the General Council.[34] Written evidence for either explanation is scanty, but Thomas, for one, voiced constant fears that after a week the initiative on both sides would begin to pass to extremists, especially in the regions, with consequent bloodshed. But the role played by ASLEF, the NUR and the railwaymen in general is more complicated than this. They were clearly the weakest link in the trade union chain, and there is no doubt that this weakness led to the final failure. Railwaymen were not drifting back to work on 12 May. But the rail unions had already spent several million pounds in strike benefit, and understood the fears of smaller TUC affiliates about the cost of the strike. The strike was anyway largely moral and ceremonial in character. Trade unions had played all their cards, and yet not brought the country to a halt. Once the moral demonstration had been made, separate unions would want to return to work in good order.

More important, the railwaymen had more to lose than any other trade unions in seniority, pensions, a guaranteed week and other privileges which set them apart, even from other members of the uniformed working class. Some 200,000 were still on a three-day week, and another 45,000 jobless, through victimization and sharply reduced traffic, five months after the surrender. Those fortunate enough to be re-hired had to sign humiliating contracts. Historians have criticized Bromley and Thomas for the part they played in 1926, but have not explained how such repercussions might have been avoided, even had the TUC managed to force the government's hand over the miners. Finally, the case against the TUC as 'betrayers of the working class' would be stronger if, as Anthony Mason has pointed out, even *one* case could be found of trade unionists refusing to obey their union's call to return to work on 13 May.[35] The outrage felt by many when the strike ended was real, but it was not powerful enough to drive from office even one of the 'defeatist' leaders. Was this because their policies won rank-and-file support?

The miners struggled on alone for seven months. Only Churchill in Cabinet, mindful of the cost to the Exchequer, tried to put pressure on the owners to moderate their terms. Since the eight-hour day they wanted could only be imposed by Parliament it might have been traded for other concessions. But Baldwin and the rest were not interested, and owners like Lord Londonderry and Evan Williams made no secret of their desire to use this opportunity to smash the MFGB.[36] The miners were supported by poor relief, their own efforts and donations from other trade unions in Britain and abroad, notably the Soviet Union. This last source angered the British Government, who used it as a pretext for breaking-off diplomatic relations after the Arcos Raid.[37] But by December the miners had been beaten back on the worst possible terms. District settlements had replaced national ones, hours were raised to eight, pay was back below the lowest 1921 levels. Moreover, the MFGB lost members to the Spencer Union in Nottinghamshire and to other company unions in Scotland and South Wales, which the owners openly encouraged.[38]

It took the TUC two years at least to recover from all this, and the MFGB much longer. Yet looking back one is struck by the marginal role the Labour Party played in the actual crisis. The part played by the Liberals, a more marginal party by 1926, is instructive. Liberals turn up everywhere, and on almost every side. Lloyd George, making his first serious bid to return to power in coalition with the Snowdenian Right, attacked the TUC over Red Friday but then supported the General Strike. Asquith deplored it, Simon said it was illegal, Churchill, now a Tory again, fought it to the limit and then tried to treat the miners magnanimously. Beveridge, Mond, Reading and Samuel in their several ways tried to solve it, while Keynes criticized the policies which led to it. Clearly, when facing the challenge of trade unions in the 1920s, Liberalism was an incoherent – though fertile – philosophy.

The Tories, for their part, lost no time in securing the fruits of victory once the lock-out had ended. Baldwin was now unable to resist his party's demands. The 1927 Trades Disputes and Trade Union Act made picketing harder, banned Civil Service and Public Service workers from joining unions linked with the TUC, and made strikes by local government workers, and all general strikes, illegal. The debates on the Bill were the bitterest since Home Rule, and outrage mounted when Chamberlain dissolved those Boards of Guardians too generous in granting relief during the emergency. Baldwin was able to prevent repeal of trade union legal immunities, but the political levy was placed on a 'contracting in' basis. Of course, such a blow at their chief opponent's main source of income came ill from a party itself dependent on secret contributions from rich men and industrialists, while Lloyd George's sale of honours was a notorious scandal of the type with which Baldwin believed he had debauched public life. Though Labour Party funds recovered later, they fell by a third immediately.

THE MOND–TURNER TALKS

These were stunning blows, so that the TUC's participation in the Mond–Turner talks in 1928 was a sign of return to useful activity. With trade unions driven completely on the defensive after 1926, and industry at the peak of its inter-war prosperity, enlightened employers like Mond, Smith and Lord Weir persuaded a score of their fellow industrialists to participate in discussions with the TUC. The talks, which opened in January 1928, took the name of Mond himself and Ben Turner, a veteran textile workers' leader and now Chairman of the TUC. Bevin and Citrine did most of the work on the TUC side and persuaded the Annual Conference in September to accept the new approach. Cook and the fiery Clydesider Jimmy Maxton attacked this 'class collaboration' as 'Mond moonshine', but Bevin defended co-operation in place of the costly conflict of recent years. His argument was typically forceful. 'It is all very well', he told Cook, 'for people to talk as if the working class of Great Britain are cracking their shins for a fight and a revolution, and we are holding them back. Are they? There are not many as fast as we are ourselves.'[39]

Reactions to the outcome of the General Strike seemed to bear Bevin out, yet the immediate consequence of the talks was disappointing, and Mondism itself was slow to bear fruit. Most historians seem to share the view of Alan Bullock and others that the talks were more influential in the long run, especially on Bevin and Citrine, but it is hard to be specific about this.[40] The TUC's favourite panaceas remained tariffs, assisted emigration to the Dominions, and a 'back to the land' reform movement. These were augmented after 1928 by Mond's favourite solution of rationalization, now a vogue concept, plus earlier retirement and a limited role for public works and public spending. This was not a very encouraging formula, especially when contrasted with the Keynesian policies with which Lloyd George led the Liberals to the polls in May 1929. The electorate favoured Labour, however, who won more seats than the other parties. Thus though MacDonald's second government was another minority administration it was much better placed than his first to tackle the task of dealing with 'the intractable million'.

Such hopes were soon dashed by the Great Depression. Previously, Labour had tried to tackle deflation peculiar to Britain. After October 1929 it became a world problem, devastating economies and financial and political institutions everywhere. As unemployment doubled and tripled, Labour was gradually overwhelmed by problems it could neither solve nor understand. Most accounts of this failure, like Reginald Bassett's, concentrate on the final crisis in the summer of 1931.[41] Robert Skidelsky's pathfinding study, written before the Cabinet papers became available to scholars, argues that the inaction of the first two years was what really ruined things. This was a failure of ideology and policy as much as nerve.[42] In this view, the rock on which all new ventures foundered was Snowden, the Treasury's favourite Chancellor but the prisoner of orthodox finance. Faced with this, Thomas's skills as a fixer could not create new jobs, Henderson's links with trade unions were useless at the Foreign Office, while MacDonald himself became increasingly preoccupied with solving the world crisis by diplomacy.

At home, the 1930 Coal Mines Act might have enforced the Samuel recommendations, but managed to please neither miners nor owners and failed to solve the industry's central problems. For some on the Left the belief in ultimate socialism became the pretext for doing nothing. They would neither save capitalism nor bury it. More energetic and fertile thinkers in the party could not win acceptance for their ideas. Here Skidelsky reminds us that Sir Oswald Mosley must be seen in his pre-fascist phase. Between 1929 and 1931 he was one of the few politicians struggling towards an early understanding that the riddle of unemployment could only be answered if it were approached via ending under-consumption, with due weight given to the role of reflation and sustained public spending to revive and control economic activity.[43]

Of course, this neo-Keynesian critique's enthusiasm for public spending now looks a little dated. Ross McKibbin's sparkling response argues that the second Labour Government did about as well as any 'progressive' party could do in the circumstances. In particular, he attacks Skidelsky's two conjectures: that international experience pointed to alternative reflationary policies, and that the Labour Cabinet was free to choose this alternative. Contemporary experience in dealing with deflation in Australia, France, Germany and the United States during the New Deal was more ambiguous than Skidelsky allows. Moreover, reflation was just not an option within the existing power structure of the Bank, the Treasury, finance, most of industry and the whole inertia of conventional wisdom.[44] Some trade union leaders were part of this dead weight. Others, like Bevin, were seeking a new way out of the wood. Even Cook switched support from Maxton's imaginative socialism to Mosley's equally bold non-socialist solution. But Cook died in 1931, leaving Mosley no other links with labour leaders.

The question was no longer, as in 1924, whether a socialist solution could be found for unemployment. As the Great Depression deepened, and unemployment mounted inexorably everywhere, it was uncertain whether there was a solution of any kind. The Macmillan Committee had been set up in November 1929 to seek one, and sustain the momentum of the Mond–Turner talks. Bevin served on it, and later defended such a step with revealing pragmatism. 'I know that I could be answered by the usual socialist philosophy,' he explained bluntly, 'but when you go on a Royal Commission you have to deal with facts as they are and the problem as it is.'[45] Yet though it may later have speeded acceptance of a managed currency, its immediate effect when it reported in July 1931 was simply to reveal the bankruptcy of orthodox finance in facing the crisis of the times.

The May Report, which followed almost at once, drew further attention to Britain's balance-of-payments problems. Worse, it went out of its way to make the point that the Labour Government was financially untrustworthy.[46] Skidelsky argues that when the financial crisis of August 1931 finally brought the government down it was largely as a result of its total lack of policy. McKibbin claims in contrast that 'The practical alternatives open to the Labour Government were not drift or reflation, but drift or deflation.'[47] It collapsed when pressure became too strong and it had to choose deflation. Yet even McKibbin accepts that there was some truth in trade-union assertions that the fatal financial crisis, as distinct from Britain's budgetary problems, was largely the result of heavy City indebtedness and unwise lending. Though the unions may have been right in saying it was the Bank's crisis, 'there *was* a crisis, and if suspension of gold payment were excluded, the solution had to be deflation'.[48]

By refusing to accept this, McKibbin concludes, the TUC could claim to have brought the government down. The fact is that they neither claimed nor wanted this. The Bank and the financial world, however, clearly did want to bring it down, and the May Report was a powerful element in this process. In the end, the government brought itself down (as it did in 1974). When the Cabinet split eleven to nine on cuts in the dole, and cuts in pay for teachers, police and other public servants, including the armed forces, no element of TUC membership was threatened. The TUC, and Cabinet ministers like Henderson, mindful of how little they had done for the unemployed in ten years, simply could not accept dole cuts. Snowden misled the Cabinet about equality of sacrifice for both rentier and working class, as well as what the Bank would regard as proper, and a majority favoured the cuts.[49] Joined by only three of his Cabinet colleagues, MacDonald formed a crisis coalition, and in October swept his National Government to the greatest electoral victory in British history, winning 556 seats, largely at the expense of Labour. The party MacDonald had split was reduced to a rump of fifty-two MPs. This 'betrayal' was worse even than 1921, further compounded by the complicity of the trade union leader Thomas in both. Despite David Marquand's recent sympathetic reassessment of MacDonald's role, there can be no doubt it scarred Labour permanently.[50]

As unemployment rose inexorably to nearly 3,000,000 by the end of the year, the Communist Party and the National Minority Movement revived their appeal to the chronic jobless, but with small success. Communist Party membership, which had grown rapidly in 1926, withered just as quickly afterwards, while the Minority Movement was moribund by 1931. As the crisis deepened in Europe, extremists of both left and right made great strides. In Britain, the National Unemployed Workers' Movement (NUWM), communist rank-and-file Vigilance Movements, and Mosley's move to fascism were all partly stimulated by economic catastrophe, and the rise of Hitler and Stalin, who seemed to threaten Western democratic capitalism from either side. Yet these movements had weak links with the trade unions.

Such 'little Moscows' as did exist, like Chopwell in Durham, seem to have been rooted in local conditions rather than a national revolutionary mood. Stuart MacIntyre's new study of other examples – Mardy in South Wales, and less familiar places such as Lumphinnans, a small mining community in the Fife coalfield, or the Vale of Leven in Dumbartonshire

– suggests this strongly. They owed little to the propaganda activity of the Red International, Trotskyites or other sectarian groupings of the Left, whose influence on British trade unions was minimal.[51] Like 'Poplarism' in the 1920s it was all to do with the type and strength of local leadership. So when Wal Hannington and the NUWM began to make an impact in 1931, the TUC made more active efforts to reach the unemployed.

Indeed, Sidney Pollard has argued that while the Labour Party proved bankrupt in 1931, the TUC put forward the only ideas to come from the labour movement. Bevin's lone attack on the gold standard was joined by Citrine and others. MacDonald, who had formed his crisis Cabinet for the sole purpose of defending gold, was soon forced to abandon it and so stimulate reflation at last. Meanwhile, the General Council had submitted its most authoritative report on unemployment to the TUC Conference in 1931. For all its weaknesses, Pollard contends, the report was well-argued 'and immeasurably superior in its economic understanding to anything that emanated from the Treasury or its economic supporters'.[52] In this view it was the trade unions who gave backbone to the Labour Party (as they also did over nationalization through public corporations) by evolving their own ideas rather than taking them ready made from outside.

Yet this neglects the extent to which trade unions were still prepared to accept unemployment, partly because of the wages/work trade-off discussed above, partly because even in the depths of the depression a majority of wage earners remained in work. They could forget that their good fortune, and the steady rise in purchasing power of their wages, was being paid for largely by the sacrifices of others. Such forgetfulness was easier when the jobless – engineers, miners, shipbuilders and textile workers – lived far away in other parts of the country. With the gold standard gone, reflation was now possible. Low interest rates, higher investment and more buoyant demand at home and abroad for new products as the world slump subsided all helped it along. Real wages continued to rise after 1931, unemployment fell from 3,000,000 to 1,000,000. When historians turn their attention from the depressed areas to emerging regions like the Midlands, and to consumer goods and private housing, they can talk of 'the booming thirties'.[53]

Thus Pollard concludes that as far as the TUC leadership in 1931 is concerned, 'the crisis turned out to have converted its majority to Keynes rather than to Marx'.[54] Politically, the TUC was effectively in control of the parliamentary party after the 1931 election. The full employment and prosperity which returned after 1945 is usually attributed to successful use of Keynesian 'demand-management'. Others have argued that the relative success of the British economy between 1945 and 1970 was due largely to rapid increases in both investment and exports.[55] This view really underestimates the part played by government, employers and trade unions alike, to say nothing of the world trading community, whose Keynesian attitudes encouraged this process.

Yet it is sobering for socialists and trade unions alike to reflect that when solutions for mass unemployment and the spectres of sickness and old age were evolved, they did not spring entirely from their own traditions. The Beveridge Report, which laid the basis for the modern welfare state with social security as of right, was the product of a former Liberal and member of the Samuel Commission. Likewise Keynes, the father of managed capitalism, had been a Liberal critic of Churchill and the return to gold. In that context, trade unions had to wait for full employment and the chronic labour shortage after 1945 to reverse that bargaining strength employers had used against them between the wars and pay back some of the hurt they suffered after 1921. But if many trade unionists were cautious, conservative or cowed by a decade of depression, their leaders faced the future in 1931 with more experience and determination than in the heady days of 1918.

NOTES AND REFERENCES

1.   R. McKibbin, *The Evolution of the Labour Party, 1910–1924*, Oxford University Press, Oxford, 1974, pp. 96–97, and see also his survey of the debate among historians p. 91 and n.
2.   P. Stead, 'Working class leadership in South Wales', *Welsh Hist. Rev.*, 6, no. 3 (June 1973), pp. 347–48.
3.   R. McKibbin, *The Evolution of the Labour Party*, op. cit., p. 112 and n.
4.   M. Cowling, *The Impact of Labour, 1920–1924*, Cambridge University Press, Cambridge, 1971, pp. 1–2.
5.   R. Smillie, President of the MFGB, coolly asking Lord Londonderry if he could produce the deeds for his vast estates, provided one of the highlights of the hearings.
6.   G.D.H. Cole, *The British Coal-Mining Industry*, Oxford University Press, Oxford, 1923, p. 8.
7.   H. Fyfe, *Behind the Scenes of the Great Strike*, London, 1926, p. 8. The best modern discussion is M.W. Kirby, *The British Coalmining Industry, 1870–1946*, Macmillan, London, 1977, esp. pp. 46–66.
8.   R.H. Desmarais, 'The strikebreaking organization of the British Government and Black Friday', *Jrnl. of Cont. Hist.*, 6, no. 2 (April 1971), pp. 112–27. See also J. Foster, 'Imperialism and the Labour Aristocracy' in J. Skelley (ed.), *The General Strike 1926*, Lawrence & Wishart, London, 1976, pp. 3–57.
9.   C.L. Mowat, *Britain Between the Wars, 1918–1940*, Methuen, London, 1955, p. 259.

10.   A. Bullock, *The Life and Times of Ernest Bevin*, Heinemann, London, 1960, vol. 1, pp. 143–80 is a useful account, which can be augmented by P. Renshaw, 'Black Friday, 1921', *History Today*, **21**, no. 6 (June 1971), pp. 416–25.

11.   W.B. Reddaway, 'Was $4.86 inevitable in 1925?', *Lloyd's Bank Review*, no. 96 (April 1970), p. 19.

12.   A.L. Bowley and J. Stamp, *The National Income 1924*, Clarendon Press, Oxford, 1927, is a forceful contemporary argument of this view.

13.   E.P. Thompson, *The Making of the English Working Class*, Gollancz, London, 1963, pp. 207–12 discusses the 'standard of living controversy' as applied to the period 1780–1840.

14.   M. Cole (ed.), *Beatrice Webb Diaries, 1924–1930*, Longmans, Green, London, 1956, p. 147.

15.   R.W. Lyman, *The First Labour Government 1924*, Chapman & Hall, London, 1957, remains the best account.

16.   For a perceptive discussion of Labour's ambivalent attitude towards the dole, see A. Deacon, 'Concession and Coercion: the politics of unemployment insurance in the twenties' in A. Briggs and J. Saville (eds), *Essays in Labour History*, Croom Helm, London, 1977, vol. 3, pp. 9–35.

17.   J. Symons, *The General Strike*, Cresset Press, London, 1957, pp. 23–24 argues that Labour let the system slip, but this is rebutted by the Cabinet Papers 27/259 (E C), p. 3, 15 February 1924.

18.   *TUC Report of Proceedings 1924*, pp. 311–18. The fraternal delegate was Tomsky.

19.   C. Farman, *The General Strike May 1926*, Hart-Davis, London, 1972, p. 34 and H. Pelling, *A History of British Trade Unionism*, Macmillan, London, 1963, pp. 173–74. D.F. Calhoun, *The United Front: the TUC and the Russians, 1923–1928*, Cambridge University Press, Cambridge, 1976, is the best study of this subject, based partly on Soviet sources.

20.   Swales's role during the General Strike was negligible, and he accepted the surrender as calmly as Arthur Pugh, saying nothing at the meeting with the government. See transcript of the meeting of the TUC delegation with Baldwin on 12 May 1926 in Symons, *The General Strike*, op. cit., pp. 235–40.

21.   S. Shaw, 'The Attitude of the Trade Union Congress towards Unemployment in the Inter-War Period', Ph.D. thesis, University of Kent, 1979, p. 66.

22.   T. Jones, *Whitehall Diary*, Oxford University Press, Oxford, 1969, vol. 2, 1926–30, p. 18 quotes H. Smith and F. Varley arguing this line on 23 April 1926. Both represented mining regions – Yorkshire and Nottinghamshire – which sold on the home market.

23. Interestingly, President Hoover thought the same during the Great Depression. See R. Hofstadter, *The American Political Tradition*, Knopf Vintage Books, New York, 1959, p. 302n.

24. Cabinet Papers, Cab. 24/179, vol. LXIII, 1926, 18 March 1926, 281–82 and Niemeyer's memo to another Treasury official, Sir Warren Fisher, 14 March 1926 in Baldwin Papers, D.3, vol. 13, pp. 153–54.

25. Baldwin Papers, D.3, vol. 11, pp. 44–45, 48–49, 352–54, 355–57, 358. For the speech scotching Macquisten's Bill, see *Hansard*, HC Debs, pp. 839–41, 6 March 1925.

26. Since pay represented two-thirds of the cost of coal production, a pay cut of 13 per cent made possible a price cut of two-thirds of 13 per cent, or about 9 per cent, as Keynes argued.

27. D.E. Moggridge, *The Return to Gold, 1925*, Cambridge University Press, Cambridge, 1969, p. 27. Government discussion of policy can be found in 'Memorandum on Ending the Mining Subsidy', Cabinet Papers, 24/179, vol. LXIII, 1926, pp. 65–68.

28. *Cabinet Conclusions*, Cab 23/50 42(50), pp. 268–69, 291–93.

29. *Daily Herald*, 31 July 1925. Baldwin denied saying this, but apparently it was twice repeated and the official minute of the confidential discussion confirms the substance. Anyway, it was a correct statement of government policy.

30. J. Lovell, 'The TUC Special Industrial Committee: January–April 1926' in A. Briggs and J. Saville, *Essays in Labour History*, op. cit., pp. 41–42. The crucial meeting took place on 19 February 1926.

31. M. Cole, *Webb Diaries*, op. cit., p. 92.

32. A. Mason, 'The Government and the General Strike, 1926', *International Review of Social History*, 14, no. 1 (summer 1969), p. 21.

33. The most recent studies based on Cabinet Papers include G.A. Phillips, *The General Strike: the politics of industrial conflict*, Weidenfeld & Nicolson, London, 1976, and P. Renshaw, *The General Strike*, Eyre Methuen, London, 1975, which places the event in a wider context.

34. Ibid. Phillips argues the former view, pp. 239–50, Renshaw the latter, pp. 171–72, 221–22.

35. A. Mason, 'The General Strike', *Bulletin of the Society for the Study of Labour History*, no. 33, autumn 1976, p. 53.

36. For Churchill's magnanimity, see his letters to Baldwin, 9 June 1926, and to W.C. Bridgeman, 7 September 1926 in Baldwin papers D.3, vol. 18, pp. 45–47, 25–27. For the owners' desire to smash the MFGB see Londonderry to Baldwin, ibid., pp. 149–54.

37. Cabinet papers, vol. XXI, pp. 424–27.

38. For Spencerism, see A.R. and C.P. Griffin, 'The Non-Political Trade Union Movement' in A. Briggs and J. Saville, *Essays in*

Labour History, op. cit., pp. 133–63 and for company unionism, D. Smith, 'The struggle against company unionism in South Wales', *Welsh Hist. Rev.*, 6, no. 3 (June 1973), pp. 367–81 and H. Francis and D. Smith, *The Fed: a History of the South Wales Miners in the Twentieth Century*, Lawrence & Wishart, London, 1980, pp. 244–308.

39. Quoted in Bullock, *The Life and Times of Ernest Bevin*, op. cit., p. 401.

40. Ibid., p. 405, See also G.W. McDonald and H. Gospel, 'The Mond–Turner Talks, 1927–1933: a study in industrial co-operation', *Hist. Jrnl*, 14, no. 4 (winter 1973), pp. 807–29.

41. R. Bassett, *1931: Political Crisis*, Macmillan, London, 1958.

42. R. Skidelsky, *Politicians and the Slump: the Labour Government of 1929–1931*, Macmillan, London, 1967, pp. 387, 389–95.

43. Ibid., pp. 167–89.

44. R. McKibbin, 'The economic policy of the second Labour Government', *Past and Present*, no. 68 (August 1975), 95–123, *passim*, esp. pp. 120–23.

45. *TUC Report of Proceedings 1931*, p. 464.

46. *Committee on National Expenditure*, PP, 1931 (Cmd 3920), p. 223, para. 574.

47. R. McKibbin, 'Economic Policy', op. cit., p. 114.

48. Ibid., p. 119 and n.

49. B.C. Malament, 'Philip Snowden and the Cabinet deliberations of August 1931', *Bulletin of the Society for the Study of Labour History*, no. 41 (autumn 1980), casts revealing new light on this.

50. D. Marquand, *Ramsay MacDonald*, Jonathan Cape, London, 1977, pp. 638–70.

51. S. MacIntyre, *Little Moscows: communism and working class militancy in inter-war Britain*, Croom Helm, London, 1980.

52. S. Pollard, 'Trade union reactions to the economic crisis', *Jrnl. of Cont. Hist.*, 4 (October 1969), p. 102.

53. J. Stevenson and C. Cook, *The Slump: society and politics during the Depression*, Jonathan Cape, London, 1977, is the fullest statement of this view.

54. S. Pollard, op. cit., p. 115.

55. R. McKibbin, 'Economic Policy', op. cit., p. 122, citing a wide range of economists.

6 Trade unions and the slump

Richard Shackleton

The 1930s was a period of enduring weakness for the whole labour movement, industrial and political. Although the last years of the decade saw some recovery in union bargaining power, and although the Labour Party recaptured the share of the poll it had enjoyed in its peak year of 1929, the unions lacked both the muscle and the will for major industrial conflicts and the Labour Party was never within measurable distance of power. The troubles of the unions stemmed partly from the wounds of the General Strike and partly from the superimposition of the world depression upon the long-standing malaise of the old export industries. Membership reached its nadir in 1933 and recovery was painfully slow. As a number of dogged defensive struggles showed, the fighting capacity of the unions was not destroyed but on the whole the 1930s was a decade of sullen industrial peace.

During the 1920s, the Labour Party had enjoyed years of almost unbroken growth and its leaders and propagandists had looked forward to the quarrying-out of a natural and permanent working-class majority of the electorate. These hopes died in the humiliating collapse of the second Labour Government in August 1931 and in the subsequent calamitous electoral defeat. The 1930s was to see a tightening of the links between the party and the unions, with the unions very much the senior partner but the *rapprochement* was not achieved without conflict and controversy.

The political history of the unions in the 1930s is predominantly the history of the relations between them and the Labour Party. That this was so was a matter of necessity, not choice. The course upon which the leaders of the TUC, Walter Citrine and Ernest Bevin, had embarked in the aftermath of the General Strike was not only one of accommodation with employers and the State but was a programme the success of which was in principle independent of the political achievements of the Labour Party. In 1937,

Bevin claimed that the trade unions were an integral part of the State, but the claim was premature: until the dire exigencies of war made it essential to secure the full co-operation of organized labour, the Tory-dominated National Government was prepared to grant only a very junior partnership to the unions. Keith Middlemas has written: 'In the decade before Labour as a party returned to power in the 1940 coalition, organized labour settled down to live with organized management, both clinging to the state in a hostile economic environment and pushing the political extremes, Right or Left, beyond the boundary of parliamentary politics.'[1] In such circumstances, the unions turned back towards the Labour Party as the central instrument for achieving their political aims. The changing priorities of both partners to the alliance and the strains between them will be explored in this chapter. One further preliminary point needs to be made: whether weak or strong, whether under radical or moderate leaderships, whether engaging in syndicalist oratory or endorsing the mixed economy, unions have, save in exceptional circumstances, resisted political interference in their industrial autonomy, as forcefully when the intervention comes from a friend as from an enemy. Accordingly, the relationship between the party and the unions in the 1930s was a one-sided one. As we shall see, the assertion of trade union control was a gradual and halting process but at no point did the unions offer a share in industrial decision making to the party, nor would they have entertained any such suggestion. Even when apparently accepting proposals for radical social and economic change, the unions were mindful of their sectional interests and narrowly-understood freedom to pursue their goals. As Robert Currie has argued: 'As ever in Labour's political thought, therefore, the goal of social change was modification (in Labour's favour), and not supersession of *laissez-faire*.'[2]

THE 1931 CRISIS AND ITS AFTERMATH

Long before the final crisis of August 1931, the second Labour Government was experiencing a rash of troubles which already appeared to have doomed it to early and conclusive defeat. The fragmentation of its support took several forms: the alienation of advanced elements within the party, particularly Mosley and his supporters and the ILP, a decline in morale in the PLP and in the government itself, a near collapse of electoral strength, all combined with distant and even hostile relations with the trade union movement. Basic to all these troubles and dissatisfactions was the complete failure of the government to check the rise of unemployment, let alone fulfil its pledge to conquer it.

In its relations with the trade union movement, the government repeated and compounded the errors of 1924. Although leading trade unionists were given places on such bodies as the Economic Advisory Council and the Macmillan Commission on Trade and Industry, there was no consistent

pattern of consultation and although intervention by the TUC might
on occasion force the government to reconsider its policies, MacDonald
and Snowden regarded regular consultation with any outside body as a
derogation of the constitution. There was no attempt on the part of the
ministers concerned to familiarize themselves with the trend of thinking
on the TUC Economic Committee, which differed radically from the
prescriptions of orthodox finance on which, despite some deviations,
Snowden as Chancellor of the Exchequer continued to rely, and no real
attempt to carry the TUC along with the government's own thinking.
Further, the government severely disappointed the expectations of several
unions: it failed to satisfy the demands of the steel and textile unions
for some measure of protection for their industries; it broke with party
policy in failing to include agricultural workers within the unemployment
insurance scheme; it sponsored a settlement to the 1930 weavers' dispute
which involved heavy wage cuts; and its 1930 Coal Mines Act fell far short
both of the declared policy of the party and of the demands of the miners.
John Scanlon's[3] harsh verdict was widely shared:

The betrayal of the miners was probably the blackest chapter of all, if for no other
reason than that the miners deserved better of the community than any other
section. Their loyalty made the Government possible. Yet what happened? Every
pledge given to the miners was deliberately broken by a series of manoeuvres that
were a disgrace to the Labour Movement. The negotiations were delayed and the
miners played with until the eleventh hour, and because they were too weak to
fight, they were obliged to accept a wretched Bill which gave them nothing.

Finally, the government failed to repeal the 1927 Trades Disputes Act.
Certainly in this case the government was hampered by its lack of a
parliamentary majority, whether or not this was the case with its economic
policy but many unions asserted that it had not fought with any great
commitment.

The second Labour Government had been able to trade on a fund of
trade union patience and goodwill. In the summer of 1930, for instance,
the *Locomotive Journal* remarked that 'the second MacDonald Government
has proved itself an active and capable Government' while noting that
'unemployment alone has failed to respond to its healing touch'.[4] As late
as June 1931, the General Executive Council of the TGWU urged members
to work to ensure the return of a Labour Government at the next election
and to remember that 'the results of the work of a government can rarely be
seen in its own lifetime'.[5] Eventually, however, the growing dissatisfaction
of the union leaders with the performance of the government and above all
with its failure to cope with unemployment, was reflected in an alarming
fall-off in affiliation payments. As the government concentrated more on
measures to curb the cost of unemployment relief than on the search for
a policy to combat unemployment itself, the decline in support became so

severe that by the beginning of August 1931, only half as much had been received from this source as in the previous year and there were reports of near panic at Transport House.

The role of the unions in the 1931 crisis explains much about their subsequent political role in the 1930s. In the early stages of the August crisis initiated by the publication of the May Report, the government took no steps to consult with the TUC and the unions were provided with no inside information on the development of the crisis. Indeed, Robert Skidelsky has argued that a series of circumstantial and wholly misleading articles in the *Daily Herald* which discounted the possibility of action along the draconian lines of the May Report represented an effort by the TUC, which controlled the policy of the *Herald*, to put pressure on the government.[6] Having been excluded for so long, the TUC burst into the crisis on 20 August and soon made it clear that it would not go along with any of the major items in the government's package of planned economies, let alone a cut in the standard rate of unemployment relief.

This firm stance both narrowed MacDonald's range of options and stiffened resistance to the proposed economies within the Cabinet. At the very least, then, the role of the unions was crucial in the ignominious fall of the government which came when MacDonald formed a National Government, from which most of his former colleagues were excluded, on 24 August. Whether this trade union role constituted a species of dictatorship was to be a vexed question in the weeks ahead and indeed largely shaped the debate about the political role of the unions throughout the 1930s. Undoubtedly the TUC role had been critical: whereas the NEC had left matters in the hands of their members in the Cabinet, and particularly Arthur Henderson, the General Council had not only taken a firm stance but had actually propounded an attractive alternative to the government's insistence on deflation: it called for the suspension of the sinking fund, new taxation on fixed-interest bearing securities, a graduated levy on the whole community to support the unemployed and consideration, at least, of a revenue tariff. This head-on clash led Snowden to conclude that 'members of the General Council had no real appreciation of the position . . . their statements appeared to be based on a pre-crisis mentality'[7] while Sidney Webb, in a much-quoted phrase, told his wife that 'the General Council are pigs'.[8]

There was little or no prospect of the TUC's plans actually being carried out and their significance lies largely in their having provided a programme round which opponents of the cuts in the Cabinet could cluster and, more problematically, in their sudden adoption by the whole loyal party, ex-ministers, NEC and all, in the aftermath of the fall of the government. For politicians who a few days earlier had been willing to go the whole way with Snowden (as a small majority had been) suddenly to adopt such a financially unorthodox and radical stance inevitably fed stories of trade union dictatorship. However, the availability of the TUC package was of inestimable value in providing a rallying cry for those who had been opposed to the planned economies as a negation of all that the party stood for but were themselves unable to formulate an alternative.

Curiously, despite the TUC's vision and firmness at the time of the crisis, it soon lost the initiative in policy-formation and the Labour Party went into the unequal struggle of the 1931 general election with a programme very much of its own devising which asserted that 'The decay of capitalist civilisation brooks no delay. Measures of Socialist reconstruction must be vigorously pressed forward.'[9] It appears that the TUC lost the initiative because its constituent unions were more divided on the question of the attitude to take towards the new government than appeared from the published statements of the General Council. While the GMWU, for instance, saw the issue in class terms ('All the Fat Men came tumbling back from the Riviera, or Carlsbad in their white-and-silver yachts in the Adriatic, screaming the place down that "we really can't afford all this extravagance".'[10]), other union journals were almost apologetic in their repudiation of the actions of MacDonald and his colleagues.

The trade union movement did, nonetheless, take a very active part in the 1931 election campaign. Somewhat ironically, the emergence of the National Government loosened union purse-strings and both the TUC and various individual unions issued forceful statements in support of the Labour Party. The General Council's *Call to the Workers* combined a vigorous attack on the National Government with a sturdy defence of Labour's vulnerable record but it avoided any commitment to the party's more radical proposals for transforming the economic structure of the country. Similarly, Ernest Bevin, who stood unsuccessfully as a Labour candidate in Gateshead, did, in his campaign, stress his own semi-Keynesian financial nostrums. These divergences were not of great importance at the time though they can be seen to have interesting implications for the events of the 1930s. Much more important at the time was the ferocious glare of publicity to which the relationship between the unions and the Labour Party was subjected. Indeed, a formidable case was made out against the political activities of the unions, a case that was developed and made more sophisticated in succeeding years.

Faced with the financial crisis of August 1931, it was argued by the critics, MacDonald and Snowden had espoused a solution which, although it was repugnant to the socialist objectives of the Labour Party, did recognize the overriding needs of the nation. However, they were opposed by a minority of their colleagues and by the TUC which refused to subject its sectional interests to the interests of the community as a whole. False to Labour's traditions as a party transcending class boundaries, the argument continued, sufficient members of the Cabinet submitted to this pressure to make MacDonald's task impossible within the confines of the Labour Party, and when he formed a National Government to carry out the necessary measures of which a Labour Government alone had shown itself incapable, the grip of the unions drove the party into a superficially unanimous opposition. Trade union MPs, in particular, gave their first loyalty to their sponsoring union rather than to their constituents or the country, largely under threat to their livelihoods should they follow MacDonald. In the view of the loyal MacDonaldite Godfrey Elton,[11] the continuing link with the unions was fatally damaging to Labour's prospects:

When the economic crisis of August broke upon the chief architects of electoral disaster, and almost their first reaction to national crisis was seen to be to whisper anxiously, 'what orders to-day from the Trades Union Congress General Council?' they were, no doubt, true to the narrow vision into which of late most of them had insensibly grown, but they were false not only to the teachings of the forerunners whose sacrifices had put them where they were but to all the future prospects of the Party they were about to ruin.

Elton affected to write more in sorrow than in anger but other polemicists assaulted the union role in politics with gleeful abandon: Conservative Central Office, for instance, raised echoes of the General Strike, asserting that 'then as now the country showed clearly that it would not submit to any dictation from outside bodies',[12] and, far more seriously, Philip Snowden lent his considerable authority to the charges in an article attacking 'Labour's Little Lenins'. 'The TUC', he wrote, 'insisted on being the master of the Government and the majority of the Cabinet tamely submitted to the intimidation.'[13]

Spokesmen for the Labour Party and the unions tried to refute this charge-sheet both in outline and in detail. They pointed out that, after all, it was the government that had, however belatedly, solicited the General Council's opinion and that rather than the party submitting to dictatorship from the unions, MacDonald and the ministers who supported him were submitting to dictatorship from the bankers in London and New York.

Although Labour fought a lively campaign with much help from the unions, their cause was hopeless, faced as they were by a powerful alliance and by the defection of three of their major leaders, and the outcome was an almost unmitigated catastrophe, in which only forty-six endorsed Labour candidates were returned.

It is hard to come to any definite conclusions about the role of the unions in the 1931 crisis but a few comments may be advanced. The refusal of the General Council to accede to the MacDonald–Snowden package certainly constituted a species of dictation since the prospects of a weakened minority government pushing through a programme of economies in defiance of the firmly expressed views of organized labour were remote. Yet the firm stand of the General Council can be justified on the grounds both of the chronic incompetence of the government in face of the crisis and of the paralysis which had overtaken the NEC. The TUC was the only body capable of preventing Snowden from committing the movement to a set of proposals that were both inhumane and economically irrational.

It is misleading to see the episode as one in which a unified trade union position was imposed upon the Labour Party. On the one hand, the economic sophistication which marked the Economic Committee of the TUC was very little diffused through the movement: much trade union thinking still reflected an ingenuous and uneasy marriage between *Das Kapital* and the Sermon on the Mount. On the other hand, the division in the Cabinet which signalled the end of the government was not a division between trade unionists and others: three of the six trade union sponsored MPs in the Cabinet supported the full programme of cuts and one of them, Jimmy Thomas, ended his long and controversial career in the labour movement by joining the National Government.

THE TRADE UNIONS AND THE RECOVERY OF THE LABOUR PARTY

In the mood of stunned disbelief which pervaded the labour movement after the 1931 catastrophe, many people in both the political and the industrial movement looked to a tightening of the links between them as a vital ingredient in recovery and as the best way of avoiding any recurrence of the events which had left the Labour Party nearly prostrate. The defeat fortified and revived the organizational links but, due largely to uncertainty, weakness and division on the union side, the political consequences were not worked out until later in the decade.

Many historians have stressed the extent of trade union involvement in the Labour Party's painful recovery after 1931. Henry Pelling entitled the chapter on the 1930s in his *Short History of the Labour Party* 'The General Council's Party': quoting Citrine's assertion that 'the General Council should be regarded as having an integral right to initiate and participate in any political matter which it deems to be of direct concern to its constituents', he concluded that '. . . the General Council of the TUC under the leadership of Bevin and Citrine abandoned its usual role of being the sheet anchor of the Party and instead moved in to take the helm'.[14] There is much to be said for this view and certainly in the last two or three years before the war, trade union power in the Labour Party was at its apogee but this state of affairs did not emerge overnight. Between 1932 and 1934, the unions were themselves too divided on basic issues and too stunned by the impact of the pit of the depression on their membership, funds and morale to exert a consistent leadership in political affairs; and the difficult years of 1935 and 1936, far from being a time of tightening of links, were a period of alienation and conflict in which mutual irritation sometimes even reached the level of talk of trade union disaffiliation from the Labour Party.

Nonetheless there was, both organizationally and ideologically, a major reassertion of the party–union links in the early 1930s. Crucial to this *rapprochement* was the revivification of the NJC as a co-ordinating body of the General Council, the NEC and the Executive Committee of the PLP. From the outset, the TUC demanded, and was granted, a position of leadership rather than equality. At the first meeting of the revived council, John Bromley of ASLEF[15] argued that '. . . while the General Council could reasonably claim to function without consultation on a purely industrial and Trade Union question, the political side of the Movement could not be quite as free, as the interests of the workers were bound up with political action'. The NEC accepted this distinction but it baulked at a notably one-sided TUC formulation which asserted that there were matters on which it would be necessary to 'preserve a definite Trade Union point of view' but saw the party's problems in a less sympathetic light: 'Under certain circumstances the Party may feel compelled to pay some regard to political expediency, and there are occasions upon which the General Council may not be able to commit themselves to a point of this description.'[16] The priority accorded to the TUC was reflected in the new constitution eventually agreed to in May 1932, under which the TUC, represented by its Chairman and six members, outnumbered the representatives of the PLP and the NEC combined, each being represented by its Chairman and two members. The constitution laid down two primary duties for the National Council:[17]

(a) Consider all questions affecting the Labour Movement as a whole, and make provision for taking immediate and united action on all questions of national emergency.
(b) Endeavour to secure a common policy and joint action, whether by legislation or otherwise, on all questions affecting the workers as producers, consumers and citizens.

This formula, wide-ranging as it was, left comfortably obscure the question of how far the National Council's decisions were mandatory and binding on the individual sections, a question which was to be settled by experience and by the growing cohesion and confidence of the trade union side as the decade progressed rather than by a paper constitution.

Why then did the NJC thrive in a way which had eluded Arthur Henderson's rather different creation of the 1920s? The main factor impelling the TUC to take the initiative in reconstituting the NJC was its disgust at the period of alienation under MacDonald and its cataclysmic dénouement. Further, the prestigious but numerically manageable membership of the National Council made it a particularly suitable medium for issuing declarations of policy on vital issues, which came to carry an authority denied to statements from individual sections, and the NJC also provided a suitable umbrella and letterhead for several campaigns, particularly the triumphant campaign against the regulations of the Unemployment Assistance Board in early 1935 which marked its breakthrough into national prominence. In July 1934, it changed its name to the National Council of Labour (NCL), a change which implied a development of its function from co-ordination *within* the labour movement to active spokesmanship and partisanship to the country as a whole.

It was only in the later 1930s that the power of the NCL became a major source of grievance for the constituency parties when it appeared to be usurping the policy-making functions of the NEC and the Labour Party Conference. But even in the early 1930s it occasionally intervened in the affairs of the Labour Party and by 1935 the NCL had established itself as the major medium for statements of policy for the whole movement and, to a lesser extent, for trade union scrutiny over the affairs of the Labour Party.

The relationship between the Labour Party and the trade unions was cloaked in an official rhetoric which diverged some way from reality although it did reflect the pre-eminent role of the unions. The Labour Party 'grew out of the bowels of the TUC',[18] declared Ernest Bevin, an obvious historical truth, if a partial one, to which the anatomical imagery imparts the suggestion of actual as well as temporal primacy. This is the keynote of the official rhetoric. Party leaders rarely engaged in public criticism of the unions whereas union leaders frequently berated the party with considerable severity. Walter Citrine expressed the ideal during an election rally in 1931: 'I want to tell you that all talk of dictatorship, of attempting to impose a policy from outside, is entirely unfounded . . . I would remind you that the Labour Movement consists of two broad divisions . . . and it has always been the policy of the Labour Movement for these two sections, in no sense rivals, but each complementary to the other . . . to work closely together and consult from time to time when any matter of policy is in question.'[19] Typically, Citrine discusses only political policy and there was no suggestion that the TUC should consult the Labour Party if an item of industrial policy were in doubt.

Hugh Dalton who, of Labour leaders, probably got on best with the union bosses, but at the same time was very aware of the problems of their political status, expressed similar sentiments from the party viewpoint: '. . . without the Trade Unions our British tree would have no roots and no stability, without the Constituency Parties it could bear no heavy crop of political fruit.'[20]

The obligatory optimism of official spokesmen was violently contested on the left where grave doubts were harboured about the political role of the unions. In particular, they were held responsible for the lamentable policy of class collaboration which, in the left's view, the party continued to espouse even after the departure of MacDonald. Not many, perhaps, shared the pessimistic view of J.T. Murphy that the Labour Party was really no more than the trade unions participating in politics and that the individual membership sections were just 'appendages of the trade unions for propaganda work and electioneering'.[21] However, Harold Laski was one of the major left-wing intellectuals in the party and he, too, placed the role of the unions in the forefront of his analysis. Writing of the state of the movement in the aftermath of the 1936 Labour Party Conference he argued that class collaboration was '. . . a cul-de-sac into which the trade union leaders have taken the Labour Movement. To get out will be a long and grim struggle, not likely to be won without bitter fighting.'[22] These strictures on the power and policy of the unions were not confined to the left of the movement and particularly in the early 1930s there was a spate of writings berating the unions not for class collaboration but for imposing a crippling and misconceived adherence to a mere sectional interest upon the party, a charge which constituted a curious mirror-image of the left-wing critique. 'It is clear [wrote Godfrey Elton in 1932] that at present the dominance of the Trade Unions is slowly paralysing the Labour Party. The Trade Unions have done, and still do, splendid work in the industrial field but in politics their day is over.'[23]

The solution preferred by Elton and others of his ilk, most notably Clifford Allen, was that the party should beg MacDonald to return to lead it, a plan which did not command very widespread support.

It is difficult to gauge the attitudes of rank-and-file trade unionists towards the Labour Party in particular and politics in general. Certainly they were not short of attempts to inform them but they had to steer a course between the caricatures of the bourgeois press (which tended to write up a supposedly unbridgeable gap between an 'airy-fairy' political wing and a solid trade union wing) and the bland exhortation to which they were subjected from the labour side. From material directed specifically at trade unionists, it appears that the Labour Party tended to regard them as canny pragmatists whose support was best ensured by stressing solid achievements and holding out the prospect of concrete benefits, rather than by lofty appeals to socialist principle or even class solidarity. For instance, a 1938 Labour Party pamphlet, *A Trade Unionist's View of Politics*, stressed such matters as the Shops Act and the Sea Fish Industry Board, on both of which the PLP had won concessions, to the exclusion of the PLP's work in opposition to the central pillars of government policy. Similarly, when dealing with the immediate priorities of a Labour Government, the raising of the school-leaving age, holidays with pay, and an improved pension scheme all take priority over the search for collective security. The same instrumental approach can be seen in an article by Walter Greenwood, who linked trade unionism and political action in a manner much at odds with the marginal and ineffective role he allotted them in his 1932 novel, *Love on the Dole*: 'People are Trade Unionists generally because they desire better conditions of life and labour. In what manner are these better conditions obtained? By parliamentary action. Hence the need of the Labour Party whose origin was Trade Unionism. Trade Unionism is the voice of the workers: the Labour Party is the voice of Trade Unionism.'[24] Such calls for support were more frequent in the 1930s than in most periods since the workers' pennies as well as the workers' votes were at stake: the 1927 Trade Disputes and Trade Union Act had, by substituting contracting-in for contracting-out, made it the task of union and party militants to prevent their political opponents from reaping the benefits of inertia, by striving to show their less concerned workmates the paramount necessity of paying the political levy which provided the life-blood of the ever-impecunious Labour Party.

There was undoubtedly much resentment among party activists about the dominant role of the unions in the organization of the Labour Party. Certainly the unions did not invariably exercise their power with any very great solicitude for the susceptibilities of the party faithful. Much of the dissatisfaction centred on the exercise of the block vote and the control by the unions of voting at Conference and on the NEC. However, the exercise of authority by the NEC was itself a cause of frequent dismay. The unions were generally represented on the NEC by men who were not General Secretaries and were in some cases of second-rate ability. They took part in all the deliberations of the NEC but it was the work of the Organization Sub-Committee which, superficially, provided the work for which their union background provided the best training. Throughout the decade, the Sub-Committee was dominated by union representatives who showed a most inadequate grasp of the difference between running a union and running a political party. Whereas in a union, geared primarily to an economic purpose and reliant above all on the maintenance of solidarity for the achievement of its objectives, loyalty to majority decisions could be enthroned as the overriding obligation of membership. Such a formula failed to do justice to the variety of social origins, the diverse and often idiosyncratic enthusiasms and the widely divergent priorities found on the political wing of the movement. Further, while the emergence of a majority in a trade union might be a dubiously democratic exercise, its legitimacy was rarely challenged with the virulence with which a large and (at least until 1937) a growing section of the constituency activists assailed decisions taken by the trade union dominated annual conferences and by the NEC. The record of the Organization Sub-Committee was depressing: the threat of disaffiliation was much too freely used against recalcitrant constituency parties while the deviations of trade unions were regarded with sympathetic understanding. The attempts of trade union members of the Sub-Committee to solve the complex feuds which so often racked local parties were frequently repudiated at grassroots level and had to be enforced by threat of 'reorganization'. Perhaps the worst example of heavy-handedness was seen in the fiasco of the League of Youth, the first but not the last demonstration of the inability of the Labour Party to run a successful youth movement.

Ben Pimlott concludes his account of the revolt of the constituency parties by asserting 'The Constituency Parties' Movement was short-lived but it brought a revolution in the Labour Party of far greater importance than anything achieved by noisier and more glamorous factional groups which captured the headlines, and claimed, with no mandate whatsoever, to speak for the rank and file.'[25]

The 1930s witnessed a partially successful rebellion by the constituency parties against the domination of the party by the union block vote. The grievances of the constituency parties' activists were manifold and the solutions proferred various but two themes stand out: first, the growth of size and contribution of the constituency parties and, second, the supposedly baneful effects of trade union dominance.

Individual membership of the Labour Party was neither adversely affected by the depression nor halted in its advance by the political catastrophe of 1931 while by contrast not only was trade union membership very slow to recover from the effects of the slump but also the aftermath of the Trades Disputes Act saw enormous gaps open up between the industrial and political memberships of some unions. Trade union affiliations to the Labour Party fell below 2,000,000 in 1932 and did not pass that figure again until 1937. The constituency parties, by contrast, were the healthiest of the party's component bodies and by 1937 individual membership had reached the impressive figure of 447,000. Although this development did not present a numerical challenge to the preponderance of the unions in the counsels of the party, the balance between affiliated and individual membership was shifting markedly in favour of the latter by the mid-1930s, stimulating demands that the constituency parties should be granted increased representation on the NEC, exclusion of the unions from voting for the constituency parties' representatives, and a greater role in decision making at Conference.

Although reformers generally prefaced their comments with expressions of admiration for the unions, the reality was that there was a considerable and growing fund of resentment. The main criticisms were that the financial contributions of the two sides were not reflected in the grossly inequitable constitutional arrangements, that the propaganda work of the constituency parties in non-industrial areas was made harder by trade union preponderance, that the unions were at best imperfectly imbued with socialist spirit and were at worst positively anti-socialist, all with the result that the party was committed to policies alien to its ideals and inimical to its electoral appeal. Ernest Bevin himself lent credence to this view in his striking and evidently accurate declaration at the 1937 Labour Party Conference that 'there are thousands of our members paying the political levy who are not conscious socialists'.[26] It was a staple argument of the constituency party militants that the TUC and its affiliated unions were not, and never had been, socialist bodies, though not many perhaps would have gone all the way with Hugh Ross Williamson who claimed that there was an unspoken conspiracy between the 'Trade Union bosses' and the National Government to maintain the present enfeebled leadership of the Labour Party by denigrating and holding down the alternative leadership which challenged the supremacy of both of them, and whose aim was 'a bold, intelligent and militantly socialist party of men of the calibre of Sir Stafford Cripps, who can neither be duped nor bribed'.[27]

The demands of the constituency party activists were alternately rejected, stonewalled and side-tracked at successive annual Conferences until 1936 when the combination of the negative attitude of the NEC and the chaotic events at the Conference itself crucially strengthened the case and reinforced the organization of the activists. The debate on the Spanish Civil War ended in the adoption of the policy of non-intervention which was passed by an overwhelming majority despite the absence of a single competent speech in favour of it. This proceeding put the legitimacy of the block vote in a very questionable light and the Conference was marked by the emergence of a Provisional Committee of constituency parties expressing a fierce resentment at the failure of the Executive to remedy its grievances and, to the alarm and annoyance of both political and industrial leaders, engaged in a partial and conditional alliance with the dissidents of the left.

At the Conference, the NEC was impelled to give a pledge to examine the grievances of the constituency parties and in 1937 came up with a series of proposals for increasing the number of constituency parties' representatives on the NEC from five to seven, allowing them to elect their own representatives without any interference and moving the date of the annual Conference from October to Whitsun in order to remove it from the shadow of the TUC in September. It was by no means certain that the reforms would be passed. The constituency party activists did not help their cause by engaging in fevered canvassing for the places on the constituency party section but the issue brought out some of the crudest statements in favour of trade-union hegemony ever heard in the troubled history of the alliance. Will Lawther declared that 'members of the Parliamentary Labour Party . . . will have to be told that the decisions of the Trade Union Movement are the decisions that have got to be accepted'.[28] The anticipated conflict did not, however, occur. At the 1937 Conference, Bevin proposed a compromise which would have involved a postponement of the reforms but when this was put to the vote there was a massive vote in favour of their immediate operation, backed by the votes of the GMWU and the NUR which had been opposed to the principle of reform. Some commentators regarded this volte-face as a splendid gesture on the part of the unions while others saw it merely as an attempt to 'do Ernie down'. 'That is the measure of Trade Union statesmanship at a crisis. Nor is it anything to be surprised at, for as Mr Dukes remarked with engaging candour a year later, "the Unions have never fought the employers half as tenaciously as they fought each other".'[29] The reforms brought only a brief respite in the demands of the more irreconcilable constituency activists.

A few words ought to be said about the contribution of trade unionists to the work of the PLP in the 1930s.

The work of the attenuated rump of Labour MPs who survived the 1931 election has been the subject of very different verdicts, with some commentators dismissive or patronizing and others claiming that it kept alive the reality of parliamentary opposition in extremely adverse circumstances. There is, however, no dispute that despite the numerical preponderance of trade union sponsored MPs (thirty-five out of the forty-six successful candidates in 1931) there was little in the way of contact between the PLP and the unions. The PLP followed an independent and advanced political line, taking its inspiration from George Lansbury and much of its detailed information from briefs specially prepared by the Labour Party Research Department. Lansbury described himself as a spokesman rather than a leader, and he was sincere in his protestations, but he was determined to maintain his small band's morale and faith in the future, and he reacted firmly against any attempts at interference from outside bodies or individuals, including trade union leaders.

The PLP received few reinforcements during the 1931 Parliament but after the 1935 election, disappointing to Labour hopes as it in many ways was, there was a wider variety of talents and social backgrounds available. There is a good deal of evidence to suggest that these reinforcements were overdue. There have always been derogatory comments about the quality of trade union MPs, but in the early 1930s, when a uniquely heavy burden fell on them, there was a rash of comments about the Labour Party treating the House of Commons as a home for retired check-weighers and so on. Typical was the comment of a writer in the *Daily Express* who argued that the power of the trade unions in the process of candidate selection (which they derived both from their financial strength and their voting power on General Management Committees) produced a system of 'rotten boroughs' but without the opening for impecunious talent that had been the saving grace of the old system. The outcome, he declared, was that trade union MPs were a bunch of 'amiable mediocrities'.[30]

Many of these men were not the ciphers they were so often made out to be but they did largely lack any appropriate training or intellectual calibre with which to justify their presence at the Palace of Westminster.

THE UNIONS AND THE PROBLEMS OF UNEMPLOYMENT

Despite all the problems associated with the rise of Hitler, the united front and the danger of war it was unemployment which presented the labour movement with its greatest challenge in the early 1930s and the issue continued to loom large throughout the decade. It was the issue which had been at the bottom of most of the tribulations of the second Labour Government and memories of the 1930s were to play a large part in the election of the Attlee Government in 1945 but the response of the labour movement was curiously ambivalent. At a time when the lives of millions were crippled by lack of work and when whole areas were plunged into seemingly unending poverty, squalor and demoralization by the decay of the industries round which they had grown up, the Labour Party's response evolved slowly away from an insistence on the impossibility of curing unemployment within capitalism towards a policy which combined a faith in a socialist future with a programme of palliatives to bring about some alleviation *before* the distribution of political and economic power was transformed. The response of both the industrial and the political wing of the movement to the practical consequences of unemployment was hampered by a number of factors: the unions were excessively rigid in their approach to the organization of the unemployed; there was indecision on the limits of justifiable protest against the government's policies; and both issues were complicated by the existence of the lively, militant, communist-led NUWM.

The problems offered a potentially fruitful field for practical unity between the trade unions and the Labour Party, aligning industrial experience and organizational capability with effective intellectual analysis and socialist idealism but these possibilities were only very imperfectly realized.

The trade unions did contribute greatly in breaking through the sterile insistence on the total transformation of society as a precondition for dealing with unemployment which hindered the Labour Party's efforts at building an employment policy in the early 1930s. At first, the influence was exercised in a muted and somewhat oblique way, yet even at the gloomiest moment of the depression, Bevin produced a carefully considered plan for reducing unemployment by raising the school-leaving age, providing adequate pensions conditional on early retirement and thus reducing the size of the potential labour force.

The most striking divergence between the reform- and crisis-orientated approaches came over the response to the New Deal, which produced an almost uniquely clear-cut contradiction between the decisions registered by the Labour Party and the TUC. From the start, the complex of measures clumsily referred to as 'Rooseveltism' found favour with the union leadership. Indeed, the TUC claimed that Roosevelt was adopting the policies which they themselves had been advocating for years. As Citrine put it: 'President Roosevelt's actions are more significant in that he is avowedly not a Socialist, and therefore his conversion to immediate reform and remedial measures which have for long been advocated by the Trade Union & Labour Movement in our own country, and by the International Federation of Trade Unions, are a convincing proof, if such proof be needed, that our policy is the only one yet put forward, which is in any way adequate to deal with the present situation.'[31] The TUC in 1933 accordingly passed a resolution which, after a ceremonial bow in the direction of the ultimate objective of socialism, praised Roosevelt's programme and called on the National Government to take similar measures to raise purchasing power and initiate national planning.

By contrast, the Labour Party a month later passed a resolution, which had the support of the NEC, proclaiming a chiliastic vision of the downfall of capitalism and the futility of measures aimed at bringing about economic recovery *within* capitalism. Such a clear-cut division between the Labour Party Conference and the TUC at which the great majority of votes were, after all, controlled by the same people, would appear to be a demonstration, if not a particularly reassuring one, of the truth of Attlee's dictum: 'The same man in his capacity as a Trade Union official may take a slightly different attitude from that which he does as a member of the Party Executive or Member of Parliament.'[32] In part, the divergence arose from the contrast between the day-to-day orientation of trade union officials towards problems of wage negotiations and unemployment benefits and the fixing of the Labour Party's eyes on electoral victory as the threshold of socialism. But the Labour Party did proclaim the view that the root of the unemployment problem lay in the decay of capitalism and although it was ready to point to the effects of the First World War, the return to the gold standard, and the policies of the National Government as factors which had exacerbated the problem, and although it never wholly lost sight of the need for palliative measures in the short term, it gave priority to the need to maintain the unemployed at a decent level of subsistence pending their relief by the achievement of socialism.

The fissure was not bridged by the adoption of Labour's new programme, *For Socialism and Peace* in 1934. For while it set out measures both of short-term relief and long-term reconstruction, no unambiguous order of priority was set down. The TUC intervened vigorously to insist that Labour should shift its emphasis unmistakably in the direction of practical measures for alleviating unemployment and improving the social services, at the expense of the more radical commitment to a rapid socialist transformation. At a time of strained relations between party and unions, this dispute caused, as Citrine put it, 'many anxious problems' and the leader of the Labour Party, George Lansbury, was deeply out of sympathy with attempts to impose policies which suggested that permanent improvements could be won within capitalism. The TUC view won through and was to find powerful confirmation in the work of the Distressed Areas Commission of the Labour Party which was established by the Party Conference in

1936. The Commission of three senior members of the NEC headed by Dalton, visited the distressed areas, took evidence from all sections of the local labour movements and produced vigorous reports condemning the National Government's failure to deal with the problem of regional decay in a determined way and propounding a large number of specific policies to revive the local economies and prevent the breakdown of communal life and local government. The proposals ranged from the appointment of a Cabinet minister for the areas to a quite ambitious plan for controlling the location of industry, but although their tone was bitterly hostile to the National Government there was little in the proposals which could not have been carried out by an interventionist capitalist government. Indeed, many of the proposals were later adopted by the post-war Labour Government. There was a good deal of criticism on the grounds that the Labour Party was wringing political advantage out of the fate of the unemployed on the basis of brief visits and banal proposals. But although, on a purely rational basis, the work would have been better undertaken several years earlier, the Commission did mark a reassertion of the possibility of limited reforms and, thus, a victory for trade union pragmatism over socialist catastrophism.

But divergencies between the political and industrial wings in the field of unemployment were not confined to the realm of policy. Difficulties even arose over the means test, the subject of so many eloquent denunciations of the unfeeling cruelty of the National Government. Although there was unanimous condemnation of the *family* means test, several in the party leadership (particularly those who, notably George Lansbury and Herbert Morrison, had experience of local government) were opposed to an open-ended commitment to provide aid to all applicants, irrespective of their resources. The TUC view, though, was uncompromisingly hostile to any means test. They were particularly concerned that trade union benefits were not exempt for means-test purposes, a state of affairs which called into question the value of trade union membership in a depression, for if, on top of enforced industrial pacifism, the financial dividends of membership were undermined, many unions might suffer catastrophic defections. To the dismay of Lansbury, the unions used their voting muscle on the NEC to impose a policy of complete abolition.

In the area of the organization of the unemployed and of mobilization of mass support against the policies of the government, the record of the 'official' movement was one of failure. Neither in building up organizations to provide activity and a sense of dignity for the unemployed nor in organizing marches and other protests did they match the efforts of the communist-led NUWM, the success of which prompted the unions and the party not to take more vigorous action themselves but to try to isolate their own supporters from the communist contagion. This negative stance appeared quite irrelevant in the distressed areas and proved impossible to enforce with uniformity.

To this dismal record there was one startling exception, the campaign in early 1935 against the regulations of the new Unemployment Assistance Board when, for a brief moment, the official movement in the form of the union-dominated NCL put itself at the head of a massive wave of protest against new scales of relief for the long-term unemployed which, contrary to declared government intention, imposed widespread and extensive cuts in the already exiguous income on which the unemployed and their families were surviving. For a time the campaign threatened the composure of the National Government and even its seemingly impregnable majority appeared vulnerable.

The NCL issued an 'Appeal to the Public Conscience' aimed at all sections of the community but at the same time it initiated a series of monster meetings at which the spirit was undoubtedly partisan and the rhetoric suffused with class feeling. By the time the campaign was under way the government had partially capitulated by withdrawing the scales and both the Communist Party and the NUWM claimed that the purpose of the NCL campaign was to head off a still-mounting 'unofficial' agitation organized by the NUWM on 'united front' lines that were anathema to the official leadership. It is, however, beyond doubt that whereas the NUWM campaign soon faded away the NCL campaign was a massive success: speakers at demonstrations were greeted with wild enthusiasm and the scope of the campaign was expanded to include the whole question of the uninsured unemployed. The status of the union-dominated NCL was greatly enhanced by the episode and it conducted activity with virtually no reference to the NEC. On this occasion, the NCL did put itself at the head of a movement of protest in contrast to the innumerable occasions in the decade when it declined to do so. This exception was probably a reflection of the way the cuts against which the protest was directed outraged the shared values of the community as a whole. Thus the 'Appeal to the Public Conscience' sought to transcend class and reached many who had no connection with the labour movement. At the same time, the struggle clearly did raise class-consciousness in working-class areas and the fury which the cuts provoked ensured wholehearted participation by the organized working class.

THE UNIONS AND THE LEFT

The 1931 crisis laid down the political context within which the Labour Party had to operate during the 1930s, confining the party to opposition with only occasional deceptive glimpses of power, and it was also one of a number of stimuli impelling the party to the left, along with the persistence of mass unemployment, the triumph of nazism in Germany and of fascism in Austria, the recrudescence of the threat of war and the Communist International's renewed appeals for a united front. The swing to the left involved not only the intellectuals of the Socialist League but, in differing degrees, very wide sections of the movement. The unions were emphatically not exempt.

There were three main elements in the attempt by the left 'to find an escape from gradualism without losing sight of Parliamentary democracy'.[33] First, there was a rejection of what was pejoratively referred to as 'the socialism of the ambulance'; of concentrating on piecemeal remedies for particular social grievances while leaving the concentrations of power in society unchanged. Second, there was a willingness to alter the forms of democracy, both to speed the process of socialist transformation and to guard against the possibility of an unconstitutional counter-attack by the defenders of the *status quo*. Third, there was a distrust of leadership within the labour movement itself, expressed in various plans to restrict a future Labour leader's freedom of action in taking office in a minority and in choosing his colleagues.

Ultimately the unions were to be crucial in checking the swing to the left but in the early years of the 1930s the unions were themselves divided, weakened and sometimes dubious of the continuing validity of their reformist methods and parliamentary orientation and did not act as an immovable barrier to the adoption of left-wing policies.

A right-wing Labour opponent of the policies of the Socialist League argued that its schemes for rapid structural economic change would be harmful to the unions: 'There are three or four million Trade Unionists, whose collective funds are as sensitive to financial perturbation as any others. Within twelve minutes of the London Trades Union Club I will find the Head Offices of twenty unions belonging to industries which would tumble to the ground at the first breath of confiscation.'[34]

Yet while in normal circumstances the stake of the unions in the established system might deter them from supporting a sudden assault upon it, the weakened state of capitalism and the near-calamitous effect of the depression on trade union membership and funds, added to the depressing experience of gradualism in action under the second Labour Government, all took their toll. Even Ernest Bevin, usually the scourge of advocates of enhanced industrial militancy and unconstitutional action, had his moment of apocalyptic vision, telling his Executive Council that he expected a further round of demands for wage cuts: 'If this be the case, I feel that whatever happens, whether we are smashed or not, we must throw all into the fight and lead the upheaval.'[35]

The depression did not lead the unions towards any head-on clash with the government or the capitalist system but it did make them less hostile and in some cases positively receptive to the ideas for structural change emanating from the left. These schemes all envisaged an enhanced role for the unions in a future socialist society in which, said Lansbury, they would find 'fresh and important work'.[36] This factor goes a long way towards explaining why enough union support was forthcoming to pass a number of left-wing resolutions against the advice of the platform at the 1932 Labour Party Conference. The *Daily Telegraph* expressed a very hostile view of these proceedings: 'The Socialist party is to be made an instrument of imposing on the nation the policy of the leaders of the trade unions and to ensure their direction of national affairs. By their control of the party machinery they are to be placed in the position which they vainly claimed last year of controlling the Prime Minister.'[37]

The trade unions were deeply involved in the complex, extended and ultimately sterile controversy over whether appointments to the boards of future public corporations should include direct representatives of the unions but they exercised no consistent direction and it is inappropriate to describe the controversy as a struggle between Herbert Morrison and the unions since the unions were themselves deeply divided. Nonetheless, the position taken by those unions (including the TGWU) which opposed the Morrisonian view that all appointments should be on the grounds of business competence alone and demanded direct representation, did reflect a changed stance towards the State after the experience of the life and death of the second Labour Government. Although there were few echoes of syndicalism, there was a fundamental stress on the issue of control. Change in industry must not merely be a change in ownership but structural change, a change in the distribution of power.

While domestic issues dominated labour politics in the early 1930s, events in Germany impinged heavily on the unions as well as on the Labour Party from 1933 onwards.

The response of the labour movement to Hitler's achievement of power may be characterized as one of horrified apathy. There was no lack of information, only of understanding. Trade union leaders had had close links with their German counterparts both through the International Federation of Trade Unions and international trade union secretariats and Citrine experienced at first hand the chilling atmosphere of the last days of Weimar, but though his analysis of what had gone wrong in Germany was in many ways perceptive, it was excessively influenced by his anti-communism. More generally, the failure of the German workers to fight and, still more, their futile attempts to conform to Nazi dictates before they were suppressed in May 1933, lost them sympathy and obscured the degree of force which Hitler commanded. The National Joint Council adopted a feeble boycott policy, testimony to a failure to comprehend the strength of the Nazi regime.

From the start, the response of the movement to events in Germany was bedevilled by the united front issue, for the Communist International promptly abandoned its 'class against class' policy, though not at once its proclivity for unmitigated denunciation of reformist parties and unions. In March 1933, the Communist Party of Great Britain, in loyal conformity with Comintern instructions, proposed to the Labour Party, the TUC and the Co-operative Movement a programme of united action against both nazism and fascism at home. These blandishments were rebuffed by the National Joint Council in a brief document, *Democracy* v. *Dictatorship*, but it was Citrine who spelled out most clearly the orthodox Labour explanation of events in Germany and of why communist approaches should be rejected. He argued that the infant German democracy had been a feeble growth which had been assassinated both by revived nationalism and by violence on the left as well as on the right and he contrasted German conditions with the far greater stability and cohesion of British society. This analysis, of course, provided comfort only if British capitalism could survive its current traumas: if Britain were to suffer an economic cataclysm comparable to Germany's it would not hold good, and there was vociferous but unsuccessful opposition mounted along these lines as well as protest against the identification of communist with fascist dictatorship as equally pernicious and inappropriate for British conditions.

Every approach made by the Communist Party of Great Britain during the 1930s, either alone or in concert with the ILP and the Socialist League, either in pursuit of a united front of all working-class parties or (from 1937) a popular front of all 'progressive' anti-fascist forces, whether working class or not, was met with summary rejection. There was, however, much more opposition to the policy of rigid exclusion than appeared from the monolithic certainties of National Joint Council statements and trade union-made conference majorities. Even in the upper echelons of the Labour Party there was no unanimity: in 1934, for instance, both the leader of the PLP and the Secretary of the Party, Lansbury and Henderson respectively, expressed grave reservations about the policy of total exclusion which found no echo in official statements.

The policy of exclusion was not imposed upon the Labour Party by the trade union leaders: doctrinaire anti-communism was rife among Labour Party officials and there was no great support for unity proposals on the NEC. However, two important qualifications need to be made.

First, the union leadership was more unified in its refusal to have anything to do with a communist alliance and debate was stultified by their implacability. Those who differed from the official line were driven either into an oppositional stance, as was the case with Sir Stafford Cripps and his allies, or into silent acquiescence. There were excellent reasons for having nothing to do with a Communist Party whose policy was dictated from outside the country and which quite failed to build a mass following. Further, an alliance would almost certainly have proved electorally counter-productive but the case for rejection was coarsened and compromised by the imposition of a bogus unanimity at the top.

Second, the opposition of the union leaders to the Labour Party engaging in any external alliance was not confined to schemes involving links with the communists. In the aftermath of Munich, there emerged a scheme for a 'National Opposition' which was free from the fatal disadvantages of entanglement with the communists, enjoyed a very wide range of support in the Labour Party from figures such as Clynes, Attlee and Dalton who were opponents of the united and popular front proposals, but which foundered on the rock of trade union opposition. Impetus was given to the scheme by the keen interest of Tory opponents of appeasement who were seeking an electoral safety-net should they break with Chamberlain. Dalton, who was deeply implicated in negotiations and was a supporter of the National Opposition scheme when it was discussed at length by the Labour Party Policy Committee, claimed that it failed because these Tory MPs lost their nerve; but it is clear that the plan fell down because the unions, both through their spokesmen on the NEC and through the NCL, imposed an immutable veto on any further negotiations and drove Attlee and Dalton into undignified and disingenuous denials that any such realignment was under contemplation. It would appear that the TUC and the union leaders were determined to prevent any external entanglements from interfering with the Labour Party's role as an instrument of trade union policy. The rhetoric laid stress on the need to maintain the 'independence' of the Labour Party but it was an independence from alliances which would necessarily qualify and dilute trade union control of its institutions and policies.

THE UNIONS AND THE APPROACH OF WAR

The part the trade union leadership played in transforming the Labour Party's policies on international relations and rearmament has often been stressed. Showing a more acute understanding of the realities of power, it is often argued, based on their day-to-day dealings with employers, they led the party away from its wholly negative attitude towards war preparations and towards a recognition of the need to defend democracy, even capitalist democracy, from its external enemies and a realistic appreciation of the necessity for confronting the aggressor powers with overwhelming force.

Labour certainly travelled a long way along this route in the 1930s yet its evolution away from its early enthusiasm for war resistance and disarmament is a complex story riddled with backslidings and contradictions. Nor was the role of the trade union leadership unambiguous. On the one hand, as hostile commentators have never ceased to point out, semi-pacifist utterances continued to emit from 'respectable' labour figures until the very eve of war and on the other the 'realism' of the union leaders did not extend to any readiness to subordinate the industrial interests of their unions to the 'national interest'.

The problem confronting the labour movement was a dual one. First, how should the movement respond to the depredations of the dictators and to the actions of the National Government in the face of them? That is, what *policy* should labour adopt? In this field there is little need to question the extent of the movement's evolution towards a realistic position. But, second, what *action* was labour to take? If the National Government really was as severe a menace as labour persistently claimed to the survival of British and world democracy, the party should surely have actively sought an opportunity to break out of the political impotence in which it was confined; and if the threat from the dictatorships was as grave as labour insisted in the later 1930s, surely the unions should relinquish their entrenched positions in industry in the interests of enhanced production and labour representatives on local authorities should overcome their distaste for their opponents and co-operate with them on schemes for Air Raid Precautions and so on. Yet the movement continued to reject any external alliance and its record on Air Raid Precautions, National Service and conscription ranged from the half-hearted to the misguided. In both cases, the role of the trade union leaders was a source of inaction rather than action, confusion rather than clarity.

In the early 1930s, debate focused not on the question of rearmament (which was not an issue until 1934) but on war resistance and in particular on whether the labour movement should adopt a policy of launching a general strike against any war in which the government of the day might seek to embroil the country. The whole labour movement was sincerely united in abhorrence of war but beyond that basic consensus there was little agreement between those on the right who, following Arthur Henderson's lead and inspired by his work at the Disarmament Conference, believed that war could be avoided by strengthening the League of Nations and the sanctions at its disposal and those on the left who completely rejected the League as no more than a front for imperialist and capitalist powers which would be more likely to use it as a cover for an attack on the USSR than as a bulwark of peace. Only the power of the organized working class, on this view, stood between the world and another war.

The unions were deeply involved in the controversy: not only would union votes determine the outcome of the debate but union power would be the sole channel for making a general strike against war a reality. As the civil servants' union leader, W.J. Brown put it: 'War is impossible without the support of workpeople. Not a unit is manned, not a shell made, not a gun is transported, save by the labours of working men.'[38] There was substantial union support for the general strike policy; ASLEF in particular was strongly committed to it despite the scepticism of its General Secretary. At the TUC in 1933 a resolution in favour of the 'general strike against war' policy was deflected by a promise by the Chairman to call a special conference but at Hastings a month later the Labour Party Conference adopted *nem. con.* a diffuse composite resolution in favour of a whole range of anti-war measures, including the general strike.

The leaders of the General Council were extremely hostile to the policy both because of the constitutional implications and of the exclusive burden it placed on the unions, and the fact that in 1933 they could not prevent and dared not even oppose its adoption is powerful testimony to the extent of the swing to the left *within* the unions. However, within a year little was left of the commitment to war resistance and the skill with which the issue was defused behind the scenes was a tribute to the reserves of power left to the leadership even when they felt it impolitic to confront the left head-on. In a complicated series of manoeuvres, the General Council pushed through a policy which did not formally repudiate the general strike as an instrument of policy but allotted it only a most marginal role and also restored the Labour Party's commitment to the League of Nations.

War and Peace, the document incorporating this skilfully engineered volte-face, was adopted both by the TUC and by the Labour Party in 1934. Within a year, its policy of support for the League even to the extent of economic and military sanctions, was to be put to the test.

The dispute within the labour movement over whether support should be given to League of Nations sanctions against Italy to halt her aggression against Abyssinia culminated in the downfall of the leader of the PLP, George Lansbury, who remained an uncompromising pacifist and campaigned unsuccessfully against a policy which, taken to its logical conclusion, might involve war with Italy. The episode has been invested with great significance not only for the development of Labour's foreign policy but also for the assertion of trade union power. J.T. Murphy argued that Bevin's famous onslaught on Lansbury at the 1935 Party Conference was not only the voice of the trade unions declaring against pacificism but also '. . . the warning of the trade unions that the policy they had formulated after the General Strike was about to dominate the Labour Party'.[39] There is, however, little evidence to suggest that the 1935 Conference marked a planned reassertion of trade union control of the Labour Party. It is easy to understand how such a view won wide acceptance. Even before the Conference, Lansbury's position as leader had become untenable: the uneasy coalition between Marxists and pacifists which had brought such triumphs as the passage of the 'general strike against war' resolution had been undermined when the USSR joined the execrated League of Nations and the worsening of the international situation rendered pure pacifism a difficult path to follow in a world of aggressive-sounding fascist powers. Lansbury seems to have realized the paradox of his position as the pacifist leader of a non-pacifist party, but by delaying his resignation he frustrated the tactics of those who wished to ease him out without an open clash and laid himself open to Bevin's vitriolic, grossly unfair but extremely memorable denunciation.

The episode was to be remembered in terms of Bevin's angry words with their strong implication of a trade union right to dictate to the party:

'Every one of us on the General Council of the TUC feel that we have been let down. We have had enough of it during the last ten or twelve years as Trade Union leaders – a very stiff time. I want to say to our friends who have joined us in this political movement, that our predecessors formed this party. It was not Keir Hardie who formed it, it grew out of the bowels of the TUC.'[40] Bevin was expressing a very personal anger at a time when relations between the party and the unions were clouded with irritation and clashing priorities but he was not speaking for the trade union leadership as a whole.

Support for sanctions in 1935 did not commit the labour movement to support for rearmament and the year 1936 saw the movement in a state of confusion and demoralization over international policy. On the one hand, the resolution passed at the 1935 Party Conference was ambiguous on whether the party would continue to oppose the actual rearmament programme of the National Government and even the full weight of Bevin's anger could not compel the leaders of the PLP to promise to cease voting against the service estimates. To make matters worse, Stafford Cripps compounded the bad publicity the party was receiving by declaring that it would be no bad thing for the British working class if Britain were conquered by Germany. On the other hand, the movement was caught up in the repercussions of the Spanish Civil War and in particular of the debate on non-intervention which the party adopted and then repudiated. It is clear that several of the union leaders including Bevin and Citrine were notably lukewarm in their support for the Spanish Republic and even after the abandonment of non-intervention continued to frustrate demands for an active policy and concrete assistance.

However, a consistent defence policy did emerge in the course of 1937 and the PLP abandoned its practice of voting against measures of rearmament. By the time of Munich, indeed, the movement had espoused a policy of firm opposition to appeasement. The role of the unions was crucial: in the absence of a Labour Party Conference in 1938, the TUC was the main forum for declaring Labour policy on foreign affairs, and, when the crisis broke, the union-dominated NCL adopted an unprecedented variety of functions: sending deputations to ministers, conducting international contacts and calling a successful demonstration at Earls Court. It issued an 'open letter' to the German people affirming the will of the British labour movement to resist aggression and plans were agreed for it to act for the whole movement should war come. In short, the NCL had become a well-informed cohesive body capable both of exerting pressure on the government and leadership within the movement.

But the emergence of a firm policy of resistance to aggression was not matched by practical developments in the trade unions' own sphere of activity. For instance, when a deputation from the General Council was due to visit Chamberlain in 1938 to discuss speeding-up the armaments programme, they made clear to the Labour Party that although they would call for a real search for collective security, the question of the pace of rearmament was a purely industrial matter between them and the government. Similarly, the unions were initially extremely cautious or hostile in responding to the government's plans for Air Raid Precautions, the growth of the Territorial Army and the Voluntary National Service Scheme. The NCL was most influential in gaining acceptance for all these measures from a union movement still suspicious of government intentions and ready to discern a threat of compulsion in the most permissive of schemes. It was therefore probably inevitable that the whole movement would declare its opposition to the very limited measure of conscription announced in April 1939. There were excellent arguments against conscription which was introduced in defiance of recent and apparently unequivocal pledges and had little immediate military rationale, but the movement's opposition to it constituted a damaging lapse from the path which the movement had been following and one, moreover, that was caused far more by trade union fears about inroads into their industrial privileges than from socialist principle. The effect of labour movement opposition to conscription did considerable harm to foreign confidence in British unity and Labour was deeply embarrassed by calls from the French socialist leader, Leon Blum, to reconsider its position. The electoral effect at home was also harmful and the most that can be said in defence of the union attitude is that their opposition was ineffective and even apologetic. The General Council deflected calls for industrial action and succeeded in preventing mass desertions from the Voluntary National Service Scheme.

Despite the reluctance of the unions to back their acceptance of the need for defence with any sacrifice of their industrial interests, the labour movement had evolved painfully but reasonably quickly away from its quasi-pacifism of the early 1930s to a position in which it faced the onset of war with greater resolution than the government.

CONCLUSION

By 1938, the union leaders were taking a strongly proprietary attitude towards the Labour Party and trade union power in the party was at its apogee. There were several reasons for this. In Bevin and Citrine, the TUC had two leaders of outstanding vigour and clarity of mind. Only Morrison and Cripps were figures of equivalent stature on the political side and while Morrison, handicapped by a four-year absence from Parliament and defeated in his bid for the leadership in 1935 by the still unregarded Attlee, continued to focus much of his energy on the local government of London, Cripps was in permanent revolt against the leadership of the movement and was a particular object of suspicion to the union bosses. More important, though, was the increased significance which the union leaders attributed to the Labour Party as a medium for the achievement of trade union policies. As the Labour Party recovered, however hesitantly, from the 1931 débâcle and as the economic prospects improved, opening possibilities of achieving real gains this side of the millenium and thus drawing the party back to the consideration of practical and limited reforms, its value to the trade unions increased. Likewise, the transformation of the Labour Party's foreign and defence policies was both in large part the work of union pressure and a factor rendering the Labour Party a more valuable instrument of trade union political purpose.

NOTES AND REFERENCES

1. K. Middlemas, *Politics in Industrial Society: The experience of the British system since 1911*, Deutsch, London, 1979, p. 214.
2. R. Currie, *Industrial Politics*, Oxford University Press, Oxford, 1979, p. 147.
3. J. Scanlon, *The Decline and Fall of the Labour Party*, Davies, London, 1932, p. 218.
4. *Locomotive Journal*, July 1930, p. 327.
5. *TGWU Record*, June 1931, p. 326.
6. R. Skidelsky, *Politicians and the Slump*, Macmillan, London, 1967, pp. 350–51.
7. R. Skidelsky, 'Crisis 1931', *The Times*, 3 Dec. 1968.
8. M. Cole (ed.), *Beatrice Webb's Diaries*, 1924–32, Longmans, London, 1956, p. 281.
9. *Labour's Call to Action: the nation's opportunity*, October 1931.
10. *General and Municipal Workers Journal*, September 1931, p. 521.
11. G. Elton, *Towards the New Labour Party*, Jonathan Cape, London, 1932, p. 20.
12. Conservative Party *Election Notes*, October 1931, pp. 25–26.
13. *Daily Mail*, 20 Oct. 1931.
14. H. Pelling, *A Short History of the Labour Party*, Macmillan, London, 1961, pp. 76–77.
15. *Minutes of Joint Meeting of NEC and General Council*, 10 Nov. 1931.
16. *Minutes of National Joint Council*, 26 Apr. 1932.
17. Ibid., 23 May 1932.
18. *Labour Party Conference Report*, 1935, p. 179.
19. W.M. Citrine, *The Trade Unions in the General Election*, TUC, 1931, p. 5.
20. H. Dalton, *The Fateful Years*, Muller, London, 1957, p. 142.
21. J.T. Murphy, *New Horizons*, Bodley Head, London, 1941, p. 310.
22. New York *Nation*, 3 Jan. 1937.
23. G. Elton, op. cit., p. 27.
24. *Labour*, September 1933, p. 4.

25.   B. Pimlott, *Labour and the Left in the 1930s*, Cambridge University Press, Cambridge, 1977, p. 140.
26.   *Labour Party Conference Report*, 1937, p. 146.
27.   H.R. Williamson, *Who is for Liberty?*, Michael Joseph, London, 1939, p. 260.
28.   *TUC Report*, 1937, p. 418.
29.   H.R. Williamson, op. cit., p. 249.
30.   *Daily Express*, 30 Sept. 1933.
31.   *TUC Souvenir*, 1933, p. iii.
32.   C.R. Attlee, *The Labour Party in Perspective*, Gollancz (Left Book Club), London, 1937, p. 73.
33.   R. Lyman, 'The British Labour Party: the conflict between socialist ideals and practical politics between the wars', *Journal of British Studies*, 5, November 1965, p. 150.
34.   *Forward*, 3 July 1933.
35.   A. Bullock, *The Life and Times of Ernest Bevin*, vol. 1, Heinemann, London, 1960, p. 519.
36.   G. Lansbury, *My England*, Selwyn & Blunt, London, 1934, p. 207.
37.   *Daily Telegraph*, 4 Oct. 1932.
38.   *War*, 15 Mar. 1933.
39.   J.T. Murphy, op. cit., p. 309.
40.   *Labour Party Conference Report*, 1935, pp. 179–80.

7 A new relationship: trade unions in the Second World War

Denis Barnes and Eileen Reid

Immediately after 1931, when the PLP came near to destruction as a result of the political consequences of the decision by Ramsay MacDonald and the major figures in the government to give priority to protecting the pound in face of opposition from the General Council of the TUC, relations between the trade unions and the government were probably as distant as at any time since the early 1900s and the influence of the trade unions on government less than at any time in that period. Their suspicion of, and hostility to, government economic and industrial policies was as great as in the 1920s and, after 1935, extended to government foreign policy. The consequences, however, given the weakness of the Labour Party and the decline in the membership and the industrial power of the trade unions in a period when unemployment did not drop below 1,500,000, was regularly above 2,000,000 and sometimes stood at nearly 3,000,000, were of little immediate political importance.

By 1945 the demands and pressures of the war had transformed the situation. The position and power of the trade unions were revolutionized by the Second World War and the relationship between governments and the trade union movement was radically changed. Fundamental in bringing about this change were the crisis of May 1940, the establishment of a Coalition Government and the appointment, by Winston Churchill, of Ernest Bevin as Minister of Labour in May 1940. Until then there was little to suggest a partnership between government and trade unions in the conduct of the war.

THE PRE-WAR YEARS

The Conservative Government under the leadership of Neville Chamberlain was fully aware of the manpower and related problems experienced between 1914 and 1918. It was expected that in a future war there would again be shortages of manpower for war production and particularly shortages of skilled labour. These manpower shortages would lead to the bidding-up of wages and, combined with other factors, present a threat of serious inflation. There could be threats to production by strikes.

The policies to be adopted to meet such problems had been the subject of debate and discussion almost from the end of the First World War. In 1922 the Committee of Imperial Defence advised that consideration should be given to plans for organizing labour and resources in the event of another war, while the problems which had been experienced between 1914 and 1918 were still in the forefront of the minds of officials and politicians. As a result two sub-committees were set up,[1] and after a report presented in July 1922, the Committee of Imperial Defence referred detailed manpower planning to a standing inter-departmental sub-committee, the Manpower Sub-Committee.

From its creation until 1939[2] the sub-committee, together with the Ministry of Labour, worked at schemes for recruiting men to the armed forces and for ensuring an adequate supply of civilian labour. The issues discussed included a recommendation that there should be a separate Ministry of National Service and, on the civilian side, the necessity for control of wages, prices and profits and for the avoidance of industrial disputes. It was not until the beginning of August 1939, however, that it was decided to give to the Ministry of Labour full responsibility in the event of war for control of the allocation and use of manpower, military and civilian, a responsibility which it had previously been reluctant to accept on the grounds that the activities in which it would be involved would interfere with its role of conciliator in industrial disputes.[3] On 8 September 1939 the Ministry of Labour became the Ministry of Labour and National Service. In this chapter our concern is with the responsibilities of the Ministry of Labour for the control of civilian manpower.

The Manpower Sub-Committee had in its final report recommended that before any Bill was produced about the control of civilian labour during a war, trade unions and employers should be brought into consultation with the Ministry of Labour. So far as the unions were concerned, past hostility meant that the omens for co-operation with government were not good; nor did the threat and outbreak of war remove trade union hostility to the government. It was not until the end of March 1939 that the Minister of Labour, Ernest Brown, met with representatives of the TUC and the British Employers' Confederation (BEC). He then put forward proposals that employers should recruit workers only through employment exchanges; that employers and workers might be approached with a view to releasing workers from less important to more important industries and that local committees of employers and trade union representatives might be set up to supervise these operations, together with a national committee to advise on general problems. On wages and industrial disputes, he said that the government intended to maintain the existing machinery of collective bargaining, but suggested consideration of the possibility that it should be compulsory to refer a dispute to an arbitration tribunal if all other attempts to reach a settlement failed.

Members of the TUC General Council met the Minister again in April, and said that they were willing to co-operate with the government, provided that it would ensure control of prices, profits and food supplies. In June, however, the General Council produced its own proposals. It suggested that joint national committees with executive powers, composed of employers and trade union representatives, should be set up for each main industry. The government should submit manpower and production requirements and the committees would then put into effect the best methods of mobilizing and transferring workers. The proposed committees should, the General Council suggested, also consider any changes necessary in the machinery for determining wages. The scheme was, not unnaturally, not acceptable to the government, as it amounted to a reduction of its authority and control. The General Council was not willing to modify its proposals.

By this time the Committee of Imperial Defence was insistent that the Ministry of Labour should produce detailed plans for the organization of labour, so that a Bill would be ready immediately on the outbreak of war. The Committee was critical of the reluctance of the Ministry to put forward proposals for legislation without first obtaining the agreement of the TUC. The reluctance of the Ministry to proceed with legislation for control of labour without the agreement or, at least, the acquiescence, of the TUC was understandable. The TUC still distrusted government intentions both on the domestic front and in foreign policy; legislation to introduce statutory controls of labour without agreement might in these circumstances result in strikes and industrial trouble.

In the face of pressure from the Committee of Imperial Defence, however, the Ministry of Labour produced a draft Bill which made it compulsory to engage workers through employment exchanges. It was thought that the TUC would not oppose such a Bill, but in discussion General Council representatives indicated that they were not satisfied with government plans to control prices and profits, and were unwilling to support the draft Bill. They protested that the government had not given them reasonable notice, and attacked the Bill as an infringement on the voluntary character of the labour market. They pressed that it should not become effective without an Order, and that any Order should be made only after the Minister of Labour had referred it to an advisory committee consisting of equal numbers of trade union and employer representatives. When the Control of Employment Bill was introduced in Parliament on 5 September, it became clear that it would be opposed by the Labour Party. The government delayed the passage of the Bill and accepted amendments which satisfied the Labour Party and the General Council.

Under the resulting Control of Employment Act, the Minister of Labour was given authority to make Orders which prohibited employers in certain industries from advertising for labour without the consent of the Minister and from engaging workers except through employment exchanges. The Minister could not, however, refuse consent to the engagement of workers unless there was suitable alternative employment of which workers were aware, and on refusal of consent workers could appeal to a Court of Referees. Before he could make any Order, the Minister had to submit a draft of his proposal to a committee, which he appointed, consisting of a chairman and equal numbers of the employers' organizations and trade unions most concerned. The Act was a compromise which seemed likely to be ineffective. If, however, the government had not produced legislation it could have been accused of surrendering to union power; if it had introduced legislation which the TUC opposed, there would have been the likelihood of industrial trouble.

THE FIRST MONTHS OF WAR: CONSERVATIVE GOVERNMENT (September 1939–May 1940)

The compromise over the Control of Employment Bill and acceptance by the government of modifications put forward by the TUC was one of the events immediately following the outbreak of war which marked a radical change in the attitude of the Conservative government to the trade union movement. At the same time, Ernest Brown met representatives of the General Council and the BEC and proposed the setting-up of an Advisory Committee with members from each side of industry and, following complaints from the General Council that the government had set up a Ministry of Supply (by the 1939 Ministry of Supply Act) without consultation, the Prime Minister, Neville Chamberlain, issued instructions to consult with the TUC and individual unions on any matter which might affect them directly or indirectly. Chamberlain's instructions were cleared with Walter Citrine, General Secretary of the TUC, before they were issued. Citrine had made it clear that the unions would collaborate with the government only if the government extended 'the fullest recognition of the trade union function on [the workers'] behalf'. A month after the outbreak of war, Ernest Brown set up the National Joint Advisory Council (NJAC), consisting of fifteen representatives from the

BEC and the same number of representatives from the General Council of the TUC. The Council was to advise the Minister on all matters relating to manpower.

The current major issue was about control of wages. The Treasury and economists outside government had been emphasizing the need for government measures – including measures on wages – to counter the inflation which would result from shortages of manpower and consumer goods. Union leaders, with the support of the Ministry of Labour, had argued in favour of the continuation of free collective bargaining, and had warned that there would be industrial trouble if the government interfered. By the time of the first meeting of the Council, increases in wages had already been agreed for shipyard workers, miners and certain steel-workers. The dockers and engineering workers were pressing claims. At the request of the employer and TUC representatives, the Chancellor of the Exchequer, Sir John Simon, was asked to discuss with the Council the problem of wages. He made points he had already made in a speech in the House of Commons the previous week,[4] stressing in particular that wage increases could not keep up with increases in the cost of living. Walter Citrine replied that workers would not support union leaders who advocated a decline in living standards. The General Council, in a five-point programme, stressed the importance of controls on prices and profits and of extending subsidies, and the undesirability of trying to restrain wage increases to meet cost-of-living increases.

While discussions on the NJAC were going on, the government had in fact decided to subsidize food prices for six weeks in order to check the rapid increase which had been taking place since the beginning of September. The steadying of food prices which this achieved did not reduce trade union opposition to wage controls or proposals to interfere with collective bargaining. The government, however, decided to continue the subsidies for six months, and the Chancellor announced the decision, although without mentioning the time limit, in the House of Commons at the end of January 1940. The Chancellor had intended to insist that unions must reciprocate by voluntary wage controls, but in the end made no mention of any such 'deal'.[5] The fruitless discussions on the NJAC continued until the Ministry of Labour persuaded the government that there was no point in further attempts to persuade the unions to co-operate on wage control. It was hoped that food subsidies would lead to a reduction in the number of wage claims, and in the vigour with which claims were pressed.

By the spring of 1940 it was clear, however, that increasing labour shortages in certain industries and competition for scarce labour were beginning to force up wages, particularly in the engineering industry. The view still held by the Ministry of Labour, that the first essential step to checking competition for workers was to convince union leaders and unions that the government wanted to work in co-operation with them and that, without this, attempts to impose manpower and wage controls might lead to widespread industrial unrest, was not readily acceptable to critics of the Ministry's policy. The critics argued that the government could delay action no longer, whether or not the unions were ready to agree to some form of wage control. The government was criticized for failing to deal with distribution of labour to essential industries and for failing to prevent employers offering wage increases to obtain labour. It was argued that there was no guarantee that food subsidies would result in an agreement to restraint in wage increases, that any such subsidies should be part of a wages policy and that the unions should be 'brought under control'. The argument was unresolved and plans for changes in policy were still under consideration when the Chamberlain Government fell and the Labour Party joined the Coalition Government of Winston Churchill.

THE WAR: THE COALITION GOVERNMENT

The formation of the Coalition Government (and the military disasters of 1940 and 1941) transformed the relationship between government and the trade union movement. The 'deadlock' which had existed between the two, and which had prevented the adoption by government of any effective manpower policies, was broken. The development of such policies based on the principle of (almost equal) partnership between government and the trade union movement – or at any rate its leaders and the General Council of the TUC – is the main theme of this chapter. It is discussed under four heads:

1. The immediate steps following the crisis of May 1940;
2. Wages;
3. Industrial relations;
4. The mobilization of manpower.

IMMEDIATE STEPS, MAY 1940

The most significant appointment to the Cabinet in terms of the labour movement (and of the country) was that of Ernest Bevin as Minister of Labour. A leading figure on the General Council for twenty years, Bevin may be regarded as the 'creator' of the TGWU, and he was by 1940 the most influential trade unionist in the country. As Minister of Labour he was, in effect, the trade union representative in the Cabinet and the key figure from the labour movement in the government. His major responsibilities were to achieve the highest level of war production and for this purpose to determine the allocation of labour between activities essential to the war effort, to contain the inflationary wage pressures which had become apparent since 1938 and which were likely to be intensified by the new situation, and to avoid industrial trouble, which would have an adverse effect on the level of production.

In the crisis of May 1940 (after the defeat of France), Parliament passed an Emergency Powers (Defence) Act under which the government could by Order exercise complete control over property and persons. This was the basis for the statutory powers to be taken to allocate manpower and deal with industrial relations and wages. The main principles of the powers which would be needed had already been decided within the Ministry of Labour. It was only with the crisis of 1940 and the establishment of co-operation with the unions that they could, with Bevin as Minister, be put into effect.

In the following months Orders were made under the Act giving the Minister of Labour power to prevent employers engaging workers except through labour exchanges, to direct people to particular jobs and prevent them leaving essential jobs, to protect them from dismissal and to regulate some working conditions. The Orders provided the legal framework for the mobilization of labour. All the Orders were agreed with the General Council and, if appropriate, with individual unions. Bevin insisted that the powers available must be agreed among government, trade unions and employers and that they must be reserved for use in the last resort. The civilian manpower operation for which he was responsible would work only if it was generally accepted, and the co-operation and active support of the unions were essential for that purpose. (His policy on wages and industrial relations was to be based on the same belief that agreement and consent must be the basis of policy and that legal powers should be used only where these had failed.) The general strategy of the operation was set out from time to time in manpower budgets which indicated the desired distribution of manpower between the services and essential civilian work.

Within weeks of becoming Minister, Bevin had appointed within the Ministry a small Labour Supply Board of industrialists and trade union officers to advise on and oversee the implementation of manpower policies. Bevin himself was Chairman of the Board and the members were Major-General K.C. Appleyard, R. Coppock, J.C. Little, A.P. Young[6] and the Permanent Secretary of the Ministry. After a few months the Board ceased to play any significant part in policy making or administration. After daily meetings for a short period it ceased to meet and some members of the Board left the Ministry. It was, however, the first example of a policy which continued throughout the war of recruiting to the Ministry people from management and the trade unions to administer wartime manpower policies. The most eminent recruit from outside was Sir William Beveridge, who was put in charge of manpower operations of the Ministry, but who also left after a comparatively short stay.

Immediately after taking office Bevin called his first meeting of the NJAC. He stated that the handling of industrial disputes would require careful consideration of the issue of arbitration, and that there might be a need to alter the arrangements for adjusting wages, though the existing joint negotiating machinery would be retained so far as it was possible to do so. He insisted that close attention must be paid to the health and welfare of workers.[7] He concluded:

We [the government] came to the conclusion that with the good will of the Trades Union Congress, the Unions and the Employers' Federation, a little less democracy, and a little more trust in these difficult times, we could maintain to a very large degree intact the peace-time arrangements, merely adapting them to suit these extraordinary circumstances.

The Council unanimously agreed to co-operate to secure the defence of the country and to set up a Joint Consultative Committee of fourteen members, seven from each side of the Council. From then on, the full Council met only occasionally, while the Joint Consultative Committee met repeatedly, under the chairmanship of Bevin, to advise the Minister on matters of common interest to employers and workers arising from the conduct of the war.

A few days later Bevin spoke to a meeting of representatives of trade unions, telling them of his plans and asking them to tell their members what was required of them. At the end of the meeting the representatives pledged that the trade union movement would use all its resources to provide the arms and munitions required.

WAGES

Of greater importance was a request to the Joint Consultative Committee to prepare proposals on how wages might be 'regulated' without industrial trouble. Recommendations were made by the Committee on 4 June 1940 and the Conditions of Employment and National Arbitration Order, No. 1305, made in July under the Defence Regulation 58AA, was largely based on these recommendations. Collective bargaining would continue, but subject to certain restrictions. The Order required that if a dispute could not be settled the parties must give twenty-one days notice to the Minister of Labour, who could then attempt to settle it by conciliation or other methods, or refer it to a new body, the National Arbitration Tribunal, which consisted of three appointed members (including the Chairman) and two selected from panels representing employers and workers respectively. Strikes (or lock-outs) before the end of the twenty-one days notice or against awards of the Tribunal were illegal.

It was clear from the limited restrictions on collective bargaining that Bevin and the government were relying on the reasonableness and sense of responsibility of unions, workers and employers. The approach did not receive universal support. *The Times*, for example, argued that the National Arbitration Tribunal might prevent strikes, but it could not ensure control of wages.[8] The first Chairman of the Tribunal, Lord Simonds, also expressed doubts. Bevin and the government did not alter their approach. They hoped to encourage the reasonableness of unions and workers by control of the cost of living.

A general prices policy was not, however, adopted until April 1941, although there were various piecemeal subsidies. The Chancellor, Sir Kingsley Wood, announced the policy in his budget speech, saying that he hoped by means of subsidies to keep the cost-of-living index within the range 125 to 130, and to hold wages at their current levels. If, however, wage increases began to spiral, the prices policy would be abandoned.[9] Bevin and the Ministry of Labour continued to resist demands that steps should be taken to control wages if prices were to be controlled. The argument for not interfering with wages was made on two grounds: first, good industrial relations depended on the unions exercising their authority in day-to-day adjustments of wages and conditions; secondly, industrial peace depended on facilities for making claims for increases in wages and having these discussed. While the Lord President's Committee, then under the chairmanship of Sir John Anderson, accepted these views, it pressed for a statement on the government's economic policy which would refer to the need to restrain wages. The resulting White Paper, *Price Stabilisation and Industrial Policy* (Cmd 6294), which had been discussed with the General Council, warned of the dangers of inflation, but to avoid any suggestion of a general 'freeze' or direct control of wages, included a statement on 'special cases' for wage increases: where productivity had increased, where there were low-paid workers or where there had been changes in the form of production.

The first important increase in wages after the publication of the White Paper in July 1941 was a rise for agricultural workers, which was followed by an increase for railway workers in December. These increases were justified on the grounds that they were for low-paid workers, but they were followed by claims from comparatively highly-paid workers in engineering and shipbuilding. These claims were conceded and there were fears that there would be a general upward movement in wages. Once again the issue of government control of wages was raised and Bevin continued to oppose a policy of government control, arguing that wage control was unacceptable unless accompanied by more general controls of other financial aspects of production. Pressure for wage increases continued, however, particularly among lower-paid workers, including the miners, whose resentment at what they regarded as lack of sympathy with their case had led to unofficial strikes. (Many men – some 36,000 in the first six months of 1942 – had been transferred from munitions factories to mines, and had incurred severe reductions in wages as a result.) The miners' claim was referred to a Board under the chairmanship of Lord Greene (Master of the Rolls), and in June 1942 a minimum weekly wage was instituted for adult mineworkers. The 'Greene Award' amounted to 2s. 6d. per shift for adult workers, almost 15 per cent of the earnings per shift of adult workers in the March quarter of 1942. The effects could not be isolated, and further increases followed for railwaymen and other groups.

Once again the government came under severe criticism for its failure to devise a wages policy, and there was a debate in both the House of Commons and the House of Lords. In the House of Commons, Bevin stressed the undesirability of setting aside the joint negotiating machinery which had brought together employers and workers, before it could be shown to have failed completely. His standing in the government ensured success for his approach. The debate in October 1942 was the last occasion on which there was a parliamentary challenge to the government's wages policy.

Some assessment of the soundness of Bevin's policy can be made by looking at the figures for increase in wage rates and increase in the cost of living. In the first month of the war the cost of living, as measured on the cost-of-living index,[10] rose by over 6 per cent; in the first year of the war it rose by over 20 per cent. In the latter period, wage rates increased by about 14 per cent, considerably less, therefore, than the increase in the cost of living. Between September 1940 and September 1941, there was little difference in the increase in wage rates and the increase in the cost of living: wage rates rose by about 8 per cent, while the cost-of-living index showed an increase of 6 per cent. Figures for the remaining years of the war do not show a great tendency for the increase in wage rates to spiral rapidly: although increases were higher than the increase in the cost of living after the introduction of the government's prices policy, the average annual rate of increase from September 1941 to September 1945 was about 6 per cent. By September 1945, wage rates had increased by about 50 per cent over their level in September 1939, while the rise in the cost of living over the same period was about 31 per cent.

It was also the case that the average level of increase in wage rates for manufacturing and related industries rose by about 43 per cent over the war period, compared with about 52 per cent for all industries and services. The increase was about 10 to 12 per cent above the increase in the cost of living over the same period. Industries excluded from the manufacturing and related industries group included railways, coalmining and agriculture, where pre-war wages had been comparatively low, and where workers were awarded higher increases. *Earnings* for workers in the manufacturing group of industries, however, rose steeply during the war period: by July 1945 the index of average weekly earnings for those workers showed an increase of about 80 per cent over the level in October 1938. This was, however, a reflection of the circumstances of employment: long hours, with overtime rates (for most of the period) considerably above the basic, and a widespread system of payment by results as an incentive to increase output.

The fears that absence of direct statutory control of wages would result in a dangerous level of inflation can, therefore, be said to have been exaggerated. Although the increase in earnings seemed at the time extremely large, certainly when compared with the years before 1939, it was in part a result of the circumstances of wartime production, when long working hours and extra effort were required. On balance the decision of the government not to introduce direct control of wages appears to have been right. Wage controls might well have been impossible to enforce and, if enforced for a period, might have ultimately been rejected with disastrous inflationary consequences and serious industrial unrest.

INDUSTRIAL RELATIONS

Quite apart from the protracted argument within government about control of wages, there was also argument about the operation of Order 1305, which made strikes illegal. In the first six months of its being in operation there were no prosecutions under the Order, although there were over 900 stoppages beginning in 1940. Bevin and the Ministry of Labour took the view that disputes, even if illegal, were best dealt with by conciliation and co-operation with both sides of industry. Prosecution under the Order would interfere with this approach. In any event, it was argued, legal action should be taken only when it was possible to enforce penalties: it was not possible to send large numbers of workers to prison; it was desirable not to make martyrs of a few. The first convictions under the Order took place in Manchester in April 1941, when six engineering apprentices were bound over for twelve months, on the sum of £5 each. The reluctance to prosecute came under criticism, both publicly and within Government on the grounds that legislation which could not be enforced ought not to have been promulgated.

As a result the position with regard to Order 1305 was reviewed in October 1941. By this time there had been over a thousand illegal strikes, with prosecution taking place on only six occasions. There was continuing trouble in the coalfields, and at the end of the year David Grenfell, a former miner and now Minister of Mines, decided to prosecute 1,050 strikers from Betteshanger Colliery in Kent. His action was supported by the Cabinet but opposed by Bevin. This was the first large-scale prosecution under the Order. Three officials of the local union branch were imprisoned (the Chairman, the Secretary and one committee member) and the miners themselves were fined. The final outcome, however, was a settlement of the dispute, more or less on the strikers' terms, by a process of negotiation with the jailed union officials, the release of the officials and non-payment of the fines. The limits to the use of the powers under the Order 1305 and the futility of mass prosecutions and imprisonment as a final penalty were exposed. There were no further wartime imprisonments under the Order.

In all, under Order 1305, there were 109 prosecutions of workers and two prosecutions of employers. In England and Wales proceedings were instituted on the authority of the Minister of Labour in 39 cases, and in Scotland, on the authority of the Lord Advocate, on 72 occasions. In Scotland almost one-half of the prosecutions arose out of trouble in the coalfields. By 1944 strikes were so frequent that the Lord Advocate[12] gave up prosecuting in Scotland, and in England and Wales in 1944 there were only three prosecutions, in two of which the Ministry of Labour lost the case, the magistrate deciding that the stoppages were lock-outs and not strikes. The last prosecution was in January 1945 when 127 boilermakers who had been on strike for 3 months were prosecuted and fined.

Bevin's reluctance to resort to legal action under Order 1305 reflected his general position that co-operation and not compulsion was the best – or indeed the only – means of achieving success in the civilian manpower operation for which he was responsible, and his belief that in any case too-frequent resort to the law would increasingly expose the weakness of Order 1305. He preferred to rely on the deterrent effect of declaring strikes illegal (an effect which excessive use of the deterrent would erode), on giving employers and unions full opportunity to negotiate and on unions 'controlling' their members. Union 'control' of members weakened as the war continued, particularly after the middle of 1943, when the incidence of unofficial strikes and number of working days lost increased rapidly. The development was understandable. The conditions of war, which necessitated long hours of work, rationing and restrictions of various kinds, inevitably led to increasing dissatisfaction. Secondly, with union officers committed to the government's labour and wage policies and preaching restraint, the tendency of workers to take matters into their own hands was bound to increase. Legal action would not have solved the problem, and where large numbers of workers were involved, it would have revealed clearly the weakness of Order 1305.

During the war, more than one-half of the strikes which took place were over wages and a large proportion of the remainder over other working conditions or arrangements, disciplinary proceedings or demarcation disputes. The industries most seriously affected were coalmining and engineering and allied industries. The most serious stoppage in coalmining, where there was continuous unrest, occurred in the spring of 1944, mainly in South Wales and Yorkshire. About 250,000 workers were involved and nearly 1,750,000 working days were lost. In engineering and allied industries most stoppages were local, and were often limited to a single establishment. Apart from those in coalmining and engineering, the two most serious stoppages (both in 1943) were in transport and the docks. In May 1943 over 12,000 bus drivers and conductors went on strike in protest against the rejection by a special tribunal of their claim for increased wages, and in August 16,000 dockers in Liverpool and Birkenhead went on strike in sympathy with workers who had been suspended for failure to work overtime.

The number of industrial disputes and the number of working days lost through stoppages increased every year from 1940 to 1944.[13] After the middle of 1943, Bevin and trade union officers increasingly blamed left-wing agitators for strikes, including strikes in the coalfields and the Clyde shipyards. To strike was an offence under Order 1305, but incitement to strike was not, and Bevin pressed for legislation which would make it an offence to incite or instigate strikes. Following the stoppage in the Yorkshire and South Wales coalfields in 1944, a new Defence Regulation, 1AA, was made by Order in Council on 17 April. The Regulation stated that 'no person shall declare, instigate or incite any other person to take part in, or shall otherwise act in furtherance of, any strike among persons engaged in the performance of essential services or any lock-out of persons so engaged'. The maximum penalties for incitement were severe: five years imprisonment or a fine of £500 or both. At the same time Defence Regulation 1A was amended to make peaceful picketing illegal.

The TUC in September 1943 supported the Regulation by a majority of less than a million and, in general, there was a good deal of doubt and controversy about it. While Bevin argued that it would have a deterrent effect, it would have been even more difficult to apply than Order 1305. It might have been possible to bring 'offenders' to prosecution, but it would have been almost impossible to establish guilt in a court of law. Harold Emmerson, Chief Industrial Commissioner, responsible in the Ministry for industrial relations since 1942, reporting on evidence collected by MI5, said that the success of political agitators depended on the existence of real grievances which were not resolved, or were not resolved quickly enough. Strikes were not fomented by political agitation but might be prolonged by it if the real causes of dispute were not dealt with. The Regulation was strongly criticized by left-wing members of the Labour Party, and Aneurin Bevan moved its annulment in the House of Commons. The Order was not annulled, but was never used before it was withdrawn in May 1945.

THE MOBILIZATION OF MANPOWER

As with his policies on wages and industrial relations, Bevin's policy on 'direction of labour' reflected his belief that the mobilization of civilian manpower could only be achieved on the basis of persuasion and voluntary co-operation; the power of direction to go or to remain in a particular job was primarily a means of indirect pressure and only to be used in the last resort. He aimed to secure co-operation by discussion and conference before decisions were reached, by information and explanation, and by paying increased government attention to the welfare and conditions of workers.

So far as discussion, conference and information were concerned, as has already been mentioned, there was discussion with the Joint Consultative Committee on the best way to avoid industrial disputes before Order 1305 was promulgated and the Order was, generally, based on its recommendations. Wages policy was similarly discussed with the Committee. The Committee was consulted on the powers taken to allocate and direct manpower. Large numbers of women were entering employment to replace men conscripted for the services and a Women's Consultative Committee was set up in March 1941 to advise on matters relating to their employment. Where large numbers of workers were to be reallocated to particular industries, managers of employment exchanges were encouraged to co-operate and have discussions with the employers' associations and trade unions closely concerned in advance of the reallocation. Bevin also spoke directly to union representatives himself, as after the passage of the Emergency Powers (Defence) Act. The welfare and conditions of workers were a matter of prime concern: their suitability for the work in question, wages, housing, food – all had to be satisfactory before Bevin would agree to the issue of any directions, or to schedule any establishment under the Essential Works Order. The functions of the Factory Inspectorate transferred from the Home Office (see note 7) were extended and the Inspectorate was strengthened to deal with these welfare issues.

There were criticisms of Bevin's policy on the mobilization of civilian manpower, including criticisms from colleagues within the Cabinet, notably from Lord Beaverbrook, as of his policies on wages and industrial relations. It was argued that the process of reallocating labour was too slow and that too much weight was given to trade union views. Other methods, however, may in the long run have been less successful. The mobilization of civilian manpower was highly effective compared with that of many other countries. Until the last years of the war there were relatively few serious industrial stoppages, and the threat of serious wage inflation was avoided. Union views were certainly a major influence on both the substance and conduct of policies, but the necessity for co-operation with organized labour had been recognized in the 1930s in the discussions of manpower policy which had stressed the need for consultation and co-operation if control of labour, wages and industrial disputes were to be possible. It is certain that this co-operation would not have been achieved without a Coalition Government and probably not achieved to the same degree if Bevin had not become Minister of Labour in 1940. There was little evidence of it during the period of the Chamberlain Government in 1939–40. The basic fact, however, is that only the immediate threat of national disaster created the partnership between the government and the trade union movement which continued throughout the war. Whatever the terms and consequences of the partnership on each side, and whatever criticisms can be made of it, it was a central feature of the deployment of manpower for the purposes of the war.

POST-WAR RECONSTRUCTION PLANS

From 1940 to 1945 trade union views on mobilization of labour, wages and industrial relations, as expressed in Bevin's policies, prevailed. His (and union) influence on related issues which could directly affect war production – rationing, prices, the protection of the civilian population – was considerable and at times decisive. The extent of union influence on the development of policies for the post-war period is, however, more difficult to assess. Certainly on one issue of major importance to them they were ineffective: Bevin failed to persuade Winston Churchill and the Cabinet to repeal or to amend the 1927 Trade Disputes and Trade Union Act or to secure a commitment to repeal it after the war. Major plans for post-war 'reconstruction', including the reform of the education system prepared for by the 1944 Education Act, the re-organization of health services, and housing policies, reflected a consensus within the Coalition Government in which the trade union influence was only one of many. The Beveridge Report on social insurance, published in December 1942, which became in the public mind the centrepiece of what was to be the post-war welfare state, was supported by the trade unions, but they did not attach high priority to it.

For the unions, the crucial pronouncement on post-war policy was the White Paper, *Employment Policy* (Cmd 6527) published in May 1944. This accepted the expansionist economic policies designed to create jobs which the TUC had pressed on governments since 1929 (though it also, of course, represented a general movement in the views of economists and politicians in all parties). It committed post-war governments to having 'as one of their primary responsibilities the maintenance of a high and stable level of employment' and to using government policies, including public expenditure, to influence demand to achieve this.

The commitment was made in general terms, and the White Paper emphasized the problems of a 'full' employment policy, as well as the conditions necessary for its success, which to a great extent rested on the efforts of employers and workers. These efforts would include keeping wages and prices stable, maintaining mobility of workers between occupations and localities and the requirement that 'trade unions examine their trade practices to ensure that they do not constitute a serious impediment to an expansionist economy and so defeat the object of a full employment programme'. In practice it was nevertheless to be the precursor of the post-war commitment to 'full employment' which was to dominate the economic policies of governments for thirty years. It was welcomed by the General Council, who pointed out that it had urged the policy on governments since 1929 but who made it clear that this alone did not meet its view of the economic and industrial requirements of the post-war period.

The TUC had been preparing for the post-war period since 1943, and shortly after the publication of *Employment Policy 1944* set out its objectives in its *Interim Report on the Post-War Reconstruction*, published in July 1944, which stated that the trade union movement was determined to have a 'decisive share in the actual control of the economic life of the nation'. The report fully supported a policy of full employment but insisted that trade unions should function without State interference and represent their members through free collective bargaining. It 'pledged' the unions to act reasonably and responsibly, as they had done during the war, so that full employment would not be prejudiced. In its specific proposals, the *Interim Report* for the most part repeated those in *Trade Unionism and the Control of Industry, 1932* and reports of the later 1930s, e.g. the establishment of a national industrial council, which would advise the government on all aspects of industrial policy and would have representatives of trade unions and employers and its own administrative staff, State control over banking, and the nationalization of the fuel and power, transport and iron and steel industries. Industries which remained in the private sector would be influenced by government through its control of purchasing and licensing and the continuation of price controls.

SOME CONSEQUENCES OF THE WARTIME PARTNERSHIP

After twenty years of opposition to governments, both Conservative and Labour, the position of the trade union movement in relation to government and in the country was transformed between 1940 and 1945. The unions could claim to have influenced – almost decided – manpower policies vital to the war effort and had worked in partnership with government to administer those policies. Ernest Bevin had become the most important national figure so far produced by the labour movement. He (and his Labour Party colleagues) had been in office for far longer than any previous representative of the labour movement. His personal standing and the wartime record of the trade union movement which he represented were major factors in the election of 1945, which returned the first Labour Government with an overall majority in the House of Commons.

The Labour Party manifesto for the election, following earlier proposals for 'reconstruction' in *Full Employment and Financial Policy*, included commitments to all the major points put forward by the TUC, and between

1945 and 1951 the government carried through a programme which gave effect to the long-standing objectives of the trade union movement.

The effective working partnership between the government and the General Council, established during the war, continued. The latter helped the government to meet the serious immediate post-war economic difficulties by continuing to accept the need for restraint in collective bargaining and by accepting the continuance in peacetime of legal restrictions on collective bargaining and the right to strike which had been introduced in the crisis of 1940. The fact that many of the personalities involved in the co-operation of the war years – on the one side Arthur Deakin, Thomas Williamson and William Lawther,[14] on the other Bevin and Attlee – were the same, was a crucial factor. The conflicts which had arisen between the two sections of the labour movement between 1920 and 1931 and which had led, for the politicians, to the near fiasco in 1931, were avoided. The trade union movement finally and triumphantly achieved the political power which had prompted the formation of the Labour Party in 1900 and the reform in the movement and the party in 1918.

There were other consequences of the wartime partnership, less dramatic but important. The insistence by the unions during and after the war that collective bargaining should continue and could be reconciled with the policy of full employment led to persistent problems for post-war governments. Full employment gave the unions greatly increased bargaining power. The 'annual wage round' was firmly established, and the annual increases were inflationary. Although the use of union power was restrained between 1945 and 1951, the outcome of collective bargaining in these years led to a renewal of the debate within the Attlee Government about the need for a 'wages policy' reminiscent of the arguments in the Coalition Cabinet in 1940 and 1941. Sir Stafford Cripps, Aneurin Bevan and others were not convinced that collective bargaining was 'the best wages policy there is',[15] though it continued to be government policy. Government commitments after 1945 to 'manage' the economy to ensure full employment, stable prices, economic growth and a balance of payments to protect the value of the pound made it, however, increasingly difficult for the government to stand aside from the process of collective bargaining. The extension of public ownership and the creation of the 'mixed economy' meant further involvement.

These changes and the need to mitigate the difficulties for the pursuit of government economic policy created by the process of collective bargaining led the Conservative Governments of 1951 to 1964 to maintain as close a relationship as possible with the trade union movement, in an attempt to continue some elements of the working partnership of the war. At least while the wartime generation of politicians and trade union leaders continued to be active in affairs the relationship between Conservative Governments and the trade unions was very much closer than in the pre-war years. The desire on the side of the government to maintain this position was underlined by the establishment in 1961 of the NEDC, though it is true that all efforts in the 1950s and 1960s to secure from the trade unions what government regarded as the necessary degree of co-operation over wages ended in failure. The Wilson Government of 1964 aimed more ambitiously to recreate the partnership of the Attlee Government, including – it was hoped with the support of the General Council – the same element of wage restraint that had been given to Bevin and Attlee. The failure of the Wilson Government marked the beginning of a decade of conflicts between governments and the trade unions reminiscent of the 1920s, except for the all-important fact that governments were now defeated by the industrial and political power of the unions.

The conflicts of the 1970s were also in part a legacy of the partnership of governments and the General Council between 1940 and 1951. That partnership had led to increasing tensions within the trade union movement. Conflict between union leaders and activists at lower levels was the inevitable consequence of the restraint in collective bargaining urged jointly by governments and the General Council. As the wartime generation of trade union leaders retired some of the activists succeeded them. After the mid-1950s important and influential members of the General Council became increasingly reluctant to work in partnership with governments and, as became evident under the Wilson Government, the General Council was unable to make any such partnership effective. The trade unions, though immensely more powerful than before the war, reverted increasingly to their traditional pre-war role of pressure groups in opposition to government.

NOTES AND REFERENCES

1. The Sub-Committee on National Service in a Future War and the Sub-Committee on the Supply of Munitions and Armaments in a Future War.
2. In early 1939 the Manpower Sub-Committee was raised to ministerial status as the Manpower Policy Committee, and a Manpower Technical Sub-Committee was created.
3. The Military Training Act of May 1939 and the National Service (Armed Forces) Act of September 1939 had already given National Service functions to the Ministry of Labour.
4. HC Debs., vol. 355, col. 160–75, 29 Nov. 1939; esp. col. 168: '. . . one of the chief contributions we can make . . . is, within the limits that are possible, to do without rises of wages and not to assume that, if there should be . . . some rise in costs, therefore automatically our remunerations must all go up on a sliding scale'.
5. HC Debs., vol. 356, col. 1154–56, 31 Jan. 1940.

6.   Respectively, Chairman of North Eastern Trading Estates and a member of the management board of the Engineering and Allied Employers National Federation; General Secretary of the National Federation of Building Trade Operatives; former President of the AEW; and Managing Director of British Thomson-Houston Company Ltd.

7.   The Factory Inspectorate, previously with the Home Office, was transferred to the Ministry of Labour in June 1940, and there was a general extension of 'welfare' activities by the Ministry. When the Essential Work Order was passed in 1941, Bevin refused to schedule any establishment unless he was convinced that the health and welfare arrangements were satisfactory.

8.   *The Times*, 22 July 1940.

9.   HC Debs., vol. 370, col. 1320–22.

10.   All items. *Source: British Labour Statistics, Historical Abstract 1886–1968*, Department of Employment.

11.   Basic hourly rates of wages, all manual workers, all industries and services. *Source: British Labour Statistics, Historical Abstract 1886–1968*, Department of Employment.

12.   The then Lord Advocate, T.M. Cooper, had openly questioned the viability of Order 1305.

13.   In general, the conciliation and arbitration activities of the Ministry increased greatly during the war period and immediately after. Over 2,300 disputes were referred to the Ministry between 1939 and 1946. About one-half of these were withdrawn or resolved by the parties themselves; about 50 per cent of the remainder were sent to the National Arbitration Tribunal, and the rest to either the Industrial Court or a single arbitrator. The Tribunal issued 907 awards, single arbitrators and boards of arbitration 365, the Industrial Court 361 and the Civil Service Arbitration Tribunal 43. *Source:* Ministry of Labour, *Annual Reports, 1939–48*.

14.   Respectively, General Secretaries of the TGWU and the GMWU and President of the NUM.

15.   The view of Sir Godfrey Ince, the then Permanent Secretary of the Ministry of Labour.

8 The vagaries of participation 1945–1960

Ken Coates

At Blackpool, on 10 September 1945, there opened the first post-war Congress of the TUC 'with loud cheers'. 'We are offered', said the President, Ebby Edwards of the NUM, 'the opportunity of making a clean new start.'[1] He then plunged straight into a discussion of the problem of safeguarding peace and controlling the atomic bomb. Fifteen years later, the start no longer quite so clean, the Congress was still preoccupied with the same issue. This preoccupation with world affairs was perhaps a symbolic indicator of the change in outlook which had come to mark the British unions. Ernest Bevin, the one-time dockers' KC, had become Foreign Secretary in a Labour Cabinet which included five other union-sponsored members, and had the support of no less than 120 trade union backed MPs in a total roll of 393 Labour Party representatives.

The trade union movement had arrived. The aspirations articulated by Ernest Bevin and Walter Citrine (still General Secretary of the TUC in 1945) after the defeat of the General Strike in 1926 had, in the main, become material facts. The war had brought the TUC into direct consultation with government on a wide variety of public issues. Congress had established itself as the unchallenged centre of trade union representation, with only a handful of public service organizations holding any substantial membership outside its ranks. While outsiders accepted its status, the TUC General Council also held unchallenged sway over the affiliated organizations themselves.

Yet the structure of the trade union movement in 1945 remained, to put it kindly, archaic. There were, in that year, 191 unions, organizing 6,576,000 workpeople, affiliated to the TUC (see Table 2).

Half these bodies organized less than 5,000 people apiece, so that they represented less than 2.5 per cent of union total membership. Nine organizations had over 100,000 members each, and together accounted

TABLE 2

Year	Total union membership (000s)	Total TUC affiliated membership (000s)	Number of unions in TUC	Potential union membership (000s)	Retail prices (1930 = 100)	Wage earnings (1930 = 100)	Unemployment (%)
1945	7,875	6,576	191	20,400	145.7	196.0	1.2
1946	8,803	6,671	192	20,481	150.8	207.0	2.5
1947	9,145	7,540	187	20,563	159.0	221.0	3.1
1948	9,363	7,791	188	20,732	169.8	239.0	1.8
1949	9,318	7,937	187	20,782	174.9	249.0	1.6
1950	9,289	7,883	186	21,055	180.5	262.9	1.6
1951	9,530	7,828	186	21,177	197.1	289.5	1.3
1952	9,588	8,020	183	21,252	215.0	312.3	2.2
1953	9,527	8,088	183	21,352	221.8	331.6	1.8
1954	9,566	8,094	184	21,658	225.9	353.2	1.5
1955	9,741	8,107	183	21,913	236.0	386.0	1.2
1956	9,778	8,264	186	22,180	247.8	416.9	1.3
1957	9,829	8,305	185	22,334	257.0	436.2	1.6
1958	9,639	8,337	185	22,290	264.6	451.2	2.2
1959	9,623	8,176	186	22,429	266.0	471.7	2.3
1960	9,835	8,128	184	22,817	268.8	502.2	1.7

for nearly 65 per cent of total membership. Of these nine, six had more than 250,000 members, and disposed, between them, of a clear majority of the votes at any Congress which they might enter with a united policy. These unions, the 'big six', were the AEU with 704,000 members; the NUGMW with 605,000; the NUM with 533,000; the NUR, with 410,000; the TGWU with 975,000; and the shopworkers' union, soon to be restyled under its modern name, the Union of Shop, Distributive and Allied Workers (USDAW), with 275,000. Thus, over 3,500,000 workers had chosen membership in one of the giant organizations. During the next fifteen years, the 'big six' maintained their ascendancy. The three biggest grew steadily, so that the AEU had reached 973,000 by 1960; the TGWU, 1,302,000; and the NUGMW, 796,000. The NUM and the NUR had risen in membership in the early post-war years, only to begin their decline with the onset of rationalization. The railwaymen suffered their first shrinkages earlier than the miners, and by 1960 they were down to 334,000. The miners had peaked at 681,000 in 1957, but were beginning to decline thereafter, and had reached 586,000 in 1960. The shopworkers grew to 355,000 in the same period, but were not successful in achieving any take-off beyond that point until years later. Of these six organizations, three were overtly general unions: the TGWU, the NUGMW and USDAW, which organized workers in chemicals as well as distribution. A fourth, the AEU, was increasingly taking on many aspects of general unionism, because it combined the organization of skilled engineers in every industry where they were employed with an increasing open, across-the-board appeal in metal-manufacturing industries. The other two were would-be industrial unions, although both shared their spaces with other craft or status-based organizations in the same field.

Beneath the level of the big six lay a profusion of overlapping and contending organizations, which were still provoking a standard apologia at the end of our period. 'Many people say', wrote W.A. Widden of the TUC staff in 1960, 'that ours is a most complicated structure – but we are proud of the reason – it is the oldest trade union movement (one affiliated union has had a continuous history since 1747).'[2] In spite of this richness of tradition, there were many other people who hoped for modernization. As Dr N. Barou, the author of a Left Book Club survey of trade unionism published in 1947, insisted: 'Adjustments to rectify weaknesses – some integration and co-ordination, some streamlining . . . could make an enormous contribution to the success of a socialist Britain.'[3]

Streamlining was not in the event to follow this appeal. But at two distinct levels, there did arise a considerable degree of effective co-ordination. First, at the national level, the dominant leaders of the big six joined forces to present the Labour Government with solid institutional support throughout its life, and to sustain the Labour Party's official leadership fairly consistently during its first years of post-war Opposition. Second, at the level of the workshop, the shop stewards' movement which had so steadily augmented its power during the war years, continued to develop cross-union links in joint shop-stewards' committees, and to carry an increasing responsibility for direct bargaining and practical union administration, sometimes regardless of strident admonitions from higher up in the formal union establishments.

If we look first at the national conduct of affairs, we find the pre-eminence of a handful of national leaders remained, throughout the period, a quite unavoidable fact. The TGWU had in practice been led by Arthur Deakin since 1940 (when Bevin was 'seconded' to the Ministry of Labour), although he held the title of 'Acting Secretary' until 1946, when Ernest Bevin was already at the Foreign Office. Deakin died in the mid-1950s, and was briefly replaced by Jock Tiffin, who in turn died within months of taking office. Thus, in 1956, Frank Cousins was elected and soon ended the post-war ethos which had hitherto ruled the union. The GMWU was taken over by Sir Tom Williamson in 1946, and he remained in the General Secretaryship throughout our period. The engineers were led by Jack Tanner, an old syndicalist who had argued with Lenin at Comintern congresses. Soon after the war Tanner became convinced that communism was a threat to the British labour movement, and thenceforward joined forces with the other union leaders. He was also involved in the foundation of the IRIS newsletter, which operated out of an office in the seamen's union building in Clapham, and intervened consistently against communist and other left-wing nominees in union elections. Tanner was briefly succeeded in 1956 by R. Openshaw, and then more durably in 1956 by Sir William, later Lord Carron. The shopworkers' amalgamation was led by Sir Alan Birch from 1949. The miners were evenly balanced. Arthur Horner, the communist General Secretary, was elected in 1946: but he shared office with Sir William Lawther, the President, who became fiercely anti-communist in the late 1940s after a long period of fellow-travelling. Sir William could be blunt to the point of uncouthness, and is well remembered for his Chairmanship of one Labour Conference in which he stifled critics with a loud instruction to 'Shut your gob'. After an unauthorized speech of solidarity with a French miners' strike, Horner was officially restrained. He was allocated a portfolio for industrial relations in the NUM, leaving political pronouncements in the hands of his opponent, who was thus enabled to join his union's weight to that of the TGWU and the NUGMW in a wide variety of crucial political decisions. Alone in this grouping of major leaders stood the railwaymen's leader James Figgins, who took over the General Secretaryship in 1948, and was to hold it until he died in a car accident in Russia in 1953. Figgins was a partisan of workers' control, and frequently found himself out of step with his TUC colleagues during the later years of the Labour administration and the early period of Labour Opposition.[4]

Not surprisingly, the early months of the Attlee administration saw major reforms which were generally, indeed almost universally, welcomed in the trade union movement. The nationalization programme was set in train. The 1927 Trade Disputes and Trade Union Act was repealed, thus transforming the financial basis of the Labour Party. After the General Strike, the Conservative Government had legislated to enforce 'contracting in', a procedure under which union members were obliged to make an individual decision if they wished to opt in to the payment of the political levy out of which unions financed their political activities, including affiliation fees to the Labour Party. Repeal meant that members who wished to withhold the payment had to make the deliberate effort to 'contract out', so that affiliated membership could only grow, at a time when there was in any case wide support for what the government was doing.[5] Above all, the post-war years were years of full employment. Unemployment ranged from 1.2 per cent in 1945, to 1.7 per cent in 1960. The highest point it reached during the whole period was 3.1 per cent in 1947, a year marked by an acutely bad winter which affected production very adversely. Otherwise there were only four years in the run where unemployment nudged above the 2 per cent mark. The significance of this development can hardly be overemphasized. Indeed, it became the cornerstone of the new doctrine of revisionism, outlined by Allan Flanders, Rita Hinden and C.A.R. Crosland during the years immediately after the fall of the Attlee Government. This received its classic statement in Crosland's major book *The Future of Socialism*, published in 1956:[6]

there has been a decisive movement of power within industry itself from management to labour. This is mainly a consequence of the seller's market for labour created by full employment

The relative strength of workers and employers does not, of course, depend solely on conditions in the labour market. It depends also on the political balance, the social climate, the degree of organisation of the two sides, and current views about the relation between wages on the one hand, and profits, employment, or the foreign balance on the other. These factors had all changed in a manner favourable to labour even before 1939. Yet the strength of the Unions was still severely limited by large-scale unemployment; and they were obviously, and knew it, the weaker of the two contenders.

The change from a buyer's to a seller's market for labour, however, by transposing at once the interests, and therefore the attitudes, of the two sides, has dramatically altered the balance of power at every level of labour relations.

At the level of the individual worker, the decisive change relates to the question of dismissal. The employee, for whom dismissal before the war was often a sentence of long-term unemployment, can now quickly find a job elsewhere; and he has lost, in consequence, his fear of the sack, and with it his docility. The employer, on the other hand, who before the war could replace a dismissed worker from a long waiting-list of applicants for jobs, may now have difficulty in finding any replacement at all; and he has acquired, in consequence, a reluctance to dismiss, and himself has become more docile. Thus the balance of advantage is reversed, and the result is a transformation of relationships at the shop-floor level.

At the level of the plant or firm, the main change lies in the altered attitude of the two sides towards their ultimate weapons of coercion – the strike and the lock-out. With unemployment, the employer can often well afford to endure a strike or initiate a lockout; the odds in the contest are on his side, while the cost of a stoppage, with stocks often high and market conditions unprofitable, may be relatively minor. But with full employment, the odds are quite different, since the workers can now hold out much longer; while the cost of a stoppage in terms of profits foregone is likely, with stocks perhaps low and lucrative market demand, to be much greater. The employers' incentive to avoid strikes has thus increased in the same measure as the workers' prospects of winning them; the implications for the balance of power are obvious.

This description may be felt to exaggerate the extent of the shift of power: but nonetheless a real shift did take place, and was reflected in the accretion of strength of the shop-stewards' movement, and the growth of plant-based bargaining systems. Increasingly, however, this was reported not as a 'gain' but as a 'problem', so that by 1960 the conventional wisdom held that unfettered trade union power created inflationary pressures. The view was succinctly expressed in the 1961 OEEC survey on *The Problem of Rising Prices*.[7]

On the strength of its record to date the United Kingdom must be judged to have failed to respond satisfactorily to the new problems posed by full employment . . . given the antiquated nature of the institutional arrangements in a number of industries, the weakness of central bodies on both sides, the lack of any clearly defined norm for arbitrators to take as a guide when making awards, there can be no assurance that wage increases will in future be kept in line with the growth potential of the economy.

It was in pursuit of solutions to this dilemma that recurrent efforts were made by successive governments to arrive at a basis for control of increases in wage incomes. These began very conspicuously after 1946, when the American loans began to run out years ahead of schedule. In October of that year the TUC rejected interruptions in the process of free collective bargaining. Substantial improvements had been won during the months since the war, including significant reductions in agreed working time, and an actual reduction in hours worked in industry as a whole. In February 1947 a major fuel crisis developed as a result of the severe snows, and commercial electricity supplies were shut off in much of the country. Soon after this, announcements of new planning initiatives were made by Sir Stafford Cripps. But in July the crisis became open, with the balance of payments sliding out of control. Herbert Morrison met the TUC leaders at the beginning of August, to sound out their attitudes to the imposition of direction of labour, the increase of working hours, and the official collection of data on wage movements. This opened a see-saw of initiatives on the question of wage restraint, at first considered unmentionable in the dialogue with the unions, but soon publicly ventilated by the Prime Minister in a parliamentary debate. The unions protested their goodwill, but held their ground in defence of collective bargaining. It was not until February 1948 that the government stopped this lengthy to-and-fro by publishing a White Paper on wage restraint. New negotiations became unavoidable, and these established that the TUC would now accept restraint, provided that food subsidies were not cut, price controls remained in force, dividends and profits were also restrained, low wages were exempted from the general rule, productivity improvements could be rewarded, differentials would not be eroded, and collective bargaining would continue. Enough movement was subsequently exacted from the Federation of British Industry and allied bodies to enable the government to announce acceptance of a dividend and price freeze, and on the strength of this the TUC called an emergency conference of union executives at the end of March, which ratified a wage freeze by 5,000,000 votes to 2,000,000, in spite of the fact that many of the General Council's reservations had remained unmet.

All of this found that the unions were, in spite of their improved image of respectability, very much less powerful in determining hard policy than had been thought. Wage restraint was to continue for two further years, until devaluation ensured that it was overturned in Congress, after a further special conference had been narrowly committed in favour of the policy. The majority, of 300,000, was not considered adequate to make the policy stick. Between 1947 and 1950 the index of wages moved from 100 to 110, of retail prices from 100 to 113, and of food prices from 100 to 121.3. From the governmental viewpoint, the policy had thus been rather successful, but within the unions themselves it produced some quite different evaluations. But whatever they thought about it, the unions found that these years began important changes in their actual behaviour.

First, the wage freeze left national claims in abeyance. Second, while full employment remained, competition by employers for unavailable labour ensured that stiff alternative wage-bidding would develop. It took the form of a rash of production bonuses, lieu bonuses, 'merit money' and systematic overtime. Notices appeared requiring hands, and blandishing 'unlimited' hours as an inducement. All these mutations in payment systems strength-ened the bargaining power of shop stewards, and brought the emphasis of active trade unionism down from head offices to the workplace itself. By the late 1950s, Hugh Clegg was complaining that 'millions of hours of unnecessary overtime' were being worked each and every week. But whether his intuition was right or wrong, the overtime rosters, necessary or not, were commonly agreed with the stewards. It was this kind of function which made workshop organization indispensable to efficient working, and impelled Clegg to report elsewhere that shop-stewards' power had been 'fostered by management'.[8] The growth of this influence was spectacular,

TABLE 3 Post-war growth of shop stewards in engineering[9]. 1. Indices of growth
in numbers of AEU shop stewards, AEU membership and number of full-time
manual workers employed in federated engineering establishments, 1949–61. 1947
= 100 UK

Date	Total number of AEU shop stewards (including conveners)	AEU membership	Number of AEU shop stewards at federated establishments (including conveners)	Estimated number of manual workers in federated establishments
May 1947*	100	100	100	100
June 1954†	120	112	119	112
June 1955†	124	114	132	116
Dec. 1955†	120	114	114	119
Mar. 1956*	124	118	124	119
June 1958†	126	120	138	118
Dec. 1958†	128	120	142	115
Dec. 1959†	130	119	146	117
Dec. 1960†	141	128	153	125
June 1961†	145	130	161	125
Dec. 1961‡	156	130	172	123
Average annual increase 1947–61 (%)	4.0	2.1	5.1	1.6
Average annual increase 1955–61 (%)	4.6	2.0	6.6	0.8

Sources: *AEU Surveys.
†AEU 'D' Returns, old basis.
‡AEU 'D' Returns, new basis.
Engineering Employers' Federation.

and is reflected in the rapid increase in the numbers of stewards, which
ran sharply in front of the rate of increase in ordinary membership (see
Table 3).

This numerical growth could not fail to cause problems for the national
leaderships, which indeed began to reveal themselves in the arguments
about wages policy, and continued after the election of the Conservatives
in 1951. Communist influence on shop stewards remained active, since
the re-emergence of the factory organizations had been marked by active
communist example in the aviation industry shortly before the outbreak of
war, and widely consolidated throughout the engineering industry during
the war years. Yet this influence had been characterized by a certain
ambivalence, since the main growth of wartime workshop representation
had occurred after the German invasion of the USSR in 1941, and the new
shop stewards found themselves mobilized in vast conferences on how to

increase war production, organized under communist auspices with the support of major newspapers. The post-war adjustment of communist policy weakened the membership of the party, without dissolving its rank-and-file trade union presence, so that the emergence of an 'informal' bargaining system represented a certain political threat to the predominantly right-wing leadership of the big union organizations, as well as an organizational challenge which was more difficult to deal with. Consequently there were frequent attempts to amalgamate the two threats, which were perhaps best encapsulated by Sir William Carron's denunciations of some of his engineering shop stewards as 'werewolves'. The TUC still reflected this kind of attitude, albeit in mellower phrases, when, at the end of our period, they published in 1960 a report, based on a study commissioned at the 1959 Congress, on 'disputes and workshop representation'. This acknowledged certain functions as proper to shop stewards' organization:[10]

The work for which shop stewards are elected and recognised in union constitutions involves three main functions – organisation, negotiation and information. The precise list of duties varies from union to union. At its widest it includes supervising agreements and safety regulations; representation about grievances; negotiation of piece-rates and of matters of local discretion (e.g. arrangement of working hours); recruitment and collecting contributions; and reports to district office about working conditions, membership position and employment prospects.

It went on, however, to point out the difficulty of co-ordinating formal union policies when extended cross-union organizations had grown up inside the factories:

Each union can allocate a sphere of responsibility for its own stewards but no union individually is in a position to bring within its rules the joint committee of stewards from several unions or the officers of such joint bodies. These bodies are of three main kinds:

i.   The joint committee of stewards from several unions in one place of work.
ii. Organisations linking a number of joint committees either from several factories under the same ownership (e.g. B.M.C.) or throughout an industry (e.g. electricity generating).
iii. Attempts to form a national centre or to call national conferences of stewards irrespective of the industry in which they work (e.g. the organisation which goes under the name of the Engineering & Allied Trades Shop Stewards National Council).

The aim of the sponsors of the third type is to usurp the policy-making functions of unions or federations of unions. Whatever the motive of those primarily responsible for the second type the effect is often to challenge established union arrangements. The first type is the most longstanding and the most numerous. No census has been taken but instances of joint activity between stewards of different unions are, in some industries, almost as widespread as workshop representation itself.

These second and third types of organization were still anathema to the General Council, although in fact they corresponded to a variety of actually-felt needs:

Some joint arrangements between stewards have been harmful. Where decisions about a programme of demands and priorities have been constitutionally taken in a union it is wrong for stewards in that union to set them aside and to follow another path through a joint shop stewards' committee on the excuse that this other path is 'official' or acceptable to one of the other unions. Where several unions are involved in one industry there are bound to be occasions where there are differences of emphasis. Naturally there are channels for bridging these differences and reaching agreements on a common approach to employers.

'Naturally' is a word which sometimes silences dissent. But in this case, 'natural' was that which happened rarely in any effective way, and could certainly not be confused with 'usually', or even 'ideally'. The truth was that numbers of shop stewards were finding some need for industry-wide or combined organization or consultation, which was very difficult even at the end of the 1950s, because of the fears it aroused in some of the most important union leaderships.

From the worm's-eye view, these admonitions were not made any more acceptable by the evident differentiation which had opened up between 'official' and semi-official or spontaneous institutions. In the engineering industry, for instance, the procedural agreement of 1922, imposed by a bitter lock-out and insisting on 'managerial prerogatives' which were in no sense appropriate to an age of full employment, leave alone social democracy, still held formal sway. As a result it was widely ignored, which meant that the official union structures were locked into a ludicrous situation, in which large numbers of strikes could not be recognized officially even though they were, on the union side, universally felt to be justified. Yet no serious attempts were made to modernize the procedures at the national industrial level.

To these tensions were added others which arose from the attempts made by the Attlee administration (and continued by its successors) to secure union consent to overall social and political policies.

A network of national consultative procedures involved considerable numbers of union officials in participation of one form or another in broader government affairs, although this clearly did not imply any substantially greater membership involvement in such matters. By 1958, this process had reached the point where V.L. Allen could identify sixty-five distinct government bodies on which members of the General Council sat. 'Many union leaders sit on committees in which they have little or no interest', he wrote.[11] This was because, where the TUC itself recommended appointments, it did so normally on a basis of seniority. The same perception is supported by Robert Taylor, who reports that Sir John Hare, Minister of

Agriculture during the 1950s, complained to the TUC 'about the lack of effort being put in by union nominees serving at that time on the marketing boards'. 'At this time', Taylor claims, George Woodcock was provoked to comment 'there was no reporting back. We never knew what they were doing. In fact, they did damn all . . .'[12] Woodcock's stringent evaluation is probably too sweeping, although certainly there were cases in which it might have been justified. But in the first, heady, post-war years, there can be little doubt that the whole cadre of trade union officials found their increased involvement in affairs to be a major extension of their recognition, status and influence. It was only later that the ill effects of such patronage began to be appreciated and discussed.

Recognition took more blatant and controversial forms as well. In spite of consistent pre-war opposition to the honours system, more and more trade union peerages and knighthoods were created. The first trade union peer was William Westwood, ennobled by Winston Churchill for services during his wartime secondment to the Admiralty. The Attlee administration enobled Reginald Cook of the Ministry of Labour Staff Association, Sir Walter Citrine, A.G. Walkden of the railway clerks', Charles Dukes of the NUGMW, and a number of politicians with trade union backgrounds. It also bestowed knighthoods on at least nine sitting General Secretaries including the miners' William Lawther and Vincent Tewson of the TUC.[13]

During the earliest years in question, these promotions undoubtedly served to evoke a certain sense that the trade union movement had 'arrived' and become a fully accepted estate of the realm. Often the recipients of such honours received numerous congratulatory messages from their members, which indicates that the respectability conferred was to some extent 'shared'. Yet the attitude of the labour movement to this process was never less than ambivalent, as is shown in the persistent rejection of any title whatever by so powerful a figure as Arthur Deakin. Nonetheless, all this indicates that senior union leaders were able to perceive changes in their accepted roles and expectations, which must have seemed important to them, however cosmetic they may appear to later agnostics.

No support would have been given to this process by the union memberships, had the post-war settlement not marked an appreciable change in their conditions.

But as the industrial relations system muddled its way through the 1950s, these acts of State patronage began to be seen in a more hostile light, as is evidenced by the increasing bitterness in the internal union polemics of the time.

This process even developed in the most crucial area of industrial reform, that of the post-war nationalizations.

The radical programme of nationalization which had been resolved by the last wartime Labour Party Conference, against concerted platform opposition, was in fact implemented. Coal, railways, gas, electricity, road haulage, iron and steel, all were to come under public ownership during the Attlee administration. But all of these industries were brought under the control of Boards appointed by an appropriate minister, modelled on the scheme worked out for London Transport by Herbert Morrison. There was no direct worker representation on these Boards, although a limited number of trade union functionaries were offered positions when the new Boards were constituted. These persons were expected to sever their direct trade union connections and were in no way accountable to their former memberships.

All this was not entirely unpredictable, because in 1944 the TUC had agreed an *Interim Report on Postwar Reconstruction* which had been drafted in consultation with the Labour Party Executive, and which proposed to introduce worker participation in the control of private industry while opposing it in the public sector. Management in this section was to be chosen for its 'competence efficiently to administer' and the resultant Boards would answer to the public through their relevant ministers 'responsible to Parliament'. Again and again governmental spokesmen took their stand on this principle, even though it soon became clear that the actual degree of public accountability offered by the Morrisonian form of nationalization was dilute indeed. Answering a Labour Party debate in 1946, Emanuel Shinwell, the Minister for Mines, insisted that the 'first principle' of the new NCB must be 'that we employ the best men for the job'.[14] Sir Stafford Cripps went further, insisting that 'there is not as yet a very large body of workers in Britain capable of taking over large enterprises'. 'I think', he told his Bristol constituents in October 1946, 'it would be almost impossible to have worker-controlled industry in Britain, even if it were on the whole desirable.'[15]

This view was widely criticized. Indeed, there was some basis for such criticism in the same 1944 *Interim Report* which was so widely cited in evidence for the agreed need for professional expertise in public enterprise management. This *Report* had also laid down the principle that efficiency also required that policy should 'be subject to the continuous influence of those whom it directly affects'. Coal was the first industry to be taken over, because the industry had become a symbol of the evils of capitalist exploitation. The miners, whose original demands for nationalization had been heavily stamped with the imprint of syndicalist and guild socialist ideas, were divided by the new institutions designed for them, much though they welcomed nationalization in principle. Both Labour Party activists and the communist opposition within the NUM reflected this division. Some communists joined the regional coal boards as appointed members, and some declined invitations. George Brown, then a young backbencher for the mining division of Belper, made a passionate speech during the nationalization debate, insisting that 'we shall cause the greatest disappointment to very many miners if we are not very careful about which people we take into the management of this new industry'.[16] He cited a plea from one of his constituents: 'Let us have no well-feathered nests for the tyrants of the past.' This judgement, he reported, 'very well expresses what is in the minds of the men'. But Mr Shinwell, from his ministerial desk, claimed that he 'had to start on a clear desk', to elaborate the Nationalization Act, in the implementation of which the communist miners' leader, Arthur Horner, 'never put the ideological precepts of his . . . affiliations before the welfare of the men he represented'.[17] Whatever individual communists thought of the NCB, it was not until 1948, after the launching of the Marshall Plan and the outbreak of a visible cold war, that Harry Pollitt published a pamphlet demanding workers' direct representation.

There were no fewer arguments in other industries, where the traditions of some of the unions were even less tractable than those of the NUM. The railways were precipitated into a major debate. Unlike the miners, the railwaymen had their own weekly newspaper, the *Railway Review*. During the three years from 1946 on, 'hundreds of yards of column space were taken up by articles and correspondence on the subject of workers' control'.[18] Immediately after the 1945 election results had been declared, the NUR's annual general meeting unanimously resolved that 'workers' participation . . . is an indispensable requisite to ensure the success of a publicly owned transport industry'. Those officials who sought to justify the Labour Party's managerialist approach to nationalization were wont to cite the fact that 'the trade unions did not control the railways in Russia', thus echoing Mr Herbert Morrison's own defence of his model for public ownership of industry, a decade earlier, during the debates which shaped Labour policy in the pre-war years. James Figgins, the post-war General Secretary of the union, stood with his rank-and-file on this matter: workers' control, he said, 'may have failed in the co-operative movement, but I am perfectly certain that we in the railway industry will not fail to solve the problem, because I know of no industry in this country where men have to display greater initiative'.[19]

The railwaymen remained obdurate, and in 1949 they were still insisting on '50 per cent workers' representation at all levels'. This commitment was shared by the postmen, whose union had always defended the perspectives of guild socialism, and continued to do so until well into the 1960s. Evaluating these and other similar responses to nationalization, Eireen White, MP, concluded in a 1951 Fabian survey of the field, that 'the issue of workers' representation is by no means dead'.[20] Dissatisfaction about the exclusion of directly elected worker representatives concerned only a minority, if a significant one: but there was also much more general dissatisfaction, even within the given Morrisonian framework, about the inadequate number of appointments given to trade unionists.

In 1948 the TUC was informed, during Congress, that out of forty-six NCB divisional appointments, only nine had been made from the unions; that the Transport Commission had one trade unionist only among its five members and the Railway Executive one out of seven. Complaints brought no perceptible change, and in 1951 the total of union appointees on national and regional boards numbered forty-four out of some 350. At the same time, seven General Councillors were among the forty-four, and Citrine passed through the NCB to be chosen as Chairman of the Central Electricity Authority.

Union members who received such appointments were often placed on the boards of industries in which they had no practical experience, and the bank clerks' complained that they were not even consulted when one member of the General Council was given a place on the Court of the Bank of England. With the return of a Conservative administration in 1951, trade union appointments were continued, but they had already lost any semblance of representativity, and increasingly frequently provoked adverse commentary among rank-and-file union members. This began to find insistent echoes among the more radical trade union leaders through the later 1950s, as is perfectly exemplified by Clive Jenkins' indictment of Labour Party policy in respect of public corporations, published in *The Insiders*, a pamphlet issued by *Universities and Left Review* in 1958. Five employee rights were itemized in this influential tract:[21]

1. Workers in an industry are entitled to a voice in workshop management and in higher policy making.
2. Their authority at local level should be absolute in such questions as working arrangements, hiring and dismissals.
3. They should be allowed to select their own supervisors (providing these are technically qualified).
4. Workers' representatives should sit on the Managing Board for their industry.
5. This scheme of sharing in power (while operated by the joint union organizations within the corporations) should be manned by employees only and *not* full-time trade union officers, who should remain primarily responsible for the negotiation of wages, conditions, and grievance settling . . .

The main concession to 'participation' in the different nationalization Acts was the agreement to write provisions for joint consultation into them. Consultation was always seen by those in office as an advisory process, although its capacity to involve workers varied with the necessary degree of ambiguity which the device incorporated in its structure. As was the case in engineering, also in mining, joint production committees had flourished during the Second World War, as part of the drive for war production. Communist support for them was broadly continued in the immediate post-war period.

As Reg Birch, the communist engineering leader in London, put it:[22]

The people have elected a Labour Government – the first of its kind in the history of the country. There are powerful interests already at work sabotaging the efforts of this Government. The workers' safeguard is inside the factory, demanding Production Committees determined that maximum production must be achieved and that no-one is to be allowed to frustrate our efforts . . . years and years of necessary work stare us in the face. The engineering workers are willing to co-operate. Nothing must be allowed to stand in the way.

Similarly passionate appeals were made by Arthur Horner to the miners: and these were not answered merely verbally.

During those fierce snowstorms of 1947, the communist spokesman of the Grassmoor miners in Derbyshire, Mick Kane, walked several miles through the blizzards in order to clear snow from the pithead area to enable production to continue. Innumerable similar efforts were made during 1947, to 'make nationalization work'. This kind of attitude persisted among rank-and-file communists long after the official policy had changed towards a contestatory and oppositional stance. As late as 1950, the President of Rufford branch of the NUM in Nottinghamshire, Bill Baker, was heatedly defending joint consultation against party colleagues, no doubt in part because he recalled the role of the wartime pit production committees in keeping open his own colliery by forcing a revision of colliery boundaries, contrary to the interests of the coalowners. But in general this kind of enthusiasm faded rather quickly, because commonly the only powers which were ceded to worker representatives were those involving unpopular disciplinary measures, such as the punishment of absentees. The reaction may have been more obviously politically motivated among the communist minority, but it was widely shared by workers with quite different political opinions.

This is not to say that joint consultation was generally rejected, or even that it did not produce certain positive results. But where it did benefit workpeople, this was invariably because their trade union strength enabled them to push beyond the prescribed advisory role, and actually to bargain on material questions.

Thus, where the balance tilted to the workpeople, they tended to see this as resulting from their own organization, and where it did not, they responded with even more alienation to all those entreaties about 'making consultation work'. Not surprisingly, the system began to generate complaints.

Even before the unions pushed forward to criticize, socialist thinkers had begun to develop similar notions, and these were sometimes outspoken. Notable among such advocates was R.H. Tawney, who was later to be lionized as a patriarch of revisionism, in the Labour Party, but whose last long article, which appeared in *Socialist Commentary*, was insistently radical on this theme. The Labour Government, he wrote, 'increased freedom by enlarging the range of alternatives between which ordinary men can choose; but it did little to remove from wage earners the sense that they belong to a class treated as instruments for ends dictated from above'. Future Labour Governments, he thought, must 'use the industries in public ownership as a laboratory where different methods of making industrial democracy a reality are tested'.[23]

These valedictory words were never to be taken seriously by Tawney's professed followers, although they were very much in the minds of the revived workers' control movement which began to reemerge in the mid-1960s.

The political meaning of these events was difficult to grasp within any narrow perspective. Numerous historians have emphasized the extent to which they 'incorporated' trade unions into government, or again represented the foundation of a consensus which involved tripartite 'corporatism' with big industry and government together. Yet as sensitive analysts such as Keith Middlemas point out, the actual movement of events does not lie so easily under the rubrics designed to explain it. The real extent of the post-war consensus rested on full employment, and would continue, in increasingly open stress, until full employment came to an end. But stress was never absent, even though it shifted in acuteness from one industry or service to another. In one period, management were adjusting to government policies by inadvertently encouraging workshop organization: at another period that same organization presented them with serious problems. Industrial management's gain was sometimes government's loss or difficulty. At one time the introduction of piecework was seen as a panacea to improve productivity: in a later age productivity was seen as crucially related to the establishment of measured daywork. Union institutions changed slowly, almost imperceptibly, through most of our period: but the changes which built slowly were to culminate in major upheavals at the ripe time. The old aspirations of the socialists for a new social order in which labour was no longer a commodity, and of trade unions for an epoch in which democracy no longer stopped at the factory gates, were never completely annulled in these complex processes. But they were compelled to assume new forms, as the institutions changed within which workpeople developed both those of their aspirations which were considered acceptable within the given framework, and their oppositional responses to that framework itself.

NOTES AND REFERENCES

1. *TUC Annual Report*, 1945, p. 8.
2. *The Place of Non-Manual Workers in the Trade Union Structure*, TUC (mimeo), 1961, p. 3.

3.   N. Barou, *British Trade Unions*, Gollancz, London, 1947, p. 8.

4.   Figgins was also unusual in the 'big six' leadership for his pro-Soviet attitudes, which were to divide him from the Bevanite left in the 1950s.

5.   See M. Harrison, *Trade Unions and the Labour Party since 1945*, Allen and Unwin, London, 1960, Ch. 1.

6.   C.A.R. Crosland, *The Future of Socialism*, Jonathan Cape, London, 1956, pp. 30–31.

7.   OEEC, *The Problem of Rising Prices*, May 1961, p. 419.

8.   H.A. Clegg, A.J. Killick and R. Adams, *Trade Union Officers*, Blackwell, Oxford, 1961, p. 181.

9.   A.T. Marsh and E.E. Coker, 'Shop Steward Organization in Engineering', *British Journal of Industrial Relations*, 1, no. 2, June 1963, p. 177.

10.   *TUC Annual Report*, 1960, pp. 128–29.

11.   V.L. Allen, *Trade Unions and the Government*, Longmans, Green, London, 1960, p. 39.

12.   R. Taylor, *The Fifth Estate: Britain's unions in the 'seventies*, Routledge and Kegan Paul, London, 1978, p. 109.

13.   V.L. Allen, *Trade Union Leadership*, Longmans, Green, London, 1957, pp. 34 *et seq*.

14.   R. Dahl, 'Workers' control of industry and the British Labour Party', *American Political Science Review*, Oct. 1947.

15.   Sir Stafford Cripps, Report in *The Times*, 28 Oct. 1946, p. 2.

16.   *Hansard*, H.C. Debs., 418, 5S, 29 Jan. 1946, C. 769–70.

17.   E. Shinwell, *Conflict Without Malice*, Odhams, London, 1955, pp. 172–73.

18.   P.S. Bagwell, *The Railwaymen*, Allen and Unwin, London, 1963, p. 623.

19.   Ibid.

20.   E. White, *Workers' Control?*, Fabian Tract 271, 1951, p. 67.

21.   'The Insiders', a Supplement of *Universities and Left Review*, No. 3, winter, 1958, pp. 59–60.

22.   R. Birch, *A Wage Based on Human Needs*, Communist Party, London, pp. 15–16.

23.   R.H. Tawney, *The Radical Tradition*, Pelican, Harmondsworth, 1966, p. 185.

Part two

CONSOLIDATION AND CRISIS

9   The trade union 'problem' in the Age of Consensus 1960–1979

Robert Taylor

The TUC has arrived. It is an estate of the realm, as real, as potent, as essentially part of the fabric of our national life as any of the historic Estates.[1]
    Harold Wilson at the TUC centenary celebration at Belle Vue, Manchester Whit Sunday 1968.

To me Socialism is not just militant trade unionism. It is the gentle society in which every producer remembers he is a consumer too.[2]
    Barbara Castle diary entry 11 February 1975.

Society today is so organised that every individual group almost has the power to disrupt it. How is their power to be channelled into constructive channels?[3]
    James Callaghan at the 1978 Labour Party conference.

It is not the intention of the trade union movement to hold back its members' wage claims if they are justified. It is our purpose to sell our labour and our skill in open market to the best of our ability while we live under the present system.[4]
    Frank Cousins, general secretary of the Transport and General Workers Union in Oxford June 1964.

OVERMIGHTY SUBJECTS?

The explosive issue of trade union 'power' came to dominate Britain's industrial politics in the 1960s and 1970s. 'The unions have increasingly demanded, with effective menaces, excessive wage increases which have inevitably led to excessive cost and price increases', lamented Reginald Maudling, Chancellor of the Exchequer under Harold Macmillan in the early 1960s in a memorandum to the Conservative shadow cabinet in May 1976.[5] He was concerned about what he regarded as the growth of trade union 'monopoly' power in conditions of full employment. In his opinion, the growing interdependence of the country's workforce made society as a whole much more vulnerable than in the past to paralysing disruption by strong unions in vital state-owned monopoly sectors of the economy like electricity supply, coal mining and the water services. Maudling argued that Britain's unions, now possessed 'the power to bring any capitalistic economy to a halt'. Apparently 'the days when the community could provide skills to replace those of a striking union (e.g. electric power workers) had now gone. The only defence left to the community was the art of political diplomacy in achieving a social consensus that would somehow try to reconcile the interests of competing producer groups with those of the nation as a whole.

No doubt Maudling remembered not merely the humiliations experienced by Edward Heath's Conservative Government between June 1970 and February 1974 at the hands of organized labour, but also the difficulties in the early attempt to establish a voluntary incomes policy between 1961 and 1964. As Harold Macmillan wrote in his diary: 'These 150,000 power workers have the whole country in pawn. Owing to the great interlocking and great complication of these plants, we cannot do what we did in the General Strike of 1926'.[6]

It was not only Conservative ministers who worried about what they feared to be the 'giant's strength' of the trade unions during the period. Labour, in power, also came to the conclusion that the trade union movement was badly in need of internal reform and had to take some of the blame for the country's persistent economic troubles because of their capacity to veto necessary structural change and stimulate wage-push inflation through the successful use of the strike threat weapon.

In 1969 the highly dirigiste Employment Secretary, Barbara Castle, produced a controversial White Paper – In Place of Strife – that was a toughly-worded critique of the inadequacies of contemporary trade unionism. On that occasion James Callaghan, then Home Secretary, rushed to the defence of the trade union establishment in a rearguard action that helped to destroy the Wilson–Castle attempt to reform the trade unions under the stimulus of statutory action backed up by penal sanctions against unofficial strikers.

But as a besieged Labour Prime Minister himself during the so-called 'winter of discontent' in 1978–1979, Callaghan also questioned out loud 'the power of the organised worker in society', where 'every individual group' has the 'power to disrupt it'.

The trade unions became the scapegoats for Britain's relative economic decline in the 1960s and 1970s. They were denounced by many political commentators and economists as the engines of inflation for forcing up money wage rates far above the levels justified by modest improvements in labour productivity. The country's self-destructive wages scramble was blamed for its high unit labour costs that injured Britain's export performance in overseas markets. Trade unions were also attacked because of their alleged perpetuation of restrictive practices that ensured an inefficient use of labour, overmanning and the preservation of obsolete craft-skill distinctions.

Trade union leaders became both objects of fear and contempt, often portrayed in colourful language as the robber barons of the corporate state, swollen with perks and privileges. In the 1960s Frank Cousins, the awkward and confused general secretary of the Transport and General Workers Union, was the union bogeyman to make the flesh creep to be followed on the pantheon of demonology by his successor, Jack Jones and Hugh Scanlon, the left-wing president of the Engineers' union. During Labour's years of political office from March 1974 until May 1979 many critics suggested that the trade unions had in fact become 'the arbiters of the British economy'. The former editor of the *New Statesman*, Paul Johnson, gave fevered voice to this prevalent orthodoxy in May 1975 when he suggested that 'huge unions, pursuing wage claims at any cost, have successfully smashed other elements in the state – governments, political parties, private industry, nationalised boards – and now find themselves amid the wreckage of a deserted battlefield, the undoubted victors'. 'They did not plan the victory', Johnson conceded and apparently 'they do not know what to do with it now they have got it. Dazed and bewildered, they are like medieval peasants who have burnt down the lord's manor'.[7]

The imagery, no doubt, reflected a middle-class prejudice against manual workers but it was symptomatic of the mood of the time among many who believed the trade unions were too powerful and needed to be brought to heel. The reality of even that time at the height of the Social Contract between the Labour Government and the Trades Union Congress was rather different to such hysterical observations and the recession of 1980–1982 with the huge rise in unemployment put the so-called power of organized workers into perspective.

This is not to deny, however, the crucial importance of organized labour in the ultimate downfall of three democratically-elected governments in the period. The stubborn but effective opposition of the TUC forced Harold Wilson and Barbara Castle to drop their plans in June 1969 to deal with unofficial strikes through penal sanctions and the imposition of a cooling-off period and the holding of a secret ballot of those concerned before the beginning of a dispute. The humiliating climb-down soured relations inside the Labour Movement and made a contribution to the eventual defeat of the Labour Party at the June 1970 general election.

In January 1974 Edward Heath felt compelled to call a prematurely early general election as part of the way of resolving the deadlock of the miners' strike and the imposition of the three-day working week. Many Conservatives as a result of that experience drew the conclusion that the brutal exercise of trade union power broke their government. This view hardened into myth but it was hardly accurate. The Cabinet chose to go to the country eighteen months before the end of the Parliament to fight on the single issue of trade union power and Who Rules? Parliament or the union leaders? The attempt to concentrate the minds of the electorate on that question alone failed as other issues emerged during the election campaign such as inflation where the government's record was far from successful. It needs to be remembered that Heath was defeated narrowly through the ballot box and not on the picket line and it was Enoch Powell with his call on Conservatives to vote Labour rather than the National Union of Mineworkers who played the decisive part in the outcome.

But there can be no doubt that the persistent confrontations between the trade unions and the Heath Government from the July 1970 dock strike through to the final denouement on the coalfields highlighted a problem for which the Conservatives could find no satisfactory answer – namely how to deal with public sector monopoly workers with proven muscle power to disrupt the economy. As Heath's then-close political adviser, Douglas Hurd, wrote later;

In a public sector dispute the employee barely suffers. Any temporary loss of income is usually covered by the union and is in any case quickly recouped out of the eventual settlement. The employer, the actual administrator of the public concern does not suffer at all, for his salary is secure. It is the public, and only the public, which suffers, first as consumer and later, when the bill comes in, as taxpayer. The public picks up the tab for both sides.[8]

Less than five years after the downfall of Heath, the credibility of a Labour government was shattered at the hands of organized labour when many trade unions smashed their way through Labour's flimsy and unrealistic 5 per cent pay norm in the 'winter of discontent' with widespread disruption of the community. The apparent but limited savagery of those events provided an eloquent backcloth for the arrival of Margaret Thatcher with her determination to pursue a 'step by step' strategy to change the alleged balance of power in industry away from the trade unions. The Labour party could no longer claim it enjoyed a positive, special relationship with the trade unions which could ensure harmony and goodwill, although a so-called 'concordat' with the TUC promising to introduce a more civilized, though voluntary, code of behaviour into industrial disputes was negotiated under pressure in February 1979 in a hopeless attempt to salvage something constructive out of the wreckage. Of course, the unions did not force the government to leave office. This followed a defeat by 311 votes to 310 in the House of Commons on a confidence motion following referendum defeats for devolution in Wales and Scotland. But there can be little doubt that the sectionalist trade union offensive of the previous winter went a long way to destroy Labour's electoral chances.

Yet the problem of trade union power was always far more complex in the period than most politicians were prepared to recognize. Trade unions never have been massive, highly-centralized, bureaucratic organizations with obedient, disciplined cadres of members ready to obey unquestioningly the orders of a professional elite of leaders. Governments might seek to do business with national trade union leaders through their representative organization, the TUC, in the belief that they could deliver their side of any national bargain. Yet the reality has always remained the reverse even during the post-war years when the arrival of full employment weakened the self-imposed disciplines of the labour market. For the most part the trade unions, and certainly the TUC itself, remained weak, fragmented bodies, vulnerable to the ups and downs of an economy in almost constant crisis.

Contrary to the critics, the trade unions exemplified in the shape of their full-time officials did not turn into social partners or agents of a British variant of corporatism during the period. In the summer of 1972 Heath did make a bold attempt to entice the union leaders into a deal to, in effect, manage the British economy but he was compelled to introduce a statutory prices and incomes policy following a ninety-day price, wage, rent and dividend freeze when he refused to swallow the TUC's shopping list of demands for subsidies, repeal of the Industrial Relations Act and bigger old age pensions. 'No Prime Minister, either before or since, could compare with Ted Heath in the efforts he made to establish a spirit of camaraderie with trade union leaders and to offer an attractive package which might satisfy large numbers of work-people', wrote Jack Jones in his autobiography, though it no doubt came as a relief to the TUC that his corporatist overture failed because Congress House would have had to face the unnerving responsibility of somehow delivering its side of a national bargain.

From the spring of 1974 the much-hailed 'social contract' between the Labour Government and the TUC proved to be at least a temporarily successful understanding but by the summer of 1975 the union leaders began to find what influence they had exerted over Ministers evaporating quickly in the face of grim economic realities, not least the frightening level of inflationary wage settlements that spiralled to an annual increase of 25.8 per cent and price increases travelling up at a rate of 26.6 per cent. Union leaders like Jack Jones and Hugh Scanlon, along with TUC General Secretary Len Murray, might be consulted and their views listened to with respect by Labour ministers. During the late 1970s union leaders became frequent dinner guests at 10 Downing Street but this gave them little positive power or influence over the key economic decision making of the Callaghan Government after the summer of 1976 even if it increased the sense of their own self-importance. Indeed, it was the increasing awareness of the lack of trade union impact on the course of events that underpinned the increasingly sour and disillusioned attitude of trade union activists that became so brutally manifest in the winter of 1978–79.

Undoubtedly, governments of both major parties wanted to make the trade unions through the TUC shoulder wider responsibilities as social partners in the running of the economy. Macmillan hoped TUC participation in the tripartite National Economic Development Council, formed in 1962, would lead to a much greater understanding among trade union leaders about the intractable character of the country's economic difficulties of low economic growth, a vulnerable currency, balance of payments problems, sluggish productivity and home-grown inflation. During the 1970s TUC nominees came to serve on a wide range of quasi-autonomous bodies known as Quangos such as the Equal Opportunities Commission, the Commission on Racial Equality, the Manpower Services Commission and the Health and Safety at Work Commission. No Royal Commission or Committee of Inquiry seemed to be complete without a TUC nominee being included. In the past, state patronage had been bestowed by governments on TUC worthies as a recognition of their longevity in office or senior position inside the movement rather than on grounds of ability or interest. But now increasingly the TUC itself began to insist on having a much greater say in the making of public appointments with the need for the work done to be accountable to the TUC. Unfairly, trade union leaders like Jack Jones were criticized for their involvement on such bodies but they were hardly sources for personal financial betterment and there is no evidence to suggest that the presence of trade union officials was either harmful or pointless. The middle-class army of the Great and the Good used by Whitehall to man public bodies might look with distaste at the intrusion on their world of trade union leaders but on balance they were a welcome addition in providing a degree of realism and commonsense not always in plentiful supply in British public life.

Such developments, especially in the era of the Social Contract between 1974 and 1979 suggested a new, much more trusting view by the TUC of the activities of the state. In its 1966 evidence to the Donovan Royal Commission, the TUC continued to argue from its traditional attitude of voluntarism, that the enforcement of minimum standards by law was only 'the second best alternative' to collective bargaining between employers and trade unions.[9] The TUC insisted that the state should stand aside by adopting what it called 'an attitude of abstention, of formal indifference' towards the conduct of industrial relations. Yet at no such stage was such a negative view allowed entirely to overwhelm the thinking of the TUC. Indeed, from the early 1960s there were signs of a significant and subtle change in Congress House attitudes. Both the 1962 Contracts of Employment Act and the 1964 Industrial Training Act were welcomed by the TUC although they made clear inroads into the old *laissez-faire* philosophy of state abstentionism from the workplace.

The TUC played an important creative role in the making of the 1965 Redundancy Payments Act, with its cash in hand incentives for workers as a way of trying to encourage a voluntary shake-out of labour in declining industries, while the 1970 Equal Pay Act was a clear recognition by the trade unions that collective bargaining alone had failed utterly to close the enormous earnings gap between male and female workers performing similar kinds of work. However, most trade unions saw no inconsistency in their demands and support for an extension of national legislation in the area of collective and individual worker rights, while at the same time they continued to defend their legal immunities under the common law from attacks by the courts. Jack Jones, the champion of workplace voluntarism, described the 1975 Employment Protection Act as a 'worker's charter' with its modest minimum benefits in areas like maternity leave, guaranteed lay-off pay, disclosure of company information and protection for shop stewards from discrimination in carrying out trade union duties. Indeed, his enthusiasm for the measure was unsurprising as he had helped 'to draft its essentials'.

The 1974 Health and Safety at Work Act also owed a great deal to TUC involvement and Congress House pushed hard for the introduction of safety representatives on the shopfloor, replete with genuine power. Some trade union leaders like Jack Jones and Len Murray were also keen to see legislation for the introduction of a system of industrial democracy, giving direct access for trade union activists on the boards of major private companies by statutory right.

But such a positive view of the benign role that the state could play in industrial relations continued to co-exist with a reaffirmation of an older, more instinctive hostility towards state intervention in the actual conduct of collective bargaining. The TUC general secretary George Woodcock warned during the 1960s that the trade unions must 'retain their independence' at all costs. He described their attitude eloquently as: 'We would just as lief you left us alone. If you do not think it is possible for you to help the trade unions then the least you can do is not to impede us'.[10] In a lecture he gave in 1970 Len Murray, who succeeded Vic Feather as TUC General Secretary in September 1973, explained that governments could not act as sole arbiter with groups like trade unions playing a 'subordinate role'. He added:

Trade unionists point to the manifest advantages of securing as great as possible a measure of consent to change and the value of industrial self-regulation, and express doubts about the competence of a government to understand the subtle and delicate processes of collective bargaining. It is the nature of governments, especially when making laws, to deal in absolutes, but absolutes leave little room for manoeuvre to accommodate the shifts and fluctuations of industrial activity.[11]

And he went on to assert: 'Trade unions claim that there are areas of activity in which they have an inherent right to act independently, as opposed to that right being created by the state and thus subject to reappraisal and modification by the state'.

The TUC simply could not agree with the successive attempts made to bring the trade unions within a new framework of law, as proposed first by Harold Wilson and Barbara Castle in their 'short, sharp' Bill they sought to force through in 1969 with its legal sanctions against unofficial strikers and again in 1971 with the passage by the Conservative Government of the Industrial Relations Act.

The first occasion almost severed the historic links between the political and industrial wings of the Labour Movement as employment secretary, Barbara Castle, in the words of her main protagonist in Cabinet, Jim Callaghan, 'galloped ahead with all the reckless gallantry of the Light Brigade at Balaclava' in the single-minded pursuit of her objective of forcing the trade unions to reform themselves.[12] It took the combined efforts of the TUC general council, the parliamentary Labour party and a growing group of dissidents in the Cabinet to prevent a fatal rupture in government–union relations. Under enormous pressure Wilson and Castle backed down and settled for a 'solemn and binding agreement' with the TUC which agreed to push ahead with its own reform programme to improve trade union behaviour.

The 1971 Industrial Relations Act looked a much more formidable instrument to deal with the trade unions. The Heath Government believed that the method of legal immunities for trade unions, so that their officials could not be sued for actions 'in furtherance or contemplation of a trades dispute', was no longer a sensible way of conducting industrial relations. But the comprehensive and major measure that the Conservatives placed on the statute book was based on a fundamental contradiction. On the one hand, it sought to strengthen the authority of full-time trade union officials over their members and build up their organization at the centre but on the other it reflected a determination to uphold the rights of individual workers through the device of the agency shop against being coerced by a trade union. The attempt to reconcile libertarian and hierarchical principles within the same piece of legislation proved to be an unqualified failure. However, it certainly gave the TUC a renewed sense of common purpose after the divisions and frustrations of the Wilson years, while at the same time the Act had 'little influence on the general practice of industrial relations' and 'few outside the ranks of newspaper leader writers and lawyers seemed concerned about the abstract relationship between industrial relations and the law'.[13] It is true that a combination of fortuitous events in the spring and early summer of 1972 brought about the early demise of the Act. The imprisonment of five London dockers' leaders in Pentonville jail for contempt of court (albeit for only a few days) pulled back a number of wavering unions (the Electricians; the General and Municipal Workers; the National Association of Local Government Officers) from defying TUC policy by agreeing to register under the new Act in order to protect their funds. The non-involvement strategy of the TUC held firm but even employers in the public sector who might have been expected to be more directly under government influence, were quite unwilling to accept that trade union negotiators should sign legally binding collective contracts with them. Moreover, after the traumas of the miners' victory in March 1972 and the climbdown by the Heath Cabinet over the Upper Clyde Shipbuilders's work in early 1971, the Act became an acute embarrassment for a government which was now seeking a new partnership with both sides of industry through the TUC and the Confederation of British Industry. By the winter of 1973–4 the measure was for all intents and purposes in cold storage, though it was still capable of provoking conflict between unions and the law, mainly because the Amalgamated Union of Engineering Workers refused to have anything to do with its provisions, not even being prepared to attend court hearings under its jurisdiction.

THE IMPERATIVE OF AN INCOMES POLICY

If the power of the state could not be used to make the unions change their attitudes however, governments of the period were anxious to win the TUC's co-operation for measures of wage restraint in the national interest. Harold Macmillan's Government could not achieve any consent from the TUC for its anti-inflationary efforts when they involved efforts to reduce pay rise expectations. The 1961 pay pause in the public sector aroused widespread unrest in the public services and the TUC refused to have anything to do with the National Incomes Commission, established in 1962. However Macmillan drew some comfort from the fact that most senior union leaders said 'little' about the Conservative incomes policy and he believed the government 'could expect quiet and uneffusive sympathy' from them for what it was doing.[14] He hoped that an incomes policy would become 'not an instrument of deflation but a weapon for more rapid growth' but in the run-up to the October 1964 general election the Conservative Government of Sir Alec Douglas-Home virtually abandoned any attempt to dampen down the level of wage increases. Not for the first time in the period the necessities of electoral politics undermined government efforts to hold the line on pay.

In its 1958 economic policy document – Plan for Progress – the Labour party argued that the future growth in money incomes would have to 'broadly keep in step with higher productivity' but the party's leaders assumed they would be able to count on the TUC's goodwill and support to realize that objective on the grounds that a Labour government would 'restore a climate of expansion, maintain fair play between different sections of the community, promote greater equality and create a price truce'.[15] Union leaders were indeed desperate to see a Labour victory after thirteen years of Conservative rule and they had no wish to upset the climate of harmony achieved by Harold Wilson after his election as Hugh Gaitskell's successor in February 1963 with any unseemly public squabble over the role of wage restraint under a future Labour government. Even Frank Cousins, the awkward General Secretary of the Transport and General Workers Union, was ready to hide his genuine doubts about an incomes policy through the use of the euphemistic phrase, 'a planned growth of wages'.

But Cousins spelt out the genuine dilemma that would face union leaders in any voluntary agreement with a government covering pay rises in an article he wrote in his union journal in October 1963. His words went to the heart of the problem. 'If we do not fulfil the purposes for which members join unions, to protect and raise their real standard of living, then the unions will wither and finally die', he argued. 'We can give leadership, we can persuade but basically we must serve trade union purposes'.[16] In the battle of all, his members were to be part of the all. In saying this, Cousins was merely expressing a widely-held opinion among trade union negotiators. Through the 1960s and 1970s most of them, though by no means everybody, were never really convinced by the political or economic arguments for a national prices and incomes policy laid out through a national agreement between the government and the unions through the auspices of the TUC. They continued to preach and practice the virtues of 'free' collective bargaining, where the forces of capital and labour fought it out in the market place to divide the limited spoils unevenly.

Every prime minister during the period from Macmillan to Callaghan reached a similar conclusion that the unfettered wage scramble was a major cause of Britain's relatively high inflation rate and ultimately self-destructive. It led to the impoverishment of workers rather than a rise in their real prosperity. Yet the unquestioning, touching faith of trade unions in what Sidney Weighell at the 1978 Labour party conference called the 'philosophy of the pig trough, where those with the biggest snouts gain the most'[17] remained without successful challenge. The concept of business unionism was unpopular among the small minority of activists who ran the trade unions in the period on behalf of the mass membership. Even the most rapacious white-collar union bargainer, with a clear-eyed aim of boosting the earnings and perks of the salaried elite he or she represented, felt obliged to pay lip-service to some vague sentiment of social equality. In Britain union activists found little difficulty in marrying a commitment to the pay merry-go-round with a belief in more state intervention in economic and social affairs. Trade unions took a benign view of the extension of state power to deal with unemployment, industrial investment, health care, education, the distribution of wealth and income through the tax system and welfare benefits for the old and the poor. The state was regarded by trade union activists as an essential instrument for the creation of a more just and prosperous society through its powers of redistribution. They refused to accept the view of many American trade union bargainers who believed they had to concentrate their activities on winning better bread and butter benefits for their members rather than ensuring all workers achieve them through social legislation. Trade union activists in Britain have traditionally regarded the Labour party as the political means of achieving reforms for everybody through parliamentary, democratic action. Before the 1960s an effort was usually made to draw a distinctive line between the industrial and political concerns of the Labour Movement. Even as late as 1966, in its evidence to the Donovan Royal Commission, the TUC suggested that the party-union alliance became strained 'if either attempts to capitalise on the loyalties which exist' between them and the strength of the relationship was said to derive 'paradoxically from the looseness of the ties'.[18]

After October 1964, however, it became increasingly hard to maintain such a position. The Labour party under Harold Wilson's leadership came to power on the basis of an election manifesto that stated there would have to be 'a planned growth of incomes so that they were broadly related to the annual growth of production' and it went on to assert that this would apply 'in an expanding economy to all incomes; to profits, dividends and rents as well as to wages and salaries'.[19] The huge balance of payments deficit – mainly the result of the pre-election Conservative consumer spending boom – did little to dampen down the early euphoria of Labour's first months in power after thirteen years in the political wilderness. But from the very beginning, the Wilson Government was under almost continuous pressure from the international money markets after its initial decision not to devalue the fixed exchange rate for sterling as a way of easing the economic crisis. Rescue operations designed to protect the over-valued currency required wage restraint at home and trade union co-operation was seen as vital in order to achieve that aim.

The unrealistic optimism of the much-heralded National Plan with a proposed annual growth rate to 1970 of 3.8 per cent was not long in evaporating. By the spring of 1965 the government was busy establishing the machinery for a prices and incomes policy that required employers and trade unions to provide early warning of pending wage claims and price rises, with the prospect of delay where necessary so that the newly created National Board of Prices and Incomes could be allowed time to scrutinize cases referred to it. As Secretary of State for Economic Affairs, George Brown tried to browbeat the TUC leadership on the eve of the 1965 Congress to swallow a compulsory 'early warning' system on pay claims. In his view, union leaders only responded to 'frequent kicks in the shins'[20] but his bullying diplomacy upset George Woodcock, the TUC

General Secretary, who believed (like Labour's already forgotten 1964 election manifesto) that any incomes policy could only stand a chance of success in the broad context of economic growth, not as an instrument for deflation. In the event, the majority of union leaders decided to establish a committee within the TUC to vet pay claims and settlements as a way of deflecting Brown's demands but this decision was only carried by 5,300,000 votes to 3,300,000 votes at the Congress, with the Transport and General Workers Union already leading the mounting opposition to government interference in collective bargaining.

The TUC's incomes policy committee proved to be a failure. 'Although it examined more than 600 claims during its first nine months, it questioned only a handful and had no real effect on the course of any of them', wrote Gerald Dorfman. 'The committee often acted on claims at the rate of 50 an hour during its one-day sessions each month. It reached decisions to approve claims without making any attempt to measure them against the 3 to 3.5 per cent present norm the TUC had agreed to honour.'[21]

Britain's economy deteriorated during the spring and early summer of 1966. The Labour party won an overall parliamentary majority of 97 in the April general election but this did nothing to strengthen confidence in the ability of the government's management of the economy. A seven-week long official seamen's strike helped to weaken uncertain foreign business opinion. Sterling came under intense pressure on the exchange markets and large sums of money began to flow out of the country. Harold Wilson declared that the government had been 'blown off course' and he introduced emergency measures that included a six-month standstill on pay rises to be followed by a further six-month period of 'severe restraint' as well as a freeze on price rises, higher indirect taxes and hire purchase restrictions. The TUC general council demonstrated its residual loyalty to the government by voting 20 to 12 in general support of the July measures but Frank Cousins resigned as Minister of Technology in protest after an unhappy period in office and returned to his old union to lead the resistance. At the 1966 Congress support for the government's pay freeze only went through by a paper thin majority in a vote of 4,560,000 to 4,220,000. The moral credit built up by Labour with the TUC during the opposition years was wasting away rapidly.

Despite the growing unease about the wisdom of Labour's economic strategy, the TUC under Woodcock was prepared to examine the role of Congress House in the administration of an incomes policy, even though it meant a greater co-ordination of power at the centre and a corresponding decline in the autonomy of affiliate unions. But by the 1967 Congress the trade unions were in no mood to give its blessing to the government's increasingly unpopular prices and incomes policy. The frustrations and disappointments experienced by Woodcock and his colleagues led eventually to the development of a more coherent economic alternative from the TUC embodied in 1968 for the first time in its own economic review which became an annual event thereafter. Congress House embraced a commitment to growth and even sought to back an incomes policy that would bring an annual rise in wage rates of 3.5 per cent with a further 1.5 per cent for local wage drift. But this suggestion only scraped through a TUC conference of union executives in February 1968 by the skin of its teeth. By that stage the Transport and General Workers under Cousins had been joined by the formidable opposition of the former right-wing bastion the Amalgamated Union of Engineering Workers that came under left domination with the election of Hugh Scanlon as its president.

Indeed, by the late 1960s the whole idea of a national incomes policy had become discredited in large areas of the trade union movement. It had not been used to bring about any redistribution of income, help the low paid or provide an opportunity for genuine productivity bargaining. The tensions and animosities aroused between the TUC and the government over incomes policy hardly seemed disproportionate to its modest achievement. 'As far as the actual earnings of manual workers were concerned the policy had little overall effect in the period 1965–1969 but slowed down the rate of increase in the first half of the period', concluded Oxford labour economist Derek Robinson.[22] In his opinion, it was 'an excessive price to pay for merely postponing wage increases'. In fact by the end of the 1960s Britain was suffering from the consequences of a major wage explosion and industrial conflict on a scale not experienced for more than forty years. The remnants of Labour's incomes policy fell apart by the spring of 1970 in the run-up to the general election as workers fought to recoup the ground they thought they had lost during the years of freeze and restraint. It has been argued convincingly that the main reason for the revolt of the rank and file between 1969 and 1972 stemmed from the rise of a 'wage-tax spiral'.[23] Between 1964 and 1968 it was estimated that gross money incomes for male manual workers jumped by 6.6 per cent but their net real income rose by a mere 0.5 per cent. The burden of direct taxation fell on the average wage earner to help pay for Labour's public spending programmes. In 1960 the average male manual worker's tax and national insurance contributions together amounted to less than 8 per cent of his earnings. By 1970 the proportion had climbed to 20 per cent. 'It seems to be the fate of Labour governments in Britain to tax employees more heavily (or restrain their real wages more effectively)', wrote Jackson, Turner and Wilkinson. 'Indeed, it almost appears as if the objective economic historical role of the British Labour party is to do (no doubt despite itself) those things to the workers that Conservative governments are unable to do'.

But the failure of efforts to achieve a credible and workable incomes policy in the 1960s stemmed primarily from the changing nature of the collective bargaining system as more and more power of decision making passed from the centre to the workplace or company. The Donovan

Commission gave due recognition to this trend as it occurred particularly in private sector manufacturing when it sought to distinguish between 'formal' and 'informal' systems. In Donovan's opinion, the existence of full employment since the end of the Second World War had encouraged the move away from national substantive industry-wide agreements covering pay and benefits, with a resulting decline in the authority of employers and full-time union officials, and at the same time strengthened the power of the lay shop stewards and shopfloor workgroups.

The Commission report concluded that 'the central defect' of industrial relations in the 1960s was 'disorder in factory and workshop relations and pay structures promoted by the conflict between the formal and the informal'.[24] The sudden unofficial strike by small groups could lay off hundreds and sometimes thousands of other workers over seemingly trivial issues and these were regarded by Donovan as a symptom of the country's malaise and the inability to integrate the 'formal' and 'informal' blamed for the strike statistics (though it is worth remembering that at the time according to the comparative figures produced by the International Labour Office in Geneva Britain came only half way down the stoppage league table among western nations). Donovan and the majority of his colleagues concluded that it was no solution to try and re-establish centralized union control through a return to industry-wide agreements and the eclipse of shop-floor bargaining. The nature of the tight labour market with too little supply and not enough demand made such a policy option unrealistic anyway. Instead, the Commission came down in favour of putting more order into the informal system through the encouragement of job evaluation and productivity bargaining as well as better facilities and greater recognition from employers and trade unions for shop stewards and greater managerial control of job incentive schemes.

In other words, Donovan wanted to use voluntarism as a means of remedying the defects of the system. Unfortunately the Commission gave little attention to the tangled connection between what was going on on the shopfloor and the imperatives of the national economy. The report acknowledged that the Confederation of British Industry made a valid point when it suggested national planning on incomes was impossible because of the fragmentation of plant bargaining. 'Incomes policy must continue a lame and halting exercise so long as it consists in the planning of industry-wide agreements, most of which exercise an inadequate control over pay', argued Donovan. 'So long as workplace bargaining remains informal, autonomous and fragmented the drift of earnings away from rates of pay cannot be brought under control'. It is unclear why the Commission thought either workgroups or trade unions should see any obvious advantage for themselves in a more regulated localized bargaining arrangement, if this meant greater disciplines and controls imposed by employers on workers.

Moreover, there is a danger in exaggerating the spread of shopfloor power in the 1960s. Trade union expansion in the public services at the end of the decade, reflected in the huge growth in membership of unions like the Public Employees and the Local Government Officers, where national pay bargaining remained paramount, revealed an awareness among new groups hitherto poorly organized of the successful role of trade unionism in protecting workers from the ravages of inflation. The growing attraction of trade unionism to white-collar and public service employees and the greater strike-proneness of workers beyond the traditional bastions of organized labour like the docks, coal industry, and car production could not be put down to the rapid spread of plant bargaining. Professor Phelps Brown believed that the phenomenon arose from a collision between rising worker expectations and the inability of the market economy to deliver the goods because of a profits squeeze. 'Collective bargaining today is not between labour and capital or employees and management for the distribution of the products of particular industries between pay and profit', he wrote in 1973, 'but between different groups of employees, for the distribution of the national product between them one with another and between them as a whole and the inactive population. Cost inflation appears basically as the process by which particular groups of employees enter and enforce claims to shares in the national product that add up to more than the total product; and the over-subscription comes out as a rise in prices'.[25]

The 1960s saw the spread of a self-regarding worker sectionalism with an erosion of older notions of solidarity and the emergence of the workgroup as a more dominant force in industrial relations. John Goldthorpe and his colleagues discovered what they regarded as a new kind of trade unionism in their study of manual workers in Luton in the early 1960s. 'Neither as a way to greater worker participation in the affairs of the enterprise nor as a political force is unionism greatly valued', they concluded. 'Rather, one would say, the significance that unionism has for these workers is very largely confined to issues arising from their employment which are economic in nature and which are local in their origins and scope'.[26] The Goldthorpe study argued that workers valued union membership as a form of meal ticket rather than an affirmation of any sense of class collectivism.

However, this did not mean that the manual workers were suddenly all becoming middle class in their lifestyles and ambitions. The embourgeoisement theory suffered real setbacks in the face of the realities of the 1960s. But nor were they in any sense a revolutionary proletariat. 'Instrumental collectivism' was how Goldthorpe described the attitude of the Luton workers. They found self-fulfilment outside the workplace in the network of family and community not through association with their fellow workers on the shopfloor.

Workplace bargaining found an idealistic and articulate champion in Jack Jones, who was elected to succeed Cousins as general secretary of the

Transport and General Workers in 1969. Ever since his days as district secretary in Coventry in the war years and after, Jones had favoured the devolution of power down through the union hierarchy to the shop stewards and away from full-time union officials. 'Our success – and indeed the success of industry itself – is going to be determined by the extent to which we can decentralise – spread decision-making amongst work people and above all get industrial agreements settled where they are going to be operated', Jones told an Institute of Personnel Management conference in October 1969. He believed in self-help on the shopfloor and decried the notion that union leaders should be in any sense boss figures. 'I am working for a system where not a few trade union officials control the situation but a dedicated, well-trained and intelligent body of trade union members represented by hundreds of thousands of lay representatives – every one of whom is capable of helping to resolve industrial problems and assist in collective bargaining and the conclusion of agreements.'[27]

Jones's romantic vision was of a decentralized trade unionism that legitimized the position of the much-maligned shop stewards. No longer were they to be treated by full-time union officials as a threat from below. Internal union reforms like the establishment of industrial delegate conferences, lay representation on bargaining teams in multi-employer and single-employer negotiations and the drawing-up and ratification of pay claims and offers by the rank-and-file activists, were designed to integrate the realities of the workplace into the more formalized and often ossified rubric and settled ways of trade union hierarchies. But how was it really possible to reconcile the inevitable parochialism and limited objectives of shopfloor bargainers with the wider needs and aspirations of trade unionism? The optimistic Benthamite assumption that the sum of diverse and often conflicting self-interests would ensure the well-being and harmony of all workers was hard to reconcile with the virulent sectionalist outbursts of the 1960s and 1970s. Far from bringing about the liberation of a thwarted worker idealism and producing a sense of purpose on the shopfloor, decentralization tended to enflame the underlying fragmented tendencies of the diverse, often competing workgroups. Certainly it failed to generate any cohesive sense of worker solidarity or a political consciousness that could provide a remotely socialist perspective for the often unedifying and endless struggle of the annual wage round.

The rhetoric of the class war and social solidarity made very little impression on most workers during the period. W. G. Runciman in his important study published in 1966 – *Relative Deprivation and Social Justice* – discovered that workers retained surprisingly narrow terms of reference when they compared their own earnings and benefits at work with those of others. Envy of the better-off was found not to be particularly widespread on the shopfloor though there remained a vague belief in the natural justice slogan of the Labour Movement – 'a fair day's work for a fair day's pay'.

What did stimulate a sense of worker grievance, however, was a disruption of wage relativities and differentials between workers doing similar kinds of work or employed in jobs that were close to each other in character and place. It is arguable that the main cause of instability and unrest in industrial relations in the 1960s and 1970s derived not from generalized trade union 'power' or a determination by the low paid to crusade for a better deal for themselves but from the archaic and often arbitrary nature of pay bargaining structures due to a lack of sensitivity and professionalism by employers and their personnel managers.

The open season on wage bargaining throughout the year and the widely-perceived belief in the concept of the 'going rate' in wage increases achieved by the early front-runners in the annual round must not be overlooked either as a cause of the unrest. The failure of the strenuous but ultimately abortive attempts at creating a national incomes policy during the 1960s was an understandable result of the fluidity and ad hoc character of competitive bargaining in a free society where no sense of discipline or consensus existed to restrain the demands of workers to better themselves and their families in an unequal society where capital rather than labour was the ultimate arbiter of events. This is why those critics who spoke so sweepingly about the tyranny of trade unionism or the muscle of union organization were wholly mistaken about the fundamental nature of the problem.

THE ERA OF THE SOCIAL CONTRACT

In the aftermath of Labour's unexpected but decisive defeat in the June 1970 general election, a number of policy makers in the party began to examine the tricky issue of Labour's future relations with the trade unions. In particular there was a short discussion on how Labour in office could seek to achieve its objectives of greater social equality and justice without any understanding with trade unions on wage bargaining. The dilemma was clear; how to reconcile the sectionalist aspirations of union members for the good life with the determination of the Socialist activist minority in the unions who sought to establish a more rational, equitable and planned economy. In an important Fabian Society pamphlet published in October 1970 Harold Wilson's former economic adviser, Lord Balogh, emphasized the dangers of union militancy for the creation of high levels of self-destructive inflation.

As he argued:

Once unions, in their wage demands and firms in their investment and other decisions, anticipate further increases in prices, they will take defensive action by increasing their wage demands and prices respectively – This would accelerate and aggravate the process. Should it intensify, the creep of inflation might become a walk, a trot, a canter and eventually a gallop. In the end it would cause unemployment and undermine the currency.[28]

Lord Balogh pointed out that trade unions were unable, as a result of their limited position in the economy, to increase the share of total national income devoted to wages. As a result, the so-called 'free' collective bargaining they practised tended to widen existing wage inequalities rather than either narrow or remove them. He suggested that what the Labour party needed was what he called a *'contrat social'*, a bargain between government and organized labour in order to avoid the mistakes and conflicts that had characterized the 1960s. In his view, a national incomes policy was an integral part of a much wider strategy designed to strengthen the influence of the trade unions in society. But Lord Balogh's ideas found few enthusiasts in the Labour party in 1970.

At that year's annual conference Jim Callaghan questioned out loud how it was really possible to secure social justice for and between workers in a pay free for all and wondered whether there was not a better way to organize the bargaining system. 'It is only fair to the next Labour government to know in advance what doors will be shut against them before you get there', he added.[29] Callaghan was soon left in no doubt about what union leaders thought about it. Jack Jones launched a ferocious verbal assault on journalists and 'some politicians' who had, he alleged, 'for the most part never been covered by a wage claim because frankly they have never worked for a living', while Hugh Scanlon suggested the Labour party might start discussing a socialist incomes policy 'when we own the means of production, distribution and exchange'.[30] Such deep hostility from Britain's two most powerful union leaders to any suggestion of an incomes policy ensured that the Labour party (whatever the doubts among the leaders) was forced to drop any open discussion about such a controversial issue, at least until the eve of the February 1974 general election and even then it was done tentatively.

However, this did not mean that the Labour–TUC alliance fell to pieces in the early 1970s. On the contrary, mainly as a result of Jack Jones's initiative, a new body was formed in January 1972 – the Labour Party–TUC Liaison Committee, which became the main policy-making body in the Labour Movement. It brought together senior figures on the TUC general council, in the Shadow Cabinet and on the National Executive Committee in what it was hoped would be a close and effective unity which would bind all sides together in common cause. Not since the revamping of the National Council of Labour after the party's 1931 general election disaster had there been such a formalized organization bringing the TUC and Labour leaders together in such a systematic, regular way.

During its first two years of existence the Liaison Committee laid down the foundations of what came to be known as the Social Contract.

Its main early sessions concentrated on creating the framework for a new industrial relations system based on voluntary principles to replace Heath's 1971 legislation. The two sides agreed that an independent tripartite conciliation and arbitration service should be created. New laws were to make it easier for workers to join trade unions, to have greater access to company information and more security when faced with unfair dismissal by their employer. But the Liaison Committee began to extend its concerns beyond industrial relations to economic policy making. In January 1973 Harold Wilson and TUC General Secretary, Vic Feather, unveiled an economic programme for the next Labour government which promised a wide-ranging package of measures to subsidize food prices, transport fares and rents, to redistribute income and wealth, to phase out National Health Service subscriptions and substantially improve old age pensions. A further statement appeared in July 1974 from the Liaison Committee that proposed a reform of the European Community's common agricultural policy. All of these various items were to find their way into Labour's manifesto for the February 1974 general election.

Indeed, during its first nine months in office the minority Labour Government carried through most of the Liaison Committee's initial set of policies. The TUC general council enjoyed an influence in that short period over the course of British politics that it had never had before and would not have again. As Secretary for Employment, Michael Foot carried through the repeal of the 1971 Industrial Relations Act and replaced it with a measure that was mainly drafted in TUC headquarters. The Chancellor, Denis Healey, in his first two budgets, met with warm TUC approval for the introduction of food subsidies, a large rise in old age pensions, a rent freeze and higher taxes on the rich. At the 1974 TUC Congress Jim Callaghan, as fraternal delegate from the Labour party, enthused that the Social Contract was 'a means of achieving nothing less than the social and economic reconstruction' of the country. The Labour party's narrow victory in the second 1974 general election a month later, appeared to endorse the 'Social Contract' approach.[31]

Senior ministers were anxious to try and keep in close contact with the TUC leadership despite the pressures of government. This was mainly done through regular dinners with the six most senior TUC members who served on the National Economic Development Council, the so-called NEDDY 'gold plated' six. But Ministers also somehow found the time in their crowded diaries to attend monthly meetings of the Liaison Committee. Both sides seemed anxious to avoid the troubles that did so much to strain relations in the 1966–1970 period of Labour government.

But relying on the goodwill of the TUC to ensure wage increases did not become inflationary was not enough. In 1974 the Cabinet agreed not to have an incomes policy. During their internal discussions before the February 1974 general election, Harold Wilson had suggested a future Labour government would seek to 'create a mood rather than a contract'[32] for wage bargaining to take place without the need for any direct government intervention. Recently-elected TUC General Secretary, Len Murray, for his part, told the Liaison Committee that the greatest disservice the TUC could do the Labour party was to 'pretend it could do more than it could' but assured Wilson the TUC would 'respond' to what a Labour government did in office to meet its demands.[33] The Labour Government abolished the statutory Pay Board established by Edward Heath to run his incomes policy in the summer of 1974 and accepted there should be a return to free collective bargaining. In a statement to the 1974 Congress the TUC stressed the need for there to be twelve-monthly intervals between pay rises; a low pay target for negotiators to ensure all workers earned £25 a week and moves towards equal pay for women. It was also suggested that 'over the coming year negotiators should recognise that the scope for real increases in consumption is limited and a central negotiating objective in this period will be to ensure that real incomes are maintained'.

However, the 1974–1975 wage round was an unmitigated disaster for the British economy with a deterioration in the balance of payments deficit to £3.8bn with basic hourly wage rate increases climbing to 32 per cent a year and price rises in hot pursuit. 'The unions defaulted on their part of the Social Contract', complained Denis Healey in his memoirs.[34] The TUC guidelines provided a flimsy, inadequate protection against the suicidal consequences of the illusory pay bonanza, which was partly fuelled by the continuation of the pay threshold clauses to protect pay against the erosive impact of inflation from the Conservatives' statutory incomes policy. However, the Labour Cabinet was unable to act quickly enough to deal with the increasing economic crisis because Wilson was trying to negotiate favourable terms for British membership of the European Community in order to hold his government together.

By June 1975, however, the eighteen months of drift over dealing with wage push inflation came to an end. Under the threat of the imposition of a new statutory incomes policy complete with sanctions against employers who broke its provisions the TUC began to reassess its attitude. The crucial change came with the transformation of Jack Jones, who, his old foe Barbara Castle noted in her diary at the time, was changing from 'the archetypal trade union villain' into 'an almost gentle, and certainly benign influence'.[35] In fact Jones played a key role in winning the consent of the TUC to a voluntary £6 pay rise for everybody earning up to £8,500 a year and nothing except incremental increases for those earning more than that figure, though the vote of support on the general council was only 19 to 13. The government took the precaution of bringing in back-up legislation which it was prepared to enforce if the £6 policy broke down.

In fact, it proved to be a great success in at least reversing the wage-price rise trend. Over the twelve months of its application to July 1976 inflation fell by half to 12.9 per cent while earnings averaged increases of 14.4 per cent. 'Not a free for all but a fair for all – that is our policy', declared Jack Jones to the 1975 Congress. 'The union I lead and myself personally have never supported the idea that trade unionism is a licence for any group to look after themselves and to hell with the rest.'[36]

But after the economic crisis of June 1975 the balance of influence in the TUC–Labour alliance moved steadily away from Congress House as ministers came under increasing pressure from other more powerful external interests like the International Monetary Fund and foreign governments like those of the United States and West Germany to remedy the country's economic troubles. Wilson and his colleagues still listened to what the TUC leaders had to say and the TUC was still consulted on some policy making but the impact of Congress House started to wane perceptibly in the winter of 1975–1976. Necessary Treasury spending cuts and the introduction of the curbing instrument of the public sector borrowing requirement failed to win TUC approval. The Social Contract was meant to cover a wide programme of action to protect vulnerable groups in society from inflation and unemployment. Instead, the dole queues began to lengthen and the government started to phase out the subsidies introduced in 1974, rejecting the TUC call for reflation of the economy in April 1976.

By the spring of 1976 union leaders began to despair about their apparent lack of impact on government policy. Jack Jones warned the phasing-out of food subsidies seemed to imply a change in strategy that took Labour in the direction of the neo-liberal market ideas of the Conservative party's new leader Margaret Thatcher, while Hugh Scanlon who had mellowed rapidly since Labour's return to office said 'almost pleadingly' that if the Budget did not ensure more investment for industry the position of TUC leaders would become 'almost impossible'.[37]

In fact, it took many weeks of argument to win agreement on a second year of wage restraint. The Chancellor Denis Healey proposed to link tax cuts to pay moderation in order to achieve trade union consent for further austerity after it became clear that the TUC would not swallow any attempt to keep wage increases in the 1976–1977 pay round of only 3 per cent. In the event, a limit of 5 per cent or a maximum increase of £4 a week and a minimum of £2.50 a week was eventually agreed between the government and the TUC, far tighter guidelines than those of the £6 policy the previous year. The TUC leaders had to admit they had not achieved all they had wanted. Indeed, Scanlon admitted to the Special Congress called to endorse the second stage of the incomes policy that the only concession the TUC won in talks with the government had been to defer an increase in school meal charges at a cost of £35m. But he warned his colleagues there was no real alternative for the TUC but to accept what the government wanted. 'We honestly believed then – and still do – that no agreement would have meant a catastrophic run on the pound that would have made what has recently happened look like chicken feed'. In fact, the outcome was again relatively successful. Earnings between August 1976 and August 1977 rose by 8.8 per cent on average, while prices rose by 15.6 per cent over the period. This produced a sizeable 6.8 per cent cut in real wages for workers, which provides an understandable explanation for the growing signs of a rank-and-file worker unrest.

Indeed, at their September 1976 Congress the TUC indicated that it was not possible to have a third wage round of nationally-agreed voluntary wage restraint. Delegates voted overwhelmingly for an 'orderly' return to free collective bargaining from August 1977 and although union leaders agreed there should be a twelve-month interval between the dates of wage agreements, they were unable to co-operate any longer with the government on any new pay norm. W. W. Daniel in a survey carried out for Political and Economic Planning in December 1976 discovered growing resistance to any further nationally agreed incomes policy from shop stewards and he warned that 'manufacturing industry represents the most likely detonation point for the pay explosion that would certainly follow the removal of restraint'.[38] The main cause for grievance among workers turned out to be the comparison between rates of pay for workers doing similar kinds of work in the place where they worked, something that Runciman had discovered ten years earlier. The revolt of the British Leyland toolmakers in 1977 and again in 1978, was a good example of the corrosive impact of the national pay policy on skilled worker wage differentials relative to the earnings of production workers in the same plants.

There was no agreement with the TUC on pay after the autumn of 1977. Earlier in the summer Jack Jones found himself forced to concede defeat at the hands of his shop steward activists at his union's biennial conference in his efforts to win the approval of delegates for a further year of reasonably agreed wage rises. His failure came as a sad blow to the government's efforts at counter-inflation for they could no longer rely on his powerful influence inside the TUC. In fact, the wage round of 1977–1978 when the government hoped to keep rises down to 10 per cent came out at average earnings increases of 15 per cent when prices rose by only 7.8 per cent. The improvement in real wages amounted to 7.2 per cent, a substantial figure. The wage restraint efforts of the government were clearly failing to win much of a positive response from pay bargainers. Indeed, as many as 57 private sector companies were deprived of government financial aid for breaking through the 10 per cent government pay rise guidelines in 1977–1978.

Neither the union leaders nor their activist members seemed reassured by this. In 1977 the Social Contract was running out of momentum. The trade unions were divided bitterly over whether to press the issue of industrial democracy on the government. A committee of inquiry under Lord Bullock had come out in favour of representation for union nominees in equal number to shareholder representatives on the unitary boards of private sector companies employing more than 2,000 people but this failed to convince the Prime Minister, Jim Callaghan, and most of the Cabinet. There was in fact little evidence of popular rank-and-file support for industrial democracy and several major unions like the Engineers, the General and Municipal Workers and the Electricians disliked the Bullock proposals. Some union leaders questioned whether their organizations might compromise their role as bargainers if they became too involved in corporate strategy. The rising level of unemployment – it passed the one million figure in October 1975 – and the deflationary policies of the Cabinet made worse by the need for support from the International Monetary Fund in November 1976 worsened relations between the government and the TUC. Congress House was unable to win Cabinet approval for selective import controls, higher social spending on welfare benefits, a more dirigiste industrial strategy and a restoration of cuts in capital public sector expenditure programmes on hospitals, schools, road and house building.

But it was what happened in the 1978–1979 wage round in the notorious 'winter of discontent' which shattered public confidence on the ability of Labour and the unions to work harmoniously together. In his memoirs Denis Healey admits that the government was 'blind' to the warnings of impending trouble as the Cabinet agreed under the influence of Callaghan and himself to introduce a 5 per cent wage norm for everybody. In Healey's view ten years later the decision to go for 5 per cent was 'typical of the hubris which can overcome a successful government towards the end of its term' and he also then recognized that 'it is difficult to operate a pay policy even with the co-operation of the union leaders for the real power lies not in the union headquarters but with the local shop stewards who tend to see a national incomes policy as robbing them of their functions'.[39]

Callaghan was convinced that the fight against inflation must be the over-riding priority and this meant a tightening rather than any further relaxation in the pay guidelines. As it was, he believed a 5 per cent target would end up with earnings rises of between 8 and 9 per cent during the pay round. Desultory discussions were held with the TUC in the summer of 1978 but no agreement emerged. Most union leaders were convinced the government would hold a general election in October as it had no overall parliamentary majority and its pact with the Liberals had come to an end. Speaking at the 1978 Congress Callaghan was less than frank with the TUC and they felt betrayed when he announced a few days later his government would soldier on into 1979. It was a serious political miscalculation and it soured Callaghan's relations with the senior union leaders like Moss Evans who had succeeded Jones at the head of the Transport and General Workers and the loyalist, newly-elected right-wing president of the Engineers, Terry Duffy, who lacked the ability and authority of their predecessors.

The 'winter of discontent' came as a shock to the Callaghan Cabinet. This was no sudden outburst of class warfare, stimulated by envy of the rich. It was hard to detect any radical political consciousness in the great revolt that started with a successful nine-week strike by Ford car workers that ended up with the achievement of a 17 per cent wage rise and was followed with what often seemed like a rolling programme of disruptive action involving lorry drivers who won deals of 17 to 20 per cent and key public service workers who launched a planned union offensive on 22 January 1979 for a £60 a week minimum wage. The action of the dustmen, hospital ancillary workers and grave-diggers added to the over-riding sourness that did so much to turn public opinion decisively against Labour and the unions. The industrial conflict was no heroic struggle of labour against capital. The victims were those who could least help themselves like the old, the sick, the bereaved, children and the poor. The campaign of the public service low paid was one they could not really hope to win, for any huge rise for them would have provoked a demand for a restoration of differentials for other more skilled workers and white-collar staff. Indeed, it was skilled workers at the end of the 1970s who had most grounds for complaint about the distortion of incomes policy rather than the low-paid public service workers, many of whom worked in part-time occupations.

The graphic inside account from 10 Downing Street in that gloomy period of self-destruction is well told by Lord Donoughue, then senior policy adviser to Callaghan. Several attempts were made to try and salvage something from the wreckage but they failed to improve matters. In early November 1978 the TUC general council split 14 to 14 over approval of a generalized statement on economic policy that was little more than a fig-leaf to give the government a semblance of credibility. It went down to unlamented defeat on the chairman's casting vote. For a time in January 1979 Callaghan seemed almost paralysed from taking any initiative as his incomes policy fell to pieces. Donoughue wrote of the prime minister 'being worryingly lethargic' and 'of sitting in a sinking Titanic without music'.[40] In retrospect Callaghan regretted he failed to declare a state of emergency to deal with the deteriorating situation for at least it would have given a display of resolve even if it would have done little to ease the crisis.

Early in February the TUC and the government worked out together a so-called concordat that paid lip-service to a longer term understanding between them on the economy and also produced some voluntary codes of conduct designed to try and put a stop to the savage scenes of secondary mass picketing that had done so much to alienate public sympathy from the unions during the previous two months. The TUC suggested unions ought to consult their members by secret ballot before calling them out on strike and it advised greater control by the unions on the numbers of people to be deployed on picket lines, especially in secondary actions. The government also agreed to create a standing commission on pay comparability under the chairmanship of Professor Hugh Clegg that suggested a serious effort was to be made to escape from the ad hockery and hand-to-mouth response of governments to the persistent difficulties posed by public service pay.

What did the 'winter of discontent' achieve? Politically it undermined the confidence of the Labour Government and shattered the belief in the mind of the electorate that the TUC and Labour could work together in harmony for the improvement of the economy. More important, it paved the way for Margaret Thatcher's election triumph in May 1979. Her populist appeal of acquisitive economic liberalism evoked a favourable response especially among skilled manual workers, many of whom voted Conservative for the first time. As many as 33 per cent of trade unionists voted Conservative and only 51 per cent Labour.

The trade union 'problem' had come back with a vengeance and made it easier for the Conservatives to carry through their step-by-step strategy to shift the balance of power in industry away from the trade unions through reforms of labour law in the 1980s that went with rather than against the grain of voluntarist traditions.

Myth is often more potent than reality in contemporary history but the economic results of the 'winter of discontent' add a painful coda to a series of events that pushed the unions and Labour out of the mainstream of British politics for over a decade. In the 1978–1979 wage round earnings averaged rises of 14.4 per cent and prices climbed by 16.5 per cent. There was in effect a 2.1 per cent decline in average real wages despite the widespread industrial militancy.

In 1979 as in 1960 the politicians seemed no nearer finding a way of working in harmony with decentralized unions through an unco-ordinated pay bargaining system to deal with Britain's serious underlying economic problems. The events of the 1960s and 1970s had highlighted in a painful way just how difficult it was to reconcile the country's *laissez-faire* collectivism with the need for stability and consensus at the centre. Above all, it was the lack of any sense of social solidarity between workers that made it so much harder for governments to win the necessary approval for their efforts to find answers to Britain's recurrent trouble of a vulnerable currency, balance of payments deficits, high unit labour costs, sluggish productivity and modest economic growth. Unlike trade unions in other European market economies those in Britain were trapped by their own customs and practices as prisoners of their past.

NOTES AND REFERENCES

1.   H. Wilson, *The Labour Government 1964–1970: A Personal Record*, Weidenfeld and Nicolson and Michael Joseph, 1971, p. 533.
2.   B. Castle, *The Castle Diaries 1974–1976*, Weidenfeld and Nicolson, London, 1980, p. 309.

3.   Labour Party Conference Report, 1978, p. 74.
4.   G. Goodman, *The Awkward Warrior: Frank Cousins, his life and times*, Davis Poynter, 1979, p. 382.
5.   R. Maudling, *Memoirs*, Sidgwick and Jackson, London, 1978, pp. 263–266.
6.   H. Macmillan, *At The End of The Day 1961–1963*, Macmillan, London, 1973, p. 44.
7.   P. Johnson, *The Recovery of Freedom*, Basil Blackwell, Oxford, 1980, pp. 15–16.
8.   D. Hurd, *An End To Promises*, Collins, London, 1979, p. 128.
9.   *Trade Unionism*, TUC, 1966, p. 69.
10.   G. Woodcock, *The Trade Union Movement and The Government*, Leicester University Press, 1968, p. 10.
11.   L. Murray, *Trade Unions and The State*, Glasgow, 1970, pp. 8–9.
12.   J. Callaghan, *Time and Change*, Collins, 1987, p. 274.
13.   B. C. M. Weekes, M. Mellish, L. Dickens and J. Lloyd, *Industrial Relations and The Limits of Law*, Blackwell, Oxford, 1975, p. 246.
14.   H. Macmillan, *At The End of The Day*, op. cit., p. 108.
15.   *Plan For Progress*, Labour Party, 1958, p. 10.
16.   G. Goodman, op. cit., p. 369.
17.   Labour Party Conference Report, 1978, p. 110.
18.   TUC, op. cit., p. 56.
19.   D. Butler and A. King, *British General Election 1964*, Macmillan, 1965, p. 85.
20.   G. Dorfman, *Wage Politics in Britain 1945–1967*, Charles Knight, London, 1979, p. 121.
21.   G. Dorfman, op. cit., p. 138.
22.   W. Beckerman (ed.), *The Labour Government's Economic Record 1964–1970*, Duckworth, London, 1972, p. 314.
23.   D. Jackson, H. A. Turner and F. Wilkinson, *Do Trade Unions Cause Inflation?*, Cambridge University Press, 1972, pp. 113–114.
24.   *Royal Commission on Trade Unions and Employers' Associations 1965–1968*, HMSO, 1968, pp. 36–37.
25.   H. Phelps Brown, *Old Wine in New Bottles*, British Journal of Industrial Relations, 8, no. 2, 1970, p. 8.
26.   J. Goldthorpe, D. Lockwood, F. Bechofer and J. Platt, *The Affluent Worker In The Class Structure*, Vol. 3, Cambridge University Press, 1969, p. 215.
27.   J. Jones, *Trade Unionism In the Seventies*, Transport and General Workers, June 1970, pp. 5–6.
28.   T. Balogh, *Labour and Inflation*, Fabian Society, October 1970, p. 21.
29.   Labour Party Conference Report, 1970, pp. 164–165.
30.   Ibid., p. 176, p. 223.

31. TUC Report, 1974, p. 396.
32. B. Castle, *Diary*, op. cit., 4 January 1974, p. 20.
33. B. Castle, *Diary*, op. cit., 20 January 1975, p. 283.
34. Denis Healey, *The Time of My Life*, Michael Joseph, London, 1989, p. 394.
35. B. Castle, *Diary*, op. cit., 23 February 1976, p. 283.
36. TUC Report 1975, p. 460.
37. Special TUC Report, 1976, p. 30.
38. W. W. Daniel, *The Next Stage of Incomes Policy*, Political and Economic Planning, December 1976, p. 28.
39. D. Healey, op. cit., p. 398.
40. B. Donoughue, *Prime Minister*, Jonathan Cape, 1987, p. 177.

10 Trade unions and the second coming of CND

Ben Pimlott

PROLOGUE

This essay was first written in the summer of 1981, when the Labour Party revolution it describes was at its height. The SDP had only just been set up, and Labour's worst-ever election defeat (partly caused by the manifesto 'suicide note' which included the unilateralist commitment) had yet to happen. The chapter is thus, in a sense, a period piece, and it reveals some of the fevered miscalculations of those unusual times. Nevertheless I have decided to leave it pretty much as it first appeared, apart from some gingering up at the start and some other minor corrections (including changes to the tenses of verbs). If I was writing it again from scratch, I would say some different things: I would suggest, in particular, that the comment by Taylor and Pritchard about the failure of CND 'to make the crucial breakthrough to the working class' proved almost as true in the 1980s as in the 1960s. I would not, however, water down the central argument.

If it was premature (perhaps downright wrong) to claim that unilateralism had become a working-class as well as a middle-class issue, my main contention had been amply borne out – namely, that because of the greater attachment of unions to the anti-nuclear idea than to other non-industrial causes, Labour's support for it would be particularly steadfast. Indeed, of all the issues which precipitated the 1981 split, unilateralism was the Labour Party commitment which endured the longest. The main reason for this was the devotion to it of big-voting trade unions and, above all, the TGWU, which continued jealously to guard the flame lit by Frank Cousins, until the bitter end. Whether or not unilateralism was a major vote-loser in the 1980s, it was certainly a policy which most leaders of the parliamentary party fervently wished to shed throughout the decade; yet the Labour Party entered two general elections unhappily committed to versions of it.

But has the end really been reached? There are reasons outside the United Kingdom which make unilateral disarmament a less immediate concern in the 1990s. Just as a decade or so ago a frosting up of the Cold War helped to revive the anti-nuclear movement, so the upheaval in East Europe, combined with rapid progress in arms negotiations, has helped to marginalize it. As long, however, as nuclear weapons continue to exist and Britain continues to possess its own arsenal, the possibility of yet another upsurge of interest in disarmament will remain.

In British grass-roots and campaigning politics, there seems to be a stock of peace-issue related energy that moves from issue to issue according to the pressures of the time. In the 1960s, passions associated with Ban-the-Bomb shifted to anti-Vietnam War protest. In the 1990s, the 'green' movements – which were themselves present at the birth of second-wave CND in the 1970s – have taken over from unilateralism as the focus for a certain type of radical concern. For the moment, unilateralism is in disgrace. But it is easy to envisage another turn of the wheel producing a Mark III revival.

If this occurs, it may be that trade unions – on the argument of this chapter – will come back to the issue with equal enthusiasm. On the other hand, the reduced constitutional power of unions within the Labour Party may make the unions matter less, at least in party political terms. But whatever the future nature of the relationship, the past loyalty of unions to the cause and the strength of feeling it aroused among many active members, suggests that unions may once again play a critical part.

FULL CIRCLE

A curious feature of the campaign in Britain for 'unilateral' renunciation of nuclear weapons is the way in which it vanished entirely for most of two decades; and then suddenly re-emerged. Until after the 1979 election, it was widely regarded, when it was regarded at all, as a distant episode without relevance to contemporary politics. Thus a book by two sympathizers (published in September 1980 but completed in July of the previous year), comparing CND with other protest campaigns, posed the question: 'Why has the Disarmament Movement failed where the others have, at least to an extent, succeeded?' The answer, the authors concluded, – and at the time of going to press the point must have seemed uncontroversial enough - was that the nuclear disarmers lacked 'political and economic muscle':

Because the Movement in the UK was one of middle-class radicalism *par excellence* and was therefore largely unconcerned with basic economic issues of jobs, investment alternatives and so on, it failed to make the crucial breakthrough to the working class. It thus failed to build up sufficiently powerful forces to confront the massive vested interests of the military/industrial/state complex.[1]

The implicit assumption was that the movement had been finally and definitively defeated, and was now as dead as the pacifist campaigns of the 1930s.

Yet, even as the authors' words appeared in print, the political earth was shaking: unnoticed by most observers unilateralism was already back on the agenda. The following month, the Labour Party Conference at Blackpool passed four resolutions on defence, two of which were unequivocally unilateralist. So revolutionary was the 1980 Conference in other ways that this development was scarcely noticed. 'As the week draws to an end such leftward lurches are no longer news,' Peter Jenkins wrote in the *Guardian*, reflecting the attitude of many commentators.[2]

Yet this decision was to have a far greater impact than the unilateralist votes of 1960 for several reasons. First, the rapid growth of the new campaign in 1980 occurred against a background of a wider and more deeply-rooted sympathy for disarmament within the labour movement. Second, on this occasion the Labour Party leadership in the shape of the NEC (though not the parliamentary leadership) was overwhelmingly in favour of an anti-nuclear policy, whereas in 1960 both NEC and Shadow Cabinet were opposed. Third – and perhaps more important in terms of Labour Party politics – the sudden re-emergence of unilateralism was as much the product of trade union interest and involvement as of the traditional alliance of 'pacifist, Quaker, intellectual, non-political, socialist, liberal, progressive'[3] groups and individuals who took the lead in the past. Thus, the rebirth of the unilateralist cause provides a particularly notable example of the use by trade unions of their political power for ends which go far beyond industrial affairs.

This chapter will examine the reappearance of the nuclear issue in British politics, and the role which trade unions played in bringing it forward.

THE FIRST CAMPAIGN

The first major anti-nuclear campaign in Britain began outside trade union and party politics. It came to be a major issue because of a coincidental shift to the left in important unions (most notably the TGWU), and an attack on Gaitskell's leadership which reflected a broader division within the industrial wing of the movement. As a result of these splits, nuclear disarmament acquired a symbolic importance. Once the wider conflict had subsided, leaving the Gaitskellite position within the Labour Party secure, unilateralism became a tainted idea, treated by serious politicians with circumspection.

The Campaign for Nuclear Disarmament was founded at the end of 1957. Canon Collins became Chairman, Bertrand Russell President and Peggy Duff Organizing Secretary. The most prominent Labour supporter (at that time not an MP) was Michael Foot, a leading Bevanite. By 1959 CND had a national network of branches, and for about three or four years the campaign was a mass popular movement, its annual Aldermaston Marches attracting up to 150,000 demonstrators. However, interest within the labour movement developed only slowly. A unilateralist resolution was defeated by five and a half million to one million votes at the 1958 Trades Union Congress.[4] It was the switch to unilateralism of the TGWU, led by Frank Cousins and carrying the largest Conference block vote, which swung the Labour Party, temporarily, against the Bomb.

After Labour's third successive election defeat in 1959, hostility to Gaitskell's leadership on other issues (including the proposed abandonment of Clause 4 of the party constitution) led to unilateralist victories at the Scarborough Party Conference in 1960. The margins were tight. Though a unilateralist resolution proposed by the AEU was carried by a majority of 407,000, a TGWU demand for the rejection of any policy based on the threat of nuclear weapons was accepted by the tiny margin of 43,000 – one of the very few important votes in Labour Party Conference history that was decided by a handful of constituency party votes. Nevertheless it was the votes of some big unions, and especially the TGWU, that really counted. Hitherto, the job of the unions had been to support the platform, which in turn backed the parliamentary leaders in a system of interlocking directorships which ensured that Conference, NEC and Shadow Cabinet normally expressed the same opinions.[5] The TGWU had for years been the rock upon which official policies were built, 'the very symbol of loyalty to the leadership'.[6] After Cousins declared his independence over unilateralism, things were never quite the same again.

There was nothing inherently socialist about nuclear disarmament. Aneurin Bevan's passionate rejection of unilateralism in 1957 had actually been one of the events that sparked the campaign off.[7] Even the communists were at first hostile. The 1960 votes, however, left very few left-wingers in the multilateralist camp, and from then on unilateralism became part of the pantheon of left-wing causes. By this time, what had started as a moral issue had been fashioned into a tool to change the leadership. When Gaitskell promised to 'fight and fight and fight again to bring back sanity and honesty and dignity',[8] he was also fighting for his political life, linking the issue directly to his own future.

After George Lansbury had been defeated on a similar issue (though from the opposite point of view) at the 1935 Party Conference, he immediately resigned. Gaitskell decided to counter-attack, knowing that victory in 1961 was essential for his survival. 'The belief that the Conference and the PLP would not long remain at loggerheads was widely held', argues one historian. 'At that time so great was the belief in Conference supremacy that few believed the divide could continue long before the Party fell apart in chaos.'[9] But Gaitskell's resistance was successful. Union support for unilateralism, shaky in 1960, collapsed in 1961. The unilateralists were already divided among themselves – some remaining purist, others seeking compromise. But it was the change of heart in the unions which really mattered. Some unions were influenced by appeals for unity. Others may have been shifted by an extremely energetic pressure group called the Campaign for Democratic Socialism, led and organized by a committed young Fabian called William Rodgers.[10] For these and other reasons, three key unions

– USDAW, the NUR and the AEU – reverted to multilateralism. As a grassroots movement and moral crusade, CND had not yet reached its peak. But by the summer of 1961, all chance of unilateralism becoming an established part of Labour policy had disappeared.[11] Before October the issue was politically dead, and Conference in Brighton merely provided the funeral. The TGWU held fast to unilateralism, but it was almost the only major union to do so. A TGWU resolution was defeated by 2,400,000 – a far more emphatic majority than the slender margins of 1960, and a clear vindication for the Party leadership.

The 1960 challenge was not repeated. The Campaign had become closely identified with one political tendency, and when that tendency failed, there was no second chance. Indeed, in one sense the 1960 majority had been an illusion – the product of a brief flirtation, not a settled conviction, on the part of many of the unions concerned. The later history of CND in its first phase seemed to show the irrelevance of rallies and demonstrations in a country firmly wedded to a two-party parliamentary system. Aldermaston Marches continued to get bigger, but serious politicians had moved on. Meanwhile, the mass movement became a Frankenstein monster which CND leaders could no longer control. Schisms widened, and a civil disobedience campaign led by the militant Committee of 100 associated unilateralism in the public mind with a libertarian and anarchist fringe. The peaceful resolution of the Cuban missile crisis in 1962, and then the Partial Test Ban Treaty in 1963, reduced world tension and hence removed the early sense of urgency. At the same time, the imminence of a general election concentrated the minds of Labour politicians on issues which they thought might win votes.

By the time Labour had won power in the autumn of 1964, CND had lost most of its former active support. Soon attention began to shift towards the more immediate cause of the Vietnam War. The Committee of 100 dissolved itself in 1968. CND remained in existence with a small membership and a skeletal staff, but the campaign 'arguably the greatest protest movement in Britain since the Chartists',[12] had failed in its main objectives. Occasional nostalgic pieces appeared in the press. A few MPs kept up their membership. But throughout eleven years of Labour Government and three-and-a-half years of Labour Opposition, the issue which had dominated discussion in the Party in the late 1950s and early 1960s was almost universally ignored. The Bomb remained. But not the Movement.

REBIRTH

Nevertheless, unilateralism had time on its side. Multilateralism was the policy of all governments. Yet after two decades and lengthy East–West negotiations, multilateral agreement had not been achieved and nuclear arsenals had become increasingly accurate and destructive. For as long as the reality – or illusion – of *détente* lasted, the nuclear threat stayed in the background. But as soon as a new round of war scares began, following the Iranian revolution, the invasion of Afghanistán and the failure of the Strategic Arms Limitation Talks, the setting was provided for a new popular disarmament movement. At the same time, government decisions about a new generation of costly nuclear weapons gave the renewed campaign a specific focus beyond the simple 'Ban the Bomb' slogans of twenty years before.

The proposed purchase of Trident long-range missiles, plans to site American Cruise missiles in Britain, and the prospect of a £5 billion public bill, began to capture headlines at about the time that the world recession and falling production were being met by government economies – with cutbacks in social services and other public spending. The emotive associations of the word 'nuclear' had already been revived by a campaign – more ecological than left-wing – against an expansion of the nuclear energy programme and the building of fast-breeder reactors. Attention began to shift from this issue back to nuclear weapons with the development of the neutron bomb. Finally, in 1979 as in 1959, a Labour election defeat precipitated a new round in the epic left-right struggle, providing a fertile seed-bed for new divisive causes.

But it would be wrong to relate the upsurge in interest that occurred after 1979 solely to current crises and disputes. It is possible to trace a very slow revival through most of the 1970s, ignored in the media and unrecognized even by participants at the time – yet providing a background of knowledge and commitment that gave CND in its second phase a much more substantial base than in its first.

One explanation of this slow recovery may be that, while unilateralism ceased to be a live issue, many former unilateralists continued to be involved in political and trade union affairs. Young, energetic and committed ex-CNDers had advanced to increasingly influential positions, helping to shape the policies of the organizations they now led.[13] In 1960, the Labour Party and union establishment was multilateralist, indifferent, or recently – and often temporarily – converted to unilateralism. By the early 1970s there were senior officials and executive members in many unions who had grown up with the CND movement and remained latent supporters. This was the basis for a 'silent majority' in favour of unilateralism – with a special strength in unions that had backed the disarmers first-time round.

In some unions, support for unilateralism became part of a sentimental heritage, so that new members were sometimes vaguely aware of the commitment without knowing why it was there. This was true of the TGWU, strongest backers of the Campaign in 1960 and 1961. Over the years a number of TGWU regional committees, including those in Scotland, London and the South-East, the Midlands and the North-West, continued to back CND. Biennial Delegate Conferences of the union discussed disarmament resolutions, usually with a unilateralist flavour, almost as a matter of course. 'My organisation has been proud to be in the front of the protest to get rid of these weapons', Frank Cousins had declared in 1960.[14] The example of these crusading days was often invoked.

But it was not just the TGWU that remained loyal to unilateralism. Even in its darkest period, CND received affiliation fees from a number of other unions – including NUPE (with a large Conference vote), ASLEF, SOGAT, ACTT, SLADE, the tobacco workers' union, the fire brigades' union, the bakers' union and the sheet metal workers' union. Several of these had been among the keenest supporters of CND in its heyday.[15]

In 1972 this support was consolidated in a Labour Party Conference resolution, carried on a show of hands, that was quite as unilateralist as anything that appeared on the order papers in 1960 or 1980: 'This Conference is opposed to any British defence policy which is based on the use or threatened use of nuclear weapons either by this country or its allies and demands the removal of all nuclear bases in this country.'[16]

It was an indication of how far the 1960 debate had really been about the leadership rather than the Bomb, of the declining status of Conference decisions, and of public and press indifference to the nuclear issue, that a decision which split the party from top to bottom in 1960 caused scarcely a ripple when it was repeated twelve years later.

Nor was this an isolated vote. The unilateralist Conference in 1960 had been swiftly followed by a multilateralist Conference a year later. After the 1972 decision, there was no reversal. On the contrary, the 1973 Conference repeated the decision of the previous year. The initiative came from the TGWU. At the transport workers' conference that summer, two defence resolutions were passed, one calling for a Nuclear Free Zone and the other demanding a cut of £1 billion in military spending and calling 'for the removal of Polaris bases and U.K. reliance on nuclear defence strategy'. This second motion was significant for a new emphasis on releasing expenditure on arms for 'essential needs'.[17] As a result, the Labour Party Conference at Blackpool the same year passed by 3,166,000 votes to 2,462,000 (a larger margin than for any of the unilateralist votes in 1960) a motion which followed closely the policy adopted by the TGWU a few months earlier. In defiance of an NEC request to remit, Conference reaffirmed the 1972 unilateralist verdict and demanded:[18]

The closing down of all nuclear bases, British and American, on British soil or in British waters and . . . that this pledge be included in the General Election manifesto.

Conference demands that Britain should cut its military expenditure initially by at least £1,000 million per year. This would release resources to expand social spending at home and allow more generous aid to poor nations.

However, the lack of the requisite two-thirds majority meant that such a policy did not go into the Party Programme; and a similar resolution in 1974 was remitted, and generally forgotten, after an eloquent plea from Ian Mikardo on behalf of the NEC.[19]

The 1972 and 1973 votes were, indeed, an illustration of the irrelevance of Conference decisions unless accompanied by external pressure. As it was, these two decisions were treated as no more than harmless nose-thumbing by unions at the Shadow Cabinet. The issue was not seriously discussed in either of the 1974 election campaigns, and Labour's manifesto commitment on defence was one of studied ambiguity.

Nevertheless, the 1972 and 1973 decisions were a straw in the wind. They indicated that a latent Conference majority for unilateralism existed, and that trade union support for a revived movement was there for the asking. In none of the three short defence debates of 1972, 1973 and 1974 did a single speaker support the principle of multilateralism. By 1975, a new element had crept in. At the TGWU Conference a resolution was passed drawing attention to earlier union and Labour Party decisions about disarmament, and expressing the belief that 'the monies saved would enable resources to be used for the expansion of social services, education, pensions and *employment creation*'.[20] The dole queues were beginning to add a new imperative. Meanwhile the NEC, increasingly left-wing in composition, was beginning to stir. In 1976 the Party Executive responded to earlier Conference decisions by setting up a Study Group on Defence Expenditure, including a number of young left-wing academics such as Mary Kaldor, Dan Smith, Ron Smith and Frank Blackaby, some of whom had been involved in CND in the early 1960s as students. The Group was chaired by Ian Mikardo and its report, *Sense about Defence*,[21] was arguably the best-researched party document on defence published since the war. In contrast to many early CND publications, it showed that the anti-nuclear lobby was capable of hard, sophisticated thinking.

Yet as a movement outside conference halls and research seminars, CND still lacked significant public support. Hence political leaders were able to disregard resolutions and policy documents, and there was no significant change in defence policy during the 1974–79 Labour Government. When did popular interest begin to revive? One former CND organizer recalls that already by the mid-1970s there were signs of renewed interest.[22] From this time until 1979, a very gradual growth of concern is discernible, partly related to the nuclear energy issue and partly to the neutron bomb: enough to keep committed disarmers optimistic, but giving no indication of the sudden upsurge that was to follow.

In November 1977 CND celebrated its twentieth anniversary by choosing a new Chairman, Monsignor Bruce Kent, a Roman Catholic parish priest who had previously been Chairman of War on Want's management committee.[23] Bruce Kent replaced John Cox, a foundation member and communist, and the change not only brought in a fresh personality and a new approach – it also helped CND to shed a (largely unjustified) image acquired in the 1960s as an offshoot of King Street. Kent had no political background as such, and in the chair (and later as General Secretary) he always adopted an ecumenical attitude towards political parties and factions. At this time, CND had a small office in Bloomsbury, 3 full-time staff and 2,000 paid-up members.[24] It saw its main task as educational – seeking to create a public awareness of the nuclear threat through leaflets, meetings and demonstrations – though its emphasis was now far more on the first two than the third.

The leaders of CND were careful not to make exaggerated claims. Yet there was already talk of a 'rapid resurgence', linked (Kent believed) to the neutron bomb, Cruise, SALT and the Russian arms build-up. Two hundred delegates turned up to the CND Annual Conference that autumn – the first occasion for a long time that there had been a substantial increase since the previous year.[25] It was a sign of CND's reviving activity that by the following spring, members had collected 160,000 signatures for a petition calling on the Labour Government to renounce any intention of acquiring the neutron bomb.[26] This provided the background for yet another Labour Party Conference resolution, again carried on a show of hands, calling on the Labour Government not to develop a new generation of strategic nuclear weapons to replace Polaris, to refuse to permit the deployment of new nuclear weapons, and to initiate negotiations for multilateral disarmament.[27]

The 'rapid resurgence' was only relative. At Easter 1979, an attempt to revive the Aldermaston March was a dismal failure. CND was much derided in the press when barely a hundred demonstrators turned up at Falconfield, opposite the gates of the Aldermaston atomic weapons research establishment. Comparisons were inevitably made with the tens of thousands who would have been there in the early 1960s.[28] Yet the fortunes of CND were about to improve dramatically. In May 1979, the Labour Government was defeated in the general election, and 1979 also happened to be the year of the TGWU Biennial Conference. While CND's anti-neutron bomb campaign was gaining some attention, the TGWU adopted a resolution which amounted to an updating of its earlier positions:[29]

This Conference asks that the weight of the T.G.W.U. be thrown in behind the growing world protest movement against the development and possible use of the latest super bomb – the neutron bomb.

Further, Conference requests that the Government be asked to make a serious contribution to the next United Nations Special Session on Disarmament by announcing that it intends to phase out Britain's nuclear weapons.

As we have seen, the passage of such resolutions had for some years been part of the ritual of TGWU conferences. In this respect 1979 was no different, and the resolution had no special significance in itself. Defence was not even debated at the Party Conference in October, and the TGWU vote was ignored by the media. Yet two key developments were about to give this resolution, and its predecessors, a special importance. One was a spontaneous, and unexpected, growth in public concern about nuclear weapons; the other was a mounting pressure in favour of a package of left-inspired reforms to the Labour Party constitution. 'As a union we are very anxious to support any motion for democratising the party', Moss Evans, the General Secretary of the TGWU, declared in September.[30] But it was to be democratization with a purpose: namely, the implementation of policies of which the trade union and the constituency Labour left approved. A revival of interest in unilateralism thus coincided with the precise moment when the issue could be used as a weapon in the political warfare that was beginning to break out.

The real renaissance of CND began at the end of 1979. Bruce Kent was later to relate the change in public mood to anxiety following a much-publicized American nuclear alert, caused by computer error, that had occurred in November. Whatever the immediate cause, from this time on CND was able to report a rapidly growing membership and a more enthusiastic campaign[31] – at the very time that the Labour Party was opening out towards the left in ways that could only help the unilateralists.

The 1979 Labour Party Conference had left the constitutional issues (mandatory reselection of MPs, Conference control of the election manifesto, an electoral college for choosing the leader) undecided. The following Conference was going to be crucially important. Meanwhile attention focused on a special Committee of Inquiry set up to look at proposed reforms, and on the quarrel between the (predominantly right-wing) Shadow Cabinet and the (mainly left-wing) NEC. Neither the Party Executive, nor the reform-minded unions, were in a placatory mood. In December, the General Executive Council of the TGWU passed a resolution calling for opposition to Cruise missiles on British soil, and urged the TUC to conduct a massive campaign on this theme.[32] Others followed this lead. Early in the New Year, the NEC decided to throw unilateralism into the cooking-pot of issues which a special Labour Party Conference (to be held on 31 May 1980) should consider.

In March, the NEC International Committee considered a policy statement incorporating 'various decisions made by annual conferences in recent years',[33] and covering defence expenditure, nuclear weapons, arms sales and the sale of weapons to underdeveloped countries. This Committee was chaired by Joan Lestor, and members included leading left-wingers such as Tony Benn, Eric Heffer, Joan Maynard and Renée Short (all deeply involved in the internecine struggles), Frank Allaun, one of CND's veteran supporters, and Jo Richardson, for several years CND's Vice-Chairman.

The Committee proposed that a future Labour government should be required to renounce the neutron bomb, Cruise and Trident and refuse to deploy nuclear missiles in the United Kingdom. Thus unilateralism had become one of the pills the parliamentary leaders would be required to swallow.

Now things began to happen fast, inside and outside the labour movement. A week after the NEC statement, the new CND campaign received an important boost. Midst a fanfare of press publicity, the distinguished labour historian E.P. Thompson launched a pamphlet entitled *Protest and Survive*, published by CND as a reply to the government's ill-timed Civil Defence document *Protect and Survive*. Coinciding more by accident than design with the NEC announcement, unilateralism suddenly made a reappearance in the newspapers. 'Nuclear disarmament now seems likely to re-surface as a major subject of political controversy', Ian Aitken predicted in April, after Callaghan had met the NEC and considered, without pleasure, their draft document.[34] At about the same time, Thompson joined forces with Ken Coates and the Bertrand Russell Peace Foundation in the formation of European Nuclear Disarmament, an intellectual-based pressure campaign calling for a nuclear-free zone 'from Poland to Portugal'.

However, no serious upset at the Blackpool Conference in October was yet anticipated. Outwardly, the Labour right gave a show of quiet confidence. 'No matter what the commission of inquiry into the party recommends', reported Adam Raphael in the *Observer*, 'no matter what the special party conference decides at the end of May, no matter what the Left gets up to in the meantime . . . the word from the Callaghan camp is that the party is about to be saved by the block vote.'[35] Early in May, the *Daily Telegraph* decided that the Labour Party was 'poised to swing right', because of an AUEW decision to back Callaghan.[36] *The Times* meanwhile came to the conclusion that the defence policy eventually agreed by the NEC for the special conference let the Shadow Cabinet off the hook.[37]

Yet already there was striking evidence that unilateralism might become much more than a pawn to be moved around the chess board in a game between Labour left and Labour right. The number of applications to join CND had doubled in six months, and the Campaign's puzzled staff were having to cope with forty or so inquiries a day. The banners were unfurling. However, Bruce Kent was adamant on one point: new CND was not going to be like old CND. 'I do not think demonstrations and marches are the major way to change public opinion', he told an interviewer. 'It is very important that the disarmament message is seen to come from normal moderate people and not from a crowd of cranks and partisan extremists on the Left.'[38] Yet there was no doubt that the left was where many of the most active new supporters were coming from. The rapid growth that took place over the next few months was not led – as in the 1950s – by liberal-minded, non-aligned notables willing to lend their names to a good cause. There were a few retired generals and former senior civil servants. But most of the expansion was a grassroots, spontaneous development, without the radical chic of the earlier movement, and with very strong Labour and trade union connections.

The Special Conference at Wembley on 31 May 1980 adopted a policy document called *Peace, Jobs, Freedom* which reiterated Labour's opposition to Cruise and the neutron bomb, but stressed multilateral as opposed to unilateral disarmament. This represented a compromise between NEC and Shadow Cabinet positions, but the important point was that it gave disarmament a higher priority than for many years past. The sense of a new urgency was reinforced by a Labour Party Disarmament Rally on 22 June, called by the NEC, and taking as its theme three specific demands: 'No Cruise missiles on British soil; no successor to Polaris; and no increase in arms spending.' This slogan did not, in fact, go any further than the Wembley document which the Shadow Cabinet had accepted. But it drew attention to an aspect of Labour policy which the parliamentary leader found embarrassing and would rather have neglected – and this had been the NEC's intention.

Political turning-points often occur when least expected, catching attackers and defenders unawares. The success of the Labour Disarmament Rally – regarded by some as just another salvo in the left–right trench warfare – took everybody by surprise. The organizers were certainly helped by a government announcement, a few days before the rally, to the effect that 160 American-owned Cruise missiles would be based in Berkshire and Cambridgeshire in order to counter the threat of Russian SS-20 missiles. No doubt there were other factors – in particular, the growing success of unemployment rallies and marches, which had rekindled the habit of demonstrating. Whatever the reason, a crowd assembled in Trafalgar Square that was estimated, even by the police, at 15,000, and by the amazed organizers at almost twice that number.

Ostensibly, of course, this was a multilateralist rally. In practice, however, it was unilateralist – as speakers and audience were both aware. Michael Foot manoeuvred carefully around the uni-versus-multi problem. All other speakers – who included Joan Lestor, Jo Richardson, Frank Allaun, Tony Benn and Neil Kinnock – called for unilateral disarmament. In order to stress the point, the party's defence spokesman, Bill Rodgers (who had been excluded from a party political broadcast on defence earlier in the month because of his multilateralist views) was not invited to what was supposed to be an official party event. This was a calculated snub, and Rodgers reacted fiercely. 'The party does believe in the proper defence of Britain', he told the press, 'and if people believe it doesn't it will be extremely damaging.'[39] But, who, and where, was 'the party' that held such views?

If the Labour Party (however such an abstraction might be defined) *had* believed in multilateralism, it was rapidly changing its mind. The June

Labour Disarmament Rally had a great symbolic importance. Not since the height of the Vietnam protest movement had a defence or international issue attracted such crowds. Unlike early CND rallies and marches, however, this one had been organized under official Labour auspices. From now on, despite CND claims to independence, the politics of the growing disarmament movement and the politics of the labour and trade union movements were to be far more closely interwoven than had ever been the case twenty years before.

On 5 June, the General Executive Council of the TGWU had decided to push the issue through the TUC as a prelude to a wider debate at Party Conference. 'We believe that all countries ought to get rid of their nuclear weapons', declared Moss Evans, 'but we believe we can make a start in the U.K.' *The Times* concluded that the battles of the 1960s over unilateralism were about to be repeated.[40] Other newspapers began to feel the same, reflecting and feeding public interest. E.P. Thompson, the Bertrand Russell of the new movement, was attracting capacity crowds in his personal crusade around the country. There were articles about Bruce Kent, and about the nuclear issue, that were no longer sneering or dismissive. Editorially all the quality papers were hostile, and *The Times* conducted a strangely passionate campaign against unilateralism in tones that indicated how little it understood the Labour Party or the changed mood within its ranks. On one matter, however, *The Times* made an accurate prediction which was presumably based on information from multilateralist MPs. 'If Labour were to become a unilateralist party there would, of course, be a much stronger chance of its splitting,' a leading article suggested on 23 June. 'A new centre party, or something of that sort, would then be a probability . . . How could any self-respecting social democrat fail to take his stand on the very issue on which Gaitskell himself declared that he would "fight, fight and fight again"?'

How indeed? Both Rodgers and the former Foreign Secretary, David Owen, the two most committed multilateralists, were finding their position increasingly difficult and humiliating as NEC members went out of their way to provoke them. Rodgers, who had led the 'fight, fight and fight again' campaign in 1961, now found himself, by a cruel irony, in Gaitskell's position but without the authority of the Party leader, and with no means to defend himself. Rodgers wrote angry articles in *The Times*, earning editorial praise for his personal stand: he was against Trident, but in favour of Cruise and of retaining a British deterrent. Yet he got little support from within the Labour Party. The majority of Labour MPs had always been multilateralist. But few leading politicians apart from Callaghan and Owen were prepared to stick their heads above the parapet now. To this extent, the threat of mandatory reselection was beginning to have its effect.

The publication in late July 1980 of the list of resolutions for Party Conference showed just how far, and how fast, what *The Times* called the 'tide of sentiment that has been evident in the party for some months now'[41] had gone. As in previous years, CND's two labour movement committees – Labour CND and Trade-Union CND – circulated model resolutions in the hope that enough organizations would adopt them to produce a good unilateralist composite for debate at Party Conference. In 1980, the secretaries of these committees found that they were pushing a door that was already swinging open. The discovery that 131 out of a total of 497 resolutions dealt with some aspect of the nuclear controversy surprised CND as much as its opponents. An indication that CND efforts did have some direct effect on the adoption of resolutions was provided by a large number (twenty-seven) that closely resembled the CND model, which urged that a future Labour government should disarm unilaterally in order to help create a European nuclear-free zone.

Some hostile commentators (such as Peter Jenkins in the *Guardian*)[42] saw the number of resolutions as evidence of a 'broad left' conspiracy. It is true that the appearance of European Nuclear Disarmament widened left-wing connections. But the tactics of CND had not changed, and to imagine that it was possible to coerce or hoodwink nearly a quarter of all constituency parties into adopting unilateralist resolutions greatly exaggerated the organizational powers of the Left. Trade union conferences provided more scope than constituency parties for a concerted campaign, because there were fewer of them, and resolutions could be adjusted according to particular union traditions and susceptibilities. The broad similarity of union defence resolutions – generally related to a new generation of nuclear weapons rather than proposing unilateralism *per se* – indicated a CND influence in drafting. But success depended on the presence of an influential group of unilateralists in the union concerned – and on the balance of political forces.

When did Labour become 'officially' unilateralist? It is an interesting question. Strict constitutionalists might date the conversion to the 1972 Conference, when a unilateralist resolution was passed and never subsequently revoked. Others might claim that without a two-thirds Conference majority, and with the PLP and Shadow Cabinet opposed, Labour was multilateralist even after the October 1980 Conference. What is clear is that, by the summer of 1980, the NEC was behaving as though the issue was already decided – anticipating the debate that was expected in the autumn. In July, the Executive decided to follow up the June Labour Disarmament Rally by officially backing a CND march planned for the end of October. Callaghan was furious. 'As far as I am concerned', he declared, 'I have never been in favour of unilateral disarmament and never will be.'[43] The NEC was undeterred. In a matter of months, unilateralism had made more progress even than in 1960.

At the TUC in September, unilateralism was one of the issues tossed between the (unilateralist) TGWU and the (multilateralist) AUEW in a struggle for power on the General Council that related as much to industrial matters and personalities as to defence. A TGWU resolution opposing any defence policy based on the use or threatened use of nuclear weapons was carried, after Larry Smith, the union's Executive Officer, had declared the need to revitalize the CND movement. Unilateralism was clearly going to be a key policy issue at the Labour Party Conference. But it was the constitution, not policy, that was the centre of attention, and few commentators were giving much thought to the nuclear issue as delegates assembled at Blackpool at the end of the month. Such was the turmoil within the Labour Party, amounting to revolution, that the steady advance of unilateralism seemed almost incidental.

REVOLUTION

As in 1979, the great constitutional debate concerned three key issues – mandatory reselection, the electoral college and the manifesto. Until shortly before Conference, it had been believed that Callaghan might avoid or postpone at least two of the changes. Now this possibility seemed to be slipping away. Callaghan was certain to lose on reselection, and would probably win on the manifesto. The electoral college hung in the balance. The AUEW (engineering section) backed Callaghan, while the TGWU and the GMWU favoured the change. This was arguably the most important reform, affecting the immediate succession, and with the forces so evenly balanced all media attention focused on it. On the eve of Conference, the NEC decided to back complete withdrawal from the EEC and re-nationalization without compensation of companies sold by the Tories. Unilateralism was added to this package of left-wing policies, regarded even by Callaghan as less crucial than the constitutional issues.[44]

For many observers, the 1980 Blackpool Conference had such an air of unreality that the passage of individual measures affecting policy seemed to have about as much significance as voting in a school debating club. The next general election was still far away. Meanwhile the barricades were up in the Winter Gardens. So much was happening so quickly that nothing seemed surprising – and all the time there was the knowledge that, in practice, Conference decisions were usually ignored. The quality press reacted with a weary cynicism. Peter Jenkins wrote that the endorsement by Conference 'of a programme of wholesale socialism scarcely caused a Monday morning eye to unglaze'.[45]

Addressing a Campaign for Labour Victory rally on Monday night to celebrate (if that was the right word) the twentieth anniversary of Gaitskell's famous Scarborough speech, Shirley Williams claimed to see a basis for party unity on the EEC and defence. 'We are going to fight to save this Party', she declared, 'and by God I think we can!'[46] But debates on Tuesday and Wednesday made Monday's deliberations seem like a friendly skirmish. In what *The Times* called 'two of the most disastrous days the party has ever experienced',[47] Conference took a number of decisions which pushed the party sharply to the left. A resolution which committed Labour to withdrawal from the EEC was adopted by a huge five million to two million majority. The manifesto reform was rejected, but compulsory reselection and the principle of the electoral college were both adopted. It was the last decision which preoccupied the newspapers on Thursday morning – midst speculation that Michael Foot might stand against Denis Healey as 'interim' leader, pending agreement on how the electoral college would be composed.

Thus, by the time that the defence issue had been reached on the fourth day of Conference, the main excitements seemed to have passed. Yet the debate had been given an important place in the week's programme. In 1973, when a unilateralist motion had been adopted on a card vote, there had only been four speeches. The 1980 defence debate, by contrast, occupied almost the whole of Thursday morning, covered five separate motions, and included nineteen speeches. There were little grounds for suggesting (as some papers did next day) that the decisions were taken absent-mindedly, in the middle of a busy schedule.

The first motion, calling for withdrawal from NATO, was lost massively on a card vote. There followed a motion calling for multilateral disarmament, a reduction in arms spending, and support for the World Disarmament Campaign. The third motion linked planned spending on Cruise and Pershing 2 missiles with cuts in social services. This one was clearly unilateralist: 'Conference calls for a commitment in the Labour Party manifesto to unilateral nuclear disarmament and for proposals to be made for producing alternative, socially useful products using existing skills and materials in the arms industry without loss of jobs and for the planned transfer of resources to the poorer countries in the world.'[48]

The fourth resolution, moved by Bill Keys of SOGAT, contained an even more uncompromising demand for unilateral steps towards multilateral disarmament and a European nuclear-free zone. It was drafted jointly by CND and the Bertrand Russell Foundation, which had recently launched the European Nuclear Disarmament Campaign:[49]

Conference, whilst acknowledging that the safety of all people would best be served by multilateral mutual disarmament in the nuclear and conventional fields, demands that the next Labour Party manifesto – and any interim manifesto – must include a firm commitment opposing British participation in any defence policy based on the use or threatened use of nuclear weapons; a pledge to close down all nuclear bases, British or American, on British soil or in British waters, and a firm commitment to disbanding defence sales organisations and reorganising arms industries to produce alternative products of social value.

Conference pledges its support for the European Nuclear Disarmament Campaign and calls upon the next Labour Government to take the necessary initiatives for the establishment of a European nuclear free zone as a major step towards world wide disarmament.

In his speech on Tuesday, Callaghan referred to 'the idealistic CND days of 20 years ago', and declared, 'I do not believe this great labour movement is going to say, "stop the world, I want to get off".' In the debate on Thursday, William Rodgers was the only speaker out of nineteen who backed him up. At least two-thirds of the PLP opposed unilateralism: none apart from the shadow defence minister dared to advance to the rostrum and meet the revolutionary storm. Rodgers was booed and hissed. The eighteen unilateralists were loudly applauded. The result was never in doubt.

Why was there no call for a card vote? A two-thirds majority would have placed the decisions in the Party Programme; less than two-thirds might have been used as an excuse to keep it out. Both sides hesitated to get a final verdict. The unilateralists were happy to see the issue decided in their favour. Their opponents were afraid that a card vote might, in the mood of 1980, make the degree of support for unilateralism only too starkly clear. Hence all three resolutions were carried on a show of hands.[50] 'When the historic milestone was passed – without a vote – there was no sign of jubilation', commented the *Guardian*. 'By this stage the Conference was obviously getting blasé. It might just as easily have been voting on a minor detail of education policy.'[51] Some confusion was caused by the passing of both unilateralist and multilateralist resolutions, and the multilateralists made the most of it. But multilateralism certainly did not exclude unilateralism as a first stage, and the intentions of Conference had been made clear.

If delegates were blasé, journalists were even more so. The defence decisions were taken for granted as a part of the general left-wing triumph: unilateralism seemed to be one of the Conference's most predictable aberrations. An article by George Gale in the *Daily Express*, the day after the unilateralist decisions, typified the language and priorities of the popular press:[52]

The Labour Party, as we all have known it, died this week in Blackpool, giving birth to a new Labour Party.

A nasty death it has been and it is an ugly, deformed and monstrous little brat which has been born.

The new Labour Party, to all intents and purposes, is Marxist.

IT REJOICES in the language of the class war.

IT IS SUFFUSED with class hatred.

IT PROPOSES to nationalize the banks, the insurance companies and the principal commercial enterprises in the country.

IT IS COMMITTED to massive increases in public expenditure.

IT IS HOSTILE to the mixed economy.

IT WANTS to abolish private education and the House of Lords.

IT WOULD tear Britain out of the Common Market.

Although it baulks at an outright renunciation of NATO, it is committed to unilateral nuclear disarmament.

Gale concluded that: 'The tinpot Trotskyist dictators of constituency Labour Parties who have swaggered through Blackpool this week – the political equivalent of the football hooligans', had carried the day.

The reality, of course, was quite different. The decisions at Blackpool came from the unions, not the local parties. There were few items on Gale's list which the constituency parties, left to themselves, would not have voted for at any Conference in the previous ten years. The changes were brought about by a union decision to move into Labour Party politics more decisively than ever before, and to throw their weight heavily against the parliamentary leadership. In some cases (especially over the constitutional issues) there was a fragility to the victories of the Left. Measures adopted by unions in 1980 could as easily be overturned a year or two later. However, as we have seen, unilateralism had a long history in many unions and might not be so easily shed.

UNILATERALISM AND THE UNIONS

Immediately after the defence debate, multilateralists gave notice that the lack of a two-thirds majority left the matter open as far as the Party Programme was concerned. However, during 1981 the anti-nuclear campaign continued to gather strength, both within the labour movement and among the general public. Organizers of the CND rally on 26 October hoped for 50,000 people; *The Times* estimated the crowd that turned up at 70,000.[53] CND membership doubled in 1980 to 9,000, and by the autumn of 1981 it had trebled again, reaching 30,000. Income also grew, and CND's paid staff expanded from three to eleven. Meanwhile the non-campaigning public showed a receptiveness not known in the 1960s. A poll conducted for London Weekend Television in November 1980 showed 44 per cent of the population in favour of Britain abandoning nuclear weapons – higher than the peak of a third reached in 1960.[54]

In January 1981, the Wembley Conference reinforced the constitutional changes and vested the election of the leader in an electoral college composed of 40 per cent trade unions, 30 per cent constituency parties and 30 per cent MPs. The retirement of Callaghan and the surprise victory of Michael Foot meant that the office of party leader was given to one of the earliest supporters of unilateralism (though now more cautious in his endorsements to avoid offending the PLP). Finally, the multilateralist cause within the Labour Party was dealt a serious blow by the defection of the Social Democrats – partly on this issue. Where was Rodgers's Campaign for Democratic Socialism now? The answer was that many of its former members had left the party, and they had no real successors. In 1981 there was no equivalent group of young, career-minded right wingers, ready to rally support behind the Shadow Cabinet. In 1961, the party leader and the NEC were against the unilateralists. In 1981 this was no longer so.

The older generation of committed multilateralists continued to speak out
– but in tones which indicated that this was one battle which, for the time
being, they would have to concede.

Indeed in the summer of 1981 (in contrast to the summer of 1961, when
the Campaign for Democratic Socialism had already tied up the trade-union
vote)[55] it was the Left which was consolidating through effective organization, not the Right. After Blackpool, Labour and Trade Union CND,
Labour Action for Peace and the Bertrand Russell Peace Foundation set
up a liaison committee with the intention of getting a commitment into
the manifesto. The 1980 unilateralism arrived like a whirlwind, and might
subside as fast. But the omens seemed far better than a generation before.

Kept alive in the labour movement by the trade unions, the fate of
unilateralism as a Labour Party commitment depended on continued union
support. In 1961 the unions had abandoned it. This was less likely in
the 1980s because the movement had a much longer heritage. Arguably
there had been a tacit majority in favour since 1972 – a dormant volcano
requiring a conjunction of party, national and international forces to bring
it to notice. An indication that more than 'tinpot Trotskyist dictators' in
the constituencies were caught up in the new mood was provided by the
agenda of the 1981 Biennial Delegate Conference of the TGWU, which
included thirty-four resolutions on nuclear weapons – equal to the number
on unemployment – compared with five in 1979. At the NUPE conference
in 1981, only four votes were cast against the removal of nuclear bases from
Britain.[56] By contrast, the 1960 pro-unilateralist votes had no immediate
background at all. The 1957 Labour Party Conference had even been offered
the spectacle of the ETU and other communist-led unions defending the
NEC against 'irresponsible' unilateralists.[57]

This chapter has been concerned with the early stages of the revival of
unilateralism. In the future, much will depend on the outcome of the
continuing struggle within the Labour Party, and it is possible that the
fashion in protest movements may quickly change. In the autumn of
1981, however, there was little sign of this happening. Indeed, there were
growing indications that what was once a sectarian cause had become one
which could be electorally popular or at least not a vote loser: a Marplan
poll in September revealed that 51 per cent of Labour voters considered that
a unilateralist platform was more likely to make them vote Labour, against
only 31 per cent who said it would have the opposite effect.[58] Evidence that
unilateralism was no longer a purely left-wing issue, but was capturing the
middle ground, was provided by the Liberal Assembly's decision against
Cruise missiles, seriously embarrassing the Liberal Party's new SDP allies,
some of whom (like Mr Rodgers) had abandoned the Labour Party partly
on this issue.

But the real reason for thinking that a counter-revolution in the Labour
Party was unlikely for some time was not fickle public opinion or attitudes

in other parties but the roots which unilateralism has established within the labour movement. Although bound up with the leftward move in the Party, unilateralism now had an independent standing which might even survive some shifting back. Both the TUC and Labour Party Conference in 1981 passed unilateralist resolutions by large margins – the last only just missing the requisite two-thirds majority needed for inclusion in the Party Programme. It was hard to see these positions being easily reversed – largely because unilateralism was so much a part of the political tradition of several major unions that they were unlikely to vote against it.

Here, unemployment indirectly helped the unilateralists – not only by pushing the whole movement leftwards. One of the most potent CND slogans linked arms expenditure to dole queues, helping to absorb unilateralism into a youth culture that was far more proletarian than that of the early 1960s. Thus, in January 1981 Melvyn Bragg drew attention to the punk-generation chant of several thousand young people taking part in a torch-lit procession across the Tyne Bridge: 'Away with Ronald Reagan/Away with Ronald Reagan. Jobs not Bombs/Jobs not Bombs/He's just a Cosmic Cowboy/Just a Cosmic Cowboy/Jobs not Bombs/Jobs not Bombs'.[59]

Twenty years before unilateralism might have been a middle class issue. The crisis of the early 1980s helped to make it a working-class one as well – the argument that money spent on American weapons might be spent on creating employment carried conviction.[60] This was a major factor with many unions – especially those linked to the public sector, and those most affected by the slump. Continued union backing for unilateralism, and hence a long-lasting electoral commitment by the Labour Party to abandon the nuclear deterrent, British or American, seemed probable as a result. Whether this would make it possible, or likely, that an incoming government so committed would actually carry out CND policies – given the hostility of the PLP and Shadow Cabinet, and the combined opposition of press, Whitehall, military establishment and Nato allies – is, of course, another matter.

NOTES AND REFERENCES

The author wishes to thank Ron Mclroy, Ray Collins, David Griffiths and Ken Coates, among others, for help in preparing this article. The views expressed are, however, entirely his own.

1. R. Taylor and C. Pritchard, *The Protest Makers: the British nuclear disarmament movement in 1958–1963: twenty years on*, Pergamon Press, London, 1980, p. 140.

2. *Guardian*, 3 Oct. 1980.

3.   M. Stewart, *Frank Cousins: a study*, Hutchinson, London, 1968, p.
       93. See also F. Parkin, *Middle-Class Radicalism*, Manchester Univer-
       sity Press, Manchester, 1968.
4.   See M. Harrison, *Trade Unions and the Labour Party since 1945*, Allen
       and Unwin, London, 1960, p. 237 n.
5.   See R.T. McKenzie, *British Political Parties*, Macmillan, London,
       1955.
6.   M. Harrison, *Trade Unions and the Labour Party*, op. cit., p. 238.
7.   R. Taylor and C. Pritchard, *The Protest Makers*, op. cit., p. 6.
8.   Labour Party Annual Conference Report, 1960, p. 201.
9.   L. Minkin, *The Labour Party Conference*, Allen Lane, London, 1978,
       p. 280.
10.   See Lord Windlesham, *Communication and Political Power*, Jonathan
       Cape, London, 1966, pp. 81–152.
11.   Yet (as Minkin points out) the campaign did bring about a significant
       change in Labour's official attitude to defence. 'Each new Joint
       Statement between 1958 and 1961 was marked by a major shift
       from the previous policy until finally in 1961 the Party leadership
       was defending a policy which unilateralists would have acclaimed as
       a revolutionary policy innovation in 1957.' (op.cit., p. 58.)
12.   R. Taylor and C. Pritchard, op. cit., p. 15.
13.   This is a hard point to prove. But it is interesting to note that
       former supporters of the highly activist Committee of 100 have been
       particularly successful in obtaining professional and administrative
       jobs since the heyday of unilateralism. According to a survey of
       former unilateralists conducted by Taylor and Pritchard, only 16
       per cent of Committee of 100 supporters were in Classes 1 and 2
       in the early 1960s; by the late 1970s, a total of 51 per cent of the
       same sample were in these categories. More than a third remained
       members of the Labour Party. (Ibid., pp. 149, 152.)
14.   M. Stewart, op. cit., pp. 94–95.
15.   Eight trade unions with a combined strength of more than 1,800,000
       Conference votes backed unilateralist resolutions at both 1960
       and 1961 Party Conferences: the TGWU, NUPE, Boilermakers,
       National Society of Operative Printers and Assistants, Sheet-metal
       workers', Draughtsmen, Construction Engineers and Fire Brigades
       Unions (K. Hindell and P. Williams, 'Scarborough and Blackpool:
       an analysis of some votes at the Labour Party Conferences of 1960
       and 1961', *Political Quarterly*, summer 1962, p. 309).
16.   Labour Party Annual Conference Report, 1972, p. 221.
17.   Minutes of the Proceedings of the Biennial Delegate Conference of
       the TGWU, July 1973, p. 21.
18.   Labour Party Annual Conference Report, 1973, p. 301. The resolu-
       tion was proposed by the Fire Brigades' Union.

19. Labour Party Annual Conference Report, 1974, pp. 304–5.
20. Minutes of 1975 TGWU Conference, p. 28 (italics added).
21. *Quartet*, London, 1977.
22. D. Griffiths. Interview.
23. *Guardian*, 11 Nov. 1977.
24. Ibid., 26 Nov. 1977.
25. Ibid., 28 Nov. 1977.
26. Ibid., 25 March 1978.
27. Labour Party Annual Conference Report, 1978, p. 327.
28. *Guardian*, 17 April 1979.
29. Minutes of 1979 TGWU Conference, pp. 34–35.
30. *Financial Times*, 22 Sept. 1979.
31. *Daily Telegraph*, 16 Nov. 1979.
32. *Morning Star*, 17 Dec. 1979.
33. *The Times*, 16 March 1980.
34. *Guardian*, 17 April 1980.
35. *Observer*, 13 April 1980.
36. *Daily Telegraph*, 4 May 1980.
37. *The Times*, 24 April 1980.
38. Ibid.
39. Ibid., 26 June 1980.
40. Ibid., 6 June 1980.
41. Ibid., 21 July 1980.
42. *Guardian*, 24 July 1980.
43. *Daily Telegraph*, 24 July 1980.
44. *Financial Times*, 21 July 1980.
45. *Guardian*, 30 Sept. 1980.
46. *Financial Times*, 30 Sept. 1980.
47. *The Times*, 2 Oct. 1980.
48. Labour Party Annual Conference Report, 1980, p. 161.
49. Ibid., p. 163.
50. A 'show of hands' is of course, a vote, though no count is taken. How did Conference divide on the defence issues? A writer for *Peace News* claimed to have spoken to delegates for unions representing 5,400,000 out of the total 6,450,000 union vote. On the basis of this information, it appeared that the first unilateralist motion was opposed by APEX, AUEW, the Communications Workers and Union of Shop, Distributive, and Allied Workers; and that on the second a total of 3,800,000 union votes were cast in favour and 1,600,000 against (*Peace News*, 17 Oct. 1980).
51. *Guardian*, 3 Oct. 1980.
52. *Daily Express*, 3 Oct. 1980.
53. *The Times*, 14 Nov. 1980.
54. *Financial Times*, 17 Nov. 1980.

55. According to Christopher Driver (*The Disarmers*, Hodder and Stoughton, London, 1964, p. 96): 'On October 19th the counter-revolution began . . . [C.D.S.] made the reasonable assumption that the Labour Party was still basically sceptical about the wisdom of unilateral nuclear disarmament . . .' Such an assumption could scarcely be made in 1981.

56. *Sanity*, June–July 1981, p. 14.

57. M. Harrison, *Trade Unions and the Labour Party*, op. cit., p. 237.

58. *Guardian*, 25 Sept. 1981.

59. *Observer*, 18 Jan. 1981.

60. See M. Kaldor, D. Smith and S. Vines (eds) *Democratic Socialism and the Cost of Defence*, Croom Helm, London, 1979.

11 The decline of working-class politics: a reappraisal

Barry Hindess

The Decline of Working-Class Politics (hereafter: *Decline*), written in the late 1960s and first published in 1971, was based largely on a study of Labour Party branches in Liverpool. *Decline* was concerned with political support for and activity within the Labour Party and it argued that there were two related and interdependent respects in which working-class politics had declined. On the one hand there was a decline in the participation of working-class individuals and on the other a decline in the significance of working-class identification as a reason for political activity. The fall in working-class participation made the Labour Party a more middle-class (or 'classless') party, so that its policies became less orientated to specifically working-class concerns and therefore led to a further fall in working-class participation.

The study of party branches in Liverpool had shown a number of striking differences between wards in the more working-class areas (which generally returned Labour councillors) and those in the more middle-class areas (generally non-Labour). With some notable exceptions ward parties in the more middle-class areas were larger, more likely to include councillors or ex-councillors among their members, younger on average and covered a wider range in terms of age and length of party membership. Parties in these different kinds of areas also differed significantly in the political interests and concerns of their active members. *Decline* argued that these differences reflected differences in social conditions in the areas concerned, e.g. in the class distribution of the population and the character of the housing stock. The figures on age and length of membership suggested that parties in the middle-class areas were able to recruit and to retain new members and were therefore in a process of growth, while the parties in the working-class areas were in a process of decline. The argument then was that those shifts in the pattern of party membership led to a corresponding shift in the pattern of interests represented in the policies of the city party and, further, that the predominance of the middle-class areas was exacerbated by the residential distribution of Labour councillors. These changes meant that the party became progressively less attractive to actual and potential members in the working-class areas, leading to further changes in the pattern of membership. Finally, it was argued that those changes at the local level in Liverpool mirrored a secular process of change in the national Labour Party, gradually turning it into a more middle-class party, less able to reflect working-class interests and therefore less able to attract working-class membership and support.

Now, there are serious weaknesses in the argument of *Decline*, only a few of which need to be noted here.[1] Critics have argued that the distinctive character of Liverpool politics must render suspect any generalizations about British politics based on it, and that the major thesis of the book constructs the myth of a golden past in which local Labour constituency parties sustained significant active working-class participation.[2] There is something to be said for both objections. Too much can be made of Liverpool's uniqueness, but to base an argument about British politics generally on the case of one city is to invite precisely that kind of objection. As for the 'golden past', reliable evidence of local party membership and activity is difficult to come by, but what evidence there is hardly suggests that Labour Party branches in the working-class areas of our cities were ever the thriving centres of political activity that *Decline* implies.

A further problem, surprisingly not mentioned by most reviewers, is that *Decline* ignores what might be regarded as the major channel of representation of working-class interests in the Labour Party, namely, the affiliated trade unions. The importance of union affiliation at the national level in the Labour Party is well known. But what is particularly important for the argument of *Decline* is that nationally affiliated unions may also affiliate to district and constituency Labour Parties. Labour Party General Management Committees commonly contain delegates from locally affiliated unions (and sometimes from various socialist organizations) as well as from party branches. *Decline's* argument is therefore misleading in two significant respects: first, in treating the pattern of *branch* membership as determining the pattern of interest representation within the party, and secondly, in treating the party branch as the only significant channel of working-class participation.

Finally, it is worth noting here a significant weakness that *Decline* shares with a great deal of political commentary on the state of the Labour Party. It treats parties in middle-class and working-class areas as representing political interests which differ according to the characters of their respective populations and the social conditions in which they live.

Now it is clear that differences in the character of the housing stock or in the extent of owner occupation may well provide the basis for the articulation of rather different concerns over, say, local authority housing policy or the level of rates. The problem with the argument of *Decline* at this point is that it treats the interests that are articulated in the different areas as if they were determined outside politics, quite independently of the political work of parties, trade unions and other significant political actors. What is at stake here is a peculiar kind of sociological reductionism in which significant elements of political life are regarded as the products of social conditions and therefore as determined independently of the activities of parties and other political agencies. Other examples of such reductionism can be found in Marxist analyses of British politics, in which the working classes are regarded as having interests determined essentially by their economic location. The working class then appears as a political force that may *react* to what Labour, or some other party, does but whose essential character is determined outside politics. But such reductionism is by no means confined to the Left. An equivalent reductionism can be found in parts of the decidedly non-Marxist arguments of Anthony Crosland's *Can Labour Win?* to the effect that the experience of affluence by workers and their families induces a shift towards a middle-class psychology, and therefore away from Labour. We shall see that these reductionisms have important political concomitants when it comes to the analysis of changes in the patterns of electoral support for Labour and of what the party should do about it.

For these and other reasons the detailed arguments and explanations offered by *Decline* are impossible to sustain. Nevertheless, some of its central claims do appear to reflect, however inadequately, important changes that had taken place in the relation between the Labour Party and its actual or potential support during the post-war period and have continued since the book was published. This chapter concentrates on those changes. It begins with a short summary of the evidence of changing patterns of voting support, party membership and popular attitudes towards Labour's stance on policy issues and its trade union connections. I then proceed to consider the two main kinds of account of these developments and of their political implications, which tend to be associated with left and right analyses of where the Labour Party has gone wrong, and argue that both are seriously deficient. I conclude by commenting briefly on the questions of how Labour might adapt its policy positions in the light of popular political concerns and its links with the unions.

THE SECULAR DECLINE IN SUPPORT FOR LABOUR

There are several important respects in which popular support for Labour has fallen since the early 1950s. Official Labour Party figures show a fall in individual membership from a peak of over a million in 1952 to about 300,000 in 1979. The extent of the change is obscured by the operation until recently of the minimum affiliation rule of 1,000 for constituency parties. Yet there is no reason to dispute Forester's claim[3] that the Labour Party lost more than half its individual membership between 1951 and 1970 (so did the Conservative Party, starting from a much higher figure). And there has certainly been some further loss of membership over the last decade.

There has also been a long-term decline in electoral support for the two major parties. In their *Political Change in Britain* Butler and Stokes note a marked weakening in the class alignment of electoral politics throughout the 1960s. Their results suggest that the image of politics as a matter of opposing class interests was most widely accepted among those who entered the electorate during the Second World War and its aftermath. 'But such an image was accepted less frequently among Labour's working-class supporters who entered the electorate more recently.'[4] They also suggest that there was a declining trend in association between class and party among all age groups throughout the 1960s. Again, the Essex election studies,[5] based on post-election surveys covering elections from 1964 to October 1974, indicate that both party allegiances within the electorate and their association with class were getting weaker. The proportion of the electorate not committed to one or other major party and the proportion not voting on class lines were substantial and seemed to be growing. The position of the Labour Party seemed particularly precarious to the Essex researchers given 'the fall in support for Labour Party principles amongst its own identifiers – in particular, its younger, working class and trade unionist core'.[6] Evidence from the polls suggests that there was a further erosion of Labour's working-class support between 1974 and 1979. While Labour's middle-class support held up reasonably well, there was a fall in support among trade unionists (especially over the winter of discontent, 1978–79) and among skilled workers in particular.[7] This decline became even more apparent in the 1983 and 1987 elections.

The polls also suggest that Labour's stand on policy issues and its connection with the unions are increasingly losing support. The Essex studies report a growth in diffuse dissatisfaction among both Conservative and Labour identifiers over the period 1964–74. But they also show among Labour's working-class supporters increasing disaffection from Labour's established policy positions on public ownership, public expenditure on social services and social security, and on racial integration – and more recent evidence suggests that this trend, too, is continuing. Of course, this lack of support for Labour's policies is nothing new. As long ago as 1960 Mark Abrams noted a similar phenomenon with regard to public owner-ship. Public sentiment 'has not suddenly turned against nationalisation – in a sense it was never greatly for it'. But there had been a decisive change within the ranks of Labour supporters: 'In 1949, 60% were in favour of extending public ownership; in 1960, 58% were opposed.'[8]

The growing unpopularity of the unions is not a new phenomenon either. Writing in 1960 Crosland could refer to Gallup poll evidence showing a 'steady 20-year decrease in the numbers of those who think the unions a "good thing"'.[9] He went on to argue that Labour's identification with the manual-worker unions was becoming an electoral liability. The popularity of the unions has hardly improved in the subsequent period. Butler and Stokes noted a growing proportion of the electorate who felt that the unions had too much power and, by 1980, a MORI poll showed that even among union members a clear majority felt that the unions in Britain had too much power.[10]

Now, these changes are not quite what the author of *Decline* had in mind, and the explanations advanced in that book are hardly adequate to account for them. But the class character of British politics is no longer what it seemed to be in the late 1940s and 1950s. Individual membership of the two major parties has fallen drastically from its post-war peak, and there has been a steady fall in electoral support for the two major parties since the 1950s. The old relationship between class and party has dissolved so that, by October 1974, class was no longer a good predictor of party identification.[11] Labour has lost support for its policy positions within the working class, and there is less inclination within the working class to see politics 'as a zero-sum game in which the gains for one class are losses for the other'.[12] This is not to say that Labour has suffered a permanent loss of working-class support. Rather, there has been a fall in identification with Labour considered as the party of the working class, and a growing electoral volatility reflecting a weakening of voter identification with one or other of the major parties.

ACCOUNTS OF WHAT WENT WRONG

These facts are well known. But, as with all facts, it would be misleading to suppose that they could be left to speak for themselves. To take account of these facts and to give them political significance is to construct an account of the ways in which British electoral politics has changed over the years. In this section I discuss the two main kinds of accounts of these facts and the lessons to be drawn from them. On the one side there are stories of betrayal, of Labour acting against the interests of its working-class base and thereby alienating support. On the other there are tales of Labour's unfortunate association with unpopular images, of secular social changes leading to a progressive erosion of Labour's traditional base of support, and of a hidebound, traditionalist organization failing to adapt itself to the rigours of the modern world. Both involve versions in which working-class politics may be said to have declined and both, as we shall see, are seriously deficient.

Consider first the stories of betrayal. The basic theme concerns a working class with distinctive economic and social interests to which Labour has traditionally appealed but which it represents inadequately, if at all. That basic theme may be elaborated in many different ways but in all cases the weakness of Labour's working-class support is seen as deriving from its failures adequately to represent working-class interests. Sometimes there may be what Forester calls a 'myth of the golden past' of working-class activism, but more significant is the supposed discrepancy between the interests of the working class and what Labour Governments do.

In its strongest form that theme is elaborated in terms of a working class having interests that cannot be satisfied within capitalist society and which therefore entail perpetual conflict, open or suppressed, with the capitalist ruling-class. In the long run, so this story goes, the interests of the working class require major social changes which may be summarized, in the words of *Labour's Programme, 1973*, as 'a fundamental and irreversible shift of power and wealth in favour of working people and their families'. The Labour Party with its union connections and its minority socialist tradition and rhetoric certainly appears to represent those interests but opinions differ as to its capacity to do so effectively. Ralph Miliband, David Coates and Leo Panitch have argued,[13] for rather different reasons, that the Labour Party has not been and cannot become an effective force for socialism. In effect, then, Labour's union connections and the socialist rhetoric of the Labour Left actually serve the interests of capital by containing the inherent militancy and socialism of the working class. Within the Labour Party, of course, the story is told rather differently, with the Labour Co-ordinating Committee, Campaign for Labour Party Democracy, *Militant* and others each adding its own particular twist. Here the all-too-many failures of Labour governments are not attributed to any inherent features of the Labour Party. Rather they are interpreted as so many evidences of betrayal of the party by its leaders, the result of which is that Labour persistently fails to realize its true potential support in the country, and in the working class in particular. The remedy is to 'democratize' the party in order to subject its wayward parliamentary leadership to the party's true objectives, thus releasing its socialist potential and its capacity for securing mass popular support.[14]

In these stories the Labour Party at once appeals to and suppresses a distinctive brand of working-class politics, and the persistent failure of Labour to deliver on its socialist promise must tend to undermine its hold over working-class loyalties. *Decline* offers a somewhat eccentric version of much the same story. Labour's failure to represent working-class interests is regarded neither as an inescapable feature of Labour Party organization nor as a simple matter of leadership betrayal. Rather it argues that differences of interest between leaders and the membership and between working-class and middle-class sections of the membership lead to persistent struggles over what interests are to be effectively represented in party policy. The victories of an unholy alliance of leaders and the middle-class member-ship mean that working-class interests lose out, working-class support is eroded,[15] and the relative strength of middle-class interests increases. The thesis of *Decline* does require, if not a 'golden age', at least a period in the party's past when the interests of the working class were represented more effectively.

At the other extreme are the stories of Labour's inappropriate image and of underlying secular changes in British society, to which Labour must adapt or slowly perish. Here the basic theme is that long-term social changes have eroded the significance of class differences in British politics with the result first that a growing proportion of the electorate no longer vote on the basis of class identification and secondly, that Labour's working-class image is a wasting electoral asset. The *locus classicus* is undoubtedly Anthony Crosland's Fabian pamphlet *Can Labour Win?* published in 1960, although similar arguments can also be found in Rita Hinden's somewhat confused discussion of 'The Lessons for Labour' or the results of the *Socialist Commentary* survey presented in *Must Labour Lose?* which appeared in the same year. Anthony Crosland argues that two interrelated developments were responsible for the trend against Labour between 1951 and 1959. First, there were problems with Labour's image: the welfare state and full employment had long since ceased to appear to be specifically Labour concerns; Labour was associated with increasingly unpopular images – nationalization, bureaucracy, controls, an endemic liability to splits; and its identification with the unions meant that it suffered from their growing unpopularity and that Labour, more than the Conservatives, was identified with a particular class. Secondly, economic development involved changes in the occupational structure, with the working class shrinking as a proportion of the employed population, and it involved a spreading affluence, increasing social and geographical mobility and the break-up of old working-class communities. The result was that in the more prosperous sections of the working class, people had 'acquired a middle class income and pattern of consumption, and sometimes a middle class psychology'.[16] In Crosland's argument it is precisely that erosion of class as a basis for Labour's political support that creates the space for the importance of party images.

Even at the time, the 'affluent worker' explanation of Labour's 1959 defeat was on very weak ground. Mark Abrams' cautious presentation of the results of the *Socialist Commentary* survey in the first part of *Must Labour Lose?* (on which Hinden's discussion in the last part was sup-posed to be based) makes that abundantly clear.[17] Working-class affluence was not particularly associated with Conservative voting. Working-class houseowners were indeed the more likely to vote Conservative. But that, Abrams suggests, should be seen as an index of the importance of housing as a political issue, and of its successful appropriation by the Conservatives. It is not a consequence of affluence as such. Subsequent academic criticism has further damaged the reputation of the affluence argument,[18] but its undoubted weakness has not prevented its resurrection in milder forms. Thus, Butler and Stokes argue that 'the betterment of the electorate's economic condition' is 'by far the most important of the social trends which have weakened the inclination to see politics in terms of class'.[19]

As for the other aspect of Anthony Crosland's argument, 'The Decline of the Working Class'[20] itself, its implications are by no means as clear-cut as he suggests. *Political Change in Britain* analyses voting and party identification in terms of a learning process in which parents' party identification and the early voting experience of individuals can have significant effects on their subsequent electoral behaviour. Thus, while changes in occupational structure may reduce the relative size of Labour's working-class constituency the demographic basis of recruitment into the expanding middle-class occupations involves a significant middle-class 'inheritance' of Labour support. In that respect it has been argued that, far from shifting as Crosland suggests to a 'classless' image, the Labour Party may have 'good grounds for consolidating its appeal to the manual working class'.[21]

But, whatever the problems with Crosland's account of the erosion of class, the greater part of his argument is concerned with what he regards as the other major determinants of electoral behaviour, namely, party images and their relation to the interests and concerns of the electors. With the decline of the class alignment 'the voters may make a *less automatic assessment* of where their political interests lie'[22] (emphasis added), and it is for that reason that party images are so important. In effect, Crosland operates with two distinct models of voting behaviour: there are those who vote 'automatically' on class lines, and those who vote on the basis of a more-or-less serious assessment of party images and their record in government. The decline of the one is significant because of the increased space it creates for the other. It is this concern with the images that Labour presents to that part of the electorate not voting automatically on class lines that is the principal legacy of Crosland's analysis.

For a more recent example of this emphasis on party images consider Austin Mitchell's Fabian Tract *Can Labour Win Again?* written after Labour's 1979 defeat. Its title is a clear gesture towards Crosland's response to the defeat twenty years before. Mitchell notes the long-term decline in the two-party share of the vote, which he attributes to 'the perception of poor performance in office',[23] and the decline in class alignment of the electorate. 'Those set loose from *class constraints* will view parties primarily in terms of their effectiveness as governments. Assessments will be a broad impression . . .'[24] (emphasis added). Here too the 'class constraint' is seen as inhibiting voter assessment of the parties in terms of image and performance – and it is supposed to do so in a way that poses a clear problem for Mitchell's explanation of changes in the two-party share of the vote. If the class constraint inhibits assessment of parties in terms of their performance in office then a shift in electoral behaviour 'due to the perception of poor performance in office' obviously requires a prior loosening of that constraint.

But, however that loosening is to be explained, its effect is that Labour's image becomes all the more important. And in a further echo of Crosland's argument Mitchell points out that Labour continues to be associated with unpopular images. To remedy that situation Labour must either change the climate of opinion or adjust its policies to appeal to 'the autonomous voters'.[25] While not regarding the pattern of opinion as completely immutable, Mitchell does see it as reinforced by the media in such a way as to prejudice 'the whole debate against Labour'.[26] In effect, then, Labour must change its policies, adopting the model of the SPD in Germany by moving 'to the middle of the road, modifying policy, toning down ideology, and becoming a much less socialist and electorally more attractive party'.[27] Mitchell's argument is both more complex and more interesting than this discussion of the place of class alignment and party image may suggest. But it is only the latter that concerns us here, as yet another example of the way political implications may be drawn from accounts of shifts in the relation between class and politics.

THE 'INTERESTS' OF THE WORKING CLASS

These different accounts of developments in the relationship between the Labour Party and its actual or potential supporters also involve divergent analyses of British politics: the one side emphasizing the fundamental role of class interests in (potentially) mobilizing political support, and the other posing the problem of electoral support in conditions where that class alignment cannot (or can no longer) be presumed. They also differ in their assessment of the political lessons to be drawn from these developments. The lessons of Labour's alleged failure to represent working-class interests depend on whether that failure is regarded as an inherent feature of the Labour Party or as something to be remedied by a victory of the 'left' within it. In the one case socialists and the working class should be persuaded to reject the Labour Party and to pursue their interests elsewhere, e.g. through the vehicle of yet another party of the Left.[28] In the other case the lesson is that Labour should return to its socialist roots, employing a system of accountability to its (socialist) membership as a means of preventing further leadership betrayal. The lessons of the tales of long-term social

changes in British society and the consequent importance of party image
and performance are quite simply that Labour must adapt to the modern
world or else slowly perish. It must move away from its identification
with the working class and develop a classless appeal, it should reduce
its association with unpopular images and seek to develop new, electorally
attractive images in their place, and it must try to appear a credible party
of government.

Fortunately things are by no means as clear-cut as any of these accounts
suggest. The arguments concerning Labour's alleged failure to represent the
interests of the working class operate with a highly problematic notion of
political interests. In order to bring out the problem here let us begin by
noting that interests are always produced in the course of argument or evaluation. The point may seem trivial but it has serious implications for the way
interests and their political repercussions are assessed. To say that interests
should be seen as products of evaluation is to say first that their definition is
always open to dispute. In that respect political conclusions derived from an
assertion of working-class interests must always be regarded as problematic,
for they may be countered by alternative evaluations of those interests. It is
to say, secondly, that interests are always articulated by particular agencies
of evaluation. The agencies in question may be individuals or organizations,
and the interests they articulate may be their own or those of others. Trade
unions may calculate their own interests and those of their members, *qua*
union members, and sometimes also they may calculate the interests of
somewhat broader constituencies, the labour movement, the working class,
the *British* workers, etc. Sections of the Labour Party and numerous other
left organizations and sects may claim to define the interests of the working
class. And so on.

Consider, for example, relations between the trade unions and the Labour
Party. Many unions affiliate to the Labour Party on the basis of a significant
proportion of their membership and they play an active role in Conference
and the determination of party policy. In addition to that direct involvement
in the Labour Party unions may attempt to reach agreement with the party
leadership over a range of policy issues. In these cases calculations of the
interests of the unions and of their members are made by the unions
themselves or the TUC. There is no reason to suppose that 'interests'
calculated at this level necessarily correspond to the 'interests' calculated
by union members. Indeed, there are well-known cases where the politics
of a union run counter to those of a majority of its members, and the
1979 election studies suggest that Labour failed to obtain majority support
among skilled workers, most of whom are organized in unions affiliated to
the Labour Party. The point here is that it can be seriously misleading to
regard the Labour Party as 'an alliance of *workers organised through the trades
unions* and constituency-based activists'[29] (emphasis added). It is the unions
as organizations that affiliate to the Labour Party, not the individual

workers organized within them. An agreement or social contract between the Labour Party and the TUC or major unions may well have its electoral attractions (and it may be desirable for other reasons) but it is not an electoral agreement between the Labour Party and the individual members of the unions concerned. Disagreement between the party leadership and the major unions may also have significant electoral consequences, as with the 1978–79 winter of discontent in which unions' assessments of their members' interests led them to reject the 5 per cent pay norm. But those electoral consequences follow from the economic and political effects of resistance by unions and organized groups within them. They are not the product of any simple reflex action on the part of the working class to an unambiguous act of betrayal of its interests by the Labour Government.

The crucial point in regarding interests in this way is that any analysis of their political significance must begin with the activities of those agencies engaged in the definition of the interests in question, and it must investigate the repercussions of those activities. Calculations of interests play an important part in political life but they do not function at all in the ways assumed by all too many arguments on the left. In particular, the use of Labour's failure to represent what are said to be the interests of the working class as an explanation of its failure to mobilize massive working-class support involves a radically different way of conceptualizing interests. The arguments require that class interests be identifiable independently of the activities of parties and other organizations in order that they can serve as the standard against which the practices of particular organizations can be judged. What makes it possible for the interests of the working class to perform that function is that they are conceived as being inherent in the capitalist structure of the economy, so that they can be furthered only by a 'socialist' policy directed towards the transformation of that structure. The Labour Party stands to gain working-class support in so far as it appeals to those 'interests' and to lose support in so far as it subsequently betrays them or reduces that appeal. Because those 'interests' are inherent in the structure of the economy, they exist whether or not significant sections of the working class recognize them as such. There can be no question, therefore, of tracing the political consequences of interests through the practices of those who calculate them and the wider repercussions of those practices. In this respect the structure of the argument invites what might otherwise seem a thoroughly cavalier disregard of the overwhelming and long-standing evidence that there has been precious little working-class support for the 'socialist' policies of the Left, in the Labour Party or outside it. Where the working class persistently refuses to recognize its real interests the explanation is to be sought in something that inhibits that recognition, the media, the 'process of legitimation' that is supposed to characterize capitalist societies,[30] a failure of leadership, or whatever. In some versions of the argument[31] the Labour Party itself appears as a major villain in preventing the working class from developing a true awareness of its interests in socialism.

I have criticized that conception of political interests at length elsewhere, and there is no space to repeat the argument here. But it is worth noting that the argument in terms of leadership betrayal suffers not only from a dubious conception of political interests but also from a highly problematic account of the history of the Labour Party and the place of socialist politics within it. This, too, I have discussed elsewhere[32] and only a few points need to be noted here. There is no denying that the party leadership often acts in ways that many socialists and party activists would deplore, and that at times it refuses to act on party policy as laid down by Conference. The Left in the Labour Party had been particularly exercised by the disjunction between Conference decisions on policy and the policies pursued by the party leadership over recent years as its voting strength in Conference has grown. But what is at issue in the stories of leadership betrayal of the interests of the working class is something more than these well-known facts. For to talk of betrayal in this context is to construct a history of the party as essentially socialist, but persistently betrayed, and to represent the party in the country as custodian of the interests of the working class. The latter depends, of course, on precisely that dubious notion of interests noted above, for it requires us to disregard the compelling evidence of working-class refusal to support the policies favoured by the Labour Left.

As for the history of the Labour Party as essentially socialist, in the sense intended by the Left, that too has little to recommend it, apart from Clause 4 of its constitution and other such symbolic pronouncements. The Labour Party has gone through several changes since its formation but it has always been a more-or-less organized coalition of political groupings and organizations, involving a variety of political concerns and ideologies. Socialism has been and remains a significant part of that amalgam, but it has never been the dominant element. The socialist organizations taking part, with the unions, in the formation of the Labour Party did so not because they thought it would be a socialist Labour Party (certainly not in the short term) but rather because of their dismal failure to attract significant working-class support as independent organizations.[33] The Labour Party, in its alliance with the trade union movement, provided a space for socialist argument to intervene within the mainstream of British political debate, a space in which the appeal to socialist principles can still have a certain legitimacy and sometimes a limited effect. That space survives today and it has, if anything, grown over recent years – and that in spite of the behaviour of the Labour Left and its many tactical and strategic errors. Indeed, it would be a serious mistake to regard that space as the sole property of the Left in the party. Many of the principled opponents of the Labour Left are also concerned to argue in terms of socialist principles and the political conditions of their implementation. Consider, for example, the refusal of at least some of the founders of the Council for Social Democracy to countenance the idea of a genuine centre party precisely because of their commitment to a particular kind of socialist politics.

PARTY IMAGES AND PARTY POLICY

Anthony Crosland's *Can Labour Win?* was an excellent example of concern with the problems of implementing socialist politics. There is little in his introductory listing of socialist principles that need be disputed by the Labour Left. But he then goes on to suggest, perhaps optimistically, that 'socialists who read this pamphlet are interested in realising these aims in practice: that is, they are concerned with political achievement'.[34] Since political achievement will depend on returning a Labour government and sustaining it in office he goes on to argue for the need to study factors affecting voting behaviour and political attitudes and especially 'to consider how the Labour Party might get itself into a better *rapport* with them'. Decisions on these matters are better based on 'information rather than on whim or hunch'.[35] What is striking about the arguments discussed immediately above is their ability to refute the problem Crosland tries to pose. They invoke a thoroughly speculative conception of class interests with serious consequences both for their account of relations between Labour and its actual or potential supporters and for the political recommendations that are supposed to follow. These accounts and recommendations depend more on an act of faith in the socialist potential of the working class than on serious attempts to grapple with the problems of furthering socialist objectives through the actions of an electorally successful Labour Party.

The alternative tradition of accounting for relations between the Labour Party and its actual or potential supporters has what might seem the very great merit of appearing to take those problems seriously. We are presented with electoral statistics and opinion studies showing, first, a breakdown in the class polarization of electoral support and, secondly, Labour's association with some distinctly unpopular political images. The argument is then that electoral success depends crucially on gaining significant support from that large and growing section of the electorate that does not vote 'automatically' on class lines. The breakdown of class polarization is taken to imply the increasing importance of party images, including popular assessments of the parties' performance in office. The conclusion is therefore that Labour must take steps to improve its image and to develop policies that will improve its performance in office.

So far, it seems, so good. Unfortunately there are major problems with the argument. First, we have seen that the argument turns on there being two distinct types of voter: those who vote 'automatically' on class lines and those 'set loose from class constraints',[36] who make 'a less automatic assessment of where their political interests lie'.[37] The claim is that the latter category has grown at the expense of the former. There are problems with the explanations offered for that supposed shift, but what must be noted here is the manner in which the distinction between the two types of voter is presented, as if some more-or-less rational process of assessment of the parties were involved in the one case but not in the other. In those terms the distinction cannot be defended. But once it is admitted that those who vote on class lines might also engage in some process of assessment then the conclusion that Labour should seek to appear less of a class party need no longer follow. Consider, for example, Butler and Stokes' argument that one reason for the weakening of the class alignment of British politics is that parties have presented the electorate with a much weaker class stimulus. In that respect, they suggest, Labour's transformation has been especially striking, adding that Labour governments' confrontations with the unions 'cannot fail to have blurred Labour's image as a class party'.[38] Butler and Stokes' analysis also suggests that the demographic basis of recruitment into the expanding middle-class occupations throughout the 1950s and 1960s involved a significant middle-class 'inheritance' of Labour support. Minkin and Seyd therefore argue that there were good grounds for Labour attempting to consolidate its appeal to the manual working class and, further, that Labour's attempts to present a classless image may have alienated significant parts of its potential working-class and middle-class support. It 'was a major error of strategy and one whose consequences cannot easily be undone'.[39]

I raise these points not in order to suggest that Labour should seek to consolidate its class appeal, but rather to bring out a major flaw in the argument. The claim is made that class has become less, and party images more, salient as a result of secular changes occurring in British society that are largely independent of the electoral practices of the parties themselves – and it is to those changes that Labour must adapt or perish. But once it is recognized that these 'secular' changes may in part be the result of Labour's all-too-successful attempts to manipulate its image and electoral appeal, then they can hardly be invoked as political givens requiring that the party's image be manipulated yet further in the same direction. Of course Labour has to live, like the rest of us, with the consequences of its past actions. Thus, even to the extent that the actions of the Labour Party and Labour governments have been responsible for, say, the declining salience of class, it remains a fact of political life that cannot now be wished away or easily reversed.

The decline in class polarization and the increasing 'volatility' of electoral support for the two major parties do indeed pose serious political problems for Labour. The difficulty with the arguments of Anthony Crosland and all those who have subsequently argued in similar vein is that their conclusions depend on what can only be described as simplistic conceptions of party 'images', of voters and their assessments of Labour and other parties. That difficulty is all the more striking in relation to the policy changes and organizational reforms that Labour is supposed to undertake in order to improve its image. The point that Labour has to consider its potential electoral support and the possible effects on that support of its behaviour in or out of office is, or should be, well taken. But what follows is by no means as clear-cut as the writings of Crosland and others would suggest. First, there are good reasons for doubting the reliability of opinion poll evidence.[40] Secondly, there is a marked disjunction between, on the one hand, the claim that party images and performance are important and the consideration of opinion poll evidence that is brought to bear on that claim, and, on the other hand, the conclusions that are subsequently drawn concerning party policy and organization.

What possible alternative to this disjunction is there? One possibility would be an utterly unprincipled opportunism that offered the voters whatever they appeared to want, something that few in the Labour Party would tolerate and fewer still openly advocate. Such opportunism apart, remarkably little follows directly from a recognition of the importance of party images and the current concerns of voters. I say that little follows *directly*, for whatever may be said to follow in either the short or the long term can only depend on a process of evaluation involving political objectives and priorities, the organizational and campaigning capacities of the party and the room for manoeuvre open to it and, presumably, assessments of how voters' concerns and images might be amenable to change. That process cannot avoid bringing into play a variety of imponderables and matters of political dispute within the party. Now, to shift more-or-less directly from electoral statistics and opinion polls to recommendations for party policy and organization is to evade that process. The result is that the policy arguments are unavoidably *ad hoc*, sometimes thoroughly sensible and sometimes utterly specious, and the recommendations are somewhat arbitrary in character. In effect, the point about the importance of party images is used by Crosland and others who argue in that tradition as an excuse for advocating whatever party reforms and policies they happen to favour at the time of writing.

CONCLUSIONS

To conclude, I have suggested that while the detailed arguments of *Decline* cannot be sustained there is nevertheless a real sense in which working-class politics can be said to have declined over the last few decades. Class is no longer a good predictor of voting behaviour or party identification and Labour has lost support for its policy positions within the working class. There are two major traditions that attempt to draw lessons for Labour from that decline and I have argued that there are serious problems with both of them. Analyses in terms of the fundamental role of class interests involve a speculative notion of interests and highly problematic histories of the Labour Party which together sustain what might otherwise seem a cavalier disregard for the evidence concerning working-class political concerns and involvement throughout this century. As against that tradition there are arguments, often involving a residual class reductionism, which attempt to pose problems of electoral support under conditions where the supposed mobilizing role of class interests cannot be presumed. These arguments have the merit of recognizing serious problems involved in the pursuit of political objectives by means of an electorally successful Labour Party. But their attempts to address those problems are flawed by simplistic conceptions of party 'images' and of how the Labour Party might adapt to popular concerns. I have suggested that discussion of these problems must be contentious since it cannot avoid various imponderables and matters of political dispute. Let me conclude this discussion by commenting briefly on a couple of these issues in order to bring out something of their complexity.

Consider, first, the question of how Labour might adapt its policy positions in the light of popular political concerns. It is well known that there is little popular support for some of the major policy positions associated with the Labour Party in the 1980s – and that Labour's electoral support holds up remarkably well in spite of that. But leaving this last point aside, what follows? Was Labour right to abandon those policy positions (or at least attempt to play them down at election time) or should it have made long-term efforts to change popular perceptions of what it regards as major policy issues? The first response is clearly one of the elements involved in Labour critiques of the party's obsession with public ownership and in the suggestion that Labour has to become 'a much less socialist and electorally more attractive party'.[41] But the second response comes to the fore in other contexts. Thus Crosland argued in 1960 that the party should select a limited number of vital socialist issues and 'propagate these insistently and purposefully for the whole period between now and the next Election'.[42] The point here is that there can be no simple answer to the question of how Labour might adapt to the unpopularity of some of its policy positions.

One crucial reason why there can be no simple answer is that attitudes are not political givens, products of an underlying social structure operating independently of the practices of parties, unions and other significant political actors. There can be little doubt, for example, that the economic policy failures of both major parties while in government have contributed to the fall in the two-party share of the vote,[43] or that the antics of Labour and Conservative governments and of both parties in Opposition have done much to discredit the ideas of planning and incomes policies.[44] Or again, the 1978–79 winter of discontent was clearly a contributing factor in Labour's 1979 defeat: not only because it demonstrated Labour's ability to come up with an unsustainable wages norm in spite of its special relationship with the unions, but also because it provided the occasion for a major campaign by the Left and union activists against the Labour Government and its policies that attracted widespread sympathy within the labour movement and was capitalized on by the right. The question of how Labour can or should adapt to popular concerns is a political question that should be decided by political debate. Evidence as to Labour's image and the content of popular concerns certainly has a bearing on that debate but it cannot determine the decision. Whatever decision is reached, the outcome of any attempt by the Labour Party to adapt itself to, or to change, popular attitudes can never be guaranteed, for it will always depend in part on the practices of other political actors.

Finally, returning to a sense of working-class politics not discussed in *Decline*, consider Labour's links with the unions. We have seen that there has long been evidence of the unpopularity of unions with the electorate, and even among union members and Labour supporters. Labour's connections with the unions would therefore seem to be a mixed political blessing. The example of Sweden over most of the last fifty years shows that close ties with unions do not have to be an electoral obstacle. And in Britain there have been times (e.g. in the 1974 elections) when Labour's ability to claim a special relationship with the unions has been an electoral advantage. Few in the Labour Party would be so foolish as to wish, let alone to advocate, the severance of those connections. But once that option is rejected then it is clear that the electoral problems arising out of the trade union connections cannot be resolved by the Labour Party alone, that they depend on the behaviour and organization of the unions and the TUC and on their relations with the constituency parties. In addition it seems clear that any credible Labour policy with regard to economic management must depend on its obtaining effective union support and co-operation. The problem here, as the experience of successive Labour governments has shown, is that effective support and co-operation requires more than a limited agreement between the leaderships of the party on the one hand and of the TUC and major unions on the other. Agreements at that level can too easily be subverted, given the character of collective bargaining in Britain and the limited forms of discipline available to the TUC and union leaderships, by particular unions or groups of workers deciding, justifiably or otherwise, that they constitute a special case.

These points suggest that the electoral consequences of Labour's union connections, the development of a credible economic policy, and the economic policy performance of a future Labour government may each depend in part on structural reforms within the unions and on the character of their links with the Labour Party. There is little space to discuss those issues here, but two things at least are clear. First, there are severe limits to the reforms that can be imposed on reluctant unions from above. The lesson was brought home to the Labour leadership by the defeat of the proposals for union reform contained in Barbara Castle's 1969 White Paper *In Place of Strife*[45] and it has been reinforced by the experience of subsequent essays in the imposition of union reform by government. Secondly, the problems posed by the structure and organization of the unions and Labour's connections with them, both for Labour's electoral appeal and for its credibility as a party of government in the field of economic management, have been with us since the 1940s – and they will not go away. What, if anything, to do about those problems can only be a matter of political debate. Labour may attempt to fudge the issues and to get by on cobbled and unstable agreements with leaders of the major unions. It may attempt to impose reform on the unions from above, thereby marking its distance from and independence of the unions. Or it may attempt to work for reforms of collective bargaining and union organization through policies capable of achieving support not only from union leaders but also from the ranks of union activists and local officials, e.g. through an egalitarian incomes policy coupled with expansion of the workers' role in enterprise management.[46] Whatever solutions may be attempted they must have major implications for the future political character of the Labour Party and its involvement in the labour movement.

NOTES AND REFERENCES

I am grateful to Julian Clarke, Phil Jones, Liz Kingdom, Ben Pimlott and Penny Woolley for their suggestions and criticisms of an earlier draft of this chapter.

1.   There are theoretical problems arising from *Decline's* attempts to combine Marxist and phenomenological positions. Some of these are noted in J.H. Goldthorpe, 'Class, Status and Party in Modern Britain', *Archives Européenes de Sociologie*, 13, 1972.

2.   R. Baxter, 'The Working Class and Labour Politics', *Political Studies*, 1972; T. Forester, *The Labour Party and the Working Class*, Heinemann, London, 1976.

3.   T. Forester, *The Labour Party and the Working Class*, op. cit., p. 79.

4.   D. Butler and D. Stokes, *Political Change in Britain* (2nd edn), Macmillan, London, 1974, pp. 200–1.

5.   I. Crewe, B. Sarlik and J. Alt, 'Partisan Dealignment in Britain, 1964–74', *British Journal of Political Science*, 7, 1977.

6.   D. Butler and D. Stokes, *Political Change*, op. cit., p. 198.

7.   A. Mitchell, *Can Labour Win Again?*, Fabian Tract 463, 1979; P. Kellner, 'The voters who switch sides', *New Statesman*, 27 April

1979, and 'Not a defeat: a disaster', *New Statesman*, 18 May 1979.

8. M. Abrams, R. Rose and R. Hinden, *Must Labour Lose?*, Penguin, Harmondsworth, 1960, p. 37.

9. C.A.R. Crosland, *Can Labour Win?*, Fabian Tract 324, 1960, p. 9.

10. *Sunday Times*, 31 Aug. 1980.

11. I. Crewe *et al.*, 'Partisan Dealignment', op. cit.

12. D. Butler and D. Stokes, *Political Change*, op. cit., p. 194.

13. R. Miliband, *Parliamentary Socialism* (2nd edn), Merlin, London, 1973; D. Coates, *The Labour Party and the Struggle for Socialism*, Cambridge University Press, Cambridge, 1975; L. Panitch, *Social Democracy and Industrial Militancy*, Cambridge University Press, Cambridge, 1976.

14. I have discussed these arguments in 'A Left Labour Government?', *Politics and Power*, 2, 1980.

15. Cf. D. Butler and D. Stokes' discussion of the weakening of the class alignment. They argue that an important factor has been that the parties, and Labour in particular, have presented the electorate with a much weaker class stimulus, which has affected turnout in traditional working-class areas. 'For voters deeply imbued with a belief in working-class interests, a movement by Labour away from these goals . . . removed the motive for voting at all' (p. 206).

16. C.A.R. Crosland, *Can Labour Win?*, op. cit., p. 12.

17. See also his 'Social Class and British Politics', *Public Opinion Quarterly*, 20, 1961.

18. J.H. Goldthorpe and D. Lockwood, 'Affluence and the British Class Structure', *Sociological Review*, 11, 1968; J.H. Goldthorpe *et al., The Affluent Worker*, Cambridge University Press, Cambridge, 1968.

19. D. Butler and D. Stokes, *Political Change*, op. cit., p. 193.

20. C.A.R. Crosland, *Can Labour Win?*, op. cit., subheading, p. 20.

21. L. Minkin and P. Seyd, 'The British Labour Party', in W.E. Paterson and A.H. Thomas, *Social Democratic Parties in Western Europe*, Croom Helm, London, 1979, p. 135.

22. C.A.R. Crosland, *Can Labour Win?*, op. cit., p. 22.

23. Ibid., p. 6.

24. Ibid., p. 8.

25. Ibid., p. 11.

26. Ibid., p. 10.

27. Ibid., p. 11.

28. R. Miliband, 'Moving on', *Socialist Register*, 1976.

29. *Fabian News*, October 1980. The extract is from an advertisement for the 1981 Fabian New Year School, 'New Foundations for Labour'.

30. R. Miliband, *The State in Capitalist Society*, Weidenfeld and Nicolson, London, 1972.

31. See note 13.

242   *Trade unions in British politics: the first 250 years*

32. *A Left Labour Government?*, *Politics and Power*, 2, 1980 and 'Marxism and Parliamentary Democracy' in A. Hunt (ed.), *Marxism and
Democracy*, Lawrence and Wishart, London, 1980.
33. For a short account and further references see Forester, *The Labour
Party and the Working Class*, op. cit.
34. C.A.R. Crosland, *Can Labour Win?*, op. cit., p. 2.
35. Ibid., p. 3.
36. A. Mitchell, *Can Labour Win Again?*, op. cit., p. 8.
37. C.A.R. Crosland, *Can Labour Win?*, op. cit., p. 22.
38. D. Butler and D. Stokes, *Political Change*, op. cit., pp. 195, 198.
39. L. Minkin and P. Seyd, 'The British Labour Party', op. cit., p.
135.
40. C. Jameson, 'Who Needs Polls?', *New Statesman*, 6 Feb. 1981.
41. A. Mitchell, *Can Labour Win Again?*, op. cit., p. 11.
42. C.A.R. Crosland, *Can Labour Win?*, op. cit., p. 18.
43. A. Mitchell, *Can Labour Win Again?*, op. cit.; D. Butler and D.
Stokes, *Political Change*, op. cit.; J. Alt, *The Politics of Economic
Decline: economic management and political behaviour in Britain since
1964*, Cambridge University Press, Cambridge, 1979.
44. J. Lereuz, *Economic Planning and Politics in Britain*, Martin Robertson,
Oxford, 1976; M. Stewart, *Politics and Economic Policy in the United
Kingdom since 1964*, Pergamon, Oxford, 1978.
45. See the account of this episode in P. Jenkins, *The Battle of Downing
Street*, Charles Knight, London, 1970.
46. Some of the issues involved here are discussed by P. Hirst in 'On
struggle in the Enterprise', in M. Prior (ed.), *The Popular and
the Political*, Routledge and Kegan Paul, London, 1981. See also
J. Elliott, *Conflict or Cooperation*, Kogan Page, London, 1978.

12 The influence of the trade unions on the ethos of the Labour Party

H.M. Drucker

There can have been few periods in the history of the Labour Party when the party's relationship with the unions was not disputed, and yet rarely can the controversy have been so important to the party as in the 1970s and 1980s. Critics of both right and left objected that the unions had too much influence over the party. Some right-wing MPs and their friends took their objection to the point of resigning from the party to form the Social Democratic and Liberal Alliance, claiming that the Labour Party was the creature of the union bosses. This they deplored both because they thought that Britain's social and economic problems cannot seriously be tackled by a party dominated by institutions which are themselves part of the problem, and because they realized that union bosses are unpopular with the public whose votes the party needs in elections.

So far, no right-wing politician or commentator has complained of the unions' role in the party on the grounds that the unions are inevitably left-wing. But from the left the complaint has been that the unions are, if not inevitably social democratic, necessarily conservative. They are seen to be props of capitalism. Their attempts to protect their members stifle a revolutionary consciousness. From the Left the cry is to create a revolutionary party free from union domination.

Party activists and students of the party alike know that there is a third position; uncritical celebration of the *status quo*. It is difficult to attend a Labour Party meeting without hearing someone repeat with satisfaction Ernie Bevin's observation that 'the Labour Party emerged out of the bowels of the trade union movement'. This chapter is partly a commentary on this three-sided debate and especially on its most recent focus: the method of selection of the party leader. It is also an attempt to argue that the debate about the relationship between the unions and the party has been lacking an important dimension. So far it has been about party politics and doctrines. To be complete it needs also to consider the party's ethos as that ethos has been and continues to be influenced by the unions. Hence the argument in this chapter is that once the influence of the unions on the ethos of the party is taken into account one has a fresh view of it and of its doctrines.

DOCTRINE AND ETHOS

The argument given here depends on the distinction between doctrine and ethos. Doctrines are what people usually have in mind when they talk of the ideology of the party.[1] Doctrines can be coherent statements of a position. Doctrines can lead to policies: Labour's doctrines commonly do. These policies are recorded in the Reports of the Labour Party Conferences. They can be accepted, rejected, enacted into law, contemptuously ignored, but above all they are explicit. An ethos is not so hard-and-fast nor so easy to describe. By the ethos of the party I have in mind what an earlier age might have called the spirit of the party; its traditions and habits, its feel. The ethos is not explicit, it is not laid down in the rules (though the notion that things ought to be laid down in the rules is part of this particular ethos).

Observers of Labour have long noticed that it possesses a number of quaint, largely unexpected rituals and traditions. When these observers were foreign, and often they were, the traditions were attributed to the party's 'Britishness'. Egon Wertheimer, for example, one of the shrewdest observers of the party in its early years, thought this was the explanation. Wertheimer described his wonder at the behaviour he met at his first Labour meeting.[2]

Even the platform offered to the foreigner an astounding sight. Here sat – a thing undreamed of - a parson with his clerical collar among the speakers of the Socialist Party. Suddenly, there was a movement in the crowd, and a young man, with the face of the ruling class in Great Britain, but with the gait of a Douglas Fairbanks, thrust himself forward through the throng to the platform, followed by a lady in heavy, costly furs. There stood Oswald Mosley, whose later ascent was to be one of the strangest phenomena of the working-class movement of the world, a new recruit to the Socialist movement at his first London meeting. He was introduced to the audience, and even at that time, I remember, the song 'For he's a jolly good fellow', greeted the young man from two thousand throats . . . . But all the more unforgettable was the impression, the visual and oral impression, which the style of this speech made upon me. It was a hymn, an emotional appeal directed not to the intellect, but to the Socialist idea, which obviously was still a subject of wonder to the orator, a youthful experience. No speaker at a working-class meeting in Germany would have dared to have worked so unrestrainedly on the feelings without running the risk of losing for ever his standing in the party movement . . . But then came something unexpected, something that, by its spontaneity, shook me, although it was a trifling thing and seemed a matter of course for all those around me: from the audience there came calls; they grew more urgent; and suddenly the elegant lady in furs got up from her seat, and said a few sympathetic words, which I understood because they were simple and came immediately from the heart. She said that she had never before attended a workers' meeting, and how deeply the warmth of this reception touched her. She said this simply and almost shyly, but yet like one who is accustomed to be acclaimed, and, without stage fright, to open a bazaar or a meeting for charitable purposes. 'Lady Cynthia Mosley', whispered in my ear one of the armleted stewards who stood near me, excited, and later, as though thinking that he had not sufficiently impressed me, he added, 'Lord Curzon's daughter'. His whole face beamed proudly.

There is much in this description which will make today's activist blush. But few would deny that Wertheimer had seen something profound.

It might be thought that such quaint habits as welcoming lords and ladies had disappeared. No doubt this particular habit has. Mosley's subsequent career, his meteoric rise within the Labour Party, his split from it during the second MacDonald minority Government (to form a centre party!) and his subsequent leadership of the Nazi-emulating brown-shirted British Union of Fascists, will lead most to be glad of the loss. But Labour still possesses habits and traditions which do not arise from any doctrinal conception, which are traceable in large measure to its ties with trade unions, and which shape much of the current controversy within the party.

THE TRADITIONAL LINKS

When speakers at Labour meetings chant that the party is nothing without the unions, they point not simply to the continuing power of the unions but also to this continuing traditional link. Socialists who want to belong to a party which is not tied to the unions are quite right to think that they had better leave the Labour Party. The party is unthinkable without the unions. This may well be an electoral disadvantage in the modern world; but it is a fact all the same.

When the party was formed in the first decade of the century many of its organizational principles were taken over unreflectively from the characteristic practices of the unions. For example, there is the notion that the party's leaders, however they are elected, should be responsible to the Labour Party Conference. There is the additional notion that the party's policy ought to be formed by an annual delegate conference and not dictated by the leadership. Many such features of the party are so well accepted now that it is difficult to recollect the position of the founders of the party who had to create a new instrument. But their task was not purely imaginative, they simply transferred to the new vehicle the traditions and habits of operation they knew well from their old organizations. The notion, for instance, that a group should be represented by one of its own members is rarely written down in the party's standing orders; but it is effective throughout the organization and it comes from the unions' common practices.

Notoriously the rules and practices of unions vary. They are so diverse that they are difficult to characterize. But they do have some important things in common. They all exemplify a form of democracy. The unions, especially the older unions, were formed by people who had slowly built them in a hostile world. Thus the unions tend to be slow-moving, defensive organizations. Their rules are remarkably elaborate and nearly self-contained. They leave little to the initiative of the unions' own leaders and less to the public law. They often incorporate generous universalistic aspirations and narrow formalistic procedures.

One important manifestation of the trade unions' influence on the party in its formative years is Clause 4, No. 4 of the party's constitution. Clause 4 (as it is universally known) commits the party to secure for the workers the full, equitably-distributed fruits of their labour upon the basis of the common ownership, popular administration and control of their industry. This is the only place in the party's constitution which states its doctrinal goals. This fountain-head of the party's doctrines has remained largely unchanged since 1918. It owes its place in the 1918 constitution to the party leaders' decision, in this as in so much else, to emulate trade union practice. The notion that a proper organization needed a principle at its head – not Labour's practice before 1918, nor the Conservatives' even now – came from the unions' ethos. There is a sense then in which the ethos of the unions preceded their doctrine into the party.

Other, more recent, examples show the constraining influence of the informal ethos on formal party practices. Elections to the NEC are a case in point. *Ex officio* and individual posts (such as the Treasurer) apart, there are three blocks of seats on the NEC: the constituency section, the trades union section and the women's section. Constituencies vote for members of the first group, trade unions for the second and both for the third. One might think that in a party riven by internal factions each claiming to be the 'true' party there would be factional fights for these places. To some extent there are. Slates of candidates from factional groups such as the Campaign for Labour Party Democracy (left) and the Campaign for Labour Victory (right) are produced for the constituency and women's sections and to a lesser extent for the trade union section.

But by and large voting is not by slate. Sitting members have a sense, as Hugh Dalton once put it, of social security about their Labour Party jobs. It is rare for a sitting member to be voted off the NEC. This is perhaps less astonishing in the trade union section where the largest unions have places more or less within their gift.

Security is less strong among the constituency party places. But even here the one startling exception, when in 1952 a Tribune-backed slate swept the board, was so obviously exceptional that it points to the rule. In many constituency parties, as Lewis Minkin has observed, the security of sitting tenants is increased by the common practice of moving that 'we support all the sitting candidates'.[3] Such resolutions regularly carry in both 'right-' and 'left-' wing dominated constituency parties.

In the trade union section the rule is that each union can nominate only from its own members and each may nominate only one member (save for those with more than 500,000 members). As Minkin notes, sitting tenants are generally secure here and the rule of 'Buggins' turn' operates to determine which member is nominated when there is a vacancy within a union. 'No King is as secure as the average trade union leader', as G.B. Shaw once observed.[4] These traditions are the most important factors in determining most places. Factional preferences only operate at the margin – where there is a vote for a vacant place. Traditions emanating from a working-class ethos of loyalty are more important than doctrine in this crucial decision.

Votes for places in the women's section show the importance of the trades union ethos even more clearly. Here the unions by tradition refrain from exercising their right to nomination for places in a section even though their votes are paramount. The usual tradition of returning sitting candidates holds and usually the only important fights are over voluntarily-vacant places. Thus, at the 1980 Conference, which was marked by bitter and closely fought right/left disputes over the method of selection of the leader of the party, the first and second places went to a right-winger – Shirley Williams (5,255,000 votes) and a left-winger Joan Maynard (4,361,000 votes). Both were long-established members of the women's section. The only real fight was over a vacant place – it went to a left-winger.

The traditions and habits of the party have been gradually willed to the party from its progenitors, the trade unions, and its paternity is plain to see. An even more recent example confirms this assertion. After Michael Foot was elected leader of the party by his PLP colleagues in November 1980 – his election owed much to the MPs' preference for a man who could heal the breach within the party – the PLP then elected the 'parliamentary committee', i.e. the Shadow Cabinet. Again the fight was mainly over the vacant places created by resignations and Mr Foot's elevation to the leadership. Again Buggins' turn prevailed. Mr Tony Benn was unable to secure a seat among the eleven places, in part because of his decision to abandon the Shadow Cabinet the previous year and his attacks on it thereafter. The PLP which had elected Mr Foot, a founder of Tribune, only weeks before, gave the vacant places to 'right-wing' backers of the defeated leadership candidate Mr Denis Healey.

Other examples of strong traditions and habits which are inexplicable if one thinks of the Labour Party solely as a power-machine can be cited. Many of them concern the party's attitude to its leaders. All point in the same direction: Labour's leaders, once elected, are secure in most circumstances. The Conservative Party is much more ruthless. Its tradition has been characterized as 'oligarchy tempered by assassination', and rightly so, for the Tory Party has forced out many of its recent leaders; having been abjectly loyal to them (in public at least) beforehand. There is no equivalent in recent Conservative history to Mr Wilson's unheralded decision to stand down as leader in 1976. The Tory Party, with its very different social basis, has a different ethos from Labour.

The existence of such habits is often overlooked by commentators. Many have been inclined to summarize the party's Conference decisions before a particular general election, observe the folding of these resolutions into the manifesto and then judge the performance of the subsequent Labour government against the manifesto. This is a literal view of the ideology and policy of the party; and up to a point it is a useful one. But we need to take care how we interpret the evidence.

RECENT CONSTITUTIONAL DISPUTES

The disputes of the early 1980s over the constitution of the party demonstrate this point. One of the most hotly contested concerned the method of selection of the leaders. Until 1981 the leader – who until the mid-1970s had been strictly the leader of the PLP – was selected by the PLP alone. In theory, the leader had to offer himself for re-election each year, but in practice few MPs were willing to oppose a leader in office and so there were few elections. Since the special Conference of January 1981 the leader has been elected by an electoral college composed of MPs, constituency parties and trade unions. This change was not achieved overnight, nor was it easily won, nor is it secure.

At first glance, one might think that the dispute was a matter of doctrine between right and left: the right wanting no change and the left wanting considerable change. This is partly correct, as is the additional perception that those who want no change include many MPs and those who want change include many constituency parties.

But these descriptions ignore a dimension of the struggle. The impetus for change came from members of many constituency parties who have been deeply angered by the behaviour of recent Labour Governments. They felt that the periods in government from 1964 to 1970 and from 1974 to 1979 were scarcely worth having. They were not willing to work again for the return of a Cabinet which might call itself a Labour government but which was likely openly and repeatedly to ignore the decisions of the Party Conference and the wishes of the party outside Parliament. These activists felt betrayed and they were bitter.

On the other hand, support for the old system came in large measure from people, many of whom were MPs, who argued that Labour would never be returned to office at all unless it offered the British people something they wanted. They did not think a party bound to a set of strident, often contradictory, and unpopular conference resolutions, could hope to win. They realized that the Conservative Party loved little better than the sight of a Labour team tied to resolutions originally dreamt up by small groups of Trotskyists and forced through hollow shells of constituency parties.

Each side to this dispute had a few skeletons in its cupboard to which the other side was not averse to pointing from time to time. Each urged a case on grounds of principle which it imagined maximized its factional interest. Each side included people who reckon that their chances of becoming leader would be abetted by this or that selection procedure. There is nothing either surprising or particularly blameworthy about this: politics is about interest and career as well as principle. My concern with the language in which the claims and arguments were made is not meant to deny these underlying realities, only to suggest that the language exercises constraints of its own.

Each side to this dispute could, and did, claim that its arguments were rooted in the traditions of the party and implied that the other was an impostor. The proponents of tighter constituency control over the party's central machinery pointed out that it was created from the bottom, across the country, and only grew subsequently to have a parliamentary centre. It was always intended as a movement which would use parliament for socialist ends: emphatically it was not intended to be just another parliamentary grouping of power-seeking careerists. Recent disappointing Labour governments had made the need for stronger machinery to guide the parliamentary party clear.

From the other side the traditions of the party were also invoked. The opponents of changes contended that the relationship between MPs and their constituency parties, and the MPs' right to choose their leader, were long-established practices. These were traditions laid down not by mere historical accident but by demi-gods: by the likes of Keir Hardie, and accepted unquestioningly by others such as Aneurin Bevan and trade unionists like Ernest Bevin.

The battle was conducted partly in terms set by the party's traditions and these traditions emanated from the trade unions. The traditions of organizing trade unions and defending them against a powerful state machine allied to a capitalist order are not easily denied even if the external conditions have changed considerably. The traditions of the party are a kind of reservoir from which all members may sup. The reservoir gives life. Its tributaries run off into fertile ground. All members of the movement are vigilant against those who would foul its waters and suspicious of the schemes of those who would pitch their tent outside the land known to be long served by its tributaries.

The ethos of the Labour Party provides a language – not simply a rhetoric

– for party debate. Each Labour Party debater imposes a considerable series of restrictions on himself: he must stick to the right language. This is noticeable to outsiders straightaway: they can hear that the debate employs certain codewords strange to their ears: emblematically each contributor begins by addressing his Brothers or Comrades. Much more difficult is using the language oneself. There are things one does not say ever and other things one says only on certain occasions. A master of the language can stretch things a bit. A leader must be able to do this from time to time. Harold Wilson, when he was in command, could move the party and the nation with a call for a revived Britain refashioned by the white heat of the technological revolution. Lesser figures could never get away with that: it is a strangely foreign sentiment. The man who can frame his proposals most convincingly within the language of the party's ethos has a considerable advantage over his opponents.

The existence of this constraining language makes life difficult for out-siders, foreigners, as well as those who would address both a Labour and a more general audience. This is one cause of the difficulty parliamentary socialists often suffer. They must keep the party happy and yet carry respon-sibilities to others. A party which puts forward candidates for public office and which wants to win power through the ballot box in effect licenses some of its members to go out into the wider world and speak the foreign language understood there. When some of these members return to tell the party that some of the things the party wants dearly – such as, in the early 1980s, immediate nationalization of the 200 largest private companies – are unpopular with the rest of the country, they are not thanked kindly. When they tell their comrades that future Labour governments will be elected only if such manifesto pledges are dropped, they become suspect. It then becomes possible for other potential leaders to use the language of the movement to suggest that perhaps some of these parliamentary members have learned to speak another language and can no longer be trusted. These members are beginning to follow the path of Ramsay MacDonald, it will be said.

A Labour leader, such as James Callaghan, who has strong roots in the party and long-nourished connections with the trade union leaders, can – for a time – get away with saying a few jarring things because he can be trusted. He has an advantage which an Oxford-educated, Hampstead academic cannot match.

In this way the Labour Party is a bit like a nominally open club. Anyone over the age of sixteen is formally invited to join if he can raise the membership fee, if he is a member of a trade union, and if he agrees to Clause 4. In fact, the test of full membership is much more exacting. One has to learn the language. With time anyone can. But full membership does cost time, and time is an asset. Of course, much of the language of the party comes more easily to working people than to others; but there is more to it than that. There is a special language of Conference resolutions and the mandating of delegates, and a whole alphabet of organizations such as the Executive Committee, the NEC, the General Management Committee and the constituency parties, and some words which seem to exist nowhere else such as 'compositing'.

Some of the trickiest constraints arise from the conflict between the interests of the unions, as they are perceived by the union leaderships of the time and the logic of socialist doctrine. For a long time, for instance, it was bad form to speak in favour of workers' control. Since the position of important unions on this subject has now changed, this favourite socialist slogan is no longer taboo. Perhaps, in the changed climate of the 1990s, it will soon become so again.

Like any good insiders' language, this special vocabulary changes subtly all the time. This imposes a burden on all who wish to keep in touch: they must remain regular attenders. A member who becomes inactive for a time is best advised to stay silent until he learns the current catechism and, more important, what not to say. Someone who is 'out of touch' quickly gives himself away by his very phrasing. Being 'out of touch' is one of the worst sins in the party. Members of Parliament are often criticized for being out of touch and those who are might well worry about their reselection.

When I first joined the Labour Party the local MP was Tom Oswald. Tom's enemies used to say that he had never made a maiden speech in the decades he served in the House of Commons. That never bothered us. When he addressed our General Management Committee he could remind us what the movement had meant to him: how he and his brothers and sisters had had to take it in turns to go to school because there was only one pair of children's shoes in the house: how he had earned a few pennies to help support his family by getting up early and running up and down Edinburgh's closes extinguishing the gaslamps. After Tom had made one of these speeches nobody cared if he were silent at Westminster. So what!

Outsiders will say that this is romanticism. No doubt it is. Perhaps Tom and others like him embellished here and there. But the more serious point is that a movement which can be won over by the kind of tales Tom would tell is clannish, defensive and inward-looking. It is a very different organization from the phantom conjured-up on television screens and in the newspapers of groups of doctrinal adolescent Trots shouting down the three old dears who bother to attend. The point of Tom's stories was to remind delegates who they were. It was a way of saying that we are a special people. We have endured exploitation and hardship and we have come through it by our own efforts and we are going to build our own Jerusalem here – soon. You could as much follow one of Tom Oswald's performances with a critical analysis of the economic performance of the last Labour Government as you could praise the Shah in the streets of Tehran.

Foreign observers such as Wertheimer are quite right to wonder about the Labour Party. There is something anomalous about an organization which is at once clannish and parochial and yet idealistic and determined to create a new world. Such anomalies annoy the tidy-minded; but the Labour Party lives with them.

LABOUR IN A NEW SOCIAL ORDER

The social conditions which produced the Labour Party no longer obtain. The ideals and dreams of some of the early Labour Party leaders have long since been translated into practice. Some of the most pressing problems confronting contemporary government arise from the unintended consequences of Labour's triumphs. We have woefully inadequate means of controlling the numerous officials employed by the industries Labour has nationalized or the local government departments which administer the public housing estates Labour worked so hard for. If you are poor in Britain today you are more likely to be abused, ignored, deceived and dismissed by some organ of the State than by some capitalist. The long-term consequences of this for the Labour Party must be considerable. The unpopularity of further measures of nationalization owes something to the hamfisted administration of the existing public industries. In the long run this will affect the ethos of the working class and unless Labour can adapt, it will cost the party dear.

At the same time as the country has been altered by government policy so the society is changing. Industry has been reorganized; the employment structure of the country has been realigned. There are proportionately fewer skilled manual labourers than before the war. The old communities which once fostered and nourished the working-class ethos have been dispersed. Some even argue that the old working class is dead. Once-solid groups have been either bought off or alienated. Fred Ridley's observations of Liverpool have led him to suggest that we are moving towards a *Clockwork Orange* world of urban desolation, individual violence and despair.[5] This new world will not produce the same working-class ethos which we have inherited. We may wonder if it will produce anything so generous or anything of value at all.

Rapid social change is not readily commensurate with any established ethos. An ethos takes time to develop. It conforms to long-established patterns of work and living. Once they are destroyed it might well simply disappear, or, worse, it might ossify. In this case the habitual patterns of the party and its normal language would continue to be invoked but with less and less meaning and with no chance of developing. The ritual singing of the Red Flag at the end of Conference has the smell about it of an ossified tradition. Who knows the words? Who believes them? But a few examples prove nothing. Within a living organization a few traditions are always dying while they are replaced by others. I raise this point here simply to point to the danger.

The rapid social change of recent decades has both posed new difficulties and opened up new vistas for the party. It is the difficulties which are the more obvious. It is hard not to believe that much of the struggle within the Labour Party in the last decade is traceable to the changed society. The interests of the various unions diverge rather glaringly. Some organize much better-paid workers than others; some grow while others decline; some organize workers in the public sector, others in the private sector; some are in a much better position to look after themselves than others. This diversity of interest was one of the factors which complicated the life of the last Labour government and made the incomes policy it was pursuing towards the end of its term impossible to sustain. Should the policy seek a percentage rise? The unions of the poorly paid won't care for that. Should it allow only for a specific pound rise (say £6 per week); the more powerfully placed unions won't stand for that for long.

If the leaders of the unions, urged on by their members, no longer see their interest coinciding with the other unions', or with the nation, the job of any Labour government – no matter how its leader is chosen – is going to be near impossible. If each workshop pushes its desire for a large rise because it cannot see the connection between its rise and a general rise in the rate of inflation then there can be no incomes policy for long. If Britain's declining industrial base and economic weight in the world squeezes all sections of society (not just workers; when was the last time average rates of profit in Britain exceeded the rate of inflation?) then governing by consent may be impossible. In these circumstances appeals by party leaders to the old language of loyalty may win support for a short time, but only at the cost of discrediting the language.

And yet, there are, on the other hand, hopeful glimmerings of change as well. In one or two small but useful ways the party has begun to shake off its early deference. It has begun to fulfil some of its earliest promise precisely at the moment when the more important industrial problems look overwhelming.

I have in mind, among other things, changes in the way constituency parties select parliamentary candidates. There long was an important difference between unions and party on this question. Union leaders were nearly always people (men) who had performed the trade or job which the union organized. They were people who had worked their way up through the ranks. The party, particularly the parliamentary party, has long been attractive to outsiders. Its leaders, including some of its most impressive leaders such as Clem Attlee and Hugh Gaitskell, were not working people. The party elected many middle-class people to high office.

A number of indisputably middle-class intellectuals won nomination in safe Labour seats and rapid promotion to the front bench with apparent ease. It is not difficult to see what the party had to offer to ambitious, talented, socially conscious members of the educated middle class. What they had to offer the party, so clannish and defensive a movement, is not so clear. The answer was not flattering to the party. Generations of local selection committees have welcomed middle-class educated men out of deference. These were the people Wertheimer met at his first party meeting. It sometimes happened that branches and constituency parties selected people who had only just joined the party. Harold Wilson was not long in the party before he became an MP and then a Cabinet Minister. Others – one thinks of Hugh Dalton, Douglas Jay, Anthony Crosland, Evan Durbin – were placed in their seats by powerful friends. Many such candidates (like many authentically working-class nominees, who were shifted around the country by their unions) had no previous connection with the constituency parties which selected them.

This willingness to select outsiders to hold responsible, honourable and possibly very powerful positions within the party was never less than strange. Overcoming distrust of outsiders was only part of the problem; there was also the never quite stilled fear of betrayal. Ramsay MacDonald and Oswald Mosley were only famous examples of betrayal. Betrayal is a deeply embittering experience – so that it becomes particularly difficult to explain why so many constituency parties were willing to take the increased risk of betrayal which accompanied selecting an outsider (of class or region) to be their candidate.

However, deference is not a sufficiently convincing explanation. Lack of choice is another factor. Before the consequences of the 1944 Education Act had worked their way through, there simply wasn't a sufficiently large cadre of sons and daughters of local working people with self-confidence and education to put themselves forward as candidates.

But this is changing. Constituency parties no longer select candidates dropped in by Transport House. There is a conflict in the PLP now between the younger generation with local connections and the older generation. This conflict is the result of a change which records a strengthening for, and a victory for, the ethos. Or rather, it records the coming of age of one of the party's oldest dreams: that it be a movement of, by, and for the working people.

Much the same could be said for the unwillingness of the current generation of trade union leaders to do as the party leader bids, and the refusal of the constituency parties to accept that the PLP alone has the right to elect the party leader. The increasing attentiveness of the current generation of trade union leaders to the wishes of their delegate conferences has made the party immensely more difficult to organize than previously. The granting of a substantial say in leadership selection to the constituency parties may awaken in them a taste for more say in other Conference decisions; where that happens, under the most recent changes to the party constitution, even less order will prevail. Meanwhile one effect of the move towards one-member-one-vote in parliamentary selections is likely to be to increase the chances of local nominees. But all these changes are victories for the movement and for one of its oldest dreams: a party controlled by the movement in the country.

To some extent, too, these victories for the ethos are self-generating. It is notorious that the new generation of Labour MPs are middle-class by occupation if not background. They are journalists and academics by career. A defeat for the old dream? Not at all. The newer generation are the children of working people. They are often very conscious that their grammar or comprehensive school, provincial university education sets them somewhat apart from their own people. For this reason, they are the more determined to demonstrate their purity of socialist faith. Much the same is true, I suspect, of the execrated constituency activists. In other words, their sensitivity to the ethos makes them all the more determined to demonstrate their loyalty to it.

NOTES AND REFERENCES

Malcolm Anderson, Paul Crompton, Michael Rush and David Welsh have helped me with comments on earlier versions of this chapter. I alone am responsible for it.

1.   A fuller account of this distinction may be found in my book *Doctrine and Ethos in the Labour Party*, Allen and Unwin, London, 1979.
2.   E. Wertheimer, *A Portrait of the Labour Party*, Putnam, London, 1929, pp. ix–x.
3.   L. Minkin, *The Labour Party Conference: a study in the politics of intra-party democracy*, Allen Lane, London, 1978, pp. 249, 253.
4.   G.B. Shaw, *The Apple Cart*, Act I (first published 1929), Penguin, Harmondsworth, 1970.
5.   F.F. Ridley, 'View from a disaster area: unemployed youth in Merseyside', *The Political Quarterly*, January–March 1981, **52**, no. 1, pp. 16–27.

13 Trade unions and the media

Jean Seaton

Union-bashing is one of the conventions of the British media. National decline, economic crisis, extremism in the Labour Party are all laid at the door of the unions, which are also regularly attacked for their conservatism, selfishness and callous disregard for individual rights and liberties. Above all, unions are seen as *sectional*–they put their own interests above those of society at large. Against this background of abuse, it is hardly surprising to find that unions are regarded by the general public with suspicion. Thus, at the height of distrust of unions in the 1970s one poll showed that 82 per cent of all adults believed that the unions had too much power.[1] Even in 1989, after a decade of political exclusion, unions were still regarded by the public with automatic suspicion.[2]

What is more remarkable is that the same polls showed that a large majority also thought that unions were essential to protect the interests of workers. Thus it is too simple merely to see unions as unpopular – the reality is far more complex. So, too, is the effect of the image of union behaviour created by the mass media – not only on the public, but on government and political parties and on the unions themselves. In this chapter I shall examine this image – and consider both its structure and its consequences for British politics and industrial affairs.

The first point to note is that press hostility to the unions – and the particular forms of partiality to which the modern audience is accustomed – has a long history. Yet, until the fairly recent past, unions were concerned not so much with getting a good press, as with getting any press attention at all. In the twentieth century, one of the most vigorous pursuers of a trade-union place in the media was Walter Citrine, General Secretary of the TUC from 1926 to 1946, whose attentions were directed to the new means of mass communication: wireless.[3] Citrine saw broadcasting as a means of educating his members, 'telling our people useful things, and reaching those who have rights but don't know them'.[4] But he also regarded coverage of union affairs in another way: as public acknowledgement that trade unions mattered. Citrine fought for the right to control how the trade union movement was presented; but the main struggle was to get recognition. By the end of the Second World War, the second battle had been largely won. The first had scarcely started.

For many years after 1945 the trade unions accepted their media image fatalistically as routine misrepresentation. It did not seem to affect their influence over government – which developed dramatically. It did not seem to affect their membership – which increased steadily. The unions accepted the dominant view of the 1950s and 1960s that the press and broadcasting were just ways of communicating to a large audience, which had no independent effect on the meaning of a message. In its evidence to the Donovan Commission the TUC claimed that there was no need for 'the movement to engage in an expensive public relations campaign to counter hostile propaganda'.[5] It was quite content with its media image, and just piously asserted that it should 'use' the media more. In a study of trade unionists' attitudes towards the media done in 1969, 71 per cent of full-time officials, 70 per cent of shop stewards, and 62 per cent of members thought that if the press gave too much attention to strikes, television was unbiased.[6]

Now, however, the trade unions' attitude towards the media has changed. The media are viewed with considerable suspicion. It is feared that the long-term political and social role of the unions is being eroded and distorted by the effects of increasingly hostile reporting. A growing concern was given urgency by the way in which the disputes of 1978–79 were represented. Many of the lowest-paid workers in the public sector, who had never previously been on strike, were appalled to find themselves pilloried as inhuman blackmailers. Phrases like 'the winter of discontent' and 'secondary picketing' which, as a TUC statement commented, have 'since passed into political mythology and in fact have come to form the basis for legislation'[7], were originally invented by journalists and given currency in the media. The subsequent defeat of the Labour Government confirmed the views of many unionists that the media were prejudicing public opinion against unions, and there was a particularly bitter debate about the role of the press and broadcasting at the 1979 TUC Conference.

Union leaders also came to feel that the media had become more personalized in their style of attack. Len Murray was hounded by reporters when he was on holiday. The newly-elected leader of the TGWU, Moss Evans (who previously had a record of good relations with the press when he was dealing with the Midlands car industry), was dismayed by the changed tone in publicity when he arrived at Transport House. He was particularly incensed by a 1979 *News of the World* report which headed an eight-year-old photograph of himself being carried on the shoulders of jubilant car workers above the caption 'How to get us out of this mess'.[8]

The TUC set up a Media Working Group in 1977 (chaired by Moss

Evans) and the reports this produced, detailing media misrepresentation, and suggesting ways of handling the media more professionally[9] concentrated unions' attention on the press and broadcasting. Indeed, in a major review of the TUC's work published in 1980, proposals concerning the reform of policy occupy twenty-nine paragraphs, while the issue of promoting and campaigning for these policies takes fifty-three.[10] In subsequent years, the unions became more preoccupied with the effects of the media than ever before. Increasingly, in the 1980s, unions became more concerned about their public image. As the old industrial unions waned and the influence of white collar unions grew, so did the desire for a new kind of respectability.

The unions' resentment at what has begun to be seen as a concerted campaign of media hostility has also been supported by a series of research findings. These have shown that press and broadcasting accounts of trade union and industrial affairs are fundamentally distorted.

News, in this kind of work, has often been seen as an ideology, in which 'balance' and 'neutrality' are impossible objectives. The constitutional independence of broadcasting organizations is seen as little more than a prop of a misleading sham. Broadcasting conventions, the different authority subtly accorded to the spokesmen of opposed organizations, the manipulation of visual material, and the apparent impartiality of the process, all the more insidiously define public perception of unions and strikes. The framework of inferred interpretation that is used to explain industrial matters amounts to a 'preferred view . . . which corresponds all too easily with a particular, albeit sophisticated, version of managerial ideology'.[11] The Glasgow University Media Group have pointed out that for the media 'industrial disputes are about "trouble" – trouble for us as consumers and members of the public, trouble for the management of industry and trouble for the nation, but never trouble for the workers involved'.[12] According to David Morley, 'the media project themselves as spokesmen of the public, supposedly sandwiched between the two mighty and embattled giants, unions and employers, and proposing that while the giants stand shoving each other, we, the poor public, suffer'.[13]

The Glasgow team went further, and suggested that in the period under examination, the effect (or, perhaps they imply, even the purpose) of media reports of industrial affairs was to fix the blame for inflation on the trade unions. The only explanation of inflation suggested in broadcast news was wage rises. The role of investment, or the lack of it, was hardly ever mentioned.

Another study carried out by Denis McQuail for the Royal Commission on the Press also showed that industrial reporting was dominated by strikes. Thirty-six per cent of all industrial stories in eight national dailies were about disputes (18 per cent, the next highest category, were stories about trade union leaders). Usually only one cause for the strike was given and in 52 per cent of the examples this was described as pay. Management were

almost entirely absent from newspaper accounts. The main 'theme' associated with such strike stories was loss of output. There was thus, McQuail
argued, 'a "modal" strike story . . . about a current dispute, . . . usually
relating to pay'.[14] Yet Department of Employment figures indicated that
nearly one-third of all strikes were caused by factors other than pay.

Many critics have suggested that the media create an unrealistic image
of British industrial relations. More days of work are lost because of
strikes and stoppages in the United States, Canada, Italy, Belgium and
Holland than here. Strikes are thus hardly a uniquely 'British' disease.
Moreover, while 70 per cent of industrial relations stories deal with the
transport, motor manufacturing, paper, printing and publishing industries
and disputes in the professions, these sectors only account for 40 per cent
of the workforce.[15] The amount of publicity a strike gets is not apparently
determined by its severity as measured by the number of workdays lost or
the number of workers involved. When the 'Bad News' team were doing
their research there was a great concentration on vehicle disputes – which
then suddenly stopped. The researchers commented, 'It is almost as if the
newsmen themselves were becoming bored with their own coverage'. The
viewer in the subsequent months could have concluded that suddenly there
were no disputes in the car industry. There were. It was merely that they
were no longer getting reported.

The 'news as ideology' explanation of this distortion is that the media
maintain the status quo, promoting false consciousness. The Glasgow team
suggested that it was not pressure of material – or indeed lack of it – nor
deadlines that determined what went into the news. Indeed the text, written
by journalists, always dominated visual material. Thus industrial news,
according to this view, is not a product of accident, haste, or scarcity. It
is chosen by journalists.

JOURNALISTIC IMAGES

Journalists write about industrial stories starting from a set of assumptions
they expect to find confirmed. In the longer pieces of the quality press these
images may be elaborated and even contradicted. In the popular press and
in broadcasting, journalists depend even more on what they expect their
audience to believe already.

Much of the recent work on the media has concentrated on the procedures
which determine how the news gets made. There are long-term political
pressures on organizations like the BBC: complicated 'case laws' which over
time have established precedents and rules; and a variety of ways in which
the crises are routinized. Researchers have shown how the product – news –
is determined within rigid conventions and practices which journalists may
respond to – but hardly even recognize. Journalists see themselves as free
agents; in practice, organization, technology and precedent all make choices
for them.

One thing researchers have not considered is the role of story-telling – particularly important in industrial reporting where the bare facts often seem dry unless arranged in a digestible narrative form. A good deal of journalism is really about fitting reality into fictionally satisfying patterns and stories, with beginnings, middles and ends. The daily necessity of meeting deadlines becomes easier if the end of a story is predicated in its start. As one TGWU official put it, journalists only have two stories to write. The first presents conspiratorial union bosses involved in back-room plots, and the other describes the 'union carthorse', based on an ignorant and brutish rank-and-file. If events in the union could not be made to fit either stereotype, he would tell reporters, 'There's no blood in this one for you boys.' Union officials gave many examples of important stories which journalists have ignored, because they came to the unions expecting to 'find' one kind of story and were disconcerted to be given something different.

Journalists construct stories from developments which confirm a newsline already current. News is as ephemeral as fashion, and also as intolerant: events which go against the grain of the current approach to a particular controversy are ruthlessly excluded. In the same way trivial scraps of information can be blown up out of all proportion if they appear to corroborate the conventional wisdom. To give one example: an academic survey into the role of shop stewards in 1976 received remarkable publicity because journalists could use its evidence to back up the prevailing view that strikes were caused, not by dissatisfied workers, but by *agents provocateurs*. Thus the survey showed that plants with high concentrations of shop stewards also had high strike records. At the same time, it stressed that there was no causal relationship between the two facts. The story was first taken up by the *Sunday Times,* largely because the paper had already carried several pieces about the Department of Employment's failure to publish accurate strike statistics. The *Sunday Times* was concerned to write about a Department of Employment 'cover-up' – and used the survey as evidence of this.

The story was then followed up in the *Telegraph,* the *Sun,* the *Mirror, Express* and *Mail,* all of which argued that the survey 'proved' precisely what it disclaimed, that shop stewards 'cause' strikes. 'The awful truth about strikes in our factories' story, which dominated the press, was a product of journalists – not the academics. But the key element in the process was the original interest of the *Sunday Times* journalists in a story they had been developing long before the survey appeared.[16]

Most journalists, of course, do not consciously write stories which impose formulae on events. They understand themselves to be following something external – exposing a story, much as a prospector discovers nuggets in the ground, and there are many devices which obscure the process from the audience as well. News often appears to have occurred quite independently of the people who have written, filmed and spoken it. This is particularly true of broadcast journalism, where the spurious realism of the form leads the audience to assume that they are seeing a complete version of what really occurred.

Industrial reporting is particularly subject to formulae and preconceived ideas. This is because it is one of the types of hard news which is most frequently handled as a 'human interest' story. Trade unionists complain that reports of the women's TUC Conference only appear if there is a 'petticoat power angle'. In general, industrial disputes are usually simplified in terms of their effects on individual children, patients, holiday-makers and so on. The 'human interest' aspect of industrial affairs distorts real developments and change to a kind of re-occurring moral fable, one in which unions are always the 'baddies'.

MORE NEWS NOT WORSE NEWS

Nevertheless, it is possible that unions' anxiety about the media is partly a reaction to an explosion in the amount of space and time devoted to industrial affairs. There has certainly been far more extensive coverage of industrial affairs since the 1960s than ever before. Whether it is more, or less, misleading than in the past is less easy to establish. Superficially there has been a marked improvement in a number of respects: industrial reporting is more professional and well researched, written by journalists with a greater expertise than used to be the case. Yet the corollary of this – a greater press interest, bordering on obsession, in the least attractive aspects of union behaviour – may have contributed to an unfavourable public image for unionism in general. Thus, strikes and wage demands get reported: sickness benefits do not. What makes a good news story may sometimes create a false overall impression because of what is left out.

The impact of an increase in the sheer volume of labour news and related coverage should not be underrated. The 1947 Royal Commission on the Press did not consider industrial reporting a sufficiently important category to study separately. In the Commission's content analysis of eight national dailies, all economic, political and social news added together accounted for 27 per cent of the news space. The 1977 Royal Commission, by contrast, found that labour relations news took up between 4 and 6 per cent of space, and more than a quarter of all the main lead stories was devoted to this subject alone. By the 1980s, some additional reporting was taking place in the ever-expanding business and finance section of the press, and a content analysis of the press published in 1989 showed an increase in space devoted to labour relations to 9 per cent.[17] Industrial news thus became one of the most prominent kinds of press story.

Another indication of the importance of industrial news is the development of a group of specialist reporters to deal with it. *The Times* appointed its first labour correspondent in 1937. It still had only one specialist journalist in the area in 1963. It now has four. The *Sun* has three industrial reporters – as many as cover parliamentary affairs. The London-based Industrial Correspondents Group (a kind of industrial lobby with a constitution and rules, which circulates lists of members to appropriate organizations) was formed in 1965 and now has nearly a hundred members. Industrial reporting is seen within the profession as an area which repays ambition and initiative. Labour correspondents get a lot of what they write into the paper. Their stories are often given front-page space. It is easier and quicker to make a reputation in labour reporting than in many more traditional areas, and many correspondents have used this specialism as a stepping-stone to other jobs.

However, an industrial reporter depends on exchange deals as much as a political correspondent. He needs information. He can give publicity. Union leaders or officials 'leak' because they want something: to gain advantage for their union, to score against management, or against opponents within the union or to influence government. Thus industrial reporters depend for their news on their personal relations with individual unionists; while the esteem in which trade-union leaders are held within large and impersonal mass organizations – not unlike political parties – depends to a large extent on the good opinion of journalists. Indeed, journalists are relatively well placed to judge public performance and private skill, to assess shrewdness and measure success.

This mutual relationship of exchange gives the unions some real sanctions over the journalists. Again, the similarity with political reporting is close; except that some trade unions do not yet feel the same imperative about press relations as politicians. Union officials can refuse to talk to a correspondent who has offended them – and they do. They can talk to his rivals. Journalists are often associated with particular sides in inter-union rivalries or even with different camps inside a union that is deeply divided. There are dangers in this situation. The 'vicarious thrill of the traffic in information', as one journalist called it, can lead reporters to misjudge events – as well as forget that in the end they are the voyeurs.

Because of the career opportunities provided by industrial reporting many journalists are dispassionate in their approach, treating the subject as impersonally as any other. For many others, however, labour affairs are an area of passionate interest and even commitment, regardless of the editorial policy of the paper concerned. Reporters inevitably know more than they write about, and sometimes even act as midwives in union affairs. Thus the growth of ASTMS in the 1960s was greatly helped by one particular *Daily Mail* industrial correspondent who was generous with both advice and column inches. Most industrial correspondents believe themselves and their colleagues to be politically on the left. They also argue that even journalists who enter the field for 'careerist' reasons develop an interest and respect for trade unionists.

Thus industrial journalists acquire and trade information in much the same way as political correspondents. Within union politics they play a similar role to that of lobby correspondents within party politics. However, although political correspondents may be close either to the Labour or Conservative Parties, the group as a whole covers all party politics. In contrast labour journalists deal with one side of industrial affairs – that of the unions. Reporting on management is dealt with largely by financial correspondents. Not only are management stories often secluded in the financial pages, they are more rarely seen as general news and even more rarely in terms of their 'human interest'. Although some entrepreneurs may be good copy for gossip columnists, Sir James Goldsmith's or Tiny Rowland's financial affairs are not dealt with in terms of their effects on individual pensioners or workers' children. Thus industrial correspondents' relationships to their subject matter are perhaps more partisan – either more sympathetic or more hostile – than those of political correspondents. Indeed, labour journalists have a special importance as part of the apparatus of bringing union pressure to bear on politicians.

The career of a specialist journalist has no clear structure. There is a contrast, as Jeremy Tunstall noted, between 'rapid job mobility before specialization, followed by a period of job *immobility* after it'.[18] Like all journalists a specialist has relative job insecurity and is only as good – more or less – as the last piece he wrote. Such pressures inevitably affect the style of what is written. Journalists, as one commented, 'know who they work for'. They want what they write printed, not put in the sub-editor's basket. Self-censorship in this, as any other area of journalism, is the most effective means of control. Nevertheless, industrial correspondents probably write with other industrial journalists in mind – and the dominant ethos of the group is, perhaps paradoxically, one of respect for as well as criticism of trade unions and their officials. Industrial correspondents are more highly-educated than they used to be – and often have closer links with academic experts than other specialist reporters.

Industrial journalists are thus closely involved in union affairs. But the complex political negotiations which establish the world of the specialist reporter – the constraints which are likely to determine how he reports union matters – do not affect other reporters to the same extent. So sensitive is the relationship between the small number of industrial correspondents, and the small – and seldom changing – union hierarchy, that non-specialist general reporters are brought in when a hatchet job (a 'rubbish the unions' story, as one journalist puts it) is required.

Unions complain bitterly of the way in which papers will 'wheel in' a politics or feature writer to cover and slant a story. These journalists, having nothing to lose, produce the 'Target for Today – Sick Children' (*Daily Mail,* 2 Feb. 1979) and 'Famine Threat' (*Sun,* 12 Jan. 1979) stories on unions. The TGWU pointed out to one newspaper that all six stories produced by one 'general reporter' were fabricated. Apart from complaining, the union had no sanction it could use, either on the journalist or the paper.

There is a similar problem in television. In the attempt to separate comment and opinion from fact the BBC developed a rigid division between the style and personnel of 'news' and 'current events' programmes. The distinction was later adopted by the commercial companies. Its consequence is that journalists preparing features and current events programmes on labour affairs are not experts in the field. Ironically, they may be particularly vulnerable to pre-established images of industrial relations because their sense of what constitutes a 'story' may well be taken from the press. The TUC has proposed that the distinction between 'news' and 'current events' should now be abandoned, and specialist journalists used more in feature programmes. The broadcasting companies have so far rejected this proposal, because it would interfere with the freedom of producers. However, it is clear that the original intention of the division is now being threatened by the practice. In both cases the unions' problem is with journalists who have no stake in the world they are reporting on.

UNION POWER AND MEDIA ATTENTION

One reason why industrial affairs receive so much attention in the media is because some unions – not always the largest – have a national power that is comparatively rare in other countries. A strike by power workers, for example, can have an impact which could not be so easily arranged in the United States or France, where unions are regionally based or weakly organized. Industrial news gets national attention partly because it has national consequences. Hence, the centralization of unions during the 1970s – because of increasing pressure since the 1960s for national wage and price agreements – brought unions more and more into the public consciousness as union affairs came to affect the lives of an ever-higher proportion of the readers of newspapers and viewers of television.

This broadening of the impact of unions, related to an apparent increase in union power, has a dramatic effect in particular cases. The most notable example is provided by the NUM, which until 1966 conducted pay negotiations on a regional basis. Cohesion, a product in part of government attempts at wage restraint, led to the first major national pay dispute since the General Strike; as a result, after 1972, the NUM and its affairs were constantly in the news and both Joe Gormley, and his successor, Arthur Scargill, became media personalities. A generation ago, a handful of journalists attended NUM conferences, which rarely rated more than a paragraph in the national press. In the 1970s and early 1980s hundreds of reporters took part in such events as a matter of course, and coverage was often detailed and extensive. Even today – despite its greatly reduced size – the NUM continues to be disproportionately newsworthy, having lingered in public and journalistic imagination as a symbol of traditional unionism.

The amount of attention paid to industrial affairs in the press and broadcasting is related to the national structure of both the unions and the media. A strike by the National Union of Waterworkers, a tiny body with 10,000 members, may affect the whole country. In the United States, the same kind of dispute would not be a national one, and so would get much less attention.

However, different unions also get different amounts of publicity for different reasons. Firstly the unions have different attitudes towards media coverage. White-collar unions have devoted more resources to handling the media. Thus in the growth of ASTMS from 70,000 members in 1968 to 470,000 in 1981, each dispute was presented with great care. Local officers of the union were given training in media management; ASTMS received attention because it sought it. Nevertheless, as Greg Philo and John Hewitt showed, despite the more interventionist attitude of white-collar unions towards the media, and the more favourable image they have cultivated, when they have used the 'militant' tactics of the blue-collar unions they have been stereotyped just as damagingly.[19]

Some unions get media attention simply because of their size. The TGWU is the largest union in the country. This means that it plays an important role in the TUC; that its attitude towards the Labour Party is decisive; that its role in economic policy is crucial. Yet size alone is not an adequate reason for journalistic interest, unless allied to power, effectiveness, or influence in controversial areas. The shopworkers' union, USDAW, though huge in size, and a distributor of widespread benefits, gets little publicity because of its lack of cohesion or ability (as the phrase goes) to hold the country to ransom. By contrast ASLEF, with a mere 18,600 members, gets continuous monitoring by the media, because of the strategic position of its members who are able to have a very direct effect on the lives of a high proportion of city-dwellers and commuters.

Thus size, cohesiveness, economic importance, national role, or even the personality of the General Secretary can all influence media interest. Political factors within the union may also determine the nature and extent of publicity. Some unions deliberately keep a low profile and shun publicity. Others actively seek it not merely to recruit members but also in pursuit of national objectives, and because of the internal politics of the union.

Again, some unions receive attention because their internal workings are relatively accessible – something which is, in turn, determined by the need or desire of groups within a union to be noticed outside. One reason why the NUM has received so much publicity, for example, is that internally it is highly politicized, and contenders for office and influence behave in 'political' ways. The NUM national executive is annually elected; and so constant electioneering means that different factions are always attempting to use the media to gain advantage for their candidates and views. Miners' leaders are better known to the public than the leaders of unions with more settled, or less democratic, constitutions, because they need to manipulate the media in order to stay in business. Such trade unionists are thus involved in a game which others can ignore: providing copy to newsmen.

The amount of attention given to a union may thus reflect the demand for publicity among its leading activists, itself a product of a particular constitutional structure and set of traditions. Yet the existence of factional politics in a union may not itself lead to accessibility. The AUEW was well known for its left/right division – but the dynamics of engineering-union politics did not create a need for public presentation to the extent that is true of the NUM.

In contrast, the TGWU, as we have seen, has a high profile because of its national role, but is also relatively closed. One reason is that it elects a General Secretary for life and in this sense has less electioneering and a more subdued internal political process. One might either conclude that there was less 'politicking' in the TGWU than in the NUM, or that its style is different and that it is carried out over longer periods of time.

The openness or closedness of a union's politics is in part a consequence of its history. The difficulties it encountered, the kind of membership it represents, and the kind of activist it has developed, as well as the career structure of union leaders within it, and the industries they organize, all affect a union's political processes. A 'closed' union may merely have byzantine internecine political struggles within it which cannot be explained without reference to the union's history. On the other hand, it may be 'closed' because it has a highly developed sense of internal solidarity. Media attention is not welcomed because it is felt to be improper.

However, one could assign unions to a two-dimensional table, with one dimension representing internal political accessibility – open or closedness, and the other degree of media attention – high or low profile.

	High profile	Low profile
Open	NUM	USDAW
Closed	TGWU	

Different positions in the table indicate different attitudes towards the media – and perhaps different political strategies as well.

Some critics have, however, suggested that the bad press that trade unions get is because of their own inefficiency. Their refusal to approach publicity professionally is merely an aspect of their failure to come to terms with their new role as Britain's 'Fifth Estate'. Many unions have no full-time press officers. Given the amount of industrial money that is spent on promoting companies and often in keeping their activities *out* of the news, it is not surprising that management has a better image.

Thus it is suggested that the British trade unions desperately need a much larger professional 'civil service' of experts, as in some other countries. When what is needed is a policy, it has been argued, union leaders rely on a 'view' based on experience. Robert Taylor has maintained that there is in British unions a 'dislike of theory and education, as well as a suspicion of the professional . . . not displayed by unions in other Western Capitalist countries. There is a mistaken pride in the merits of self reliance and the virtue of working on a shoe string.'[20]

It has also been suggested that the unions have the status and power of a great national institution, but have refused to learn to act like other large-scale organizations. To some extent this is borne out by research which concludes that manual unions in particular have a very passive attitude towards the media and that unions in general concentrate almost exclusively on the press – apparently oblivious to the fact that broadcasting is a far more important source of information for their members. Yet it could also be argued that the unions' own contribution to the media had very little effect on the final reporting of their affairs.

UNION STYLE, POLITICS AND THE MEDIA

Most union leaders rise from the ranks: their positions are achieved through their organizational, negotiating and political skills in the context of the unions. Union leaders are public figures – often facing the media more frequently, and under more challenging conditions than the majority of politicians. Unlike politicians, however, their careers on the way to the top are not built on public performance but on the creation of confidence and authority within a specialized group. At the same time, there is a broader code rooted in working-class culture and labour movement tradition – which active unionists uphold, and which is less easily appreciated by those who do not share it. Above all, there is a belief in 'unity as strength', collective action, solidarity and the sense of belonging to a union that transcends individuals, or even individual unions. 'There is', wrote Vic Allen in his early study of Arthur Deakin, 'an ethical basis for decision in all trade unions, for the decisions taken in them must in some way be related to the objectives and traditions of trade unions.'[21]

Trade union political style has two aspects, neither of which is translatable in press or broadcasting terms. One is set in the formal convention of civic life, wedded to procedure, precedent, and rules as the best safeguard of fairness. The other is the secret style of negotiation and bargaining. The successful trade union leader may well be a very skilled communicator in these situations but not in the context of the very different conventions of the media. This is not to say that there are not persuasive and legitimate 'unionate images' (to use Vic Allen's phrase) available for use in the media – 'tough common sense' is one such model. But their range is limited.

Trade union style is thus instrumental, aimed at demonstrating union efficiency at delivering wants to an already committed audience. Trade unionists for the most important part of their work do not need the media. The press and broadcasting are largely irrelevant to much of the work they do. So they have developed a style that is not, like party political style, based on verbal dexterity or oratory. Consequently it does not easily adapt to the middle-class drawing-room, or university seminar, techniques adopted by commentators and interviewers on radio and television.

DO PEOPLE BELIEVE WHAT THE MEDIA TELL THEM ABOUT UNIONS?

Research into the content of media accounts of union affairs often assumes that the public accepts the messages which the media project. While the long-term effect of biased reporting is likely to be cumulative it is also worth considering whether messages are so simply accepted. There is, after all, a difference between manufacturing an ideology and making people believe it.

Paul Hartmann's work tackled this problem directly. His study showed systematic differences between social classes in attitudes towards strikes. All of his samples depended heavily on the media for their information. However, while there was general agreement about the basic reasons for strikes – pay and economic conditions – white-collar workers tended to give more prominence to the non-economic causes of strikes like the 'failure of communication'. But the most significant class differences emerged in the distinction between abstract reason and direct experience. While 71 per cent of white-collar workers could give abstract reasons for justifying strikes, only 55 per cent of them could think of a particular strike they had approved of. In contrast 75 per cent of the manual workers could provide abstract justification, and 73 per cent could also cite examples of strikes they had believed correct. Only 20 per cent of the white-collar group had ever been on strike themselves – whereas 53 per cent of the manual group had. Middle-class women were particularly likely to blame strikes on 'greed'. Only 43 per cent of blue-collar workers against 64 per cent of white-collar workers thought that unions had too much power.[22]

Thus, for the working class, immediate experience is still more influential than abstract general ideas. This is in keeping with other research findings. Lockwood *et al.* in their classic study of the Coventry car workers as long ago as the early 1970s pointed out that 'it is evident that in the eyes of our semi-skilled workers the unionism of the work-place is very largely distinct from what they regard as the official activity of the union to which they happen to belong'.[23] The union for these workers meant a familiar organization. As Blumler and Ewebank pointed out, 70 per cent of their sample could name their shop steward.[24]

Indeed, other research has shown that while the working class abstractly endorses the dominant 'aspirational' values – that success is the result of hard work, that society is open, that anyone can get on – they are far more cynical about their own opportunities. People see success in their own work-place as being determined by graft – not merit.[25]

Thus while people are quite prepared when questioned to endorse the 'polite consensus' that unions are too strong, too sectional, too greedy, and so on, it is not clear that they really believe this to be the case. Alternatively, they may dissociate their abstract rejection of unions in general from their practical reliance on their own union in particular. The long-term effects of the media image may well be changing what people believe to be a 'respectable' opinion. However, when the interests of an individual are at stake, such views may not affect behaviour. This raises the problem of whether the disjunction between concrete experience and the capacity to generalize from it in order to understand the situation of other groups is growing wider – and whether the media image of unions has diminished the ability to sympathize with other workers involved in industrial action.

Certainly trade union officials all had examples of the way in which distrust of the media was localized. Car workers in the Midlands who were very bitter about the way in which the media dealt with their own disputes, unquestioningly accepted the image of the 'drunken Scottish car worker' which dominated reports of troubles in the remaining Scottish plants. However, while people may fail to generalize from their own experience, their own experience nevertheless is an important source of resistance to media stories. Indeed, the TUC has repeatedly asked the Independent Broadcasting Authority and the BBC to investigate the feelings of specific groups of workers involved in disputes about the way in which their action is reported. While research may have shown general satisfaction with broadcast news, the TUC's evidence showed that those who were the subjects of reporting often believed themselves unfairly treated.[26]

The evidence seems to suggest that middle-class respondents accept the middle-class dominated media images of unionism more readily than do working-class ones. This is hardly surprising. What is not clear is the extent to which the effect of personal experience on what people believe about unions (as opposed to what they might derive from the media) is merely a residue of some much more generalized working-class solidarity; or whether, on the contrary, people have seldom generalized from their own experience. We need to know whether the public is more, or less, vulnerable to media images than it used to be. Contemporary evidence shows that there are real blocks to a passive acceptance of media images of the unions – but it is far more important to know the tendency of public vulnerability over time.

Of course the public does not simply accept the media as an unbiased source of information. Only 6 per cent of one sample in 1976 'trusted' press news. Indeed, even television news, which had been repeatedly shown to be a very authoritative source of information, is losing its credibility. In 1962, 62 per cent of the BBC's own sample found the Corporation's reporting impartial. By 1970 this had declined to 47 per cent, and distrust was particularly marked among the young. In 1989, only 39%, according to one survey, always believed what they were told on television news.[27]

But there are other bases for public attitudes towards unions, apart from personal experience and the media. Although the media are by far the most important source of most trade union members' information about unions, 31 per cent of Blumler and Ewebank's sample had recently seen their own union journal. There are scores of union publications, their individual circulations often running into hundreds of thousands. It is reasonable to assume that the vast majority of copies remain unread. Nevertheless, the union house journals do fulfil an important function, especially among union officials and activists.

One of their jobs is to spread 'good' news by making members of a particular organization aware of its own achievements. 'What our members want to know is, for example, what was actually won by tanker drivers, or Ford workers, or in a fair wages case, rather than lengthy and otherwise commendable articles explaining how terrible the world is,'[28] comments one editor. Unions concerned to attract new members – for example, women or high-tech home workers – have recently improved their methods of communication, with better news-sheets and more specialized information services for different categories within their membership.

THE POLITICAL EFFECTS OF THE MEDIA'S IMAGE OF UNIONS

The political consequences of misleading reporting are not confined to their effect on public opinion. Press, government and trade unions all perpetuate the myth that unions can manipulate a passive membership to do whatever union leaderships think appropriate. Successive wage and price policies were based on the assumption that what union bosses agreed to, their members abide by. It is part of the media view of any kind of socialism as a Stalinist centralism. The media image implies that general secretaries have dictatorial powers. This is not the case. The media are often concerned with the undemocratic nature of unions: they give less attention to those consequences of democracy they find unpalatable. Indeed, it is even arguable that governments are the real victims of the media image of trade unions, crediting unions with more power than they actually have, and accepting the press view of trade unionism as if it were that of the electorate.

The political elite are probably the most avid consumers of the media (as well as being one of the main sources of its information and values). It has been suggested, for instance, that Barbara Castle's aggressive attitude in *In Place of Strife* was derived from the media. From the press and broadcasting she had concluded that there was widespread public support even for the imposition of penal sanctions.[29] In turn, when Harold Wilson tried to modify the reforms to make them more attractive to the unions, the media paid little attention to his proposals; hence union leaders were unimpressed by them. In 1972 and 1974, during its battle with the miners, the Conservative Government seems to have made a similar blunder, mistaking media opinion for that of the public. In the 1980s, the Thatcher administration used media stereotypes as part of its anti-union campaign, with more success early in the decade (as during the miners' strike) than at the end of it (during the ambulance drivers' dispute).

Another section of what Colin Seymour-Ure has called the 'political public' has also been affected by media images of the unions – journalists themselves. The starting point for many stories about unions, particularly in broadcasting, is evidently the story line being developed in the popular press. The process then becomes circular – with reporters searching for the stories which they already know. Bias then is compounded on bias.

The common-sense model of the relationship between politics, trade unions and the media, which suggests that the media influence what the public thinks about unions, is too simple. The trade unions do have to demonstrate that they have public support in order to influence government. But as well as the two audiences of public and government, they must also persuade and convince their members, and among those the active members. The media are not merely channels of communication, they influence the whole political life of unions.

Indeed, the most serious consequences of a hostile media image affect the unions themselves. The media help to determine what unionists think about unions. One possible effect may be to have forced the unions into a narrower sectional concern with wage bargaining. The unions complain that the massive routine work and campaigning which they do for their members is never recorded. The impact of union agitation on health and safety, maternity and equal opportunity rights, as well as their day-to-day advice on insurance and legal affairs are ignored by the media. This means that these achievements are not recognized by union members. Thus, an increasingly cynical membership may believe that the only purpose of unions is to pursue wage settlements. Several trade union officials commented that they believed people were increasingly unwilling to join unions except when there was an issue which involved their own self-interest. Such statements are hard to assess. The very strength of unions has always been that they exist precisely to serve the self-interest of their members, and people tend to assume that, in some past golden age solidarity and idealism were stronger. Nevertheless, the scope of union activity may be limited by an increasing instrumentalism fostered by adverse media coverage.

Perhaps more clearly, crude stereotyping has inhibited the unions' capacity to reform. As Taylor has suggested, 'behind the often impressive façade of union head offices there is often little more than an empty shell'.[30] Some critics have suggested that they need more efficient bureaucracies in order to fulfil their function as a pressure group more effectively. Trade union education needs developing, both to train officials and to educate members. Yet the unions have been least able to reform, or indeed to reconsider and formulate their role, when under attack. The media image of the unions in Britain has impeded the unions' capacity for change. Obliged to defend entirely honourable objectives as if they were excusing crimes, the unions have become over defensive.

NOTES AND REFERENCES

The author would like to thank Larry Smith, Paul Routledge, Alan Brown, Brendan Barber, Regan Scott, George Apland and Sue Challis among others for help in preparing this chapter. The views, however, are entirely her own.

1.   MORI Poll, Attitudes towards trade unionism, *Sunday Times*, 5 Mar. 1978.
2.   NOP survey, *Guardian*, 7 Jan. 1989.
3.   His efforts are examined in Jean Seaton and Ben Pimlott 'The Struggle for Balance' in Jean Seaton and Ben Pimlott (eds), *The Media in British Politics*, Gower, London, 1987, pp. 133–153.
4.   W. Citrine to G. Lucker, *The BBC Written Archives*, File R34, p. 107, 10 Jan. 1937.
5.   The TUC, *Trade unionism: evidence to the Donovan Commission*, 1966, p. 13.
6.   J. Blumler and A. Ewebank, 'Trade unionists, the media and unofficial strikes', *The British Journal of Industrial Relations*, 1970, 8, no. 1, p. 29.
7.   TUC Media Group, *A Cause for Concern*, TUC, 1980, p. 29.
8.   *News of the World*, 21 Jan. 1979.
9.   See TUC, *How to Handle the Media: a guide for trade unionists*, 1979; *A Cause for Concern*, 1979; *The Truth Behind the Headlines*, 1980; *Critical Viewing and Listening*, 1981.

10. TUC, *The Organization, Structure and Service of the TUC; Consultative Document*, 1980.
11. Glasgow University Media Group, *More Bad News*, vol. 2, Routledge and Kegan Paul, London, 1980, p. 164.
12. Ibid., p. 401.
13. D. Morley, 'Industrial conflict and the mass media', *Sociological Review*, 1976, **24**, p. 258.
14. D. McQuail, 'Content analysis of the press', *Royal Commission on the Press. Working Paper No. 4*, July 1977 (Cmnd 6810–4), para. 107.
15. Ibid., p. 74.
16. See P.K. Edwards, 'The awful truth about strikes in our factories: a case study in the production of news', *Industrial Relations Journal*, **10**, no. 1, pp. 7–21.
17. *The Royal Commission on the Press*, 1947–49, Appendix I, p. 209 (Cmnd 7700). *The Royal Commission on the Press*, 1974–77, Working Paper II, p. 103 (Cmnd 6810); Harris and Marplan, 'Content of the National Press by Category', 1989.
18. J. Tunstall, *Journalists at Work*, Constable, London, 1971, p. 94.
19. G. Philo and J. Hewitt, 'Trade Unions and the Media', *Industrial Relations Journal*, **7**, no. 3, 1976.
20. R. Taylor, *The Fifth Estate* (2nd edn), Pan Books, 1980, p. 16.
21. V. Allen, *Trade Union Leadership*, Longmans, Green, London, 1957, p. 16.
22. P. Hartmann, 'News and the public perception of industrial relations', *Media, Culture and Society*, 1979, no. 1, p. 262.
23. J. Goldthorpe, D. Lockwood *et al.*, *The Affluent Worker: industrial attitudes and behaviour*, Cambridge University Press, Cambridge, 1968, p. 111.
24. J. Blumler and A. Ewebank, 'Trade Unionists, the media and unofficial strikes', op. cit., p. 39.
25. See M. Mann, 'Social cohesion in a liberal democracy', *American Sociological Review*, 1970, pp. 117–40.
26. It is not only strikers and unionists who are offended by reporting of their affairs. Professional groups like doctors are often outraged by what they see as the misleading oversimplification of television journalism – when, that is, it is directed at them.
27. Glasgow University Media Group, *Bad News*, op. cit., p. 21. BBC Audience Survey, 'Reliability and the News,' Research Report No. 23, 1989, p. 7.
28. R. Scott, 'A David against the media Goliath?', *Labour Monthly*, November 1979, p. 516.
29. See G.A. Dorfman, *Government versus Trade Unions in British Politics since 1968*, Macmillan, London, 1979, pp. 19–27.
30. R. Taylor, *The Fifth Estate*, op. cit., p. 59.

14 The changed political role of unions under a hostile government

William Brown

INTRODUCTION

The relationship between governments and trade unions is rarely better than uneasy. With their ready access to a mass membership and their control over the most potent civil sanction of the strike, trade unions are usually seen by governments as, at best, making their task harder and, at worst, a major challenge. For trade unions, on the other hand, the government is not only by far the largest employer, it also has the power to shape both their economic and their legal environment. The consequence is an unending negotiation which British governments, until 1979, generally approached with the resigned attitude that trade unions were a regrettable necessity.

In Britain the attitude adopted towards trade unions by the government has been of particular importance. They lack the legal underpinning of a constitutional right to strike or the guarantees of union security which are to be found in most Western countries. Instead British labour law provides trade unions with the curiously roundabout protection offered by 'immunity' from being sued for the damages arising from certain forms of strike action. This device is open to tinkering by government and the courts. It also has the disadvantage of not endowing union officers with the authority that usually flows from their being written into more legalistic collective bargaining procedures. British unions are, in brief, peculiarly vulnerable to a hostile government.

This vulnerability was barely appreciated until recently. It might have been exploited by Edward Heath's short-lived Industrial Relations Act of 1971, had that not been boycotted by the unions, neglected by employers, and shunned by his government in its anxiety to obtain TUC support for wage moderation. Trade union complacency about their political and legal status was increased by the Labour governments of 1974–79. The administrations of Harold Wilson and James Callaghan, with their fragile parliamentary positions, allowed trade union leaders unprecedented influence over both economic and legislative policy through the Social Contract. After occupying this dominating political position, the trade union movement was pathetically unprepared for the shocks that were to face it when Labour lost power in 1979.

This chapter is concerned with the transformation of the unions' political role under the Conservative governments led by Margaret Thatcher. It is necessary to start with an account of their changed circumstances at the hands of her government. But it would be wrong to over-emphasize the government's role. The principal influence on trade union behaviour has always been the strategies followed by employers and it is necessary to take account of these. The ground is then clear for an appraisal of the new political role towards which trade unions appear to be groping.

STRIKING A NEW BALANCE

The Conservatives came to power in 1979 committed to 'striking a new balance' in the relationship between unions and employers. After an uncertain start, and greatly assisted by the fact that unemployment more than doubled in two years, the policy evolved into three distinct strands. The first of these was a succession of laws that reduced unions' protections from court action. The second was a series of strategic confrontations aimed at breaking strikes. The third was the weakening of union bargaining strength by increased product market competition. We shall outline these in turn.

The five Employment Acts passed between 1980 and 1990 started with an unco-ordinated rag-bag of measures, some of which were aimed at the relatively unimportant issues of the closed shop and picketing. But the legislation steadily built on the emerging experience of its own effects. Combined with the Trade Union Act of 1984, it finally amounted to a coherent reduction in trade unions' freedom to strike. By the end of the decade the type of strike action available to unions had been substantially reduced and the procedural demands on strikers had been substantially increased. Most important were the provisions whereby both 'secondary' strikes and unballoted strikes were no longer immune from court action. The legislation also had important consequences for the internal government of trade unions. Besides the balloting requirements for strikes, members of all union national executives henceforth had to be elected by full postal ballots of the whole membership. A ballot of members has to be held every ten years if a union is to use its funds for political purposes. Considerable assistance was made available to discontented members who wish to pursue allegations of union maladministration. It was made illegal for unions to discipline members who refuse to take part in official strike action, and unions were made responsible even for unofficial action if they had not expressly repudiated it.

The government's sponsorship of set-piece confrontations has been important in demolishing the reputations of some of the most powerful sections of trade unionism. The earlier strike battles occurred in the public sector: the dismissal of the senior shop steward at British Leyland's Longbridge plant, the steel strike, the 'flexible rostering' rail strike, and the expulsion of the civil service unions from the Cheltenham intelligence centre. The most important government victory was that of the year-long miners' strike, after which a split and shrunken union was unable to prevent a hundred pit closures by the end of the decade. Later the government gave active encouragement to employers in the private sector and helped in the defeat of unions in shipping, national newspapers, the docks and independent television. There can be little doubt that the example of these victories strengthened many other employers in subsequent bargains.

The third policy strand affecting Britain's unions was that of measures to increase product market competition. These were not primarily aimed at labour. Central to the government's analysis was the view that trade unions were responsible for low productivity because of their defence of 'restrictive working practices' and that, consequently, weakening unions would facilitate productive innovation. A more tenable position is that working practices are allowed to become restrictive from management's point of view when labour has been badly managed and inadequately trained. It is, consequently, not weakened unions but product market crises that shake employers either into bankruptcy or into more effective management methods. For many British employers the greatest crisis came with the soaring value of sterling at the start of the decade. For others it came with technical innovation – examples being the Channel ferries and television. In the public sector the main crises were precipitated by the threat of privatization. It has been product market threat, not labour market opportunity, that has forced many employers to manage their labour better.

CONSEQUENCES OF LEGISLATIVE CHANGE

The conduct of collective bargaining has changed substantially during the 1980s. In order to assess how this might have influenced the political role of unions it is necessary to separate out the effects of government policy from those of changed employer strategies. We start with the consequences of the new laws.

Perhaps the most obvious change that occurred in the 1980s was the decline in strikes. Table 4 provides data on these, averaging over five-year

TABLE 4   Strikes – Average annual statistics 1960–89

	Stoppages reported	Working days lost (w.d.l.) per 1000 employees	% of all w.d.l. arising from stoppages of > 500,000 w.d.l.
1960–64	2512	139	22
1965–69	2380	168	20
1970–74	2917	629	43
1975–79	2345	509	43
1980–84	1363	484	67
1985–89	887	174	54

Source: Employment Gazette

periods to overcome the 'lumpiness' of strike data. It will be evident that the average number of strikes declined substantially over the decade. The measure of working days lost per thousand employees per year also declined very substantially from the levels of the 1970s, but not as low as those of the 1960s. These patterns are illuminated by the third column which shows how the 1980s were dominated by large strikes, which is mainly a reflection of disputes among the large bargaining groups of the public sector. It should be added that the 1980s witnessed a decline in strike incidence worldwide, possibly connected with the international picture of increased unemployment and diminished inflation, so that Britain's position in the international 'league table' of strike incidence was barely changed.

The new legislation probably contributed to reducing the number of stoppages rather than the number of working days lost. This is because unions wishing to avoid fines, injunctions, and sequestration of their assets have to approach a strike with greater procedural caution. This discourages the sort of small strike that hitherto might have occurred over a perishable grievance such as a dismissal. Balloting on strikes has itself become something of a substitute for strike action, with 92 per cent of ballots going in favour of strikes and usually leading on to management concessions. On the other hand, once a strike has been called, the gravity of the new procedures, and the need for balloting on the strike's termination, probably makes the action go on longer. The net effect is likely to be to shift the focus of strike action from smaller to larger issues and to shift the authorization of strike action from shop stewards towards full-time trade union officials.

This centralizing implication for union government is considerably more evident in the many legislative measures that were intended to make unions more accountable to their members. The balloting requirements for union executives required a minority of unions to alter their constitutions. They are unlikely to be reversed by a future government because future union executives are unlikely to question the democratic credentials of their own election. For those unions that have moved from having their executives elected indirectly through local delegates, direct elections tend to increase the importance of control of the union journal and to stimulate the development of factions organizing electoral slates. The requirement for full postal ballots does not necessarily increase membership turnout; the TGWU's workplace ballots for its executive of 1988 yielded a 39 per cent turnout which fell to 21 per cent under the full postal regulations in place by 1990. But the legislation does help unions with the costs of these arrangements, and in the four years up to 1988 the Certification Officer refunded £4.2 million for the costs of electoral and strike ballots.

Another unexpected consequence of the legislation came from the 1984 requirement to hold a ballot if union funds were to be used for political purposes. This posed a threat to the source of approximately three-quarters of the income of the Labour Party. Contrary to all predictions the first round of ballots revealed a high level of support for political funds. By the end of the decade, of the fifty-three unions which had balloted on the issue, only one (the First Division Association of top civil servants) had voted against. Approximately 80 per cent of union members were thereby in unions with approved political funds. As a direct result of the new legislation, at least twenty unions now have political funds for the first time.

A more far-reaching consequence of the legislation has been its incidental effect upon the centralism and professionalism of union management. Unions have been obliged to computerize their membership records, to maintain address lists, to keep more systematic financial accounts, to run more orderly elections, to gain greater influence over their shop stewards, and to communicate better with their members. Their power to discipline non-strikers may have been removed, but strike solidarity has always been sustained by peer-group pressure rather than disciplinary procedures. Outweighing this weakening of formal disciplinary powers is the greatly increased need for unions to tighten up internal discipline because they have become so much more financially vulnerable to procedural clumsiness by their shop stewards. It was because the National Union of Seamen could not control their Dover branch in 1988 that they suffered some £2 million in fines and legal costs and temporarily suffered the paralysing experience of having their head office taken from them by the official sequestrators.

The consequences for trade union behaviour of these governmental efforts to 'hand unions back to their members' are in many ways perverse. It is certainly not clear that they have caused unions to become more 'moderate', a term loosely and variously applied to reduced strike-propensity, diminished sectionalism, and closer accord with government policy. The lecturers' union NATFHE responded to its first full ballot for a general secretary in 1989 by electing someone far to the left of its established executive. Nor can strike ballots of the rank-and-file be expected to yield more 'moderate' strike decisions than before. Union leaders owe much of their success to their ability to build continuing bargaining relationships with their management opposite numbers; the give and take of bargaining is a strong teacher of moderation. When the rank-and-file make decisions by direct vote they tend to be more aggressive in prosperity and more timid in adversity than would be their elected representatives.

This major set of innovations in British labour law, collectively the greatest change since 1906, has reduced trade union power in some respects, but has had equivocal consequences for the 'moderation' of union behaviour. What may prove to be of greater importance is that, by forcing trade unions to tighten up their internal discipline, it is likely to be a major counter-balance to the fragmentary tendency of recent developments in collective bargaining. It is now necessary to describe these.

CHANGES IN COLLECTIVE BARGAINING

If government attitude were the major determinant of trade union fortunes, the 1980s would have been a decade of massive collapse. The combination of hostile legislation, public sector defeats and the recession might have been expected to force unions into the defensive corner that they have retreated to in the United States. Table 5 compares the membership experience of British with overseas unions.

TABLE 5   Union membership as percentage of all employees 1970–85

Country	1970	1975	1980	1985
United Kingdom	48	51	53	43
Australia	50	54	52	51
Canada	36	34	34	34
France	23	23	19	na
Germany (FR)	37	39	39	37
Holland	37	38	37	29
Ireland	52	53	55	46
Italy	33	42	43	40
Japan	35	34	31	29
Sweden	74	79	88	88
United States	27	25	23	16

Source: R Price in R Bean (ed) *International Labour Statistics,* 1989

Union membership in Britain did indeed decline substantially during the 1980s – from 55 per cent of employees in 1979 to perhaps 42 per cent in 1989 – but it will be apparent from the table above that, for example, Holland, Ireland and the United States had comparable experiences. France probably had a similar decline and Japan's unions contracted faster later in the decade. But it would be a mistake to read too much into the British figures. Probably at least half of the loss of union membership in Britain arose simply because of structural change in the economy with the contraction of some highly unionized manufacturing sectors and the growth of less unionized private services.

Indeed, the evidence from many surveys all suggests that there has not been a substantial retreat from collective bargaining by British employers, at least in the sense of recognizing and dealing with trade unions. A CBI survey of the same members in 1986 as it had surveyed in 1979 reported no net change in union recognition. The official Advisory, Conciliation and Arbitration Service (ACAS) was still commenting on the rarity of union de-recognition at the end of the decade. Where unions have been hit is where they have always been weak – among managerial groups, among part-time workers, among small employers, and among the unskilled – and here the widespread shift to less secure labour contracts has taken its toll.

The coverage of closed shops, in which union membership is necessary to retain a job, has diminished substantially from a little over 5 million employees in 1978 to perhaps 3½ million in the mid-1980s. But here again it is likely that change in the structure of industry has had a greater impact than employer opposition. A more reliable indicator of employer attitudes to unions is the extent of the 'check-off', the practise whereby employers collect union members' dues on behalf of their unions. Between 1980 and 1984 the use of the check-off, already almost universal in the public sector, spread substantially in the private sector to cover almost 6 million employees. Shop stewards, the representatives elected from among employees, continue to be the women and men with whom employers prefer to deal, rather than the full-time officials on the unions' own pay-rolls. The main change over the decade in this respect has been that there are now fewer shop stewards who are permitted by employers to spend all their working time on trade union activities.

Lying behind this resilience of workplace trade unionism is the continuing decline of industry-wide agreements in the private sector. Until the middle of this century the main form of collective agreement in Britain had been one concluded with trade unions by associations of employers (rather than individual employers) and covering whole industries. Gradually, however, employers opted out of these, the larger employers first, so that whereas in the 1950s perhaps four in five of private sector employees covered by collective bargaining had a 'multi-employer' agreement, by the late 1970s this proportion had declined to two in five and, by the mid-1980s, to one in five. By the end of the decade still more multi-employer agreements had collapsed, both venerable ones, as in engineering and shipping, and relative newcomers, as in commercial television and banking.

The driving force behind the growth of 'single-employer' bargaining was the effort of firms to tighten their internal controls over pay and productivity. It was aided by the government's belief in the 1980s that industrial training was best provided for by employers pursuing their individual self-interest, without the compulsion or assistance of statutory industry-wide institutions such as the Training Boards. The consequent rapid decline in training during the recession increased the pressure on employers to protect their own interests so that what training was provided was increasingly in-house and as non-transferable as possible between firms. Employers sought to trap their more valued employees into company-specific job descriptions, pay structures, and career paths, and to isolate their internal union organizations procedurally.

The consequences of these developments for the union movement have been profound. At the end of the war, national union leaders had dominated pay bargaining and had a major influence on training arrangements. Members' subscriptions paid their union negotiators' salaries and, if necessary, their fellow unionists' strike pay. Unions were perceived as being essentially external to the individual enterprises and the interests and allegiances of members were largely linked to bodies such as district committees and to job titles that transcended their individual employer.

The growth of the workplace-based joint shop steward committee as the dominant mode of organization, at first in traditional manufacturing but then more widely, broke this down. It was both a response to and a stimulant of single-employer bargaining. Despite the growth of union membership during the 1970s, the number of union-employed full-time officials altered little; the big growth occurred in shop stewards and in the full-time shop stewards who were paid for by management. With the decline of multi-employer agreements and industry-wide training, the national union officials ceased to have substantial influence over the most important features of their members' employment contracts. Instead trade unionism in many of its traditional strongholds became workplace oriented. It was becoming increasingly isolated from the concerns and influence of a wider trade union movement. It was becoming increasingly dependent upon the management of the employing enterprise for its procedural status and bargaining facilities. Although the rise of the shop steward was applauded by many on the left of the movement, it was fair-weather trade unionism. It was bargaining on the cheap.

This explains the superficial resilience of workplace collective bargaining through the hardships and hostility of the 1980s. For managements sufficiently well-organized to innovate, workplace-based unionism is relatively compliant. Technological innovation is the basis of most productivity improvements and for most technological innovation the management of labour is only part of the problem, an excuse rather than a reason for holding back. Trade unions at the national level are sometimes reluctant to accommodate change because it may challenge some skill or technology which is a part of their organizational identity. If unions can be dealt with within the enterprise, it is often possible to offer retraining and individual guarantees that can ease such anxieties.

One of the remarkable features of the recession of the 1980s was that individual workers queued up to accept the minor cash payments accompanying voluntary redundancy despite dreadful employment prospects outside. While national union officials resisted the implied job losses, shop steward organizations, faced with a *fait accompli,* bargained over the share-out of the savings. Shop steward organizations were even more ineffective at resisting factory closures. Even in the good times little had been achieved by the 'combine committees' of shop stewards which had tried to link up factory steward committees within some multi-plant companies. In the recession, workplace-based unionism was powerless in the face of coherent company-wide managerial strategies, with the more truculent workplaces in the front ranks facing closure. The lesson was rubbed home very publicly when Michael Edwardes dismissed Derek Robinson, the convenor of stewards at British Leyland's massive Longbridge works in 1979. Not only did he stay dismissed, but the other individually powerful British Leyland workplaces, many close by, were incapable of mobilizing effective resistance.

Employers have found it easier to work with this relatively compliant form of trade unionism rather than eradicate it. It is not that these more 'domesticated' union organizations are necessarily docile, they are not, but that their survival depends more upon the survival of the enterprise of which they are a part. The style of collective bargaining has changed, with unions relegated more to a consultative than negotiatory role on non-pay matters. More issues have been dealt with on an individual rather than collective basis. A superficial feature of the procedural isolation of union organizations within their enterprise has been the publicity given to bargaining devices such as pendulum arbitration (of which experience has been poor), 'no-strike' deals (which means bipartite compulsory arbitration and has limited practical use), and 'single-union' agreements.

It was the issue of single-union agreements that provoked the greatest internal crisis for the Trades Union Congress of the 1980s, which led in 1988 to the expulsion of the electricians' union, the EETPU. It is an issue that reflects many of the problems with which the changed circumstances of collective bargaining confront the union movement in the 1990s. A single-union agreement does no more than provide one union with exclusive recognition rights for a particular workplace. There is nothing new about them, although twenty years ago employers often avoided them in apprehension that too much influence would thereby be given to the local union district committee. The substantial diminution of external union influence over training, pay and work methods has removed this anxiety.

Underlying the threat the issue poses to unions is the fact that many of the larger unions are in effect 'open' to all sorts of members. Distanced from the technologies and skills which once defined their recruitment territories, unions such as MSF, TGWU, GMB and AEU are omniverous, hungry for any membership that will deliver dues. On some 'greenfield' sights this has meant that they have vied with each other to present attractive procedural packages to management in order to win recognition. On some 'brownfield' sights they have connived with management to oust other unions already in place, in contravention of the TUC's Bridlington Agreement of 1939. The TUC has a very effective Disputes Committee that processes these territorial disputes, and all the major unions have been at different times winners and losers from its judgements. The crisis of 1988 arose because the EETPU for once refused to abide by two of its decisions. It was symptomatic of the weakness of the trade union movement by the end of the 1980s that the EETPU considered that it had more to gain by advertising itself to employers as a user-friendly union, than by remaining within the TUC.

THE POLITICAL CHALLENGE FOR TRADE UNIONS

The events described have confronted Britain's trade unions with a double problem. The first part concerns their dealings with the state. In the course of a decade their political influence has tumbled and the legal basis on which they operate has been seriously weakened. The state has also become in many ways a hostile employer, not only in its truculent attitude to bargaining but also in its efforts to fragment public sector bargaining units and to increase their exposure to outside competition. Collectivism in the public services has been under sustained attack, from the subcontracting of jobs of lowly hospital ancilliary staff and council workers to the usurping of the professional controls of more exalted lawyers, doctors, lecturers and teachers.

The second and largely unconnected problem has been the fragmenting effect of the shift to single-employer bargaining and in-house training in the private sector. The threat this poses is less to membership numbers than to the solidarity of the trade union movement. The prospect that gives the more far-sighted leaders lost sleep is to be seen in an extreme form in Japan's enterprise-based unions. Their zeal in maintaining the competitive position of their separate enterprises has been such that overall living standards have been severely held back, although the uniting of the trade union federations in the 'New Rengo' in 1989 suggests that the Japanese tide might finally be turning.

The British union movement has been slow to respond to the gravity of its position. As late as 1988 the TUC Conference voted not to be involved in the Training Agency which replaced the training part of the Manpower Services Commission, thereby opting out of one of the few opportunities still remaining to influence the process of skill acquisition. Subsequent back-tracking in construction and some other industries has emphasized the short-sightedness of the decision.

Individual unions have, however, shown an increased awareness of the need to provide their members with routine benefits rather than just emergency collective bargaining services. Many unions now offer a range of financial and other advisory services to their members; some offer advisory services to employers as well, on matters such as health and safety. There is an increased interest in being less reactive, and in getting members to shift the focus of their demands from simple pay matters towards improving the quality of their working lives through better career opportunities and working conditions. These developments have been facilitated by the spate of union mergers during the 1980s, but the decade has also seen unions raise their members' dues back towards the levels of the 1950s from the relatively low point they had fallen to by the late 1970s. Unions have made extensive use of professional advice in winning over employers and in recruiting the growing mass of workers on unconventional employment contracts.

Perhaps the most interesting development for the union movement during these bleak years was the creation in 1984 of the Unity Trust Bank. David Basnett, the ex-leader of the GMB, was instrumental in bringing together major trade unions and the Co-operative Bank in what has developed into a highly successful financial institution with assets by 1988 of over £100 million. Apart from acting as a conventional bank it manages unions' financial services schemes, pension schemes, and investment portfolios. It has recently established a public relations consultancy and a balloting agency, and gives assistance on diverse matters of union concern from coping with sequestration to funding the 1988 Wembley Mandela Concert. With several union general secretaries on its board, the influence of the Unity Trust is likely to grow substantially.

A widespread verdict on the Labour Party's period of government from 1974–79 was that the trade union movement became too heavily involved, both in drawing up legislation and in economic management, and that this reduced its room for manoeuvre and damaged its public reputation. Partly as a result of this there has been a cautious reappraisal of their relationship. At constituency level the varied and tortuous rules providing unions with considerable influence over parliamentary candidate selection are likely to be changed under the Party's own reforms aimed at giving votes to individual members, thereby diminishing union influence. At the national level, where the unions hold almost 90 per cent of Conference votes, a process of reappraisal was started in 1988 which may lead to the union vote amounting to no more than 40 per cent. Although superficially a reduction in power, these reforms would benefit the union movement by providing it with a less partisan public image and with a less compromised bargaining relationship with a future Labour government.

There is one safe prediction that should inform all discussion of the political role of British unions. It is that government hostility towards them will not continue indefinitely. Having survived the traumas of the 1980s, trade unions are going to find governments of whatever party courting them for assistance during the 1990s. At least four issues make this likely. The first is membership of the European Community, which will draw Britain into a group of countries whose labour laws provide unions with substantial rights and guarantee employees a variety of minimum entitlements. The second is the extreme disorder into which the pay structure of the public services has been allowed to drift in the 1980s, which will require radical and collaborative restorative work. The third is the crisis in occupational training, for which some sort of statutory solution may be necessary. Finally, there is the fact that the 1980s formula of high unemployment and radical labour legislation has not reduced Britain's severe inflationary tendencies, and with this realization comes the painful prospect for politicians of once again having to talk to unions about pay policies.

The difficult question is not whether future governments will show less hostility towards trade unions. It is whether unions will learn from the experience of the 1980s.

15 British unions and Europe

Denis MacShane

An integration of Europe, whatever its precise form, which broadened the basis of her economy, eliminated customs barriers and competing currencies, and enabled the basic industries of food, fuel, iron and steel, and engineering to be organised to serve a market of two hundred million persons, would unquestionably be followed by a general increase in economic prosperity and political strength; but the particular sacrifices and temporary embarrassments entailed by it would not be a trifle. Reason is on its side; but the natural human egotism of interest and emotion; of locality, class and occupation; of regional loyalties and national pride, will rally to resist it.

R. H. Tawney, *The Western Political Tradition,* 1949

At the beginning of the 1980s, Europe hardly existed for British trade unions. The standard textbooks read by students of the British trade union movement mentioned the European Community in passing, if they mentioned it at all.[1] Descriptions of European unions were available from academic writers[2] but British unions rarely referred to events or developments affecting continental labour. There was little experience of British unions or groups of workers making common cause with unions in Europe. The TUC was an important member of both the International Confederation of Free Trade Unions (ICFTU – set up in 1949) and the European Trade Union Confederation (ETUC – set up in 1973) but during the 1970s and 1980s the TUC Congress regularly adopted motions expressing hostility to British membership of the European Economic Community or specific policy proposals or directives associated with the European Commission in Brussels. While TUC officers charged with compositing motions ensured that calls to withdraw the TUC from its participation in various European bodies were not adopted, the British trade unions shared with the Labour Party a generalized hostility to the European Community evident well into the 1980s.

Yet by 1990 a revolution had taken place. Unions were competing with each other to be more European than the most fervent supporter of the

EC ten years previously. Major unions such as the General Municipal and Boilermakers' Union and the Manufacturing, Science and Finance Union produced detailed reports setting out the ways the two unions hoped to be active in Europe. The President of the Amalgamated Engineering Union, Bill Jordan, constantly referred to Europe in speeches and sought to establish a permanent linkage with the West German metalworkers' union, IG Metall. In 1988, the TUC invited Jacques Delors, president of the European Commission, a man who a few years beforehand would have been contemptuously dismissed as a 'Eurocrat', to address its Congress. His speech there was seen as a major challenge to Margaret Thatcher's hostility to the social policy espoused by Delors, a challenge all the more pointed in that Delors chose to deliver it in English, in England and to the very group of people – trade union officials and activists – that Mrs Thatcher had vilified, spurned, and sought to weaken and if possible eradicate from Britain's political and economic life.

Two years after Delors' speech Mrs Thatcher left office following disagreements within the Conservative Party over Europe. The TUC and the unions could justly say to themselves that in giving such priority to Europe and offering, in 1988, such a platform and profile to Jacques Delors to promote his social-christian democratic values and vision against those of the then prime minister, the British unions set in motion a delayed revenge over their most bitter twentieth century opponent.

The TUC followed up its offer of an anti-Thatcher platform to Delors by setting up a special European committee, publishing guidelines for its affiliates on aspects of European Community policy and politics and suggestions for improving the knowledge and activities of British unions in the European sphere. In 1989, the TUC took out advertisements in the national press, urging voters to participate in the elections to the European parliament. Although not a specific endorsement of the Labour Party's candidates, the TUC advertisements emphasized the social policies associated with the EC and disavowed by the government. Pro-Labour TUC strategists could feel well pleased with the result of the elections in June 1989 which produced impressive gains for the Labour Party and set the seal on the general reorientation by the early 1990s of the whole of the British labour movement towards a positive engagement with Europe. The revolutionary upsurges in east and central Europe in 1989 further underlined the salience of European engagement.

THE END OF ILLUSIONS ABOUT NATIONAL ECONOMIC SOVEREIGNTY

In the years after the Second World War, most leaders of the British trade unions were fairly described as 'keen internationalists but reluctant

Europeans'[3] and the process that led to their becoming enthusiastic Europeans is one of the major political turnarounds in recent trade union history with significant consequences for the future of the TUC inside Britain and Europe as well as its choice of strategy and tactics. In his *Socialism and European Unity,* published in 1983, Michael Newman discussed the failure of the Labour Party in Britain and the Socialist Party in France to transcend their national priorities and move towards effective supranational democratic socialist policies within a European context. In each country, the supremacy of domestic politics meant that in Labour's case, 'the Community must not be allowed to impinge on the sovereignty of the nation-state or Labour's freedom to determine its own policy' while in France, the Socialists 'feared that acceptance of a European socialist programme would provide fuel for PCF (the French Communist Party) and Gaullist propaganda attacks against the Socialists for subordinating themselves to foreigners.[4]

Newman concluded with the following assessment.

If the left confines its activities to the nation-state, it is unlikely that major progress can be made. Yet thorough-going cross-national cooperation would be possible only if the national solution ceased to be the dominant influence on left-wing parties, and this could probably only come about only if political power was already seen to exist at supranational rather than national level. . . . At some stage it is likely that the relative failure of the left in each country to attain its goals will bring about a transformation of consciousness. No doubt this will only occur when there is a clear change in material circumstances.[5]

Not long after Mrs Thatcher's third election victory in 1987 it appeared that Newman's tentatively posed three conditions – a decline in the belief in national solutions, the emergence of supranational political power, and a change in material circumstances – had been met.

The collapse in the belief in national solutions was hastened by two glaring examples, one from the left, one from the right. The programme of the French socialists on arriving in power in 1981 was one largely based on a policy of national economic development in the shape of state takeovers of key industries and an expansion of domestic demand. While the first served to strengthen France's industrial sector (at a time when Britain was sacrificing hers) the second proved disastrous within the context of an open European market. Imports flooded into France to meet the surge in demand. The franc fell. Inflation took off in part due to the generosity of the increase in the minimum wage and the cut in annual working time. The policies of the French Socialists were well-meant, and if they had been applied on a European scale, would have put an end to the unemployment, running at between 14 and 19 million west Europeans during the 1980s, that so disfigured that *Enrichissez-vous* decade. But precisely because they were implemented only nationally with the appeals of President Mitterrand for a general relaunch of the European economy falling on the deaf ears of the fiscally conservative Germans and the then savagely deflationist British, the attempt by the French Socialists to find a national solution corresponding to their political intentions was unsuccessful. After a year, the French switched course, adopting income control, and more conservative economic policies dressed up as modernization.

The lesson was not lost on the British labour movement. As one trade union official wrote in a Fabian pamphlet analysing lessons that Labour might draw from France:

To seek to implement policies without the fullest reference to what is happening beyond national borders (assuming that one is not prepared to seal off the country in some starkly authoritarian fashion) is to invite disaster as the French discovered.[6]

The other country which provided a more dramatic example of the decline in national economic sovereignty was the United States. Moving from being the world's biggest creditor to the world's biggest debtor in the space of a decade, stressed the message even to British trade unionists who did not closely follow international economic developments that national economic solutions no longer made sense.

One alternative appeared to stand out. Mrs Thatcher, aided by oil revenues, the easy-credit fuelled boom between 1984 and 1988, and unexamined by the most supine press in Europe, purported to give the impression that England had indeed found a national solution to economic problems. National power, provided it was guided by someone of supreme will, could re-establish economic growth. Manchester School capitalism in one country was possible, so her admirers argued.

Yet, if anything, her attacks on the Delors vision of greater European unity, animadversions on the social policy associated with the European Commission, plus minor squabbles over health warnings on cigarette packets and immigration control in the Channel Tunnel, served to increase rather than diminish public awareness of the remarkable transfer of power to a supranational authority that had taken place under her reign.

The signing of the Single European Act, the dropping of national economic and fiscal controls to create a Single Internal Market, and the search for greater currency harmony implied a transfer of power to European institutions without parallel in British history. That was the formal and measurable transfer of power to supranational bodies, in this case the European Community and its component institutions. Not so visible was the power now exercised by the international financial community and multinational companies over key sections of the British economy. A graph of the pound's movement in the course of the 1980s looks like a roller coaster, while in important areas of manufacturing such as the car industry and consumer electronics it was necessary to invite in Japanese companies such was the inability of British capital and management to perform adequately. The shrinking of nationally-controlled sectors of the British economy to the profit of external bodies was clearly evident at the end of the decade.

Finally, there was some evidence that the material decline of Britain in comparison with other northern European states was getting through to, if not the public as a whole, at least an influential section of it. Ross McKibbin put it like this:

There was a time, within the living memory of much of the public, when abroad was vacated with relief and home was where things worked, not least the sanitation. Nowadays, however, abroad must induce very different reflections. Anyone with half an eye can see what a mean and run-down little country Britain has become: what do the *Daily Mail* readers who set out at Victoria and alight at the Gare du Nord think of the miracle as they pass from one public sector to another? Presumably, for many people, the Continent is now a place where the phones work and where you can eat the food and drink the water.[7]

The statistics of Britain's relative and absolute decline were well enough known[8] to enter the consciousness of the most ardent trade union believer in national economic solutions to Britain's problems and convert him (or, rarely amongst the elected leaders or staff of the unions, her) to, if not a belief in, at least an understanding of the need for trade unions to look beyond simply national horizons in the search for policy, power and partners to achieve the ends set by the labour movement.

THE COLD WAR IN UNIONS

Two other factors contributed to the breakdown of introspective nationalism and anti-Europeanism and the embrace of European politics by the TUC and its affiliates. The first was the dying down of the Cold War. In a classic exposition of the international work of western trade unions in the 1950s Lewis Lorwin argued that the tasks of unions and their international federations lay in

Organizing workers, in combatting Communists, in extending trade union rights and in promoting political freedom.[9]

The priority given to 'combatting Communists' all too accurately reflected the tenor of international trade union work for much of the post-war period.[10] The ETUC refused to accept into membership the biggest of the three French trade union confederations, the *Confédération Générale du Travail* (CGT) on account of its membership of the Soviet-dominated World Federation of Trade Unions, the communist rival to the International Confederation of Free Trade Unions to which the west European trade union national centres, for the most part, belonged.[11] Other factors kept the

CGT without the ETUC, notably the intense hostility of its rival federation, *Force Ouvrière,* and the CGT's opposition to the European project which it denounced in identical terms to those used by the French Communist Party. On the other hand, the Italian CGIL did become an ETUC member, despite its closeness to the Italian Communist Party. The CGIL however had broken its links with the WFTU by the mid-1970s and its entry into the ETUC was supported by the two other Italian federations.

In the course of the 1980s a marked change could be seen in the dominant place hitherto occupied by the Cold War in trade union internationalism. Firstly, the arrival of Polish Solidarity threw into turmoil the Leninist model of democratic centralist trade union organization previously existing in communist countries.

The surge of support amongst European trade unionists for Solidarity based, as it was, on the clear working-class demands and trade union organizational form of the Polish union remained in force after the suppression of Solidarity by the Jaruzelski régime in December 1981. Contacts between the TUC and East European unions, who were obliged to endorse the repression of Solidarity, dried up. When they gingerly resumed after the arrival of Mr Gorbachev in power in Moscow, Norman Willis, the TUC's general secretary, vigorously endorsed British union support for Solidarity when he addressed the congress of the Soviet trade union confederation in 1987. He earned a rebuke from the congress chair but Willis's intervention signalled the burial of uncritical 'fraternalism' with the state-controlled unions in communist countries.

By 1991 the trade union scene in Eastern Europe and the Balkans had changed utterly. The Czechoslovak unions under democratically chosen leaders had joined the ICFTU. The East German communist unions disappeared as East and West Germany merged. In Hungary, Bulgaria and Romania, independent unions were formed, while the official union structures sought to adapt themselves. Even in the Soviet Union some three hundred new unions were created. The economic and social difficulties thrown up by the East European revolution posed new challenges for European trade unionism as a whole. Curiously, in Poland, the birthplace of the process, Solidarity was weak and divided with a dwindling sense of union purpose in the face of Lech Walesa's political ambitions.[12]

Discussions of foreign policy matters in the TUC in the 1950s, 1960s and 1970s had often fractured on left–right lines. These represented either Atlanticist, pro-NATO values or support for policies espoused by those who believed that, for all its faults, the Soviet Union remained a workers' state and a symbol of progress for international labour.

By the 1980s an older generation of TUC leaders whose views had been formed in the 1930s and 1940s retired to be replaced by their successors for whom the Soviet invasion of Prague was as reprehensible as the American bombing of Vietnamese villages. This new generation no longer attached the same importance either to Communism, or to anti-Communism as a main priority of international trade union work. They were more interested in terms of making links to combat multinationals, or to promote peace. Here the work of the European Nuclear Disarmament campaign with its insistence on the linkage between democratic rights in East Europe and demilitarization in the West was particularly influential amongst the large contingent of British trade union delegates attending its annual conventions each year in the 1980s.

Trade union international activity in the 1980s transcended the old east-west divisions. In countries like South Africa and South Korea, major new labour movements developed. In Turkey, Chile, Brazil and the Philippines, radical unions, carefully eschewing the kind of simplistic pro-Western or pro-Soviet profiles which had been demanded of third world unions in the first thirty years after the war's end, emerged as important political players and they sought international contacts with the TUC. A new, fractious academic school was built around international labour studies and in 1983, a new journal, *International Labour Reports,* was launched with articles aimed at trade union activists. [13]

While domestic trade unionism seemed in the doldrums, with many commentators talking of the 'marginalization'[14] of the trade unions in Britain, internationally, and in Europe in particular, the TUC and its affiliates found new areas of activity during the Thatcher years.

A NEW ROLE FOR THE TUC

Europe has helped to give a new presence and cohesion to the TUC in two distinct areas. Firstly, the TUC has developed a new role as the co-ordinating and representative body in the European sphere. This happened at a time when the British government refused to deal with the TUC as a representative body in the national sphere and at a time when the TUC's co-ordination function was coming into question as the result of an accelerating pace of mergers creating so-called 'super-unions', some of them (the TGWU, the enlarged GMB and the MSF – itself considering a merger with the TGWU) covering such a wide variety of occupations and industries as to be mini-TUC's in themselves.

British unions are not well equipped to handle the technical aspects of international affairs. Few, if any, have a professionally staffed, multi-lingual international department. The TUC, on the other hand, has experience, contacts and expertise in this field and was active in the 1980s participating in and organizing meetings and links with European unions.

Secondly, the issue of Europe in the broadest sense had become a dominant political issue at the end of the 1980s with increasing support for greater British involvement in Europe. The TUC having been pilloried as out-of-date and irrelevant in the first half of the decade found itself in the van of forward-looking political thinking in its turn towards Europe. Delors' speech at the TUC congress in 1988 was one of the most important political interventions by a foreigner addressing himself via television to the British people in post-war political history. Mrs Thatcher's furious reaction, expressed in her speech at Bruges a few weeks later, set off a debate about Europe in which many of the media comments as well as the results in the elections to the European Parliament suggested that the TUC and not the prime minister had caught the public mood. TUC activity in Europe also corresponded with the realignment of the Labour Party toward an active political engagement in Europe and reflected the increase in Europeanism at the expense of Atlanticism in labour movement circles.[15]

In short, Europe offered the TUC a new organizational role and political profile. Astute officials at the TUC seized the opportunity but there was more to the TUC's European involvement than political far-sightedness. What took place in the 1980s was the growing convergence of British industrial relations and trade union praxis with that of continental Europe. Of course each country retained its national peculiarities of trade union form, legislation, political profile and relations with employers and government but developments in three areas for British unions made them much closer to their continental *confrères* than at any previous time in their history.

TOWARDS A EUROPEANIZATION OF INDUSTRIAL RELATIONS

Firstly, the law was introduced to regulate unions in a way without parallel in Britain. Employers had recourse to courts in disputes and judges intervened in industrial relations. Laws also regulated internal union procedures and prohibited the closed shop. By the end of the 1980s, unions were shaping their bargaining and industrial action plans in regular consultation with lawyers and the entry of judicial, legal procedures into industrial relations and union practice was accepted as a norm. This legal codification corresponded more closely to continental practice. Although the government avoided setting up a properly constituted labour court system, the end effect of ten years of legal intervention and regulation in labour affairs had been to bring Britain more into line with the rest of Europe, where codification and labour courts play an important role in resolving disputes, checking arbitrary decisions by employers or *ultra vires* actions by workers, and providing an alternative to the British union tradition of shunning legal regulation and intervention.

The Conservative Government, it should be stressed, introduced its labour law bills with the intention of strengthening the employers' hand not with a view to continentalize labour relations. Nonetheless, lawyer and judicial intervention in what previously had been a sacred voluntary baliwick did willy-nilly bring British union–employer relations closer to continental practice. The European influence was felt by the Labour Party industrial specialists when the Shadow Employment spokesperson, Tony Blair, announced that Labour accepted that the closed shop was incompatible with the European Social Charter and would no longer be supported or enforced by any future Labour government. Rows over the closed shop had been a constant feature of industrial relations politics in the 1970s. Europe has helped Labour bury the closed shop as an issue and future source of controversy.

Secondly, there was a transfer of attention from the union as the sole voice of workers to seeking direct relations with the workforce itself. The political aim of the government and the employers was to by-pass unions. Some unions, notably the electricians, supported this trend and in exchange for being the only union recognized by the company, helped set up company councils on which workers and managers jointly met to resolve certain problems. According to the *Financial Times,* 'Many non-union Japanese companies retain quite collective systems of employee relations, involving teamworking, quality circles and company councils.'[16]

This development also pushed British labour relations closer to the European model of company-based works councils acting as the first level of workers' representation in the workplace. In most continental countries, works councils are legally enshrined, with their powers and rights laid down in law. The French socialist government, with its Arroux laws in the 1980s sought to strengthen the workplace representation and rights of employees as it was difficult to see any mechanism of giving further power to French unions, divided as they are on political lines. There is a difference between a French *comité d'entreprise* and a German *Betriebsrat.* In France, the enterprise committee is a joint body on which managers sit. In Germany, the works council consists only of workers. But in both cases, and unlike Britain, the legally-enshrined focus of representation is a workplace body.

In Germany, the works councils operate a kind of dual-power system with the unions, the former acting to safeguard workplace interests and provide the representation channels for the German codetermination system of industrial democracy, while the unions control strategic bargaining matters, notably on pay and hours, as well as operating a regional and federal political organization on behalf of their members. Sweden was an exception to the Europe-wide system of works councils. But even in that labour movement-dominated country the works environment committees had major legal powers invested in them so that their decisions on work organization or production, although taken in the name of environmental questions, amounted to workplace-based intervention beyond the dreams of the most militant shop stewards or convenors' committees of the 1960s and 1970s in Britain.

In themselves, works councils were as effective as the law, the overall strength of unions in each country, and the determination of each company's employees. Works councils are a recognition of the right of employees to have some collective relationship with the company. In Britain, that right has been jealously guarded by unions, though even at the height of trade union membership, union penetration in Britain rarely exceeded about 50 per cent of the employed workforce.

In addition to the employer push in the 1980s towards greater company orientated forms of representation, the law also forced unions to consult more closely any group of workers likely to be involved in industrial action. Even friendly supporters of the National Union of Mineworkers agreed that the failure of the NUM leadership to call a ballot of its members was the disastrous mistake at the beginning of the 1984–85 dispute from which the union never recovered.[17] So the turn to the workplace as the centre of industrial relations activity and to workers grouped within the company at the expense of the union was evident in Britain throughout the 1980s. What did not happen was a formal recognition of this trend by the legal creation of works councils though one eminent TUC adviser, Lord McCarthy, suggested that some form of works council might be appropriate in a Fabian pamphlet published in 1988[18] but his suggestion did not work its way into general trade union policy. On the other hand, several British unions participated in European-wide works councils, which we will discuss later. In that sense, the idea of a works council, commonplace on the continent, was seeping into British trade union consciousness.

The third way in which British unions found themselves Europeanized was the most important. It can be put simply. For the first time in trade union history, unions in different European countries, including Britain, were confronting the same problems, using the same language, demanding the same solutions, at the same time and were conscious of doing so in a European as well as a national context.

Any attempt at comparative labour history between, let us say, the founding of the International Working Men's Association in 1864 and the two enlargements of the Common Market in 1973 (Britain, Denmark and Ireland) and in 1986 (Spain and Portugal, Greece having joined in 1981) stumbles across the problem that at any moment in those hundred years the specific priorities of workers in the various European countries are radically different according to the state of political or economic relations in individual nations. As late as 1975, the first change in the Iberian peninsular was the creation of political democracy. Basic industrialization was the most important task for France and Italy in the post-war period at a time when British steel, coal, shipbuilding and car production seemed unchallengeable. The establishment of basic social security and pension rights was the cause of major German strikes in the 1950s and 1960s at a time when these were taken for granted in Britain. French workers needed the convulsion of their general strike in 1968 to secure wages and conditions that had been obtained through longer and less dramatic processes in other countries.

By the 1980s, while national peculiarities naturally continued to exist, it was striking how the priorities, pressures and *paroles* of European unions had become similar and were marching in step. The workings of a capitalist common market had created amongst unions a common concern about unemployment; about new technology; about the arms race; about the internationalization of the economy; about the creation of part-time low-paid jobs; about the division of workforces into so-called core and periphery sections; about new anti-union laws or policies adopted by many European governments. Unions became notably greener and changed their rules to give more place to women.

The most important single union campaign in the 1980s was over the reduction of the working week and this was seen very much as a European-wide issue in which unions drew support from the success and achievements in other countries. The German metalworkers, for example, referred to the 39-hour week secured in Britain and France at the beginning of the 1980s in their campaign to break through the 40-hour week which they succeeded in doing after a seven-week strike in 1984. In turn, the British engineers took heart from the German example and cited European precedents when they took up the cudgels for a reduced working week in the winter of 1989–1990.

For a decade when unions were said to have lost power and weight the reduction in working time was a common European achievement resulting in significant gains for workers. It took different forms in different countries – a reduced working week, increased holidays, or earlier retirement on full pension. But each time the reduction in working time had to be fought for and the gain represented a permanent victory of European workers, which unlike wage increases, could not be swallowed up by inflation.

So the TUC's use of Europolitics was not simply a tactical move to seize a portion of political high ground from which it had been excluded by Mrs Thatcher. Instead the TUC's turn to Europe reflected a new European ideology and practice visible in all European unions and stemming from common experiences, a convergence of economic, political and social problems, and a sense that Europe, as much as the nation, was the playing field for effective trades unionism in the future.

THE EUROPEAN SOCIAL CHARTER OF WORKERS' RIGHTS

The debate over the Social Charter was the most notorious symbol of this process. Social (which adjective in EEC jargon means pro-labour), aspects of the Common Market had never been afforded high priority in the work of the Commission or Council of Ministers. It had not been until 1973, fifteen years after the Treaty of Rome, that European unions had overcome sufficiently their divergences to create the European Trades

Union Confederation, and even then communist unions in France, Spain and Portugal did not join.

The pro-union legislation in many countries in the 1970s was reflected in EC proposals for European-wide laws on extending information rights for workers in transnational companies in Europe (the Vredling proposals) and for some form of industrial democracy involving workers sitting on the boards of companies (the fifth directive). Both stemmed from developments in national labour legislation. Information rights had been extended in most northern European countries in the 1970s while industrial democracy, in the specific form of workers or union nominees sitting on company boards, had been set up, or existing systems strengthened in Nordic countries, West Germany and the Netherlands and had been discussed in Britain by Lord Bullock's commission on industrial democracy set up in 1974.

However, by the time these national developments worked their way into European proposals, the political climate and sense of union ascendancy, visible in Europe especially in the first half of the 1970s had dramatically altered. The arrival of conservative governments in Britain and Germany meant that there was not the necessary support in the Council of Ministers to adopt any such laws. Anti-union hostility, reinforced ideologically by the Reagan administration in the United States, and turned into a cultural crusade by media proprietors eager themselves to reassert employer power over print and broadcasting unions, was a constant feature in many European countries in the 1980s.[19]

Three factors changed the relatively weak position of unions. The long period of growth in the second half of the 1980s (in EC member countries, 2.5 per cent in 1985, 2.6 per cent in 1986, 2.8 per cent in 1987, 3.8 per cent in 1988), marked an end to the long period of recession commencing with the first so-called oil shock in 1973. Unemployment also came down between 1986 and 1988, particularly in Britain where official (if contested by many labour market experts) figures showed a decline from 3 million unemployed to under 2 million.[20] Every EC country, with the exception of Denmark, showed an increase in employment in 1988 and 1989. This tightening of the labour market showed up in increased real wages for employed workers in the second half of the 1980s.

Increase in Real Compensation of Employees Per Head in EC 1985–1989	
1985	0.9
1986	2.3
1987	2.1
1988	1.75
1989	1.5 (estimate)

Source European Commission

Tragically high as the unemployment figures remained at the end of the 1980s, the fear of losing a job or the wholesale closures that had weakened union strength earlier in the decade had, at least for the time being, faded. Unions were winning real increases in wages for their members in addition to the reductions in working time already mentioned.

A second factor working in the unions' favour was the existence of socialist governments in France and Spain, and up to the middle of 1989 in Greece. Spanish growth far outstripped the European average and was achieved under a government of the left. The two presidential victories for François Mitterrand in 1981 and 1988 placed a roadblock across the full Thatcherization of Europe. Even in Germany, despite the longevity of the Kohl administration, powerful regional governments were held by the left in the 1980s. Socialist control of, or presence in, coalition governments in the 1980s in Italy, Belgium, Denmark, the Netherlands and Greece kept alive contacts and negotiations between government and unions in Europe when they were all but dead in Britain. Critics of the policies of Felipe Gonzalez in Spain or Mitterrand in France concluded that in both cases they had betrayed socialism and adopted Thatcherite solutions to the economic problems they confronted.[21] In Spain, trade union concern about the policies of the country's socialist government led to a rapprochement between the socialist UGT confederation and the communist Workers Commissions (CC.OO). Both unions which had been bitter rivals before and especially since the Franco era took part in a general strike protesting against the economic policies of Felipe Gonzalez. The strike, in December 1988, shut down the country. It was the biggest European general strike since the May events in France 21 years previously.

Yet the response of Gonzalez was to seek accommodation with the unions. He called for more dialogue with the unions and while insisting on his policies of growth, investment, capital accumulation, and a lessening of the corporatist structures he had inherited from Franco, made clear he was available for dialogue with the unions and that he continued to regard the UGT as a sister organization to the Socialist Party with its leaders enjoying a privileged access to the government.[22]

It is not necessary to enter into the merits of the policies adopted by Mitterrand, Gonzalez, Papandreou, or, when he headed the Italian government, the Italian socialist leader, Bettino Craxi. The point rather is that Europe in the 1980s has had a significant number of governing parties whose ideological pretensions have been of the left and which have never embraced the Thatcher–Reagan root and branch hostility towards trade unions.

A third factor, after the more favourable economic climate and the continental willingness to engage in dialogue with unions that favoured the TUC at the end of the decade, was the move towards greater European integration signified by the Single European Act, the setting of 1992 as a goal to complete the internal market, and the acceptance of a role for trade unions as part of social Europe by the European Commission president, Jacques Delors.

Jacques Delors, as minister of finance in the first socialist government in France after 1981, publicly stated that he considered himself a representative of the CFDT confederation in the government.[23] Some French socialists prefer to locate Delors in the post-war tradition of socially responsible Christian Democracy, with his presence in the French Socialist Party (which he only joined in 1973) a matter of convenience rather than socialist conviction. In the cynical view of Peter Jenkins, it was not surprising that

ostensibly socialist governments, such as in France and Spain, should be sensitive to the charge that 1992 is an out-and-out capitalist enterprise, which it is. 'Social Europe' is their morsel for workers. Everyone knows that little will come of it apart from fine-sounding declarations.[24]

Jenkins represents a London provincialism out of tune with European developments. Certainly, governments wanted unions as junior partners, as collaborators in growth, as policemen of social peace. But the very act of accepting unions, who arrived with their own priorities and analyses, inserted a factor into the elaboration of political developments that was unacceptable to the ruling Conservatives in Britain. Mrs Thatcher did not want German-type unions, or Swedish-type unions, or even Japanese-type unions. She did not want unions of any sort at all.

This was made clear in the debate around the Social Charter. The 'Community Charter of Fundamental Social Rights' – its formal title – was drawn up in 1989 and approved by the Council of Ministers that year. In a statement that did not go down well in 10 Downing Street, the leaders of the EC governments declared that

in the course of the construction of the single European market social aspects should be given the same importance as economic aspects and accordingly should be developed in a balanced fashion. . . .

The Internal Market must be achieved in a climate of close cooperation between employers and workers so that economic and social change take place in a socially acceptable manner. To this end social achievements must be preserved and economic cohesion strengthened.[25]

The communiqué noted that the EC Social Charter had been accepted by eleven out of twelve government delegations, Britain being the odd person out. Even after John Major replaced Margaret Thatcher as prime minister, the Employment Secretary, Michael Howard, insisted that Britain would continue alone amongst the twelve in rejecting and resisting the Social Charter. A distinction needs to be made between the symbolic value of the European Social Charter as acknowledging the rights of workers in Europe and the concrete proposals associated with the Charter's action programme which were criticized by some European socialist MEPs and trade unionists when they were published.[26]

Delors himself had made clear that he proposed no uniform European-wide collective bargaining model, and references to a minimum wage were dropped. References to industrial democracy were muted and each country was left to develop its own system under three broad headings – the German model of co-determination, the southern European model of joint management–worker works councils, or the British model of consultation and voluntary collective bargaining between employers and unions.

BEYOND THE SOCIAL CHARTER – THE WEAKNESS OF PAN-EUROPEAN UNION ORGANIZATION

The excitement over the Social Charter had provided a favourable wind for the becalmed vessel of the TUC, as well as other unions in Europe, but it was a wind that could not last forever, nor was it so powerful as to replace the need for the TUC, and other British unions, to re-think their organizational and bargaining strategies in the light of the growing importance of Europe.

For some labour movement theoreticians, the challenge of Europe and the new economic and social relations developed in the decades since the end of the Second World War required a cultural change of immense proportions. A world based on the principles of efficiency, hard work, and self-denial has been replaced by one in which self-fulfilment reigns supreme. 'Responsibility for others is replaced by responsibility for oneself', writes Rainer Zoll, the German sociologist. Moreover, adds Zoll,

If the European trade unions do not want to become corporast associations representing only restricted groups of relatively protected workers they must accept the fact of social and cultural differentiation of the working class; on the one hand an extreme differentiation of social structure including, for example, the unemployed, the marginalized and well-paid engineers, and, on the other hand an extreme cultural differentiation between workers attached to the old model of self-denial and those searching for self-fulfilment.[27]

The demand for a new unionism corresponding to the re-composing workforce, the increase in part-time work, the needs of women workers and the impact of the informatics revolution on work organization were further common themes dominating most European union debates in the late 1980s.

Although unions called for greater European activity there was little evidence that they were willing to undergo the internal changes necessary to bring this about. The involvement of the European Commission in the Social Charter debate reinforced the search for a corporatist solution in which the European Commission took over the role of British government as a partner for the TUC. Necessary and valuable as contact with governing authorities may be for the power and prestige of unions, the real strength of any trade union movement resides equally in the pressure it can exert on employers from the base and, linked to this, the quality of its organizing, propaganda, bargaining and research staff.

On both counts the evidence was that British and other European unions were not willing to go through the necessary radical changes to deal with Europe. The European trade union secretariats were woefully under-financed and under-staffed. At the ETUC, fewer than ten full-time secretariat officials were expected to cover the enormous range of issues regularly placed on the ETUC agenda by the TUC and other European trade union confederations.

There are an estimated 10,000 lobbyists in Brussels working to present a company perspective to the officials of the European Commission. Against them the European Metalworkers Federation, which proclaimed itself the co-ordinating body for some 8 million metalworkers in the Community, had a general secretary, his assistant and two typists. Bruno Trentin, the Harvard-educated general secretary of the left-wing CGIL confederation in Italy suggested that unions should consider transferring certain of their functions to European union secretariats. In Trentin's view 'each national union should give up, consciously and constitutionally, part of its power, delegating it to a body which would be answerable for its own actions to national union structures'.[28]

There was no formal response from other European union leaders to the Italian suggestion though the Danish LO has called for 'more resources – finances, premises and personnel . . . for the European trade union organisations'.[29] The practical Danes were right. A transfusion of more than power was necessary if the woefully under-staffed and under-financed European union organizations were effectively to co-ordinate union activities. The high-quality, multi-lingual and dedicated staff working in the European union bodies have found themselves stretched hard to take initiatives beyond their basic duties of organizing meetings, adopting resolutions, and arranging seminars and the occasional demonstration. All this was worthwhile and symbolic but hardly amounted to a real demonstration of trade union power at the supra-national level.

At the heart of the problem lay the question of sovereignty and the pyramidical organization of unions. Transnational contacts have been jealously guarded by union leaderships partly as a perk of office, though this is much less the case today when trips to Brussels, Frankfurt or Milan no longer carry the same cachet as once upon a time a trip abroad did.[30] Nonetheless, whereas middle-rank union officials are free to decide to travel hundreds of kilometers within their national boundaries in pursuit of their business, any trip to the continent, even if the same time and expense and distance is involved, usually requires sanctioning at the highest level.

Another problem is the political sensitivity of transnational contacts. Ever since 1920, when Lenin split the international trade union movement, contacts between unions in different countries have been bedevilled by political rivalries. International union federations have demanded that their affiliates do not enter into organizational relationships with unions who belong to rival internationals. Often this has been described as a trade union Cold War and the principal source of rivalry has indeed been between socialist and communist unions. Not always appreciated in Britain, where the all-embracing politics of the TUC was held up as a model in contrast to the sectarian continentals, was the deep rivalry in some countries between socialist and christian trade unions.

The collapse of communist régimes in East Europe opened the possibility that international communist trade union organization, and a specific communist trade union profile in opposition to democratic socialist unions would fade away as a mechanism dividing unions in Europe.

The way then was open to much greater horizontal linkages between workers in Europe and the obvious way to achieve this was to bring together workers employed by the same company operating in different countries.

EUROPEAN WORKS COUNCILS

Some efforts had been made to create European-wide company councils in the 1980s. In one form or another, councils existed in companies such as Ford, General Motors, Thomson, Unilever, Carnaud, Gillette, Airbus and Nestlé. The organization, powers and rights of these councils varied considerably. Some, such as in the car industry, had been set up by the International Metalworkers Federation and were restricted only to federation affiliates, thus excluding the communist CGT in France and the communist CC.OOs (Workers Commissions) in Spain. General Motors and Ford refused to recognize these bodies. Others set up in French-based European firms were sanctioned by management but remained only consultative bodies, obtaining no more information than what French legislation provided for.

Workers at Airbus Industrie, for example, the pan-European consortium which assembles Airbus planes, were unable to get recognition for a works council at Toulouse as the French-based management refused to accept that it should deal with a joint committee representing workers from different countries. A complicated legal case ensued based on the precise status and obligations under French law of Airbus Industrie but if ever there was one European firm whose employees might claim common European representative rights it was the producers of the European Airbus. Their difficulties highlighted the extent to which pan-European works councils uniting employees in the same firm were very much at an early embryonic stage, if they existed at all. Employers showed no desire to help the embryos grow into lusty life. In the case of Unilever, the company refused claims for representation at a European level so British unions wrote to the European Commission asking for their intervention. Again, it was an appeal to the top rather than effective pressure from the base that was brought into play. Certainly, by the end of the 1980s no European works council had secured negotiating rights.

Despite company opposition such European works councils are the logical way forward but certain major obstacles remain. Firstly, the nominating body for delegates may be either the workforce or the union. If the former, then the union loses its valued control over international contacts. If the latter, then the direct and necessary workforce-to-workforce linkages may be taken over by a full-time union bureaucracy.

A second obstacle is the administration and cost of such European workers' councils. If more than two or three languages are used then translation and interpretation costs can easily run into several thousands of pounds. Few British unions have multi-lingual officials staffing a vibrant, well-resourced international department and the brave efforts of some officials to learn a foreign language does not provide the background technical knowledge necessary to be completely at home in industrial relations, bargaining, accounting and other concepts and jargon used by different groups of workers and unions in Europe.

Important possibilities have nonetheless been opened by the technology of electronics communications. Faxes and electronic mail installed by unions in every factory or workplace of a European firm could permit instant communication between workers on questions of production, hours, subcontracting, terms of employment and use of short-term or temporary employees as well as pay-rates. In West Germany, the General Motors works council has drawn up a one-page set of data to be filled in every two months by all GM factories in Europe. It requires no complicated translation and would provide a European picture of GM operations from a union perspective. Such Euro-union networking has its own momentum and leaves management less able to impose its divide-and-rule tactics upon different sets of workers in the different European countries. Even if European-wide collective bargaining is unlikely given national legal and bargaining traditions there are common strands of mobilization on working time, controlling overtime and temporary work, women's rights and child care which would benefit from instant linkages between workers at the company level, rather than delayed notification by circular from union head offices.

The basic political question of whether vertically organized, hierarchical structures exemplified by existing trade unions can adapt to horizontal networking based on open communication has of course not been solved. A reform of trade unions in terms of structure, organizational practice and public profile had been discussed by many activists, union leaders and theoreticians in Britain in the 1980s. The growing realization of the creation of a European capitalism and the Social Charter proposals have meant that the TUC and British unions have to grapple with the twin needs of increased international work not in terms of declamatory resolutions but as an extension of basic union representation, organization and bargaining and of Britain's political place in a Europe undergoing closer integration and major upheavals in its eastern half.

In 1980, it was possible to look at the TUC and Europe under three headings. At the *political* level, the TUC opposed EEC membership. At the *institutional* level, the TUC participated in European union bodies. At the *organizational* level, British unions did little to link up with their opposite numbers on the continent to form European-wide bodies to confront employers. By 1990, politics, institutional activity and organizational demands were all pushing in the same direction. It was one of the most significant changes in British trade unionism this century. The impact of Europe had thus changed British trade unionism and opened up the potential for major advances.

NOTES AND REFERENCES

The author would like to thank Peter Coldrick and David Foden for their comments.

1.   H. Pelling, *A History of Trade Unionism,* Penguin, London, in its 1976 edition, makes no reference to Europe. Nor does Lord McCarthy's, *Trade Unions,* Penguin, London, 1976, also a standard collection of readings. K. Coates and T. Topham in their *Trade Unions in Britain,* Spokesman, Nottingham, 1989, have a useful chapter on the TUC's international activity and describes briefly aspects of European unionism.

2.   W. Kendall, *The Labour Movement in Europe,* Allen Lane, London, 1975 and A. Carew, *Democracy and Government in European Trade Unions,* Allen and Unwin, London, 1976, are two examples. One problem with such books is that the organizations, structures, policies and personalities they describe can change quite rapidly in a short space of time.

3.   The phrase is Ben Pimlott's, used to describe Hugh Dalton and Ernest Bevin in his *The Political Diary of Hugh Dalton, 1918–1940, 1945–1960,* Cape, London, 1986, p. 425, but it sums up the attitude of that and succeeding generations of Labour Party and TUC leaders.

4.   M. Newman, *Socialism and European Unity. The Dilemma of the Left in Britain and France,* Junction Books, London, 1983, p. 278.

5.   Ibid., p. 279.

6.   D. MacShane, *French Lessons for Labour,* Fabian Society, London, 1986, p. 5.

7.   *London Review of Books,* 17 August, 1989.

8.   They are well listed in G. Brown, *Where there is greed . . . Margaret Thatcher and the Betrayal of Britain's Future,* Mainstream, London, 1989.

9.   L. Lorwin, *The International Labor Movement,* Harper, New York, 1953, p. 339.

10. See G. Busch, *The Political Role of International Trade Unions,* Macmillan, London, 1985, and D. MacShane, *International Labour and the Origins of the Cold War,* (forthcoming).

11. ETUC attitudes towards communist unions are covered in B. Barnouin, *The European Labour Movement and European Integration,* Pinter, London, 1986, pp. 24–40.

12. See D. MacShane, 'Eastern Europe and Trade Unions' in *International Labour Report,* July 1990 and D. MacShane, 'Workers of the World Unite' in *History Today,* September 1990.

13. See R. Munck, *The New International Labour Studies,* Zed, London, 1988 and P. Waterman, *For a New Labour Internationalism,* The Hague, 1984.

14. See, for example, C. Leadbetter, 'A convoluted path to non-unionism', *Financial Times,* 9 June 1989 or D. Felton, 'Unions' backs to the wall', *Independent,* 7 July 1987. However, analyses common in the mid-1980s that Britain was entering a strike-free era, looked dated not long afterwards as ambulance workers, railway workers, BBC staff, dockers, London Underground staff and engineers went on strike for varying reasons and with varying effect. Unions were weaker than a decade before but writing of their marginalization or an end to strikes in Britain seemed premature.

15. On this see J. Palmer, *Europe without America? The Crisis in Atlantic Relations,* OUP, Oxford, 1987.

16. *Financial Times,* 9 June 1989.

17. See R. Hyman, 'Reflections on the Mining Strike' in *The Socialist Register 1985–86,* Merlin, London, 1986.

18. W. McCarthy, *The Future of Industrial Democracy,* Fabian Society, London, 1988.

19. An account of the extremely limited European legislation in favour of workers up to 1988 can be found in the European Trade Union Institute's report, *The Social Dimension of the Internal Market: Workers' Rights in European Companies,* ETUI, Brussels, 1988. As the author laconically notes 'such legislation remains to this day extremely thin on the ground', p. 29.

20. All figures are taken from the European Trade Union Institute's report, *Collective Bargaining in Western Europe in 1988 and Prospects for 1989,* ETUI, Brussels, 1989.

21. See D. Singer, *Is Socialism Doomed? The Meaning of Mitterrand,* Oxford University Press, New York, 1988.

22.　See 'Gobierno y sindicatos empiezan a negociar la politica de empleo', *El Pais,* 12 January 1990.

23.　Jacques Delors quoted in H. Hamon and P. Rotman, *La deuxième gauche. Histoire intellectuelle et politique de la CFDT,* Seuil, Paris, 1984, p. 344.

24.　*The Independent,* 7 March 1989.

25.　European Council Communiqué, Madrid, 27 June 1989.

26.　See, for example, Christine Crawley MEP in *Tribune,* 17 November 1989.

27.　R. Zoll, 'European Unions and the New Individualism' (Unpublished paper presented at the Warwick University symposium, 'Industrial Relations and the European Community', March 1989.)

28.　B. Trentin, CGIL general secretary quoted in *Labour Research,* August 1989, p. 5.

29.　'The Internal Market and the Social Dimension. The Position, Objectives and Strategy of the Danish Trade Union Movement', LO, Copenhagen, 1989, p. 31.

30.　The author became a member of the NUJ's National Executive Committee in 1974. Older members of the NUJ executive used to call the union's International Committee the 'outings committee'.

16 Unions and Labour in the 1980s and 1990s

Philip Bassett

In the faded gilt splendour of Blackpool's Winter Gardens, a peculiar drama was played out. It rocketed around the TV and radio bulletins, raced its way across newspapers, and ricocheted throughout the Labour Party and the trade unions. It was a direct and searing clash between the party leader, Neil Kinnock, and the party's largest trade union, the Transport and General Workers'. Nominally, it wasn't actually *about* much. Kinnock – once a firebrand left-winger, now the best manager of the party in recent times – was delivering his annual party conference speech to the 1988 Labour gathering. His team of young, smooth, professional aides were pleased with it; it was very much in line with the modernizing Labour Party, reaching out primarily through the medium of television to try to claw Labour back towards electability after its shattering electoral defeats in 1983 and 1987. Kinnock was due to speak in mid-afternoon. But hours before he even rose to his feet, his thunder was being stolen in the most forceful and difficult way imaginable. Ron Todd, the general secretary of the TGWU, was to speak the same day at a rally organized by the Labour left newspaper *Tribune*. The coincidence was just that: the paper's rallies were normally later in the week, but had unusually been brought forward. Even so, the TGWU seized its opportunity. The left-led union had been growing increasingly distant from the Labour leadership as Kinnock's pragmatism – or to his critics in the party, his rightward scuttle – became ever more dominant. Warnings had been filtered through in private; now the warning cones were to be hoisted in public. Todd's speech that evening, when it came, was almost an afterthought to its impact: in telling, acid language – the speech had been drafted by a researcher from Transport House, who was castigated about it so violently by Labour insiders (including being showered, Judas-like, by thirty silver coins) and the press that he hurriedly left town – Todd launched into the style of socialism favoured by the filofax-ferrying young turks now clustering around Kinnock. Journalists had received advance copies of the speech – then working for the *Financial Times,* I was given one an hour or so before lunch – and word had got to Kinnock's aides. Their first reaction to the TGWU general secretary's planned remarks was uncharacteristically misplaced: it doesn't matter, it doesn't count, who listens to dinosaurs like the T&G now, Neil's speech is the *real* meat. They were wrong. What actually counted, not just as a news story but as a much deeper indicator of current strains in the Labour Party, was neither Kinnock's nor Todd's speeches in isolation – but the *interplay* of the two. What was important about the incident was how it seemed to touch upon one of the fundamental elements of the party – the relationship between the unions, which founded it, and the political party itself – and how that relationship both was and is changing.

That the relationship *has* changed, and perhaps changed quite fundamentally, is now clear. As the 1990s opened, the implicit deal between the unions and Labour looked substantially different to how it had looked not just a decade earlier, but throughout most of the 1980s. With Labour's poll fortunes soaring, and union membership numbers still in decline, the power relationship which had characterized the deal was all but completely reversed. Control was with the party – more particularly, the party leadership around Neil Kinnock. A far cry from the unions' overweening presence in the 1970s, they now knew their place – and that place was markedly different. Achieved, largely unseen, by a combination of organization, persuasion, hard work, stealth, indifference, hard-facedness and careful, urgent politics, the change looked at once to be a major unsung achievement for the party, and to have far-reaching implications for future relations, especially if Labour were to be elected to Government at the next general election.

LABOUR-UNION RELATIONS IN THE 1980s

Labour's links with the unions are strong, and deep. They are firmly rooted. But they are not constant. They are not removed from change. They have served the party, over the years, both well and ill at different times. They give it strength, and solidity. They give it income, and organization. They give it pain, and trouble too, not necessarily in equal portion, or with equal effect. When general elections come round, it is the unions – or at least, the handful which are the *real* Labour paymasters, like the TGWU, the GMB and NUPE – which dig into their coffers (under particular strain in the 1980s as membership continued to fall while employment, the unions' recruiting market, grew) to get Labour's show to a point not where it can compete financially with the Conservative Party, but where it is at least on the electoral road. Despite the opportunity for Conservative gibes which that funding leaves open, it's hard to imagine Labour functioning (especially at election times) without it. In that sense, and repeated almost endlessly at regional and constituency level, the impact of the unions on the party is hugely beneficial to Labour. But what of the other end? What of the negative impact? What of the damaging political body blows which the unions can and do rain down on the party?

The industrial action in 1978–79 is only the largest and most telling example, with the most long-term impact. Some left-wing union leaders still try to reallocate responsibility for what happened in those strikes. They point – with some justification – to a particularly ill-informed, maladroit and ill-judged decision by the Labour Cabinet in 1978 to set a pay policy ceiling at 5 per cent after a number of years of tight incomes policy pay restrictions, and in the knowledge that Labour's largest union, the TGWU, had already set its course at its biennial conference the previous year on a return to wholly unfettered collective bargaining, against the passionate advice of its then-leader, Jack Jones. They point as well to what was to them an irritating misjudgement by Jim Callaghan, then the Prime Minister, not to go for an election in autumn 1978. Both points have a clear validity: but they pale beside the impact of what the *unions* did over the following months. The extent and impact of the range of the industrial action over that winter unquestionably sealed Labour's fate, and were the harbingers for the changes in social, economic and most importantly, political climate which followed and which taken together had such a devastating impact on unions – their membership, size, structures, finances, power and indeed their very existence – in the 1980s.

So if the interlinking of unions and the Labour Party has had its plus and minus points for both parties, then inevitably, the effects of Labour's opposition years in the 1980s and within them, the electoral and operational irrelevance of the party – in particular in the early and mid-parts of the decade – have brought about change in the Labour–union relationship. Informal contact – the relationships which Labour leaders build up over time with key figures in the trade unions; relations at which both sides traditionally work hard and which can be highly productive – are traditionally, though privately, the most effective method by which either side brings its demands and wishes to bear on the other. That relationship was formalized in 1972 with the formation of the TUC-Labour Party Liaison Committee, which brought together representatives of the unions and the party and which became a key instrument for delivering the economic restraint the Labour government wanted and the legislative changes the unions sought.

With the advent of opposition for Labour, little changed – at first. TUC and Labour Party meetings continued regularly, were serviced regularly, produced shopping lists of economic and legislative demands regularly. Labour and union leaders genuinely believed at the time – hard though it seems now to credit it – that a Conservative government was an aberration, that there was a real prospect of Labour returning to power at the next

election. The sheer scale of Labour's defeat in 1983 – the party's worst-ever
general election result – started the long process of bringing both Labour
and the unions to terms with the new economic, social and political realities.
Their own interrelationship was part of that. Significantly, the TUC's key
distillation of the post-83 election 'new realism', a document called TUC
Strategy, contained virtually nothing about the unions' Labour aspects.
Significantly too, it was that, rather than its stringent analysis of union
ills (all of which worsened subsequently), which allowed left-wingers in
the trade unions to damn it. Nevertheless, the TUC Strategy document
was an important step in the process of bringing the unions to terms with
the fact that no longer could they be an arm of government, particularly
a government which no longer existed: writing briefs, analysing events,
putting up ideas, acting as though they were a research arm for a Labour
administration. Even so, the enfeebling of formal links between Labour
and the unions still took time. Meetings of the Labour liaison committee
still happened, though at less regular intervals, and there was still some
semblance of internal importance vested in them by the party and the
unions. Gradually, though, as the decade wore on, and especially after
the 1987 election defeat, their value became increasingly questionable, and
their function increasingly moribund.

Hardly surprising: when it came down to it, what could each side
provide for the other? Labour could offer not much but future promises
of legislation, of rolling back the changes in the law which the Conservatives
were introducing. But as the Conservatives' years in office grew, as their
programme of legislation lengthened, the prospect of simply reversing what
had taken place grew increasingly impracticable. Employment law alone
provided a daunting corpus to flip back: five major acts of Parliament. What
also changed, though, was the perception of the Conservatives' legislation:
the view that parts of it – perhaps large parts of it – were of benefit to
employee relations in Britain, and to trade unions more particularly. Not
only would wholesale repeal of the Conservative legislation be of questionable value to industrial relations, not only would doing so not attract the
support and backing of all union members, let alone those not in unions, but
it would do nothing to help, and might well even damage, Labour's election
prospects – which, as the period in opposition stretched longer and longer,
were becoming for Neil Kinnock's Labour leadership *the* crucial objective
for everything the party, including its affiliate unions, did. As far as the
Conservatives were concerned, trade unions overreaching themselves were,
at the start of the decade, both the mechanism by which they came to power,
and one of the principal problems they had to resolve once they were there.

Legislation to lance the boil, as they saw it, was therefore both inevitable,
and had to come early. Equally inevitable, therefore, was that Labour would
take the Conservatives' employment law changes as an early target for
change for a future Labour government. But as the range of moves by

the Tory administration started to unfold itself, other priorities began to emerge: with the value of reversing employment law issues questionable in itself, the need for Labour to look to other Conservative changes became much stronger. Employment law started to slip down the shopping list. The position was further complicated, too, by the inability of Labour and the unions to agree a programme with which to replace it. For much of the decade, many of the sensitive areas of employment legislation were avoided by the party and the unions. What to do about secondary picketing, about union recognition? Don't know. Don't do anything, then. By the beginning of the 1990s, that was changing – but only because Labour had realized that there were many aspects of employment law policy which were real electoral beartraps. Fresh in the mind of many in the party was the 1987 general election campaign. The Conservatives' first party election broadcast tried to play the union card: to the stirring strains of Holst on the soundtrack, the film wove skilfully together old newsreel clips from the Battle of Britain in 1940 with shots from the winter of discontent – rubbish piling up in Leicester Square, bodies not being buried in Liverpool. Apart from the logical inconsistency of the attempt – how could the Conservatives claim the unions still to be a problem, when much of the Government's rhetoric of achievement was precisely that its employment legislation had 'solved' the union problem – it simply didn't click: it didn't grip the public, or even the politicians, as an electoral issue. Poll evidence on problems facing Britain put the trade union issue at 1–2 per cent, at the very bottom of the pile. Or at least it didn't click until part-way through the second of the three-week campaign, when in a television interview Kinnock merely re-stated then-current Labour policy on secondary action – to the immediate and hostile chorus of Labour-sanctions-return-of-mob-picket-rule.

For the unions' part, what had they to give? Not much – and as the decade wore on, not seen by the electorate to be much. From being a plus point for Labour – Labour is the only party which can work with the unions, went the line, resting on the implicit assumption that a party *had* to be able to work with the unions – the unions had distinctly become a minus. Essentially, delivering pay restraint had proved in 1978–79 to be a pipedream. The Conservative government actively wanted no truck with the unions; no deals; no meetings with Ministers; no beer and sandwiches at No 10. But Labour found that not only couldn't the unions deliver anything on pay, the party didn't much want them to: the benefit of approaching, crab-like, a cloudily-worded so-called deal with the unions, called different things like National Economic Assessment and other titles but essentially circling wordily and warily around the idea of pay restaint, was more often that not outweighed both by the difficulty and embarrassment of getting it (plane-loads of English union general secretaries and outriders from the Labour leadership on selling trips to the Scottish TUC to make sure the ball was started running right down through the spring union conference season to slam home at the autumn TUC and party gatherings), and when it had finally been agreed, the likely exposure of it to forensic ridicule by opposing politicians and smart-alec TV journalists, picking holes in its wording, thinking and rationale.

NO BEER AND SANDWICHES

Neither side, then, had much to offer the other in concrete terms. But the working deal between Labour and the unions was still on, still in place. The promise was still there: money for us, preferment for you. But what was clearly happening, particularly as the final election of the 1980s began to loom, was a clear shift in that bargain – a shift which favoured the party, and especially Kinnock, and under which union preferment was essentially implicit: your best chance of advance lies in *our* chance of advance. So stick by us, do what we do, do what we say, and you'll then be well placed for whatever's going, come victory. *Not* a shopping list of demands. *Not* us paying supposed debts. Just: your chances aren't bad, but all you can do is take them when they come, not lay down what they are. In other words, the beginnings of a redefinition of a relationship. It couldn't, of course, be done overtly. Formally, publicly, what was said was clear and constant: Labour is rooted in the unions, we've always been together, we always will be together.

That line was helped by Labour's choice of employment spokesmen during the period: both John Prescott and Michael Meacher were keen to preserve the traditional party-union links in the traditional way. Many, if not most, of their policy proposals in this area reflected that view. Neither was felt in the Kinnock camp to be not just a safe enough bet on the subject, but the right kind of bet; and from the unions' part, the by-now dominant new realist strain at the top of trade union councils had its doubts not about Prescott and Meacher's honesty, integrity or commitment, but about whether or not the lines they were pursuing were sending out the right signals – to Kinnock, to union members, to non-union employees, to employers, to the electorate. The Prescott–Meacher traditionalism had its awkwardnesses – at one party conference fringe meeting, for example, when Meacher was running the line that a future Labour government would insist on union recognition being granted by employers when unions could show a membership of 50+ per cent, one senior Labour advisor grunted dourly and said: 'This lad's got a *lot* of reading to do' – but its value was in sending out the comforting signals that the *union* traditionalists needed, that in a changing world, the Labour party was still their home, their base, their power block, still the area where – if nowhere much else – they *counted*.

Behind the rhetoric, it wasn't much like that. Occasionally, little glimpses of the real agenda poked out: a chance remark here, a quote in an interview there, as some senior Kinnockite politician or advisor, on or more usually off the record, suggested that there just might perhaps not be all that much value to Labour in continuing to hitch its wagon solely to an institution, the unions, whose social stock seemed to be falling so rapidly, whose place in their own market – employment – seemed to be increasingly *less* secure, *less* powerful, *less* important. These wider points combined with some narrow facts: with the departure of Bryan Stanley, the burly right-wing ex-NCU general secretary, from Kinnock's office, there were few if any people around the leader who even knew much about the unions, let alone cared about them or respected them.

That led to mistakes. The Kinnock camp couldn't easily have it both ways: no, the unions don't matter, who needs them? – and then when they discovered they did, they didn't know the form, didn't know how to swing things, didn't know enough about the union structures to get things done. Take as one example the one-member-one-vote drive. Following the 1987 election defeat, Kinnock's attachment to this as both policy and principle was made manifest in a resonantly clear desire from those around him that the unions should swing behind the policy in order to get it through the party conference. There wasn't much briefing on this. There wasn't much contact. It was just generally known that this-is-what-Neil-wants. It was duly delivered, even in the most hostile of environments, like the TGWU, where ironically enough it went through simply because the then-chairman of the union's general executive council, the pro-Kinnock Brian Nicholson, voted for it on the executive, and then voted for it again using his chairman's casting vote – providing by two votes executive support for a one-member-one-vote policy which then got through the TGWU's notoriously difficult biennial conference. But even close Kinnock supporters in the unions were irritated. 'We'll do it for him', said one at the time. 'Of course we will. But he bloody well could have come and *asked* us – not just expected it would be done.' The difficult balancing act being performed by the Kinnock group with the unions – wanting some things, but at arm's length – was helped by close working, not so much at general secretary·level, but by a key group of young Kinnockite officers at research and similar levels, who knew each other well personally and professionally, and who managed by virtue of that personal contact to get things done, easing deftly round some of the personal and structural problems that sometimes reared their heads higher up in both the party and the unions.

The new Labour–union relationship was most graphically presented in the 1987 general election. Fund-raising within the unions for Labour had been erratic throughout the decade. The principal mechanism, called Tulv (Trade Unions for a Labour Victory) had been riven by factional political differences, and had badly split. But the experience of the political fund ballots campaign, in which the unions geared themselves to meeting the overtly party political and unfair challenge of a section of the otherwise-valuable Trade Union Act 1984, was important. Driven by a political imperative from Norman Tebbit, then the Employment Secretary, this part of the Act required unions with political funds – repositories under law for the political levy payments which in many unions form part of their subscriptions – to ballot their members on whether they wanted them to continue. With questionable legitimacy, Tebbit was using a piece of Government legislation for obviously party political purposes – aiming clearly at reducing, or even ending, Labour's source of funding in the unions. In what was one of their few real unarguable successes of the 1980s, the unions met the challenge head on – and defeated it roundly. Not only did all the unions involved retain their political funds, but some others which had never before had them successfully balloted their members to establish them. Some of the experience, discipline and rigour of this campaign was translated to direct Labour fund-raising when Tulv was replaced by Trade Unionists for Labour (Tufl). This managed to prompt and co-ordinate fund-raising more successfully than its predecessor, though its stark assessment after the election still showed that the political donations from unions for the campaign had not measured up to their promises. But even with this shortfall, the unions financially had just about managed to do what they had always done for Labour: to come to the aid of the party.

So that part of the relationship was still in place. In addition, Labour's campaigns directorate made great use of union organization, which not only was better on the ground than that of the party (or in some cases, at least existed where Labour's in practice didn't), but – a major plus as far as the leadership was concerned – was less likely to be in the hands of committed leftists who, despite the public purges of the 1980s, still held sway in many constituency parties and who would be less likely to be in sympathy with the Kinnockite reforming drive. This use of union resources – people, offices, equipment – ran at all levels: from injecting able pro-Kinnock officials into Labour's Walworth Road headquarters to assist actively in the campaign unit, to using cars provided by one particular union to ferry around senior party campaigners.

What clearly wasn't in place, what was clearly different, was the traditional quid pro quo. Previously, teams of union officials had been out in elections, banging the drum for Labour on a succession of public platforms, standing alongside the Parliamentary spokespeople, standing alongside the party leaders, raising their profile, being seen with people who at the very least had the opportunity to win power, even if it wasn't realizable. Not this time. Look for the unions in Labour's 1987 election campaign, and you look in vain: few appearances, few speeches – even by union leaders (largely right-wingers) thought to be sufficiently modern, presentable, Kinnockite, like John Edmonds of the GMB general union, Brenda Dean of the print union Sogat 82, Bill Jordan of the AEU engineering union. The implication was clear: what the new Labour party *didn't* want was the old-style party-union relationship actualized – there in practice, there on platforms, there in speeches. Remodelled Labour saw the unions as a positive disadvantage. The hope was that they could at best be neutralized, turned into an electoral factor which had no impact one way or the other. The realization – hard though it was for the unions to take it, particularly when they were still being asked to dig for Labour into their backpockets, already hit hard by the spiralling down of union membership throughout the decade – was that they couldn't ever be turned into an electoral plus in the Thatcher climate.

That balance, *that* change was what the Labour–union relationship had become – and was a clear indicator of the direction it was likely to take in the future. Its strains, for some unions, were great: Ron Todd's Filofax speech was a perfect manifestation of some of them. For others, though, they weren't. Few union leaders enjoyed an untrammelled relationship with Neil Kinnock, particularly during the period over the summer of 1988 when he was, or was believed to be, at his most bunkered, his most aggressive, his most depressed. Even those who were on all fours with the new Labour Party vision of the future union relationship muttered privately that they found him difficult at times, inaccessible, quick to anger. But as the resurgence in Labour's fortunes continued, as the policy review – largely driven by a key union figure, Tom Sawyer from the NUPE public employees' union – proved to be not only an effective bridging mechanism from the 1987 defeat to the sharp rise in Labour's fortunes by the end of the decade but also an instrument for real policy change in some major areas, especially defence, so Kinnock's own confidence and performance seemed to return. With it came renewed and now quite fundamental revaluations of the union relationship that seemed to set the course for the two sides into the 1990s.

CHANGE IN THE RELATIONSHIP

Neil Kinnock's dissatisfaction with the way Labour ran itself increased, ironically enough, in exact relationship with his control over it. When Kinnock took over the leadership, most of the principal mechanisms of the party – and especially the national executive – were opposed to the leadership line. By the end of the decade, most issues – even the most contentious ones – were rolling through the executive with only two votes (Dennis Skinner and Tony Benn) consistently against the leadership. The revolution on the NEC, after sustained work by Kinnock and the leadership team, was an achievement both extensive and extraordinary. Much of the leverage for that change came through the trade union votes on the NEC; the core of Kinnock's loyalists lay there. Not having to worry about voting on the NEC allowed Kinnock a freedom of manoeuvre not enjoyed by any of his recent predecessors (none had put in the effort to achieve it, either). But important though that was, it wasn't enough.

The problem of the Conference needed to be addressed. At the heart of the annual Labour Conference lay a two-fold difficulty, made much worse by the now-largescale impact of television and the need to make the fullest use possible of televized conference coverage in order to present the party to the electorate – not as a party wracked by doubt, division and debate (the natural TV impression of a party conference spending its time discussing policy), but as a party presenting via the TV camera a smooth, homogeneous, polished and, above all, attractive face.

The Conference problem was and is interlinked. Both the constituent voting parts of the Conference – representing affiliated unions and con- stituency parties – were, in different ways, highly unsatisfactory in the way they operated. On the one hand, the CLPs were active, vocal, questionably representative of local Labour voting – as opposed to party constituency activist – opinion, often opposed to the leadership line, a bastion of the left. However, for many in the party, the CLPs at Conference were the only available method of trying to keep a restraining hand of socialist principle on a leadership which to this point of view seemed hell-bent on abandoning it. Inevitably, they'd be outvoted, but they could at least make their point in front of the very TV cameras the leadership so wanted to exploit to make a rather different impact. Equally inevitably, it was hardly surprising that the leadership should find this an unacceptable state of affairs. Time and again, policy proposals put forward by constituency delegates were battered back by the union section, which controlled 90 per cent of the Conference's votes. Time and again this saved the leadership. The paradox remains, of course, that the very mechanism by which this salvation was repeatedly delivered was one about which the leadership had real reservations, and was one which looked particularly bad on TV for the new, modernized Labour Party: the block vote.

Arguments about the block vote within the Labour Party are far from new. Far from simple, either. Of course, there are simple views about it. Proponents of the block vote system – under which individual trade unions have available a large number of votes based on the numbers of affiliation fee-members they choose to declare, regardless of their actual membership size or of the numbers of their members who pay the political levy – simply say it should stay, that it is wholly in line with the Labour Party's tradition and practice of representative democracy, reaching decisions which are both collective and collectively adhered to. Opponents of the system argue that it is inherently undemocratic, that votes of enormous size are cast on behalf of people who either have no or little say in reaching the decisions which they are meant to reflect, or worse, are utterly unaware of the moves being taken in their names because of inefficient representative systems within individual trade unions. Pragmatists steer some way between these poles. For them, the block vote has both values and liabilities: it operates as a moderating bulwark against excesses, of either the left or the right, but it does present one of Labour's more obviously unattractive faces. It keeps the hot-heads in place, but at the price of handing large amounts of power to grey men – usually men – in the unions. Politically, arguments against the block vote are seen by many as suspicious: at best, that they come from the Labour right. At worst, they are seen as key anti-Labour vehicles from Conservatives, or worse still, from ex-SDP leaders, who were seen as largely benefitting from the block vote when they were still in Labour, and only started to castigate it when they had left, when it no longer offered them any protection or advancement.

Gradually, though, the variegated and near-static raft of positions on the block vote began to shift in the late eighties. The key to it was a new initiative to expand greatly Labour's *actual* membership, rather than the paper membership as exemplified by both the union block votes and the CLPs' arithmetic base. Against the background of the successful Conservative emphasis in its employment legislation on the primacy of actual trade union members rather than their supposedly representative structures of leadership, a new emphasis was placed by then-rising Labour stars like Gordon Brown on the idea of a *mass* party with a much larger number of real, participating members. After years of seeing actual party membership bucket along in the low hundred thousands, what was being suggested here was not much less than a wholesale revolution: that Labour's structural, financial, organizational and operational problems – to say nothing of improving dramatically its electoral chances by solidifying as far as was possible a guaranteed, committed, sizeable popular vote – could all be substantially eased, and perhaps even all but resolved, by the simple expedient of more people joining. An evangelical-style recruiting drive, then. Labour adopted the idea, and though initial results of the drive were far from wholly encouraging, its implications are extensive.

If Labour manages to increase substantially its individual membership, its impact on the Conference problem – and therefore, on the very heart of the Labour–union relationship – will be of a large order. Take first the constituencies. Traditionally, each constituency Labour party is assumed to have at least 1,000 members for voting purposes. This gives the CLPs a total of up to 653,000 deployable votes. With actual membership at the beginning of the 1990s at less than 300,000, this is clearly a gross *over*-representation. If real party membership were to more than treble, to around the 1m mark, where would that leave the representative position of the CLPs? Given the low attendance at local Labour Party meetings, it is highly questionable that the CLPs should simply absorb the expanded votes represented by the increased individual membership to which the constituencies have, by and large, contributed little to obtain: increased individual membership was very much a drive promoted from and carried out by the Labour Party centre.

Take, too, the unions. With an expanded individual membership, their claim to represent aggregated individuals becomes even less credible, particularly since the chosen route to individual membership is through attractive subscription rates for union members and is being carried out in great part by union, rather than party, organizers. The crucial question, unresolved at the start of the 1990s and probably likely to remain unapproached until – or if – the idea of a mass membership starts to look like becoming a reality, is how that mass membership would be reflected within the Labour decision-and policy-making machinery. Partly, of course, that depends on what that machinery is by the time a mass party was reached – policy commissions, rolling policy programmes, biennial conferences, whatever. Representative reflection, by means of either the union or the constituency votes, seems largely inappropriate, and might even be wholly inimical to the very idea of mass, individual membership. Balloting is impracticable: on large, single issues – possibly. But on the range of policy and constitutional issues likely to come before Labour at any one time, balloting would either be impossible, or would move swiftly towards the possibility of endemic corruption through low turnouts, leaving as with both the CLP and union block votes, a nominally representative vote in effect in the hands of committed activists.

But despite such important questions, the sheer prospect of mass membership of the party was enough, coupled with a political imperative from the Kinnockites towards applying throughout the party as far as practically possible the one-member-one-vote concept (much to the chagrin, if not the venom, of the remnants of the Bennite left), to see the reconsideration of the union block vote move from the realms of right-wing revisionism or worse, to become an active issue with broad support. Not, of course, completely on the basis of attachment to the purity of the idea: political opportunism inevitably reared its head. Some unions on the left, for instance, saw the possibility of change as a way of increasing left-wing influence in the party against what they saw was the majority right-wing bulwark. This was especially marked given the change in position within the party of its biggest union, the TGWU. Traditionally, nothing moved in the Labour Party without the T&G. Party seers like Lord McCarthy describe the TGWU as the Godfather of the Labour Party. Under Jack Jones and his predecessors as general secretaries of the union, there were times – many times – when it behaved exactly like that. At the height of his power and authority, poll evidence saw Jack Jones as a more powerful figure than the Prime Minister. Of course, it was easier then: it was simply easier for men like Jack Jones and Hugh Scanlon of the engineering workers to be seen as major figures not just in their unions, not just in the unions generally, not just even in the Labour Party but in the country as a whole. Easier, because of a number of factors, including a tight labour market, rising inflation, a friendly legislative power environment. With conditions like those, all likely to lead to increasing union membership rolls, there were few union leaders who would not have been able to seize the opportunity of looking good, of looking powerful – and, indeed, of being powerful too. As the biggest union in the TUC and the Labour Party, and with representational structures which reflected that, what the T&G said counted: it didn't happen every time, but when Jack Jones said he wanted something – equal pay legislation, for example; or flat-rate pay policies; or the conciliation service ACAS – he very often got it.

As the last in a long line of strong T&G leaders (autocratic to their opponents), Jones managed to maintain real authority and drive even as he went ahead with his programme to decentralize power in the union, to push control down to the favoured level of shop stewards, who were virtually seen as polymathic Renaissance men, able, willing and capable of doing all, and more, that was asked of them. But after Jones, things began to look different in the union. Moss Evans, Jones's successor, was widely seen to be a less powerful force. Into the power vacuum started to step the differing left- and right-wing factions within the union, who took its general executive council – not previously a hugely important body in the union – as both their mechanism to achieve power, and their battleground. The bitter internecine fighting which followed left a gaping hole within both the Labour Party and the TUC. As TGWU leaders had endlessly to watch their backs, so the union's influence outside its own walls diminished. Right-wing union leaders were successful, for instance, in getting through the TUC a fundamental change in the structure of its governing General Council which in effect ended the extensive powers of patronage which the TUC's larger unions, and the TGWU in particular, had both wielded and enjoyed wielding.

But as the left consolidated its control within the T&G, the opportunism of the right had to be matched by new tactics from the TUC and Labour Party leaderships. Though a former TGWU official himself, Norman Willis at the TUC both had and wanted to rely on other unions as well as the T&G for advice, guidance and influence. In the party, the position was both more sensitive and more crucial. Even though the Bennite left had failed in one of its early 1980s ambitions of gaining full control over the party's election manifesto, it became increasingly clear that the left's impact on what Labour offered, and at least as importantly and perhaps even more so, on how it was *seen* by the public, could still be extensive. On occasion after occasion, the left combined to force through policy decisions which made the Kinnockite leadership unhappy. They didn't necessarily feed through directly into the manifesto, but their electoral impact was unquestionable. Kinnock began to realize that this was not something with which you could do a deal.

Defence became the key issue. Labour's defence policy of unilateral nuclear disarmament was widely seen as one of the principal reasons which had prevented people from voting Labour. Changing it became electorally inevitable – and practically likely in any case, as the real level of change in the Soviet Union envisaged by Mikhail Gorbachev started to become clear. It wasn't an easy issue for Neil Kinnock, as a unilateralist himself of long standing. But he determined that something had to be done. In a post-election TV interview on a Sunday current affairs programme, Kinnock appeared to indicate some shift away from full-blooded unilateralism. Kinnock's advisors knew what they were doing; they were pleased with the interview, pleased that the new line had emerged, and had begun to establish itself; it was pre-planned, pre-determined. They knew, too, that the interview came at the start of one of the TGWU's quarterly executive council meetings. The feeling was that Kinnock would see it through; he would tough it out. It didn't work out like that. Faced with what left-wingers on the T&G executive saw as the worst example yet of Kinnock's rightwards revisionism, the union hit back: it refused to nominate Kinnock, a T&G member and a T&G-sponsored MP, for his election due that year as party leader. That was damaging – in actuality, and as an indicator of where at that stage the power still lay in the union–party relationship. With such indications of implacable opposition, the impetus for change in the defence policy faltered. To the public, and to Labour's political opponents, the picture was clear: the brothers were still in control; the Labour dog was still being wagged by the union – and in particular the T&G – tail.

For Kinnock, it was a blooding experience. Gradually, the realization came among the leadership that putting Labour into power was likely to be dogged interminably, if not perhaps completely, by such union bulwarks as the TGWU. Perhaps more importantly, there came a gradual realization that this negative could not only be neutralized, but even turned into a positive: that if change could be achieved *without* the TGWU, then not only would the objective – the policy change itself – be obtained, but public brownie points could be won by doing it in the teeth of opposition from the T&G. The Kinnock camp set out to put together a delicately-balanced coalition of votes which could win without the TGWU. It was a high-risk strategy. Such a coalition would inevitably make those within it nervous: the T&G wasn't the power it once was, but it was still semi-overtly pitting yourself against the established power of Labour's largest union. On the defence issue itself, it was nervous for Kinnock. Success would turn on whether or not the left-led NUPE public employees union would turn away from complete unilateralism, and despite Tom Sawyer, NUPE's deputy general secretary, being both a key Kinnock ally and a powerful figure within the union, it was far from certain. Sawyer eventually brought home the bacon, and the vote looked set. Not completely, of course: Labour conferences over the years have been riddled with instances of particular union leaders happening to miss key votes, happening to be out of the room at the time, happening not to have voted the expected way by mistake. But the coalition held: the defence change went through, and

Labour reaped the benefits not just of doing it, but of doing it in spite of the TGWU. The union was the loser. Edged out of the central, inner councils of the Labour leadership, its shift was illustrated well when its inner tensions exploded again early in 1990. Ron Todd, its general secretary, had to order the first postal elections for the union's executive to be re-run after more than 9,000 ballot papers were stolen and fraudulently filled in to support particular candidates. News interest in the story – inevitably high – was assisted by the T&G's status in the party, that as Labour's biggest union, what was bad for the T&G was bad for Kinnock. A good line, but one which strictly was unusable precisely because of the shift in the union's influence, precisely because Kinnock had shown he could do without the T&G on even the most sensitive of issues. The reality was that Kinnock could certainly do without trouble in the TGWU; but if he got it – well, it could now be faced down.

Circumventing Labour's biggest union on the most delicate issues is a measure of the change in the traditional union–Labour relations which the Kinnock camp had managed to achieve by the start of the 1990s. It wasn't a question, as some on the left had charged and some of Labour's opponents outside the party on the political right had always urged, of the party breaking its links with the unions. Financially, apart from anything else, such a move would be at the very least ill-judged. What it constituted was Labour *redefining* those links – not formally, not in the sense of issuing consultation papers to change the very structures of power (though it was doing that too, by this time, on the block vote itself), but in practical, operational terms. The public might not know it. Labour's opponents either might not know it, or might not want to know it. But the fact of the matter was clear: each side in the party–union relationship now knew who was boss – and it wasn't any longer the T&G, or more widely Labour's unions. The party – more specifically, the party leadership, centring around Kinnock – now had the whip hand.

INTO THE 1990s

But will it last? Will this new, redefined relationship be sustained? Will it be possible, will it be sensible, for each side in the union party dance to maintain this new, readjusted equilibrium? Or will the pressures of doing so prove too great? Or, equally, will circumstances alter so extensively that there will no longer be any advantage to one or the other side in doing so – and a more radical re-evaluation (either way) have to take place? Inevitably, these are imponderables. All the indications are that there has been a shift – a single, important shift – in the union–party relationship, and one which by and large is to the advantage of the party leadership. But just as the relationship in the 1960s and 1970s looked strong – indeed, all but immutable – it was, in fact, subject to change and adaptation, so this apparent redefinition could equally well be temporary, open to change, subject to reversal.

The crucial determinant is the obvious one: who wins the next general election. Oddly enough, the relationship between the party and the unions would now probably be least likely to change if Labour were actually to be elected to government. In a sense, the changes which have grown in the last part of the 1980s have been predicated upon that, because being elected looked possible for the first time in a decade. Despite the sound and fury, despite the smooth glossiness of the 1987 general election campaign, few in the party hierarchy privately believed that Labour could or would win. By the beginning of the 1990s, everything looked different. There was everything to play for. Publicly, many people and organizations started to get interested in Labour, started to feel that for the first time for as long as many people could remember, they now needed to know what Labour thought about things, what it felt about things, what it wanted, what it proposed. Privately, the interest was even more extensive. Key City figures, leading businessmen, senior civil servants, newspaper editors, TV executives all wanted to know, and all used whatever contacts they had to try to find out what Labour was doing.

Of course, if Labour loses, then all bets are off. Having then taken the party unsuccessfully through two general elections, and perhaps more importantly, having set the party on a particular course which the electorate would then have rejected twice in both its partly- and fully-formed guises, Neil Kinnock's own future as leader would be questionable. It might be questioned most strongly by him, before others; he might well feel that all he had to give in the job had been given. On the other hand, as his response to his own and Labour's downtime in 1988 showed, he's not much of a quitter: his own natural ambition and aggression would tend to keep him going. But even if he didn't question his position, others clearly would. The left would argue that all the rightward shifts, all the revisionism, had done nothing in terms of its own projected success – winning elections – and had simply been at the price of abandoning proper, pure socialism. Given the eclipse in the power and influence of the left in the party and the unions – at leadership, if not at activist level – there would be little or no reason why the left would not want to try to seize the chance for change. The right might well simply feel that Kinnock had not achieved his promises, explicit and implicit; that the drive for electability had not paid off – not as a strategy, but under him as leader; that for all his efforts, especially organizationally in trying to tackle the left within the party, Kinnock had been unable to shake off his original tag of being operationally and intellectually lightweight. One way or another, the knives would be out. If that were the case, and a dispatch – or, indeed, Kinnock falling on his own sword – were done, then the thrust of the Kinnock operation in a number of key areas, including the Labour–union relationship, would be up for wholesale re-evaluation under a new party leader. That new leader, depending on who it was and broadly from which wing of the party he or she stemmed, might want to build on the work Kinnock had done, to use it, to take over some of his achievements in a range of areas; but they also might not.

Equally, the unions might want to look hard at whether or not their Labour links were best serving them. Or at least, theoretically they might. Significantly, after a good campaign, no such re-evaluation was undertaken after Labour's 1987 defeat. It *was* after the 1983 election, but that was in the first flush of the rise of the political centre, and especially of the then-still unsplit SDP, which even managed to pick up at the time overt union support from one or two prominent union leaders. With the fissuring of the centre parties, their repeatedly-failed attempts to pick up the pieces, and the inevitable collapse of their concerted voting challenge, the option of a political link with a party other than Labour is not a serious one. Indeed, where could the unions go? Who would have them, even if there was any kind of concerted or coherent attempt made to switch political allegiance away from Labour? – either to another party, or more along the lines of the AFL–CIO, the US equivalent of the TUC, which although it both favours and has links with the Democrat party, is an effective cross-party lobbying force in Washington along the lines of many other pressure groups battling to promote their own interests. The unions' money might in theory be attractive, though the likely practical problems about getting it would be enough to deter many parties from really wanting it. But in fact none of that matters. As an interest group, the unions' impact throughout the 1980s on Labour had been at least as much negative as it was positive, if not considerably more so. No political party other than Labour would be likely to want the unions; the problem for the unions is that in all practical terms, even if all else were equal – and the likelihood in practice of any sizeable or representative group of unions being able to reach an agreement on a political switch is so tiny as to be virtually dismissable – their political allegiance is, oddly enough, not really in their gift.

It is a matter of demand, rather than supply. This was a crucial realization for some close to Kinnock: if the unions have nowhere else to go, why should we do things on *their* terms? If they have nowhere else to go, why shouldn't they do things on ours? Interestingly, the steps Labour had taken by the start of the 1990s to redefine its relationship with the unions, and the prospects for that relationship throughout the decade, echo the Conservative government's strategy towards the unions at the start of the 1980s. Then Conservatives were warned from both within and without their ranks that tackling the unions was not on, it was too dangerous, look at what happened in 1971 with the Industrial Relations Act, and in 1969 for Labour with *In Place of Strife*. But piece by piece, step by step, the Conservative government went ahead. Each piece was not necessarily ultimately valuable in itself – but the cumulative effect of all the steps certainly was. Labour's change in its relationship with the unions took roughly the same approach.

There might, of course, be different union demands – a different shopping list, or indeed the resuscitation of the shopping list. But under a new Labour leadership, the prospects of any such shopping list being delivered for the unions would be even less than they have been in the 1980s. A new Labour leader to the left of Kinnock would, in theory, be more likely to be responsive to any union demands of this order. But if the electorate had again just rejected at the polls a Labour party which was in all but name a fully-fledged social democratic, neocentrist party – which in effect is what the Kinnock new model Labour party actually is – and voted instead for a further term of a party substantially to the right, it might reasonably be supposed that it would be unlikely to elect in the foreseeable future a more left-leaning Labour party. Equally, if a Labour leader were elected who was further to the right than Neil Kinnock, then a union shopping list of demands would probably get even shorter shrift than the notion received in the late 1980s from the Kinnock camp. So a radical shift in the unions' position on their relationship with Labour looks either unlikely or impracticable.

A similarly radical shift from the party's point of view only looks likely if Labour loses. If Labour wins, it will put into practice what it now has – or what it will have by the time the election actually comes. What that will be by then is an extension of, not a fundamental change from, the position at the time of writing. That doesn't mean necessarily any formal loosening of the links between the two parts of labour – the political and the industrial. But it does mean a continuing reshaping of those links, a continuing emphasis on the primacy of the party, and especially of the party leadership, over the unions.

Take, as one instance, the vexed question of pay. Pay has been the rock on which successive Labour governments have foundered. Incomes policy, in overt or disguised form, has been a central plank of Labour's economic strategy in recent Labour governments. Historically, incomes policies tend to run a highly familiar course: reluctant acceptance by unions structurally and philosophically opposed to them, but hamstrung either by electoral or political considerations into accepting them, at least for a particular period of time. As the pay restrictions inevitably associated with incomes policy bite, in order to achieve the economic targets linked to it, so union frustration grows. That frustration escalates, until it reaches a point at which the original reasons for agreement with the incomes policy can no longer obtain. Without a safety valve – some mechanism like productivity deals, to a greater or lesser degree of speciousness – or even with one, eventually the lid blows off: usually through strikes, with damaging social and, in the longer-term, political consequences. Throughout the 1980s, the Conservative government drew huge political benefit from *not* having any formal incomes policy. No deals with the unions drew electoral approval. Not having any pay limit meant there was no macho bargaining target, nothing to aim at, nothing to exceed.

Not without cost, of course. It became increasingly difficult for the Conservative government to adhere on the one hand to the purity of market forces, to say that business operations were a matter for those individual businesses, and not for governments, and on the other repeatedly to try to exhort employers to settle pay deals at lower levels. But despite that operational contradiction, the attractions of a no-incomes-policy for Labour are apparent – apparent, as well, to both the party and union sides of the relationship. Not only do Labour leaders by and large not want to receive *that* call from the TUC, suggesting a meeting to discuss early ideas for a preliminary draft of what might, when it had gone through the full range of committee structures, form the basis of some kind of compact between the party and the unions which might ease round to talking generally, within an overall framework, about the concept of earnings in the economy; but, as importantly, not many union leaders now want to see that call made either.

They don't believe that for their own interests, the advantages of such an arrangement would outweigh the disadvantages. Many union negotiators have lived under nothing but the no incomes policy, free collective bargaining of the Thatcher years. They've at times been unhappy with it, but they've learned to live with it. Indeed, many of the employees they represent have done particularly well out of such a system. Provided they have remained in employment, provided they withstood the labour shakeout of the early years of the 1980s, in many cases their pay rises have kept pace with and probably exceeded the inflation rate. They've done all right, Jack. It might well be that the greatest resistance to the idea of formal incomes policy comes not from the formal bodies of Labour or the unions, but from employees themselves.

It will be employees too, in their guise as electoral participants, who will determine whether the ending of the Thatcher years, and the replacement of Margaret Thatcher as prime minister by John Major after the extraordinary leadership wrangle in the Conservative party at the end of 1990, will have any significant effect on the Labour-union relationship. Directly, it may well not, simply because the changes in employment law of the Thatcher years, which have included legal provisions aimed directly at the Labour-union deal (with ballots on union political funds required by the Trade Union Act 1984), were so extensive as to convince Conservative ministers under the new party leader that, barring completely unforeseen circumstances, there looked little scope for further employment law reform in advance of a general election. Though they privately yearned for the electoral plus-value industrial relations issues have previously given to the Conservatives, ministers accepted by 1991 that there was little public support for further reforms before the next election. That is not to say that the replacement of Mrs Thatcher as both party leader and prime minister will mean no further changes at all in the 1990s. Indeed, one of the little-noticed but important long-run reforms of the 1980s, directly impacting upon the Labour-union relationship, is still there, still ticking away as an unaddressed problem. The 1984 Act required not just balloting on union political funds, but reballoting every 10 years. So in 1995, the relationship will be openly and publicly re-tested. Labour and union leaders are already privately nervous at the prospect. If Labour loses the next election, the vote may see an overt weakening of the union links, as union members may conclude there is little real point in supporting a party which seems incapable of getting itself elected. If Labour wins, the prospect is almost as bad: what would in effect be a mid-term referendum by Labour's key supporters on the performance of the government, at a point in the electoral cycle when governments' fortunes tend to be at their lowest. The change in the Conservative leadership may have its greatest impact on the Labour-union relationship, though, by decreasing Labour's overall electability: by the end, Margaret Thatcher was in some ways Labour's greatest electoral asset. Her going was a direct result of real Conservative fear about her negative electoral impact, her unpopularity, her loss of what had been one of her greatest features – a rooting in real populism.

In the end, the basic determinant of the relationship between the Labour Party and the trade unions will be at that level: putting it crudely, people – people as employees, people as union members (or not), people as electors. Coping with the shifts in their traditional bases was for both Labour and the unions one of the greatest difficulties of the 1980s. It is not a process which is yet complete – nor, probably, is ever likely to be. Some on the left are especially dismissive of the idea of a changed working class, of an economic, social, attitudinal and political reshaping of the roots of Labour and union support. But both the unions and the Labour party have had to try to come to terms with such change – with an occupational shift which has seen the continuing demise of blue-collar jobs and a rise in white-collar work, and a continuing move away from the core of full-time male employment to more complicated patterns of work, often using women more extensively; with a shift in jobs and population from the north to the south, from the old cities to new and reinvigorated market towns; with a move from work in traditional heavy industries, to work in services, private and public; with a growth in owner-occupancy, linked firmly to mortgage-based economic dependence on markets and interest rates, in ways inconceivable say fifteen years ago; with the growth of people actively operating as consumers, and interested in – perhaps even driven by – the view of the world which that might generate.

Keeping track of and pace with these developments has been an immense job for both Labour and the unions. There is a view that all these changes, and others linked to them, are inimical to both union membership and likelihood of voting Labour; indeed, the general election voting record of union members, has seen the Labour vote slump from more than 70 per cent early in the 1960s to a low point of 33 per cent in 1983, picking up considerably to 43 per cent in 1987, and following Labour's poll growth thereafter. Whatever the implications behind those figures, it is clear that to survive, let alone thrive, as separate entities – leaving aside as linked bodies – both Labour and the unions will continue to need to look to their markets: the people who either vote for them or buy their services. How far they want Labour and the unions to maintain their links will be how far they will be able to; and that in turn will govern whether the 1990s will see similar clashes to Ron Todd and Neil Kinnock ramming against each other in Blackpool.

LIST OF CONTRIBUTORS

SIR DENIS BARNES was Senior Research Associate of the Policy Studies Institute. He was formerly Permanent Secretary of the Department of Employment and Chairman of the Manpower Services Commission. He is co-author of *Governments and Trade Unions: the British experience 1964–79*.

PHILIP BASSETT is the Industrial Editor of *The Times*. He was formerly Labour Editor of the *Financial Times* and Labour Correspondent of BBC Television. He is the author of *Strike Free: New Industrial Relations in Britain*.

WILLIAM BROWN is Professor of Industrial Relations at Cambridge. He was previously Director of the Industrial Relations Research Unit at Warwick University. His publications include *Piecework Bargaining* and *The Changing Contours of British Industrial Relations*.

KEN COATES is M.E.P. for Nottingham, Special Professor in Adult Education at Nottingham University, and a Director of the Bertrand Russell Peace Foundation. His books include *Work-Ins, Sit-Ins and Industrial Democracy* and (with a co-author) *Trade Unions in Britain*.

CHRIS COOK is currently Head of the Political Archives Survey at the London School of Economics. He was formerly head of the Department of History, Philosophy and European Studies at the Polytechnic of North London. His publications on modern British Politics include (with co-authors) *Post-War Britain: A Political History* and *The Slump*.

HENRY DRUCKER is Director of the Campaign for Oxford and was formerly Senior Lecturer in Politics at Edinburgh University. He is the author of *Breakaway: The Scottish Labour Party, Multi-Party Britain, The Doctrine and Ethos of the Labour Party, The Politics of Nationalism and Devolution* (with a co-author) and editor of J. P. Mackintosh, *On Scotland*.

BARRY HINDESS is Professor of Political Science in the Research School of Social Sciences at the Australian National University, Canberra. His books include *The Decline of Working Class Politics, Politics and Class Analysis, Freedom, Equality and the Market,* and *Reactions to the Right*.

JOHN LOVELL is Senior Lecturer in Economic and Social History at the University of Kent. His books include *Stevedores and Dockers, British Trade Unions 1875–1933* and (with a co-author) *A Short History of the TUC*.

DENIS MACSHANE works for the International Metalworkers' Federation, based in Geneva, and is a former President of the NUJ. His books include a biography of *François Mitterand and International Labour and the Origins of the Cold War* (to be published by Oxford University Press in 1992).

BEN PIMLOTT is Professor of Politics and Contemporary History at Birkbeck College, University of London. He is the author of *Labour and the Left in the 1930s* and *Hugh Dalton,* which won the Whitbread Biography Award.

EILEEN REID is a Research Fellow of the Policy Studies Institute. Her books include (with co-authors) *Education and Personal Relationships, Differentials for Managers and Skilled Manual Workers in the United Kingdom* and *Governments and Trade Unions: the British experience 1964–79*.

PATRICK RENSHAW is Senior Lecturer in American History at Sheffield University. He is the author of *The Wobblies* and *The General Strike,* his latest book *False Promises: American Labour and Consensus Capitalism, 1935–1985* will be published this year.

DAVID RUBINSTEIN taught social history at the Universities of Hull and Tours from 1965 to 1990. His main publications have been on the history of labour, housing, education, recreation and womens' emancipation. His biography of Millicent Garrett Fawcett is due to appear later this year.

JEAN SEATON is Senior Lecturer in Sociology at the Polytechnic of the South Bank. She is co-author of *Power Without Responsibility: The press and broadcasting in Britain,* and joint editor of *The Media in British Politics*.

RICHARD SHACKLETON was Lecturer in History at Birmingham University. He is co-editor of *Essays in Birmingham Labour History*.

JOHN STEVENSON is Fellow and Tutor in History at Worcester College, Oxford. His books include *London in the Age of Reform, Popular Disturbances in England, 1700–1870* and (with co-authors) *Popular Protest and Public Order* and *The Slump*.

ROBERT TAYLOR is Scandinavian correspondent of the *Financial Times,* having previously worked as labour correspondent for the *Observer* and *Sunday Times.* He is the author of *Lord Salisbury* and *The Fifth Estate: Britain's Unions in The Modern World*.

CHRIS WRIGLEY is Reader in Economic History at Nottingham University. His books include *David Lloyd George and the British Labour Movement, A History of British Industrial Relations* (ed.), 2 vols, *Arthur Henderson* and *Lloyd George and the Challenge of Labour*.

Index